DATE DUE

NOV 3 1986	MAY 0 8 2002	
APR 2 7 1987		
OCT 1 2 1987	OCT 2 7 2003	
APR 2 5 1988		
MAY 9 1988	NOV 1 3 2003	
NOV 0 6 1990		
DEC 1 0 1990		
JAN 0 8 1991		
MAY 2 2 1991		
APR 2 7 1993		
AUG 5 1993		
MAR 1 4 1995		
DEC 1 6 1995		
MAR 0 5 1997		
AUG 0 7 1998		

Demco, Inc. 38-293

The Meaning of Love
in Human Experience

===

The Meaning of Love
in Human Experience

REUBEN FINE

A Wiley-Interscience Publication

JOHN WILEY & SONS

New York/Chichester/Brisbane/Toronto/Singapore

Library of Congress Cataloging in Publication Data:

Fine, Reuben, 1914–
   The meaning of love in human experience.

   "A Wiley-Interscience publication."
   Includes index.
   1. Love.   2. Mental health.   3. Psychoanalysis.
4. Psychotherapy.   I. Title.
BF575.L8F52   1985   302   84-27070
ISBN 0-471-87114-1

Printed in the United States of America

10 9 8 7 6 5 4 3 2

To Marcia, the ideal love companion

Sotuknang went to the universe wherein was that to be Tokpela, the First World, and out of it he created her who was to remain on that earth and be his helper. Her name was Kokyangwuti, Spider Woman.

When she awoke to life and received her name, she asked, "Why am I here?"

"Look about you," answered Sotuknang. "Here is this earth we have created. It has shape and substance, direction and time, a beginning and an end. But there is no life upon it. We see no joyful movement. We hear no joyful sound. What is life without sound and movement? So you have been given the power to help us create this life. You have been given the knowledge, wisdom, and love to bless all the beings you create. That is why you are here."

Hopi Legend (Hopi = peace)

Do you not know that it is our inheritance from remote times that no one loves another, but that always, brother against brother, and son against father, we try our utmost to injure one another?

Geoffrey Plantagenet, Count of Anjou
(time of the Crusades)

—

. . . Love being foremost in my thought,
It was a thing I never forgot.
I chose love as my primal skill,
And therefore it is with me still.

Chaucer: *The Book of the Duchess*
(14th century)

Love is like a fisherman's hook. Without the hook he could never catch a fish, but once the hook is taken the fisherman is sure of the fish . . . When one has found this way, he looks for no other. . . . Therefore wait only for this hook and you will be caught up into blessing, and the more you are caught the more you will be set free. . . .

Meister Eckhardt: from the sermon *Eternal Birth*
(14th century)

Preface

Whenever and wherever the topic of love is broached, everybody listens. Some laugh; some cry; some shout for joy; some are cynical. Love does indeed make the world go 'round. It is the central human experience. To be indifferent to love is to be indifferent to life.

And yet a strange anomaly exists. While poets have rhapsodized and sung about love at all times and in all places, scientists have found little to say about it. A recent book on the chemistry of love claims to pinpoint the biochemical reactions that make up love. Even Freud, who in 1908 wanted to set up an academy of love in Vienna, became increasingly disillusioned, and ended up claiming that the aim of life is death. Most people who write about love do so to urge it as the answer to everyone's troubles, not to subject it to a careful inquiry.

My goal in this book is to examine love from a scientific point of view. The proposition that love makes people happy is not self-evident; many, including eminent scientists, have questioned it. Yet all the evidence is there, even if it is disregarded. This evidence comes from every discipline that deals with humanity: psychology, psychiatry, anthropology, history, and so on. A world in which mass murders can be blandly denied is not one in which the power of love can be proved. So what we usually see is long discussions on whether hostility is instinctual or not, rather than on why so many people turn away from love, disheartened and discouraged by their failures.

The substantiation of the supremacy of love must first of all deal with the surrounding society. This leads to one of the most fundamental of all distinctions: that between love cultures and hate cultures. Love cultures are those in which the predominant feelings of people toward one another are positive and affectionate; hate cultures are the reverse. Many would doubt that there are love cultures, yet a careful examination of the anthropological record shows that love is as instinctual in human nature as hatred. There are no pure love or pure hate cultures; it is always a relative matter. But the distinction can be made and the data provided.

The first chapter presents five love cultures and five hate cultures. Hate cultures are more familiar to us than love cultures, but some love must be permitted if the society is to perpetuate itself. A little reflection discloses the surprising fact that many "primitive" cultures are far more loving than many "advanced" ones. In fact, the thesis could be presented that love tends to flourish more when the society is small; as soon as it gets too big, quarrels, fights, and murders begin to appear. The older idea that primitive peoples are more "savage" than we are is as distorted as the notion that animals are "beastlike."

Whence then comes the idea that hatred is so ingrained in human nature (as, e.g., Lorenz maintains) that it can never be eradicated or even well contained? It is a generalization from the history of western culture. Here is the second major thesis: Western culture, from the time of the Greeks to the present, has been largely a hate culture. Wars, famines, murders, genocide, slavery have been there from time immemorial. If historians have focused so much on the achievements of western civilization, it is only now that they are beginning to realize on what misery these achievements were based. The glory that was Greece and the grandeur that was Rome may have existed, but the toll that they exacted in human lives and suffering is incalculable. As for Christianity, the religion of love, its performance has been so mixed that George Bernard Shaw after 19 centuries could quip: "Christianity is a good idea, someone ought to try it."

Next I turn to the religious images of love. While all religions have in one form or another urged their believers to curb their violence, they have also with rare exceptions been indifferent to the sufferings of those outside their religion. And many times they have even urged their adherents to go out and destroy the enemies, thus preaching hatred rather than love.

Chapter 5 deals with the question: Can animals love? Here a surprising conclusion emerges from a careful perusal of the facts: In general, animals are loving creatures. They gather together in groups that could justifiably be called love cultures, they take care of their young, at times they even nurture the old and the sick among them. Only few animal species are so destructive that they will kill or hurt their conspecifics without reason; and the human being is one of these species. Somehow evolution has taught most animal groups to live together in peace and harmony. When they do become injurious it is for specific reasons; once these reasons are out of the way, they give up their rage. In this respect, as in so many, humankind has much to learn from animals.

Chapter 6 takes up the question of how children learn to love. Here the answer is unequivocal: Children learn to love by being loved. Any interference with the love given to them by their parents or other caretakers has very serious consequences, including serious illness or even death. Unfortunately human beings are strongly influenced by their childhood; once their minds are pointed in a certain direction, it is hard to change them. So if the world is to be made more loving, it must start in childhood.

In the next chapter a number of clinical observations are offered. As a practicing analyst I have of course been confronted with the major problem of getting people past their undigested hatreds. Regardless of what problems a person comes to an analyst with, sooner or later it becomes clear that there is a lack in their love lives, and that the problem cannot be satisfactorily resolved unless the love problem is remedied. Hence the therapist is somebody who teaches others how to love. It stands to reason that in order to do so he or she must have had some therapy, which taught him or her how to love. Just as children can learn to love only by being loved, the therapist can learn to treat others only by being treated himself or herself.

In Chapter 8 I discuss the social controls that affect the appearance and management of love in any society. For while love seems to be a completely private feeling, like all feelings it is strongly influenced by the surrounding milieu. Here it appears that there has always been a longing for love in all people. One of the ways in which this longing for love has been expressed is in the formation of separate communities (called intentional love cultures) in which the participants can lead their own lives in peace and harmony. Unfortunately these ideal communities all come from or exist within hate cultures, and sooner or later the forces of the surrounding culture tend to destroy the love groups. There are only rare exceptions.

Also, the meaning of love to the individual will vary with the nature of the surrounding culture. In a hate culture such as ours has been for millennia, love most often becomes a refuge, away from the miseries of the everyday world. Hence come the contradictory aphorisms, such as "All the world loves a lover," as contrasted with "All who love are blind." Refuge love is the predominant form of love in our culture. In fact, many people, wise to the ways of the world, will deliberately avoid being too loving because they can anticipate that their affectionate feelings will lead others to exploit them. In a hate culture it becomes dangerous to love too much.

In Chapter 9 I take up the theories of love that have been put forth through the ages, from Plato to the present. By and large the theoreticians (with the exception of the psychoanalysts) have had little to offer. Many philosophers have not even been aware that love must apply to human beings; many others have not even discussed the subject. Since people have had to defend themselves against the ravages of a hate culture, this turning away from love becomes understandable. Philosophical detachment may help to avoid pain, as among the Stoics, but it will not lead to loving human relationships.

The one man who stands out as the great theoretician of love is Freud. Actually, the entire body of his work is one long and detailed examination of the vicissitudes of love in the members of our society. Among the most central of his insights is that love and sexuality can never really be separated, as so many had tried to do through the ages. The nineteenth century, out of which he came, could be described as dominated by the image of sexless love; the twentieth, in a misinterpretation of his doctrines, as dominated by the image of loveless sex. Both love and sex are essential to a full life.

Yet Freud, for all his greatness, was also incomplete and inconsistent. My debt to him is, it goes without saying, enormous. But my goal has been to round out his theories, to correct his errors, to review the evidence that has accumulated since he worked, and to present a more comprehensive view of the field than he did. It is also to be noted that as he grew older Freud became increasingly disenchanted about the possibility of setting up a love culture. But, as he says, he was primarily a conquistador, opening paths which others could follow.

Chapter 10 offers an integrative view of love, which I call the analytic ideal. This takes off from Freud's proposition that the normal person is the one who can work and love. In sum, the theory is that the human being attains the greatest degree of happiness if he or she can love, be sexual, have pleasure, have feelings, yet be guided by reason, have a role in a family, have a sense of identity, have a role in the social order, work, communicate, have some creative outlets, and be free from psychiatric symptomatology. It is my contention that this analytic ideal is the one that has in a positive way been at the root of the constructive efforts in the history of psychoanalysis, though it is only rarely formulated as it is here. It is also my thesis that it is attainable, and that it is a philosophical outlook that if adopted will vastly improve the lot of modern humanity.

Finally, the last chapter takes up the implications for psychotherapy of this whole approach. This has already been touched upon to some extent, but it is expanded here. People who come to therapy without ever having loved anybody are almost impenetrable. The average patient comes with a history of neurotic love disappointment. He or she must first learn to get over the neurotic distortions of love, then move on to a healthy love. No attempt is made to gloss over the difficulties inherent in psychotherapy. Yet it still offers a novel theory of human suffering and happiness, a theory that is gaining an increasing audience and increasing respect. There are of course other theories of therapy; these I call the peripheral approaches, in contrast to the central scheme of psychoanalysis and its offshoots.

I wish to express my thanks to Herb Reich of John Wiley & Sons for his expert editorial assistance and encouragement of this project.

As for me, writing this book has been its own reward; it is a subject that I have been much occupied with throughout my life, both personally and professionally. To borrow Henry James's excuse for writing about Venice: "I hold any writer sufficiently justified who is himself in love with his theme."

REUBEN FINE

New York, New York
December 1984

Acknowledgements

Grateful acknowledgement is made to C. C. Thomas and Co. for permission to quote passages from E. Freid, editor: Artistic Productivity and Mental Health, and to Mrs. Alice Folus for permission to quote her poem Carrie from New Poems for 1977.

R. F.

Contents

1

Love Cultures and Hate Cultures

The first significant observation that has to be made about cultures is that there are some cultures that foster the experience of love, while there are others in which hatred and violence are strongly encouraged. Naturally, "pure" cultures of love or hate are not to be found. When the predominant relationship of one person to another is based on love, we call that a love culture; when the predominant relationship is based on hatred, we call that a hate culture. It thus becomes a relative matter whether the forces of hatred or the forces of love have the upper hand. The question can be answered only on the basis of an intimate study of the society involved.

In the wake of the horrendous genocide of World War II—and other examples of genocide that persist—it has been assumed by some animal psychologists, foremost among them Nobel laureate Konrad Lorenz (1963), that aggression is innate in human nature. The most spirited refutation of this theory has been offered by the anthropologist Ashley Montagu, who described a wide variety of friendly, peaceful, or love cultures. He argues:

The long extended period of infant and childhood dependency necessitates females who as mothers, are efficiently able to minister to the dependent needs of their young over a considerable number of years, and of males who, as fathers and husbands, are capable of the cooperative behavior necessary for the development of the nuclear family. . . . In the small population of prehistoric man, which means during more than 99% of man's evolutionary history, love and cooperation were vitally necessary and indispensable forms of behavior between members of the band if that band was to survive. [1974, pp. 8–9]

FIVE LOVE CULTURES

It will be helpful to examine some of the love cultures in more detail, to see what else they have in common and what problems they show.

The Gentle Tasaday

The Tasaday, a small group of perhaps 24 or 25 persons when they were first discovered in 1971, live in a rain forest in the Philippines. They are undoubtedly the most primitive group ever encountered, living essentially in the Stone Age. When first discovered they had no idea of what warfare meant. This is all the more remarkable since they were surrounded by other Philippine tribes who were quite aggressive and warlike. It was conjectured that they were probably a small group who had strayed away from the larger ones around them and remained isolated in the rain forest for some 400 to 500 years (Nance, 1975).

Several trained anthropologists visited the group, but the total amount of time spent with them by professional observers did not exceed a few months. Still, even in this short time, the essentials of their life-style could be ascertained. Most striking was that not a single instance of hostile or aggressive behavior among adults was ever seen (Nance, 1975, p. 44). The German ethologist Eibl-Eibesfeldt visited them briefly and confirmed the apparent absence of aggression among them.

The group is a food-gathering and hunting type, though after the outside world came to them they learned how to kill animals more deftly than before. They live in caves, where they seek shelter from the rain. They are extremely affectionate, hugging and kissing even strangers almost whenever they can.

They lavish their affections on their children especially, giving them a lot of attention and making them feel important. Children are always the first to be fed and frequently are carried and fondled, nuzzled and played with. If they misbehave, they are disciplined or distracted in a firm but gentle way, never slapped or struck by an adult.

The Tasaday have a sense of modesty, especially about their bodies. The adults keep their genitals covered at all times—whether for protection from bugs or from witches could not be said. Even when they bathe the G-strings and skirts remain in place. The observers never saw anyone above age 3 or 4 urinating or defecating; they always slipped away to a private place.

In sex, there is an incest taboo. They appear to be monogamous. There can hardly be any taboo on premarital sex, although here the group was too small to determine details. In front of the observers they joked and spoke openly about sex; for instance, one morning a young man asked a woman, "Did you do it last night?" and she replied, "Yes, three times."

Joking and humor seem to be one of their main forms of recreation. One young man, Bilayam, one of the main informants, was always clowning. When they were discovered, a number of television crews and newspaper reporters went to see them, and they frequently treated the visitors in a humorous manner, though at times they also showed quite a bit of fear of strange objects and people.

All told, they are described as a pretty happy people—not quite the Garden of Eden, but almost as close to it as you can get. However, the idea of venturing into the outside world does appeal to some of them. Since they are under the protection of the government, which has a special program to protect minorities, what will happen to them eventually is impossible to say. They have no real religious beliefs or mythology, but their intelligence seems to be high, as indicated by their intimate knowledge of the vegetation in their world. The ethnobotanist who investigated them was convinced they were true food gatherers who had only recently learned to trap and hunt.

Mangaia: The Island of Peace

On the island of Mangaia, which means "peace," as on many islands of Polynesia, love is expressed through sexual permissiveness. A closer consideration of the culture allows for some important empirical data to be collected on this all-important relationship between affection and sensuality (Marshall, 1971).

Mangaia is a small island 5 miles across in its widest section; one can easily walk around it in 1 day. Its population at the time it was studied in the 1950s was in the neighborhood of 2000.

The Mangaians are completely obsessed with sex from birth to death. Sex between the marriage partners takes place freely in the presence of the children. Adult women even suck the penises of little boys (the ethnographer calls it "lingual manipulation" but this is presumably what he means). They say that "one needs a sexual story to make all the people happy and work fast."

At around 12 the boy undergoes superincision, in a most painful manner.* He is then a man and is free to begin his sex life. In spite of the freedom there are of course, as always, taboos. One of them is that while sex is practiced freely in the home, it is not discussed, so boys and girls have to learn from their playmates or others outside the home. The Mangaian youth acquires fully as detailed a knowledge of the genitals as the average western physician. Many words for various parts of the sexual apparatus exist that are not even found in other languages; for instance, there are four different words for the clitoris, which is also described as blunt, or sharp, or projecting, or erecting, or protruding.

Circumcision involves not only the removal of the foreskin but also the provision of detailed sexual information. The expert teaches the youth about such matters as cunnilingus, kissing and sucking of breasts, and a means of achieving simultaneous mutual climax.

Premarital sexuality is universal. Children are often born before the parents marry, and they are one of the reasons for marriage. The wife is expected to be a "devil in bed." Marriages nowadays are based on love more often than on any other criterion. The two partners will have experienced one another sexually and in other ways and found one another highly satisfactory. In spite of this mutual pleasure, extramarital adventures are widespread. This does not prevent the spouses from being jealous; this feeling is freely admitted, but it is claimed that women have it more than men. Still, there is a double standard, in that a man who has been with many women is "like a bull," while a woman who has been with many men is compared to a pig.

---

* Various forms of this custom are found in central Polynesia. On Mangaia the operation is described by Marshall as follows (Marshall & Suggs, 1971, p. 113): "The foreskin is retracted, and the anvil inserted; then the skin of the penis is pulled tightly over it and slit down the medial dorsal line through the white cartilaginous underlayer—statedly, right up to the stomach, in most cases. The more carefully done and the more lengthy the incision, the neater is said to be the final result. Mangaian men are quite concerned over the appearance of the superincised organ. An insult of major social magnitude, only slightly less severe than reference to a man's smegma, is to imply that a man has a 'dog-eared' penis, with pendulous skin below the shaft."

One of the most important and striking findings is that all Mangaian women reach orgasm, and bringing a partner to orgasm and experiencing simultaneous orgasm with her represent an important part of the man's sexual pleasure. The term for orgasm is the same as that for the achievement of perfection, pleasure, and comfort. Another term for orgasm is the English word *knockout*.

The various sexual difficulties that are found in our culture are virtually unknown in Mangaia. Only one or two homosexuals* could be found. Sexual fetishism, aphrodisiacs, circle intercourse, orgies, and copulation with animals are absent. There is a sexual outlet available for everybody; no one is deprived of a partner, regardless of looks or background.

Lest all this sound too idyllic, there are also negative features. Venereal disease has been brought in by sailors and Mangaians who have visited other islands; syphilis is still unknown, but gonorrhea exists and is treated by penicillin injections, with no shame attached to having the illness. Herpes is not mentioned. While there are no professional prostitutes, some women will have sex with outsiders to procure a little extra cash or other favor. Though they are supposedly tolerant of infidelity, some women are so enraged by it that they starve their babies to death to get even with their husbands. To get even with his wife for transgressing, the husband may cut off the head of his wife's pet goat.

Divorce is rare, but there are a number of matings in which the wife is substantially older than the husband; in one tabulation, of 101 couples (not necessarily formally married), 23 female partners were older than their mates, while only nine were of the same age. There is a widespread Polynesian belief that older women take better care of younger men. They are said to cook better, be thriftier, and be more likely to spend whatever money they have on their young mate or another man; they are also thought to be less likely to be unfaithful.

There is a peculiar taboo against the sexes being seen in public together. If a man and woman are together anywhere it is assumed that

---

* It is highly likely that the official statements of some of the mental health associations do not accurately reflect the views of their members. Robitscher (1980, p. 177) states the following: "The controversy about the disease status of homosexuality refuses to die. It is not only an important issue in itself but it represents a philosophical divide that is more significant than the individual question. Five years after the APA action to delist homosexuality, the debates continued. When *Medical Aspects of Human Sexuality* surveyed 10,000 physicians who were members of the American Medical Association, 69% said they still considered homosexuality to be 'usually a pathological adaptation, as opposed to a normal variation,' and only 18% considered homosexuality a normal variation. Harold Lief, a psychiatrist, . . . suggested, as many others had, that the APA had been influenced by 'political and social considerations.' "

they will have sex. Incest also occurs with some frequency, according to the ethnographer.

Perhaps the worst feature brought out is the constant pressure on both sides for sexual achievement. Before marriage the boy boasts about how many times he can do it a night; after marriage the emphasis is on whether the man can manage to do it every night. Very little overt aggression is recorded, although occasionally a man will beat his wife to make her "give in." We have already mentioned the woman's revenge on her adulterous husband by starving their child to death.

The greatest dread of the Mangaian male is that he will become impotent, a condition they call *tira*. They attribute it to an overindulgence in sexual activity. There is so much shame attached to this condition that full information could not be obtained, even though it is said to be common.

With such a strong emphasis on actual sex, the affectionate component recedes into the background. One informant said that a man gets close to his wife only when he is past 50; others, however, stated only that when mates get older they feel sexual jealousy.

No doubt more careful investigation would also reveal other negative features. But it cannot be denied that the Mangaian culture comes close to living up to its name.

The Ifaluk: Kindliness and Concealed Hostility

Ifaluk is a tiny atoll in the Central Carolines of Micronesia, inhabited by about 250 people. They were almost completely isolated from the world until the 1940s, probably because of Ifaluk's small size and geographic location. In 1947 Dr. Melford Spiro and Dr. E. G. Burrows spent an extensive period there. Both of them published books on the people. (The present account is taken from Spiro, 1959.) When they were first visited by the anthropologists in 1947, the traditional culture was intact and functioning.

The Ifaluk ethos stresses kindliness, cooperation, and nonaggression as paramount values. Very few natives could remember a single instance of murder, rape, robbery, or fighting, nor did the anthropologists witness such behavior in the course of their study. Whereas aggression is almost entirely absent from interpersonal relations, cooperation and sharing are characteristic features of social life. People are generous with food, property, and assistance. It is as unthinkable for a woman not to offer a passerby some of the food she is cooking as it is for a man not to assist a fellow in the construction of a canoe.

These characteristics of Ifaluk social behavior, the anthropologists felt, are rooted in Ifaluk personality, at least in its conscious aspects. Thus 48% of the subjects claimed to find happiness in knowing that others were happy, while 31% were saddened by the sadness of others; 63% of the subjects stated that the possession of property was the best thing that could happen to them, for then they could have gifts to give visitors or to the chiefs who would offer these gifts to strangers. Finally, the overwhelming majority of praiseworthy acts involved generosity, while most of the blameworthy acts involved aggression. It is not accidental that with one unimportant exception all the activities for which the children reported being punished involved aggression.

The Ifaluk live a peaceful, comfortable life, on the lagoon side of the two inhabited islands of the atoll. The typical residential group as well as the primary economic and socializing unit is the matrilocal extended family.

Marriage is monogamous, but premarital sexual intercourse is both practiced and sanctioned. Extramarital affairs, although not formally sanctioned, are practiced with impunity as long as they are conducted privately and with propriety. The subsistence economy is based on fishing and horticulture, the former being men's and the latter women's work. Although there is some economic specialization, true division of labor does not exist. Leadership in all group activities and formal social control are exercised by five chiefs who inherit their positions.

Notable in the culture is the paucity of anxiety-producing or conflict-provoking stimuli. The climate is pleasant, the diet abundant; there is little call for long or strenuous work. Ifaluk social structure seems to evoke as little conflict or anxiety as its physical setting. There are no social classes based on wealth. There is no economic competition, while distribution methods preclude the possibility of economic distress as a result of old age, illness, or death. There is little if anything in the economic system to evoke feelings of hostility, insecurity, or anxiety. Politically, too, there is little to cause any grievance. The five chiefs exercise their authority benevolently and informally. Respect and love are the typical attitudes of the people toward their unusual leaders. The kinship system likewise reveals few potential points of discord. Reciprocity and cooperation characterize the various kinship relationships. Joking relationships and avoidance taboos, which serve to engender as well as to express tension, are absent, nor is there any great pressure to achieve, so that there is no discordance between sanctioned goals and sanctioned means.

An inordinate emphasis on food impresses any observer. Preoccupation with food is expressed in a number of ways. It is a favorite and almost ubiquitous topic of conversation. Its distribution is an invariable part of every secular and religious meeting. The opportunity to eat leads people to stop any other activity, however important. The presence or absence of food is a basis for linguistic expressions of emotional states. Thus the Ifaluk word for happiness means "good belly," while the word for sadness means "bad belly," that is, an empty stomach.

The people have a compulsive need for coconut toddy, a whitish sappy liquid obtained by tapping the flower stalk of the coconut tree. Toddy is consumed every morning and every evening. The daily collection of toddy is one of the most important tasks of all men. When, due to rain, toddy cannot be collected, the people become moody and morose.

There are two threatening experiences in the life of the child as it grows up. One is the daily washing of the infant at dawn in the cold water of the lagoon. The second is the replacement of the child by a new child. This almost invariably leads to what Spiro (1959) calls "sibling illness." Of 24 children who were recently "usurped" by newcomers, as many as 96% chronically displayed the following characteristics: fighting and attacking, willful disobedience, destruction of property, temper tantrums, difficulty eating, night terrors, thumb sucking, crying and whining, shyness, and negativism.

The sibling illness is overcome, but feelings of anxiety and hostility apparently remain at the unconscious level. Hostility is revealed most clearly in individual and cultural fantasy. Thus when the chiefs recount the legends of the early history and colonization of Ifaluk, according to which Ifaluk conquered and completely wiped out the populations of other islands, they become animated and enthusiastic, detailing these warlike acts with relish. Religion offers another outlet for hostility. The functionally important supernaturals are the ghosts, souls of departed ancestors. There are two types of ghosts—beneficent and malevolent. The evil ghosts are more prevalent, pointing to a projection of repressed hostility.

Further evidence of hostility was found in dreams and projective devices. Almost 70% of the dreams collected from over 50 persons were of an aggressive nature; the dreamer was either attacking or being attacked. Likewise in the Thematic Apperception Test almost 50% of the themes are aggressive in character: quarreling, fighting, physical conflict, and murder.

On the other hand, in other projective forms, such as song, which is one of the few outlets of an artistic nature, the themes are largely love and sex, and they are generally quite happy, although loss is also feared. A typical song is the following:

> My sweetheart comes to me
> Stays close beside me;
> Our feelings are the same,
> I understand what he says.
> He told me: "I'll never leave you."
> I asked: "Truly?" and he said, "I wouldn't lie to you."
> He is like a vein in my body,
> Grips me like breadfruit roots underground.
> He loves me too much to leave me;
> Wherever he goes, the thought of me is with him . . .
> He rejoices at the sight of me,
> Takes me in his arms.
> We go into the woods together,
> Find a pleasant clearing;
> There we lie down side by side,
> Where the gabwi grows low about us.
> I take off my skirt, spread my legs,
> Show him my genitals.
> He admires my thighs,
> Caresses me with his hands,
> I adore his caresses.
> We prepare a bed and lie down
> Under the coconut leaves,
> Out in the woods where nobody comes,
> We lie face to face, or from behind,
> He clasps me tight.
> If he leaves me I will be in despair . . .
> Flower in my ear . . .
> Fragrant mango flower . . .
> It is well.

Although there is repressed hostility in the culture, and some anxiety, on the whole this is a true love culture, where the positive features greatly overwhelm the negative ones. Spiro (1959) uses the culture to show that aggression is never absent from human existence. But while this is true, there is a vast difference between aggression projected to malevolent ghosts who are merely the subject of conversation and the mass murders and massacres that are the hallmark of the most vicious hate cultures.

The Hutterites: Religion and Conformity

The Hutterites are the descendants of the Anabaptists who arose during the tormenting religious wars of the sixteenth century. They decreed rebaptism of the adult, which in those days was forbidden and punishable by death. Chased from one country to another, they finally found a home in the Rocky Mountains of the United States and Canada about 1875, where they have lived ever since. They now number about 85,000. (There are many descriptions of the Hutterites in print. The account here is taken from Hostetler, 1974.)

The Hutterites have attracted attention because of the almost complete absence of violence. Their history since 1875 shows no cases of murder, arson, severe physical assault, or sex crime. No individual has warranted the diagnosis of psychopath. Divorce, desertion, separation, and chronic marital discord are rare. Only five marriages are known to have dissolved since 1875. Personal violence and childish or amoral forms of behavior among adults are uncommon, even in persons with psychotic episodes. There are no psychoses stemming from drug addiction, alcoholism, or syphilis. Only two persons have ever committed suicide. During World War II about one-third of the men between the ages of 20 and 40 served in camps for conscientious objectors.

The Hutterite way of life is strongly communal. Religion is its focus. Their whole educational system, beginning with nursery school, orients the people to look for blame and guilt within themselves rather than in others. Physical aggression is taboo. Everything is owned in the name of the church. They eat in a common dining room, pay medical bills from the communal treasury, and work at jobs assigned to them by managers elected by the males of the colony. Their indoctrination begins in infancy and is maintained by daily religious instruction and later by daily attendance at church. They spend their entire lives within a small and stable group. Their homes consist only of bedrooms, all furnished in an almost identical manner. The women take turns cooking and baking for everybody. Everyone wears the same kind of clothes. They are not encouraged to get an education beyond the elementary grades; thus there are no doctors or lawyers among them. Professional services must come from the outside.

While it has low rates of mental illness, the Hutterite culture deals with the deviants it does produce in a kindly and sympathetic manner. The onset of a symptom serves as a signal to the entire community to demonstrate support and love for the afflicted one. They do not approve of the removal of any member to a "strange" hospital, except for short periods to try shock treatment. All deviants are looked after by the immediate families. They are treated as ill rather than crazy. They are encouraged to participate in the normal life of the community, and most of them do some useful work. Most get well, and no permanent stigma is attached to them after recovery.

Because of the widely held opinion that there was no mental illness among the Hutterites, in the early 1950s a team consisting of a sociologist, a psychiatrist, and two clinical psychologists examined every member of the group. When they were examined so closely a number of persons were discovered to be quite disturbed. The predominant illness was depression, with a rate of 9.3 per 1000 aged 15 and over; this compares with a worldwide incidence of manic-depressive insanity of 3 to 4 per 1000 (Eaton & Weil, 1955). On the other hand, the incidence of schizophrenia was remarkably low, with only nine persons discovered in the entire population who had ever had any of the classical symptoms.

Dynamically, these conclusions can be interpreted as showing that, in this regulated, loving community, a lack of excitement and individuation led to a high incidence of depressive feelings; life was just dull. By contrast, the loneliness and despair that characterize the schizophrenic were almost entirely absent.

Little is known about the sexual adjustment of the Hutterites. It may be assumed that as in similar religious communities it is gratified in marriage but otherwise highly repressed.

The Mountain Arapesh: Emphasis on Cooperation

The Arapesh, a culture described and studied in detail by Margaret Mead (1935), are a people living in New Guinea. There are three groups: mountain dwellers, plainsmen, and beach dwellers. The major part of her discussion is devoted to the mountain dwellers.

She describes the mountain dwellers as happy and cooperative. Headhunters, so common in other parts of this area, are absent here. People go about unattended, without fear. Laughter stirs easily, at the slightest hint of humor; someone relates a small incident and everyone laughs uproariously and happily. Visitors are welcome and pressed to stay.

Quarrels, fights, warfare play a minor, virtually insignificant, role in their lives.*

The central emphasis in the society is on cooperation and growth. The Arapesh lack the conception of human nature as evil and in need of strong checks and curbs. They regard both men and women as inherently gentle, responsive, and cooperative, able and willing to subordinate their own needs to the needs of those who are younger or weaker and to derive a major satisfaction from doing so. Both parents take great pleasure in the tender, loving care of the child as he or she grows toward maturity. The child to the Arapesh is not a means by which the individual ensures that his or her identity will survive death. In some societies the child is a mere possession, perhaps the most valuable of all. But such a picture is meaningless to the Arapesh, whose sense of possession even of the most basic material object is so blurred with a sense of the needs of and obligations to others as to be almost lost.

To them the world is a garden that must be tilled, not for one's self, not in pride and boasting, not for hoarding and usury, but so that everything—yams, dogs, children—may grow. There is a lack of conflict between old and young, a lack of any expectation of jealousy or envy, a total emphasis on cooperation. Cooperation is easy when all are wholeheartedly committed to a common project from which no one of the participants will benefit personally.

They have very little sense of struggle in the world. Life is a maze through which one must find one's way, battling with neither demons within nor demons without, but concerned always with finding the path, with observing the rules that make it possible to find and keep the path. These rules, which define the ways in which sex and growth may and may not take place, are many and complicated. From the time that children are 6 or 7 they must begin to learn them, by early puberty they must be taking responsibility for their observance, and by the time they are adults a careful, meticulous observance, which will make yams grow beneath their hands and children come to their households, will be established. There is no other major problem in life, no evil in the human soul that must be overcome.

Their hostility is handled by projection. Upon those who do not share this mild and loving attitude toward life, the plainsmen, the Arapesh attribute the responsibility for all their misfortunes, for accidents and fire, for illness and death. Their own supernatural guardians

* For a striking comparison with the Plains Arapesh and confirmation of Mead's work see D. F. Tuzin, "Ritual Violence among the Ilahita Arapesh," in G. H. Herdt, 1982, Chap. 8. See also C. R. Hallpike, 1977.

punish lightly and always for a breach of one of the rules by which humans live in comfort with the forces of the land, or because they have failed to keep separate the natural potency of female functions and the supernatural forces that aid and abet men. But the plainsmen kill for profit and for hate. They take advantage of slight breaches in the warm wall of affection by which an Arapesh community is encircled; they convert these slight breaches into illness and death, a result that no one of the Arapesh intended. When someone dies the Arapesh find no one guilty, but they do attribute it to the hostile act of a disgruntled blackmailer or to some impersonal anger in another community far away, a community that, losing one of its own people, has paid the blackmailer to revenge the death upon someone whose name they will never know.

Nevertheless, whenever one of their young men dies, they pay the plainsmen to kill another such young man, in some distant community, so that they may obey the traditional forms and say to the ghost: "Return, thou art revenged." They hate only the distant; the only exception is the arrogant, swaggering, bullying sorcerers who boldly advertise their inhumanity, their willingness to kill for a price. Thus with the aid of the plainsmen and this formula of distant, impersonal revenge the Arapesh exile all murder and hate beyond their borders and are able to call any one of 50 men brothers and eat trustingly from the same plate with any one of them.

Whenever there is some hostility, the expression of which is generally random, unpatterned, and uncontrolled, they resort to sorcery to redress the balance. Thus sorcery becomes one of the major outlets for their aggression, otherwise completely inhibited.

In sexual matters they recognize no temperamental difference whatsoever. A scene that culminates in intercourse may be initiated by his holding her breasts, or her holding his "cheeks"—the two approaches are regarded as equivalent, and one is as likely to occur as another. However, they deny spontaneous sexuality to both sexes and regard the exception as occurring only in women. Both men and women are conceived of as capable of response only to a situation that their society has already defined for them as sexual. So they feel that it is necessary to chaperone betrothed couples who are too young for sexual intercourse to be healthful for them, but they do not feel that it is necessary to chaperone young people in general. Sex takes a slow course. It follows on the heels of affectionate deep interest but does not precede it and stimulate it. Both men and women are regarded as helpless in the face of seduction. In such an atmosphere sex is very pleasant, but the emphasis on sexual excitement and orgasm is lacking.

Most interesting is their marriage custom. When a girl reaches the age of 7 or 8 she is betrothed to a young man about 6 years her senior. Once betrothed, the girl goes to live in the home of her future husband. Here the father-in-law, the husband-to-be, and all of his brothers join forces to "grow" the little bride. Upon the young adolescent husband-to-be particularly falls the onus of growing yams, working sago, hunting for meat with which to feed his wife.

The Arapesh believe that parents should be able to control their children whom they have grown, and on the same principle they believe that husbands should be able to control their wives; they have grown them, they are responsible for them, they are older, and they have better judgment. The whole organization of society is based upon the analogy between children and wives, together representing a group who are younger, less responsible than the men, and therefore to be guided.

It is about small girls that the Arapesh are most romantic. Young men will comment with enthusiasm upon the feminine charms of a 5-year old and sit about entranced by the coquettishness of some baby whose mother, for amusement, has decked her out in a grass skirt. There is no sexual emphasis in this; to regard children as sexual objects would be incredible to the Arapesh.

Although she insists that they are rather rare, Mead devotes a good deal of space to various aberrant personalities. These have a very difficult time. They are not subjected to the rigid discipline that they would receive among a people who deal seriously with such temperaments. A woman like Amitoa, who murdered her child, continued to live on in a community; similarly a Subabibis man who murdered a child in revenge for his own son's fall from a tree was not disciplined by the community, nor by the child's relatives, because they lived too far away. The society actually gives quite a good deal of leeway to violence, but it gives no meaning to it. With no place for warfare, for individual exploits of bravery and strength, for strong leadership, violent men find themselves treated as almost insane. Thus violence is handled by ostracism; Jean Briggs reports a similar phenomenon among the Eskimos with whom she worked and lived (1970, pp. 214–223).

SUMMARY COMMENTS ON LOVE CULTURES

Other love cultures could be described. Enough has been presented to justify certain important conclusions.

1.   There are love cultures. This proposition, which has been so vehemently denied, is the most significant of all. How these love cultures came about we do not know, but evidently in the haphazard way in which various human cultures have come into existence, some have learned to stress love, affection, tenderness, and cooperation, while others have learned to stress hatred, antagonism, harshness, and competitiveness. A further conclusion is that if this has happened by accident, so to speak, it can also be brought about by conscious effort.

2.   The major characteristic of the love culture is the general feeling of harmony, which is absent in hate cultures.

3.   It must be recognized that some form of aggression is universal. In most of the societies described it takes the form of projection to outside elements, other cultures (as among the Arapesh), or supernatural forces (as among the Ifaluk). However, there is a vast difference between projected aggression that leaves the everyday lives of the people relatively free of hostility and worry and constant or intermittent violence, warfare, fighting, and murder. The major difference is that between actual violence and mere thoughts of harming others or fears of being harmed.

4.   Usually love cultures allow wide latitude for sexual expression. The most striking example is the Mangaian Culture, in which no one is left without a love partner and in which frigidity (lack of orgasm) in women is unknown. Impotence in men is rare until relatively old age. In other cultures, however, sex is less important, as among the Arapesh, who describe it only as an easy, comfortable feeling, or among the Hutterites, who condone it in marriage but forbid it otherwise.

5.   In general, persons living in these cultures are fairly happy and contented with their lives. The severe expressions of emotional conflict and mental disorder so characteristic of our own society are rare among them.

6.   Within our own culture distinctions could also have been drawn between happy families and unhappy ones (see Beavers, 1977), but this would have taken us too far afield. In general, the descriptions apply to the majority of the people in the culture, not to everyone. There are always and everywhere individual differences that require more detailed examination and more careful explanation.

But in any case the main point has been established: There are cultures in which the predominant mode of relationship among people is one of love and affection. Now we will look at hate cultures, in which the predominant mode of relationship is one of hatred and antagonism.

FIVE HATE CULTURES

It is certainly easier to find examples of hate cultures than of love cultures. This has been interpreted to mean that aggression is so deeply ingrained in human nature that it can at best only be modified, never eradicated (e.g., Lorenz, 1963; Eibl-Eibesfeldt, 1979). How this argument stands up is a matter to be discussed more carefully after all the data in this book have been assembled and digested.

The Aztecs

Because the Aztecs were conquered and subsequently slaughtered by the Spaniards, there has been a tendency to regard their customs as "quaint," overlooking the extraordinary sanguinary cruelty present in them. There are many sources that detail their history, but the account here is based on Davies (1981) and Vaillant (1950).

After they had been forced to submit by the Spaniards, the Aztecs remained there, and some of their conquerors described their civilization in the greatest of detail. It was there for all to see. In some respects, in some areas of Mexico, little has changed since the conquest.

Of the various peoples of what is today Mexico and Guatemala (meso-America), the Aztecs emerged somewhere around 1400 as a warrior group that held the rest of the area in subjection. One aspect of this subjection was human sacrifice, on such a vast scale as to be almost unbelievable. Bernal Diaz states that 100,000 heads were displayed on the skull racks of Xocotlán, while Andres de Tapia claimed to have counted 136,000 heads on the great skull rack of Tenochtitlán (Davies, 1981, p. 218). While these figures have been questioned, there is no doubt that the numbers were in fact huge.

The greatest recorded sacrifice of all time took place in 1487, in the reign of Ahuitzol, to inaugurate the Great Temple. The emperor, together with two allied rulers and his leading official, led the way, accompanied by throngs of priests; both they and the victims were dressed as gods. The captives, duly painted and feathered, had been formed into interminable lines that stretched along the main causeways into the city. The performance was watched by a huge crowd, since the people of neighboring towns were ordered to come to the capital on pain of death; no one was exempt, and not a man, woman, or child was to be seen in their home streets. The sacrifices lasted 4 whole days. When Ahuitzol and his royal colleagues wearied of gashing open the victims' breasts and plucking out the hearts, the priests took up the knives in their places.

Tradition relates that the victims numbered 80,400, a figure repeated by several sources. Davies (1981) considers this too high, but whatever it was, the number murdered (a better word than *sacrificed*) was extraordinarily large.

The standard way of killing was to cut out the heart of the victim, splayed on the sacrificial stone: Four priests held the victim's arms and legs, while the fifth slashed the ribs and tore out the heart—a process once euphemistically described as a "cardiectomy" in a tourist brochure. Some victims were drowned; those chosen for the ninth month were burned, while the main offering of the eleventh month was sudden decapitation. The symbolism attached to these months is not clear. Prolonged torture was generally absent.

These sacrifices were an integral part of the whole culture, not a frenzied release of momentary passion or hatred. There were in all 18 monthly feasts, held in honor of the rain gods, and for each of these different kinds of sacrifices were prescribed. For instance, for the first of the 18 feasts, blood offerings were made, sacrificial banners hung, and children sacrificed.

> *And there they took children, known as "human banners"—those who had two cowlicks of hair and whose day signs were favorable. They were sought everywhere and bought. It was said: "These are precious blood-offerings. [The rain gods] receive them with rejoicing; they are thus satisfied and given contentment." [Davies, 1981, pp. 218–219]*

In all, seven different places are named where these sacrifices of children took place. At first men wept for them, but "if the children went crying, their tears coursing down and bathing their faces, it was said and understood that indeed it would rain. . . . Therefore men were joyful; thus were their hearts at rest" (Davies, 1981, p. 207).

For the second month prisoners of war were sacrificed to the Flayed God. The captors smoked tobacco, danced with their victims, took mementos of hair from the tops of their heads, and made offerings of blood from their ears. Then the prisoners were led up to the temple and slain by the priests. The bodies were rolled down the steps and carried off by the old men to the temples of the different districts of the city, where they were cut in pieces, a thigh of each being set aside for the emperor Montezuma. Each captor called his blood relations to a feast, and each one was cooked a bowl of a stew of dried maize and human flesh.

And so on it goes for each of the 18 months. Sahagun, a Spanish friar who compiled the most extensive record of the culture, summed up the Aztecs' attitude to the prisoners' fate:

And this betokeneth our life on earth. For he who rejoices, who pos-
sesseth riches, who seeketh and coveteth our lord's sweetness, his gentle-
ness—riches and prosperity—thus endeth in great misery. For it is said:
"None come to an end here upon earth with happiness, riches and
wealth." [Davies, 1981, pp. 206–207]

While most attention has been paid to the bizarre sacrificial sequences, it must also be asked what kind of culture this was, which sent so many people to their deaths religiously (the word is used advisedly). Clearly it was a nation of lords and slaves, and the slaves simply had to submit to their fate. While no one has really raised the issue, it is clear that in such a culture love must have been almost completely absent. The rationalization that the sacrificial victims were assured that they would go to a special heaven is little more than that—a rationalization after the fact. Once under the yoke of the Aztecs, the only recourse for the individual was to be resigned to his or her fate.

After conquering the Aztecs in 1521, the Spanish, a hate culture in their own right, rapidly regimented all available Indian labor to mine, farm, and produce export goods in factories. This commercial explosion took a terrible toll of the Indians. Disease, malnutrition, dangerous chemicals (e.g., mercury), the absence of safety devices, and the general cruelty of the Spaniards decimated the population. One authority estimates that the population of Mexico was reduced from between 30 and 37.5 million before the conquest to a mere 1.5 million between 1520 and 1650 (Davies, 1981, p. 457).

Vaillant tends to idealize the Aztecs, describing them as a people who "could exist harmoniously together in considerable numbers" (1950, p. 123). While he describes the unending cycle of wars and sacrifices, he says that the "symbolism of their sacrifice has, nonetheless, its own barbaric beauty" (1950, p. 205). Yet as he describes the culture, there is constant fear, rage, and murder. They divided the year into 18 monthly cycles of 20 days each, leaving 5 "useless" days. Every year during these 5 useless days they were in constant terror that the world would not continue. They let their fires go out and destroyed their household furniture. Fasting and lamentation were the order of the day while the populace awaited catastrophe. Pregnant women were shut up in granaries lest they be changed into wild animals, and children were marched up and down and kept awake for fear that sleep on that fatal evening would turn them into rats. As soon as the priests were assured that the world would continue, they killed a victim (Vaillant, 1950, p. 200).

Other features of a hate culture were prominent. Children were trained by rigorous corporal punishment, although it is alleged that this started only when they were 8. This discipline ranged from pricking the hand with the maguey spine to exposing the child to the chill rigors of a mountain night, lying bound and naked in a mud puddle (Vaillant, 1950, p. 110).

The list of crimes punishable by death or physical violence that was nearly fatal is almost endless, including theft, especially of precious substances, murder, even of a slave, black magic, adultery, and incest. Even Vaillant admits that "Aztec law was brutal" (1950, p. 121).

It would be hard to find a body of literature that is more mournful than that of the Aztecs. There is a feeling of despair that runs through everything they wrote. A typical poem is the following:

> **Fatal Death**
> Where can we go where there will be no death?
> For this my heart cries.
> Be strong; nobody is going to live here!
> Even the princes are carried to death.
> So desolate is my heart.
> Be strong: nobody is going to live here.
> [K. GARIBAY, 1970. TRANSLATION IS AUTHOR'S.]

This constant brutalization under the Aztec lords no doubt played a part in the decimation of the population after the Spaniards took over. Mexicans of today are still noted for their indifference to death and resignation to their fate.

The Jivaro: "I Was Born to Die Fighting"

The Jivaro are a group of Indians in Ecuador whose history goes back to the days before the conquest. They were the only group in South America whom the Spaniards could not pacify; before that even the Incas had been unable to defeat them. For centuries they remained isolated from the outside world, famous mainly for their witchcraft, killing, and head-hunting (the *tsantsas*, or shrunken heads). It was not until the middle of the nineteenth century that some continuous contact was established with the white world. But the interior Jivaro, who lived beyond a steep mountain range, still had no constant contact with whites when the anthropologist Michael Harner went to study them in 1956 and 1957. (The account here is based on Harner, 1973.) He also returned there in 1964 and 1969, noting that considerable changes had occurred in the intervening period.

Historically, the Jivaro's complete isolation goes back to the revolt against the Spaniards in 1599. Infuriated by the treatment given to them by the conquerors, they secretly arranged for an attack on the city of Logroño, the governor's residence. Almost all of the inhabitants were massacred, except for the young, serviceable women, who were carried off. The governor was tortured to death by having gold forced down his throat. After that massacre the Jivaro were left to themselves until fairly recently.

The entire culture is violent in the extreme. There is no formal political or kin organization because of the fears that all people have of their neighbors. They live in isolated houses—typically one man, two wives, and six children—that are built like fortresses. The man sleeps with a gun next to his bed and a dog at his side who will wake him if an enemy approaches. There is so much slaughter among the men that the ratio of adult females to adult males is two to one.

The admired man is the one who has succeeded in killing three or four other men on one of the *tsantsas* raids. In fact, the life cycle of the man centers strongly around his wish to acquire power by killing. A central belief in their system is that of the three souls: the *arutam* soul, the *muisak* (or avenging), and the "true," or "ordinary," soul. Of these, the *arutam* and the *muisak* are the most important. In the system of thought around the *arutam* soul the Jivaro seek security from the ever-felt menace of death.

Possessors of a single *arutam* soul cannot be killed by any form of physical violence, poison, or sorcery, although they are not immune to death from contagious diseases such as measles and smallpox. Thus they are relieved from daily anxiety about being murdered. A Jivaro who is fortunate enough to possess two *arutam* souls cannot die of any cause whatever.

The *arutam* soul is acquired largely by men, in certain traditional ways. It is considered to be so important that a boy's parents do not expect him to live past puberty without one. Women sometimes obtain *arutam* souls, but it is not considered so essential for them.

A boy begins seeking an *arutam* soul at about the age of 6 years. Accompanied most commonly by his father, he makes a pilgrimage to the sacred waterfall in his neighborhood. By various devices, such as bathing and ingesting hallucinogenic drugs, the boy (or young man) then acquires an *arutam*. After nightfall, when he is home, he goes alone to sleep on the bank of the nearest river. He then has a dream in which there is a visitor, an old Jivaro man who says to him: "I am your ancestor. Just as I have lived a long time, so will you. Just as I have killed many times, so will you" (Harner, 1973, pp. 138–139). Without another word the old man disappears, and immediately the *arutam* soul of the unknown ancestor enters the body of the dreamer, where it is lodged in his chest.

Upon acquiring an *arutam*, the person feels a sudden increased power in his body. He is then seized with a tremendous desire to kill, and it is ordinarily only a matter of a few months before he joins a killing expedition. If he is a young boy, he will accompany his father. The rare women who possess *arutam* souls kill primarily by means of poisoning food or manioc beer.

Harner describes the killing expeditions as follows:

Jivaro killing expeditions usually attack the victim's house just before dawn. Late in the afternoon of the day prior to the attack, the expedition halts in the forest about a quarter of a mile from its intended objective. There, in their concealed location, the participants must "declare" what kind of arutam they had each seen. The younger men form a circle around several of the most experienced killers, who then ask each man in turn to describe the arutam that he had seen. As each man young and old does this, the soul of the arutam leaves his body forever, to roam the forest again as a wind, for arutam souls "are satisfied with one killing. . . ."

The warriors, having made their declarations, are ready to attack the following morning. Although each of them has just lost an arutam soul, the power of that soul remains in the body, only ebbing away gradually. The complete loss of this power is generally believed to take about two weeks. Since the power decreases slowly, the members of the killing party still retain enough of it the next morning so that they cannot be killed by the enemy in battle. If one of their number is killed in the attack, the other members of the expedition simply consider the death to be evidence that the deceased had already lost his arutam soul without realizing it. As soon as the expedition kills its intended victim, all its members again become entitled to obtain the soul of a new arutam upon their return home.

Sometimes the attackers fail in their assault on the intended victim's house. When such a failure occurs, the expedition must immediately choose a new victim and go after him at once, usually without return-

*ing home. If these men failed to kill someone, they would not be en-
titled to obtain new arutam souls, and without new arutam souls, they
would expect to die within weeks or, at the most, months. Since it is
therefore a matter of life or death to them, the members of the killing
party invariably find an enemy, or at least some stranger, to assassinate.
When the killing is accomplished, they return home and each immediately seeks to encounter an arutam again and thus to get himself a new
soul. [1973, pp. 138–139]*

The dead man (or woman) has a muisak, or avenging soul. The sole
reason for existence of a person's *muisak* is to avenge his or her death.
This soul therefore attempts to kill the murderer, or if that is not
possible, a son or a wife of the murderer. Technically, the avenging soul
is called a *muisak* only while it is in the corpse, thus in the shrunken
head (*tsantsa*) or its immediate vicinity. When the human head trophy
is not taken and prepared, the *muisak* is able to travel as far as it likes
from the corpse and to form into one of three kinds of demons, all of
which can kill a human. Thus their whole lives center around the knowledge that it is kill or be killed.

It is not surprising that with this constant desire to kill, or ward off
being killed, the people are very scattered. Nowhere is there any concentration in a village; that would be too dangerous.

The household is the close-knit economic and social unit rather than
the neighborhood or tribal society as a whole. Each house is usually isolated about half a mile or more from the next. The man is formally head
of the household and informally generally dominates the family. Men
strongly prefer to have two or more wives, but the demand for wives
usually exceeds the supply.

Marriage is based on romantic love, a concept that Harner (1973)
claims is strongly developed among the Jivaro (this seems highly paradoxical and dubious, in the light of everything else we know about
them). Young men frequently play love songs and thereby magically
cause their sweethearts to think of them, no matter how distant they
may be. Love potions are also used.

But while premarital sex is condoned, though it should not be too
open, extramarital sex is a serious offense that can be punished by
mutilation or death. Thus when a man learns that another man has
had sex with his wife, he has the right to cut her lover's scalp, whether
he discovered him in the act or not. If the husband discovers them in
the act, he may kill the offender or mutilate the genitals of the woman.

Similarly, if a woman discovers her husband in the act, she is expected to slash his scalp with a machete; she rarely attacks the other woman. The husband then leaves for about a month. If a man repeatedly commits adultery, his wife has the right to poison him. Of course, then the brothers and sisters and other close relatives of the man will attempt to murder her in retaliation.

In general, no natural causes of death are recognized. Death is always due to witchcraft or sorcery and leads to a seemingly endless cycle of retaliatory acts. Revenge thus is one of the major emotions of the society.

Infanticide is regularly practiced only in the case of deformed children. It is accomplished by crushing the infant with a foot. Sometimes unmarried girls kill their babies immediately upon birth if they have no expectation of marrying the father.

Child rearing is a mixture of extreme permissiveness and equally extreme cruelty. The baby is nursed until 6 or 7; Harner states that it is not unusual to see a woman with one child at each breast. Toilet training is likewise left until quite late. One reason for this is that at night they are afraid to let the child out of the house for fear that he or she will be hurt or murdered. Adults likewise simply use the floor as a toilet at night at times because of the fear of assassination if they leave the house.

After the first 2 weeks or so of the baby's life, the mother returns to the garden, while the father is out hunting or killing. The garden work is arduous, and the infant is often left alone for hours at a time. Other mothers who are nursing do not feed the infant, and wet-nursing is unknown. As a result the baby is always hungry. One song goes:

> Dear mother, dear mother
> Come soon, come soon,
> The baby is crying,
> The baby is crying,
> For lack of your milk it will die,
> For lack of your milk it will die.
> Dear mother, come quickly. . . .
> [Harner, 1973, p. 86]

If children are bad, they may be spanked or hit with nettles. But if they continue to be bad, the parents may resort to the harshest punishment ever used. They drop a large quantity of hot peppers into a small fire and force the children to remain over the fire under a large cloth until they become unconscious. When they recover, they may be admonished that if they again misbehave they will have all their hair burned off. Another harsh punishment is to give children hallucinogenic drugs if they are too disrespectful of their fathers.

No dolls in human form are permitted. Play among children is discouraged. Life is a grim business from birth on.

When about 4, a boy learns the art of blowgun hunting. By about 9 his skill normally has advanced to the stage where he is killing larger birds lurking in the trees around the garden.

Postpubescent boys perform most of the tasks of their fathers, including participation in the defense of the home and in attacks on enemies. When a boy reaches the age of about 16, he formally undertakes to establish his adult status by going into the forest, killing a tree sloth, and making a *tsantsa* of its head.

The real *tsantsa* feasts, which follow the murder of an "enemy," are the chief social occasions of the tribe. One informant observed: "The desire of the Jivaro for heads is like the desire of the whites for gold" (Harner, 1973, p. 192).

There is a series of *tsantsa* feasts, the last two totaling 11 days of unremitting festivities. There is plenty of beer (manioc beer) and unlimited supplies of food. These feasts are participated in with a great deal of joy and a cumulative sense of euphoria.

There is ritual circle dancing, which continues from dawn to dusk, night after night. Since most of the people are drunk, they also let themselves go sexually. Ordinarily this would lead to vengeance and murder, but at the *tsantsa* feast it is believed that the avenging soul of the murdered man will be able to take advantage of any disruption of the binding ritual by escaping from the *tsantsa* to cause an ongoing fight to culminate in a death. Therefore, any fight that erupts is immediately stopped by the others. Thus this feast, with more than 100 participants at times, centers around the indisputable evidence of a triumph over a common enemy.

The leaders are all outstanding killers and shamans. Most young men express a desire to kill and take pleasure in doing so.

Shamanism is dominant. About one of every four adult men is a shaman. The essence of their power is their magical darts, which are viewed as invisible spirit helpers that normally reside in the shaman's body. A local bewitching shaman hierarchy also sometimes acts in concert as a "raiding party" to go together to kill, through witchcraft, a common enemy in another neighborhood.

Direct suicide by men is unknown. But men sometimes undertake killing expeditions that are so dangerous they become tantamount to suicide. Women often commit suicide when they are treated badly by their husbands or when they have committed adultery and are fearful of the consequences.

Obviously this is an extreme hate culture. There is a universal fear of death, which leaves them only for brief periods, and then for magical reasons, for instance, possession of two *arutam* souls.

When Harner revisited the Jivaro in the summer of 1969, killing had diminished considerably, although, as he says, they had learned to conceal the evidence of murder in the ways perfected long ago in "civilized" societies. There are now Ecuadoran army garrisons, airstrips have been built, and the old ways of life are becoming extinct. But in spite of the changes, there is still a climate of hostility and unrest that recalls the conditions of the Jivaro revolt of 1599.

Nazi Germany: World Conquest and Holocaust (1933–1945)

The discovery of the incredible destruction of the holocaust, in which some six million Jews were systematically murdered as the "final solution," has in some ways served to obscure the real structure of Nazi Germany. It was in every respect a total revolution, from a conflicted, civilized modern state, not too different from other European countries, to a bloody hate culture, based on paranoia, revenge, and murder. Full details of the nature of the state came to light only after the defeat of the Germans and the opening of the archives.

By now the basic facts are so well known that they will not be repeated here. Instead, the psychological characteristics of the system and its leaders will be examined more closely.

One of the great paradoxes, which historians are still trying to unravel, is that Hitler from the very beginning did not conceal his intentions. His story was that Germany had lost World War I because of a stab in the back by the Jews, and revenge would be secured. When he was on trial for the unsuccessful putsch of 1923, he frankly stated: "The November 1918 revolution will be avenged and heads will roll!" (Shirer, 1960, p. 141). Germany would be reunited and would conquer the world. Propaganda based on the "big lie" was to be used as a major weapon in both peace and war.

Since Germany had long been known as the country of "poets and thinkers," Hitler's fulminations were not taken too seriously until the last minute, when war could no longer be averted. For as soon as he came to power (again, paradoxically, by legal means), he began to turn Germany into a military fortress in which everything was subordinated to the "new order" and victory by force of arms. In the meantime big lies were published all over the place, until people eventually got the idea that nothing he said was worthy of belief.

While the war story is well known, less publicized is the total transformation of Germany into a paranoid state. Its chief myths were the superiority of the Aryan race and the degeneracy of the Jews. Gay and Webb state that "in its thoroughness, its pretension to scientific truth, and its horror, the insistence on racial purity—the most characteristic trait of Nazism—goes far beyond any modern anti-Semitism and far beyond any nineteenth-century racial thinking that was not certifiable as insane" (1973, p. 1038). This judgment by two competent historians that Hitler was insane has been much disputed; yet it explains much of what happened.

The security of all citizens ended when the gestapo (secret police) was established in 1933, shortly after Hitler took power. Thereafter it became a state within a state, subject to no law or control. It set up an army of spies and informers who terrorized the populace. Any accusation was likely to be followed by immediate arrest, torture, and death. While the activities of the gestapo have been most often described in terms of the occupied countries, it was active in Germany as well, from the beginning to the end.

By the end of 1933 some 50 concentration camps had been set up all over Germany to punish the "enemies of the regime" (Shirer, 1960, p. 271). At first these camps did little more than punish the inmates, blackmail them, and occasionally commit murder. But as time went on, they became increasingly destructive, until they turned into total extermination camps, in which people were murdered by the millions. At Auschwitz, toward the end, 6000 people a day were being murdered (Shirer, 1960, p. 967).

Increasingly, control over the entire population was established. By a decree in 1943 all men from 16 to 65 and all women from 17 to 45 were mobilized for the tasks involved in "defending the Reich" (Gruchmann, 1977, p. 412). Here, too, the paranoid element comes in: Everybody knew that Germany was out to conquer the world, but the official propaganda line was that the country was "under attack." When the Nazis managed to build their dangerous buzz bombs in 1944, they called them "revenge weapons," that is, revenge for the Allies' bombings of Germany.

The mobilization of the entire population meant that *everybody* became subordinated to the interests of the state. There was to be no deviation of any kind. The press, literature, theater, university teaching, and the military were completely dominated by the new order. Family responsibility for crimes was reestablished: In 1944 Hitler decreed that if soldiers at the front surrendered or did not fight to the last, their families would be held accountable and punished (Gruchmann, 1977, p. 413).

Wartime mobilization was merely a continuation of peacetime *Gleichschaltung*, or "equalization," that had been a Nazi principle from the very beginning. The culture of the past was to be replaced by a "new order." Though not too well defined, this concept meant that all vestiges of the humanistic ideals of the past were to be rooted out totally.

The first noticeable celebration of this destruction of the past culture was the burning of the books in May 1933. Goebbels verbalized the symbolic meaning of the book burning: "The soul of the German people can again express itself. These flames not only illuminate the final end of an old era; they also light up the new" (Shirer, 1960, p. 241).

Thereafter government bureaus were set up to guide and control every sphere of cultural life. All persons engaged in these fields were obligated to join their respective chambers, whose decisions and directives had the validity of law. Not a single living German writer of any importance was published in Germany during the Nazi period. Almost all of them left, led by Thomas Mann, who engaged in futile radio broadcasts to the German people during the war, from his exile in America. Those who did not emigrate were silenced or murdered. Every manuscript of a book or a play had to be submitted to the propaganda ministry before it could be approved for publication or production.

Music fared best, because the Germans had such a rich store of it. Further, a number of prominent musicians remained in Germany and lent their names to the Nazi cause or were Nazis through and through.

In the theater, the playwrights were so ludicrously bad that the public stayed away from their plays, which invariably had short runs. The president of the Reich Theater Chamber was a certain Hans Johst, an unsuccessful playwright who once had publicly boasted that whenever someone mentioned the word "culture" to him he wanted to reach for his revolver (Shirer, 1960, pp. 242–243).

In art, one of the first acts was to cleanse Germany of its "decadent art" (such as Picasso and Rembrandt) and to attempt to substitute a new "Germanic" art. Some 6500 modern paintings were removed from the museums and replaced by what Shirer calls the "worst junk" he had ever seen; they have virtually disappeared since. When the House of

German Art was opened in Munich in 1937, Hitler said: "With the opening of this exhibition has come the end of artistic lunacy and with it the artistic pollution of our people" (Shirer, 1960, p. 244).

One of the peculiarities of the Nazi mind was the obsession with "legality." Everyone knew that the press was completely controlled by the government, but a press law had to be published (October 1933) that made journalism a "public vocation" and ordered editors to keep out of the papers anything which in any manner was "misleading to the republic."

In education, Bernhardt Rust, who earlier had been dismissed as a provincial schoolmaster because of "instability of mind," was named minister of science, education, and popular culture. He boasted that he had succeeded overnight in "liquidating the school as an institution of intellectual acrobatics" (Shirer, 1960, p. 248). The whole school system was soon completely Nazified. In a speech on May 1, 1937, Hitler declared: "This new Reich will give its youth to no one, but will itself take youth and give to youth in its own education and its own upbringing" (Shirer, 1960, p. 249). This was to be just another step in the total destruction of the family.

In spite of the obvious absurdities, one Nazi after another sang the praises of the Nazi achievements in science. Professor Philip Lenard of Heidelberg said: "Science, like every other human product, is racial and conditioned by blood" (Shirer, 1960, p. 250). Another professor, Rudolphe Tomaschek, claimed: "True physics is the creation of the German spirit. . . . In fact, all European science is the fruit of Aryan, or better, German Thought." In 1937 they even began publication of a journal called "German mathematics" (Shirer, p. 250).

Yet for the most part the German professors did not oppose the Nazi regime. In 1933 some 960, led by such eminent names as Sauerbruch, the surgeon, Heidegger, the philosopher, and Pinder, the art historian, took a public vow to support Hitler and the National Socialist regime (Shirer, 1960, p. 251).

The persecution of the churches began more moderately but eventually ended in the same way. Both Protestants and Catholics were persecuted (Hochhuth in his well-known play *The Deputy* raises the question of why the pope did not intervene more actively, when he knew that Catholic priests, monks, and nuns were being persecuted and murdered by the Nazis). Eventually, the practice of religion as we know it was destroyed (Shirer, 1960, p. 240).

Religion was replaced by a "National Reich Church." Rosenberg, in his statement of doctrines of the new church (Shirer, 1960, p. 240), specified that on the altars there must be nothing but *Mein Kampf* (the most sacred book to the German people) and to the left of the altar there must be a sword.

Women were relegated to a subordinate role as caretakers of children. Goebbels put it as follows:

> *The mission of woman is to be beautiful and bring children into the world. This is not at all as rude and unmodern as it sounds. The female bird prettifies herself for her mate and hatches the eggs for him. In exchange, the mate takes care of gathering the food, and stands guard and wards off the enemy.* [Mosse, 1981, p. 41]

But the sexual–mothering role of the woman went much further. As early as the mid-1930s, "stud farms" were set up in various parts of Germany where young girls could stay to have children for the führer. Hitler's grandiose scheme was to exterminate all the non-Aryans in Europe and repopulate the continent with "racially pure" Germans. By 1980 the Greater Reich was to be populated by 120 million Germans (Hillel and Henry, 1976, p. 81).

As time went on, and an increasing number of men died in battle, the need to replace the lost manpower was felt more keenly by the army. Hence they increased the number of homes where girls could live and have children, as well as demanding of all German soldiers that they should produce more children. These homes were known as *Lebensborn*, a typical Nazi neologism, composed of *Leben*, or "life," and the medieval *Born*, or "fount"; hence *Lebensborn* means "fount of life." (Incidentally it may be noted that the "purification" of the German language from any foreign contamination was another one of the Nazi programs; thus *radio* became *Rundfunk*; *telephone* became *Fernsprecher*; and so on.)

The men, generally soldiers on leave, obviously used the *Lebensborn* girls for sexual purposes; they cared little about what became of their children. As for the girls, they had no use for the men, either. In the correspondence of the girls there could be found no hint of love or even affection for the children they had just borne. These girls were generally about 15 or 16. For them sexual intercourse was a duty to the state and had nothing to do with pleasure. All that mattered for either men or women in this transformed culture was the greater glory of Hitler and the German nation. This was to be achieved by ruthless extermination of all enemies both within and without, and by production of more Germans. Since there were also many children in the occupied countries who looked Aryan, they were included in the scheme, and wholesale kidnappings were carried out. No one knows how many, but certainly several hundred thousand is not an exaggerated estimate (Hillel and Henry, 1976, p. 81).

Thus, had the war lasted longer, the entire traditional family system would have been destroyed and a new kind of society created. In this society the individual and love were to play no essential role; all persons had to submit to the dictates of the state. Hitler himself was unmarried (he married Eva Braun only a few days before he committed suicide), and he set the example for the rest of Germany.

Another aspect of the Nazi psychology that has been much discussed is the restoration of slavery. If even the German as an individual was not important, of what value could the foreigner be? Labor was needed to operate the factories, so the occupied countries were used to provide this labor; it was essentially slave labor.

By the end of September 1944 some 7.5 million foreigners were toiling for the Reich. Nearly all of them had been rounded up by force, deported to Germany in boxcars, usually without food or water or any sanitary facilities, and there put to work in the factories, fields, and mines. They were not only put to work but were also degraded, beaten, starved, and often left to die for lack of food, clothing, and shelter. Since they were in the eyes of the Nazis "subhuman," no justification was needed for this return to slavery.

What could be said of love in this culture? It was virtually non-existent. Even the top Nazis did not fully trust one another; thus a year after he came to power Hitler ruthlessly exterminated his friend Ernst Roehm and followers in a bloody putsch.

It is not surprising that the reaction of the occupied "slaves" was a violent one once the Nazis were defeated. One official estimated that between May 1945, when the Nazis surrendered, and September 1945, when relative order was restored, some six million Germans had died in Russia, the Russian zone, and eastern Europe (Crawley, 1973, p. 46). In addition, there were some nine million refugees who had left the eastern zone for the western (Crawley, 1973, p. 46). The surplus of women over men in West Germany was more than seven million (Crawley, 1973, p. 60).

Yet within one generation the Germans did recover from these horrors, and within two generations West Germany had become one of the most powerful states in Europe. Seemingly the hate culture, with its total transformation of human relations, was replaced by the same kind of culture that had existed before Hitler and that can be found in western Europe and in the U.S.

How different was the culture of Nazi Germany from that of the Jivaro? Largely it differed in the mastery of technology; in human terms they were on the same plane, living primarily to kill. Because of their technology the Nazis could think of conquering the world; the Jivaro were content just to kill their neighbors.

One other difference lay in the twisted personality of the Nazi leader, Adolf Hitler. Volumes have been written about him, and we shall not go into that topic here. Suffice it to say that there is general agreement that he was a perverted murderer, unable to relate to women, an evil genius at times in military matters, at other times given to a total abandonment of sound military principles, sick in body and mind at an early age, drawn to all kinds of magical potions. The recently published diaries of Hitler's "doctor," Morell, reveal that the quack physician prescribed for Hitler a number of harmful drugs (Shirer, 1960, p. 1102). The Jivaro did not have any such leader; perhaps if they had they too would have embarked on an attempt to conquer the surrounding areas.

The Tauade: Bloodshed and Vengeance

The Tauade are a group living in Papuan New Guinea, off the coast of Australia. A major administrative center is only 80 miles from Port Moresby by air. Some parts of the area have been under government and mission influence since the first decade of the century. The account here is based on Hallpike (1977).

The characteristic settlement pattern has always been one of relatively discrete tribes inhabiting spurs around the main valleys. Except for the occasional existence of dance villages, these tribes do not reside in a common settlement but are dispersed in clusters of small hamlets. However, these hamlets tend to be clustered close to one another as defense against the ever-present threat of an attack by an enemy. Land is plentiful, and food is rarely a problem.

The basic mode of social control is provided by the opposition of forces—violently in the case of vengeance, and peaceably where compensation is given for an injury. There is no idea of a meeting between disputants or of mediation by some respected arbiter.

Reciprocity is a dominant theme of their society and can be summed up as "paying back." Compensation and vengeance are both known as "payment," and their identity is more than purely verbal, since it has its roots in the basic purpose of "making the insides good." Thus an injured party may first take physical vengeance on his or her enemy, after which they will exchange work and/or other valuables to wipe out the hurt that each has sustained. In general, vengeance is more significant than peaceful reciprocity.

Women do the work of garnering the food, while the men look forward to fighting and killing. There is rather intense hostility between men and women. Men try to arrange marriages for daughters or sisters for two main reasons: first, to create an alliance with some other esteemed man; and, second, to obtain the sister of the man in question as payment for the woman he has provided.

Children seem to be unimportant. The desire to have large numbers of children seems absent. Some men with several children give one or two away to friends and relatives for adoption, or even sell them. A striking number of couples are childless; in some cases it would appear that this is the result of an abortifacient, a species of vine eaten with cinnamon and ginger.

Women are necessary for the social success of the men. Conversely, women are free to desert their husbands, impugn their manhood, or engage in adultery. Conflict and violence erupt when a man and a woman do not have the same desire.

Marriage is monogamous, but polygamy is permitted on occasion. All marriages are unstable, but the polygamous ones are especially so. In one tabulation the anthropologist found that only 46% of the marriages had remained intact (Hallpike, 1977, p. 131).

Women have considerable freedom, to desert their husbands, or to drive away other wives they may acquire, if they are strong enough. Dances are always followed by a rash of desertions by wives, leaving their husbands to cohabit with guests whose dancing had attracted them. One anthropologist who visited them in the 1930s recorded one dance that led to 25 killings. Even today dances often have similar consequences, though on a smaller scale.

The men are constantly trying to control their women, to make them marry other men with whom they wish to become allied, and to keep their own wives, or kinsmen's wives, from being seduced. At the same time they are themselves always looking for a chance to seduce other men's wives. Women are seen as having strong sexual appetites. In cases of adultery, especially where the woman comes from a different tribe, the man will plead in court that she forced herself upon him. Thus women incite men to sex and violence and admire men who are prone to violence.

Within the family, affection and grief are most intense. The relationship between siblings is especially close. The younger brother is expected to help and assist the older brother, while the elder brother is regarded as superior in status to the younger. But within the family, when affection and trust are disappointed, violent emotions erupt as well.

The greatest ceremony of the tribe is the large dance, to which all hamlets contribute. Ostensibly the purpose is to honor the bones of the dead, and by implication their spirits, before they are laid to rest and forgotten. Yet it is obvious that what they really want is to gain renown for generosity, hospitality, wealth, and stamina in dancing. For these occasions special villages are built, requiring many months of preparation; there may be as many as 70 houses for guests, of which many will be for men only; the chiefs of the host and guest tribes will have a large men's house at the top of the village. There are great displays of food by the host. Guests may be entertained for months, and pigs are killed over this period, but the ceremony culminates in a great dance on the night before the main pig killing. At the present time the tradition of the big dance, to which the guests proceed through the intervening tribal areas, dancing and killing pigs as they go, continues.

They are very open with their emotions. While there is a great deal of hatred and violence, there is also considerable love and compassion, easy tears at a reconciliation or a parting, and genuine sentiments of hospitality and generosity to strangers. All actions are explained in terms of the condition of the insides. Thus if a man is angry they say: "His insides were like fire," while if he is conciliatory, they say: "His insides were like water."

But their greatest passion is their desire for warfare and violence. Not too long ago there was still cannibalism in the area. In one case a chief, Gopa, returned from a raid with the bodies of five strange men. The five bodies had been cut up and cooked in stone ovens, and men, women, and children had eaten the flesh. When the administrative officer asked the chief why he had killed these people the chief replied, "You know our fashion. We look at these people; we look at them for a long time. We say they are there; good we kill them. We think of this all the time, and when our bellies get too hot, we go and kill them. No more" (Hallpike, 1977, p. 208).

Their thirst for violence and vengeance comes out very clearly in some of their legends and depictions of culture heroes. In one legend violence rose to such a crescendo of apocalyptic fury that everyone was exterminated and "the country belonged only to the animals" (Hallpike, 1977, p. 227). They explicitly state that they respect madmen because they are like the culture heroes.

In another legend they say that long ago their country was inhabited by nonhuman beings of gigantic power, who carved out the river valleys and who were of immense fertility, often with penises like those of horses or like 40-gallon drums. They were also extraordinarily homicidal. They roamed over the country raping and pillaging, smearing people with feces, shoving lengths of wood up people's anuses or down their throats, or flying up into trees to urinate on the people.

In reality they have lived for a long time in a state of continual warfare. In one valley warfare is probably a weekly occurrence. In 1934 one report stated that there were daily fights in the area.

When a member of a tribe is killed, no attempt is made to retaliate upon the murderer in person. It is sufficient that any member of the killer's tribe pays with his or her life, and in some cases the injured tribe is satisfied if their victim comes from the general area of the killer's tribe. But when a party of warriors has succeeded in killing one of their opponents, there is a tendency for the attackers to run away, almost in fear of their enemies' wrath.

Chiefs have considerable freedom to go where they wish, because of the fear of reprisals that killing them would provoke, and also in some cases because they are good fighters. But if any ordinary person offends a chief by not giving him a present, or if anyone in the tribe has a score to settle, he risks death by going too far. Some travelers are killed without even the justification of vengeance.

The greatest degree and frequency of intertribal violence seem to occur between tribes occupying adjoining territory on the same side of a valley. Sometimes when land is cleared for gardens and vegetation is burnt the fires get out of control and destroy pandanus trees, gardens, villages, and people. At times fighting between tribes becomes so intense that one of them withdraws temporarily until the rage of its enemies has cooled. When large-scale fighting impends, no formal challenge is given, and the object is to ambush the enemy, if possible, while they are cutting up pandanus nuts in the forest or cooking a pig in the bush. The party is surrounded and then charged, and as many as possible are slaughtered. Each tribe has a nucleus of redoubtable warriors who provide the core of their tribe in battle. In one tribe one of the warriors seems to have been virtually a homicidal maniac. One of the principal reasons for the continual warfare has been the inability of the tribes effectively to control the aggression of the individual members, while at the same time vengeance for their acts is liable to fall on any member of their tribe.

In short, the Tauade, like the other hate cultures described, love to fight, seek vengeance, and kill. In summing up the characteristics of the culture, Hallpike writes:

Tauade pig-rearing, feasts and dances, fighting and vengeance are not biologically adaptive, or even socially useful in any objective sense. . . . The traditional life of the Tauade was a prolonged fantasy of power, a religion whose rites were burning villages; the cries of warriors and victims; feathers and blood; dying pigs; and the monstrous figures of dancers singing tumultuously in the darkness of the ranges. These were . . . savage men in the grip of a collective obsession with blood and death. For them, work in their gardens was a boring necessity, to be shifted on to the women as far as possible, valuable only as the foundation of the real business of life—the pursuit of glory. [1977, p. 253]

The Sorcerers of Dobu: Magic and Paranoia

One of the purest hate cultures ever described is that of the Dobuans, who inhabit a small island off the coast of New Guinea. Rea Fortune provides a first-hand description of the Dobuan cultures (1932). The account here is based on Ruth Benedict's famous work *Patterns of Culture* (1934).

Dobuan institutions exalt animosity and malignancy to the highest degree. Dobuans live out without repression humanity's worst nightmares of the ill will of the universe, and according to their view of life virtue consists in selecting a victim upon whom they can vent the hatred they attribute to human society and to the powers of nature alike. All existence appears as a cutthroat struggle in which deadly antagonists are set against each other in a contest for the goods of life. Suspicion and cruelty are their most trusted weapons in the strife. They give no mercy, as they ask none.

Unlike some of the neighboring islands, Dobu has not been blessed with nature's bounty. The tiny scattered villages now number no more than 10 or 15 inhabitants, and still the food supply is so tenuous that the natives risk hunger.

Perhaps because of the difficulties of their life, the Dobuans are noted for their dangerousness. A couple of generations ago they were cannibals, but cannibalism has disappeared with white rule. Now they are feared for the harm that they can do. They are said to be magicians who have diabolic power and warriors who halt at no treachery.

They have no chiefs nor political organization. Like the Jivaro they are so fearful of one another that they do not aggregate in large numbers. Their social organization is arranged in concentric circles, within each of which specified traditional forms of hostility are allowed. No one takes the law into his or her own hands except to carry out these culturally sanctioned hostilities within the appropriate specified group. The largest functioning Dobuan grouping is a named locality of some 4 to 20 villages. It is the war unit and is on terms of permanent hostility with every other similar locality. Before the days of white control no man ventured into an alien locality except to kill or to raid.

The one source of affection in the society is the line of the mother's relatives (maternal lineage), which never dissolves, even with marriage. Within this group of relatives property is inherited and cooperation exists. It is called "the mother's milk," or *susu*. While it includes the brothers of the women in each generation, the children of these brothers are not included; they belong to their mothers' villages, groups toward which there is usually a major enmity.

Marriage must be with someone outside, thus forcing an alliance between two groups that are hostile. But marriage brings with it no amelioration of hostility. They have a kind of "shotgun" marriage system. Since puberty the boy has slept each night in the home of an unmarried girl. He rises early and leaves before anyone else is awake. After a certain point he gets careless and sleeps too long. Thereupon the girl's mother blocks him from leaving the house, and he is trapped for the public ceremony of betrothal. From this time on he has to reckon with the village of his wife. But there is no public laughter or teasing; everything is managed with dour formality.

Nor is marriage a happy alliance. Faithfulness is not expected of either party, and whenever a man and woman are together it is suspected that they are there for sex. Usually there are grounds for being suspicious. Sexual prowess is one of the major sources of self-esteem. As a result the common marriage house is so difficult to maintain that it continuously threatens the marriage and often destroys it. Thus broken marriages are five times as common in Dobu as in Manus, another Oceanic culture (Mead, 1953).

Apart from sexual conquest, the other source of self-esteem is ownership of property. Here there is constant competition. The good man, the successful man, is the one who has cheated another of his goods and his place. For this magical incantations are of great importance. There is fierce rivalry for magical formulas, and they are never owned in common. The bitterest conflict for the possession of magical incantations is between the sister's sons, who rightfully claim the magic of their mother's brother, and the latter's own sons, whose close association with their father in the household and common cause with him in gardening make a counterclaim strong enough to secure recognition.

The privacy of the garden is respected. But a good crop, produced by magic, is a confession of theft. It is supposed to have been alienated from the gardens even of one's own *susu* by dangerous sorcery. The amount of the harvest is carefully concealed and reference to it is an insult.

There are special charms for inflicting disease on another person. When a person finds himself or herself the victim of a disease, he or she communicates with the person who has caused the disease. The disease can be cured or ameliorated only by the corresponding exorcism owned by the same sorcerer. Usually sorcerers, if they are induced to exorcise the disease, do not themselves visit sufferers. They breathe the exorcism into a vessel of water brought by relatives of the sick ones. The vessels are sealed, and the sufferers are bathed with water in their own homes. The exorcisms are often thought to stave off death and permit deformity.

Suspicion runs to paranoid lengths, and a countercharm is always suspected. There are spells for specific diseases. Beyond that, powerful men have an even more potent weapon, known as *vada*. Sorcerers can confront the victims themselves, and such is the terror of the sorcerer's curse that the prey fall writhing to the ground. They never regain their minds and waste away to a destined death.

Naturally there is a constant fear of death. When someone dies there is an immediate inquiry into who might have caused it; death from natural causes does not exist. If the person is married the greatest suspicion falls upon the surviving spouse. As a result the wife is at least as much feared by her husband as the husband is by his wife. Men attribute to women a special technique of villainy that strangely resembles the European tradition of witches on broomsticks. After death the house of the dead is abandoned. The survivor is in subjection to the kin of the dead. The mourner must be released from subjection by further payments by his own clan to the clan of the deceased.

Murder may be committed by nonmagical means as well as magical. Poison is as universally suspected as sorcery or witchcraft. No woman leaves her cooking pot a moment untended lest someone gain access to it. Yet sorcery and witchcraft are by no means criminal; no person can exist without them.

What can love mean in such a society? Evidently there is some affection in the mother's lineage, and there is some affection between parent and child. The clan has some cohesiveness. Outside of that there exist only enmity, suspicion, paranoia, sorcery, witchcraft, hatred—and misery. Dobuans do not laugh in public. Life must be a horrible experience for them.

SUMMARY COMMENTS ON HATE CULTURES

1.　Even superficially, the five hate cultures described are markedly different from the five love cultures depicted earlier. While there are some features common to all cultures, a basic difference between love cultures and hate cultures is readily demonstrable.

2.　The major characteristics of the hate cultures is a general atmosphere of hatred, violence, and discord, accompanied by an ever-present fear of death. This fear of death is quite justified, since murder can occur on the slightest provocation, or even without provocation. These are all societies in which killing is a major activity, in sharp contrast to the love cultures, where killings are rare or unknown.

3.　There is some love present, but it is largely limited to the family and the tribe. The Jivaro have a "buddy" system in which a strong tie is set up between two adult males; somewhat similar customs are found in the others. But these love relationships are rarely completely reliable. Every individual lives in an ocean of hostility.

4.　The desire for vengeance is omnipresent. Since no natural causes of death are recognized, there is an endless cycle of murder and retaliation, apparently brought to a halt only by pressure from the outside.

5.　Reliance on magic and sorcery is widespread. Again this is entirely comprehensible, since rational considerations fail to explain the mysterious events that occur in the culture (O'Keefe, 1983).

6.　Sex is for conquest, accompanied by little or no affection. Marriages are unstable because the partners do not trust one another. A characteristic difference is the much more lenient attitude taken toward adultery in most love cultures (except for the religious Hutterites). Adultery carries with it a connotation of theft rather than of pleasure. In general, sexual pleasure as such, though obviously present, is not emphasized; what is emphasized is conquest, prowess, glory, power. While love is often mistakenly identified with sex, it is noteworthy that even in a country like the United States the slang words for the sex act carry a hostile rather than a loving connotation. The most extreme form of the destruction of marriage is found in the Nazi "stud farms." Had the Nazis won the war, the entire traditional family structure would have been wiped out.

7.　Women are devalued; their major functions are to provide food, take care of the children, and provide sex. In retaliation they fight against the men by whatever means are at their disposal, such as adultery, or in some cases murder of the husband. Thus there is constant internal warfare between men and women.

8. Since women are devalued, children are of little consequence. Public laughter is frowned upon, and so is playing for fun. The children too have to serve the purpose of the greater glory of the men.

9. In general, going "beyond the information given" (Bruner, 1973), it can safely be said that life for the members of these cultures is miserable in the extreme. Negative emotions, such as revenge, dominate their entire way of living.

10. Individual differences always can be found.

CONCLUSION

For the present, love can be defined simply as friendly feeling (affection). A love culture is one in which friendly feelings predominate; a hate culture one in which hateful feelings (hostility) predominate. One major thesis is that people are happier in a culture dominated by love than in one dominated by hatred.

Furthermore, the nature of the love experience will be different in the two types of culture. For, as will also be argued in more detail later, the reigning values of the surrounding society have as much of an impact on the individual as do his or her own idiosyncratic experiences. Hence there can be no complete definition of love as such until the relationship of the individual to his or her society is fully explored. This will be the final task, undertaken after all the other evidence has been presented—historical, anthropological, sociological, economic, psychoanalytic, psychiatric, and psychological.

2

Western Civilization as a Hate Culture

PART 1. FROM THE GREEKS TO THE MIDDLE AGES

Once the essential differences between love and hate cultures have been established, the next step is to enquire which of these western civilization has been. On this important point there can be little doubt: In the main, western civilization, from the time of the Greeks on, has been a hate culture: It still is. The solution that modern psychology has introduced is that the nature of the hatred can be understood, and a reasonable way out can be proposed. But first it is essential to see in broad outlines what the nature of the hate culture has been.

Such an approach will undoubtedly meet with a negative reaction from any traditionally minded historian. Before agreeing with such a reaction it would be well worth our time to look at the data that we have enumerated. For, as Burckhardt (1852) commented, history is the record of what one age finds of interest in another. In the familiar historical accounts, only the routes to progress have been charted; the massacres, barbarism, enslavement, and unspeakable horrors have been forgotten or passed over quickly. But since World War II, and perhaps because of the existence of nuclear weapons that can destroy the world, humanity has become increasingly concerned with hatred. And so the past has to be examined in a new light. Prevalent opinion has altered to such an extent that a reputable historian (Howard, 1976) can now speak of Christianity and Islam as two "warrior-religions," while another (McNeill, 1982) describes warriors as "macro-parasites" who by specializing in violence are able to secure a living for themselves without themselves producing the food and other commodities they consume.

Through the ages the balance between love and hatred has changed, sometimes drastically, sometimes slowly (Hunt, 1959). In looking at what has really happened in western history, this balance between love and hate must constantly be borne in mind. Since our emphasis is on love, the dominant forms of love in any particular cultural epoch and their meaning in relationship to the larger society will be given primary consideration.

For ease of discussion, six periods in western history and their dominant attitudes to love will be discussed. No attempt can be made here to summarize all of western civilization; only certain features can be presented. The six periods and their related love concepts are: (1) the ancient Greeks and bisexuality; (2) the Romans and cruelty; (3) Christianity and asceticism; (4) the twelfth-century discovery of romantic love and its later elaborations; (5) social and religious reform movements from the sixteenth century on; and (6) the making of the modern family from the eighteenth century on. In this chapter we will discuss the first three periods; in the next chapter we will take up the second three.

ANCIENT GREECE

The aspect of love among the ancient Greeks that has attracted most attention is their bisexuality. In the most recent authoritative discussion, Dover (1978) agrees that homosexuality was freely practiced by the Greeks, who did not view it in any derogatory light at all. However, this view must be qualified in a number of ways. First of all, Greek homosexuality was limited to the love of an older man for a younger (pubescent or just postpubescent) boy. Once the boy passed puberty, the love affair had to come to an end. There are other surprising restrictions and peculiarities. Homosexual love between two adult men of comparable age was unknown (Dover, 1978, p. 203). Further, the usual position in which two men had sex was one in which the older man thrust his penis between the legs of the younger. Anal intercourse was also known, but fellatio, surprisingly, was virtually absent. The boy was not supposed to initiate the sex act; he had to wait for the older man to start it. Further, there was no social niche for men who wished to remain homosexual all their lives; homosexuality was confined to puberty, except for monetary reasons. Even though homosexual prostitution was widely practiced, it was frowned upon.

Dover (1978) compared the pursuit of the young boy in ancient Greece to the pursuit of the shy young maiden in modern England. Thus the emotion of love among the ancient Greeks was strongly centered on the young boy. Dover shows that this kind of love did not exist in Homeric times; somehow it came into being in the eighth or seventh century B.C. To answer this question of why the boy was so desirable, it is essential to look at the larger picture of Greece.

The cultural achievements of Greece were so brilliant that few people have taken the trouble to see what connection there was between them and the whole social structure. Whitehead (1955, p. 20) once said that every problem that Plato discussed is alive today; others have seen the core of later thought in Aristotle. But where did these men stand in their own times? We are surprised to learn that in 399 B.C. Socrates was brought up on charges of not believing in the gods in which the city (Athens) believed and of introducing new divinities. He was also, it was alleged, guilty of corrupting the young. The penalty proposed was death. After a 1-day trial before a jury of 501 men, in accordance with the law of that time, 281 voted that he was guilty, and 220 that he was not guilty. A month later he drank the hemlock and died. Thus a great man, ever since revered as a profound thinker, was condemned and murdered by his contemporaries (Finley, 1963, p. 136).

The Greeks first entered the scene as a world power in their wars with the Persians, who formed the dominant empire of the sixth century B.C. Around 500 B.C. the Greek cities rebelled against the tribute exacted by the Persians. Many years of warfare followed, in which Athens and Sparta, later bitter rivals, cooperated. In the great sea battle at Salamis in 480 B.C. the Persians were routed by the Athenian fleet (Finley, 1963, p. 61). Persia was anything but crushed, but internal dissension within the empire took the Persians off the backs of the Greeks, who could then develop independently.

Athens has rightly gone down in history as the first democracy, and it did indeed have a democratic system for some 200 years. But it was a democracy based on slavery and the oppression of women. At the time of the Peloponnesian War in 431 B.C. the population is estimated to have been about 250,000 to 275,000, of whom 60,000 to 80,000 were slaves. Adult male citizens, who were the only ones with rights, numbered perhaps 40,000 to 50,000. The total area of Athens as a city-state was about 1000 square miles, about the size of Luxembourg (Finley, 1963, pp. 54–55).

After the retreat of the Persians, the two major rivals on the Greek mainland were Athens and Sparta. Both built up leagues based on allies. Athens had a maritime empire, at first voluntary; later secession was forbidden. The subject cities had to pay Athens an annual tribute, which Athens disbursed as it wished. Some contemporaries began to refer to Athens as the "tyrant city." When the island Mytilene rebelled during the Peloponnesian War, the Athenian assembly at first voted to execute the entire male population of Mytilene and to make slaves of the women and children. This seemed to arouse some guilt, and they executed "only" 1000 ringleaders (*Encyclopaedia Britannica*, 15th ed., vol. 14, p. 22).

Thus the sense in which Athens can be considered to have been a democracy and to have given the idea of democracy to mankind is an extremely limited one. In particular, the qualities of mercy, justice, love, kindness, concern for the poor, and others that we associate with democracy found little emphasis among the Athenians.

The reality was that Athens, especially after 450 B.C., was a military empire whose strength lay mainly in its battle fleets. The clash with Sparta, which had its own league began in the 450s but did not break out into full-scale warfare until 431, the Peloponnesian War. In this war, Athens was completely defeated. Perhaps one-third of its population, including its leader Pericles, died in the two plagues between 430 and 426 (Finley, 1963, p. 138); many were killed in the war. Athens disappeared as a center of political importance. Sparta, the victor, tried to assert itself for a while but was unsuccessful. Greece as a political entity remained unimportant until the Macedonian Philip and his famous son Alexander appeared later on in the fourth century. But the Athenian democracy had long since disappeared.

In attempting to clarify the decline of Athens and of Greece in general, attention must be paid to the psychological characteristics of the community, which have as a rule been overlooked in contemplation of the immensity of its achievements. But great achievement, as the world has repeatedly had occasion to note since, is unfortunately compatible with all kinds of horrible social conditions. What were their hatreds, their loves, and what went on in their ordinary lives?

The sociologist Eli Sagan (1979) has recently cast a fresh eye on the

Homeric epic and on the whole Greek history to penetrate more deeply into their psyche. He begins with a quote from Nietzsche:

> *Thus the Greeks, the most humane of men of ancient times, have a trait of cruelty, a tigerish lust to annihilate—a trait that is also very distinct in that grotesquely enlarged mirror image of the Hellenes, in Alexander the Great, but that really must strike fear into our hearts throughout their whole history and mythology. . . . When the victor in a fight among the cities executes the entire male citizenry in accordance with the laws of war, and sells all the women and children into slavery, we see in the sanction of such a law that the Greeks considered it an earnest necessity to let their hatred flow forth fully. [Nietzsche, 1968, pp. 32–33]*

Sagan then goes on to show that Greek culture was dominated by a commitment to sadistic violence, a love of killing, the "tigerish lust to annihilate." It is to the failure of that violence that we must look for the ultimate reason for its decline and fall.

Sagan shows that *The Iliad* emphatically describes literally hundreds of instances of men being killed in the fighting. In these passages there is no ambivalence, no ambiguity, no irony, no indication that these killings are anything but the brave heroic actions of manly, courageous heroes. The heroes' work is killing; they do it with passion and efficiency; they are heroes because they accept the fact that they themselves may die in such labor.

It is of course true that Homer was a poet, and that *The Iliad* is in the last analysis a work of fiction. But it was an epic poem that was near and dear to the heart of every Greek. It embodied their national ideals far more correctly than the open reasonableness of Socrates, or the refined dialogues of Plato. The Greeks, like others before them, and many since, wanted to conquer the known world, a purpose for which any amount of violence and destruction was justified.

The bloodthirsty wishes of the poem reflected the bloodthirsty wishes the Greeks sensed in themselves. For example, at one point Homer writes: "Hector was tugging at the body of Patroclus. He had stripped him of his noble armor and now he wanted to behead him with his sharp sword, drag off the trunk, and give it to the dogs of Troy" (Homer, 1950, p. 319). Homer, Sagan argues, justified aggression with four distinct positions: (1) violence and courage are identical; (2) the killing is accomplished without the aid of magic; (3) the gods love violence; and

(4) animals and humans are violent by nature. In a very real sense all four of these propositions were accepted as self-evident by the Greeks.

In an analysis of the famous history of the Peloponnesian War by Thucydides, Sagan also shows that the war was primarily a war of conquest, that it was fought with the cruelest of means (e.g., threats of genocide to reluctant allies), and that neither Thucydides nor his hero Pericles felt the slightest qualms about the attempted conquest.

In the account given by Thucydides, Pericles, who held Athens up as the "school of Hellas," comes through like any dictator justifying his aggression. Athens, he says, is frankly a tyranny (usually abhorred by the Greeks) but: "Your empire is now like a tyranny: it may have been wrong to take it, it is certainly dangerous to let it go" (Thucydides, 1982, p. 161). At another point Pericles boasts that military glory is man's highest good. As in other military dictatorships, men are dominant; women are there to submit.

> *Mighty indeed are the marks and monuments of our empire which we have left. Future ages will wonder at us, as the present age wonders at us now. We do not need the praises of a Homer, or of anyone else whose words may delight us for the moment, but whose estimation of facts will fall short of what is really true. For our adventurous spirit has forced an entry into every sea and every land; and everywhere we have left behind us everlasting memorials of good done to our friends and suffering inflicted on our enemies. . . . To me it seems that the consummation which has overtaken these men [dying in battle] shows us the meaning of manliness in its first revelation and in its final proof. . . . Perhaps I should say a word or two on the duties of women to those among you who are now widowed . . . the greatest glory of a woman is to be least talked about by men, whether they are praising you or criticizing you. [Thucydides, 1982, pp. 148–151]*

A new look at Pericles is also necessary to grasp the psychology of the Greeks. Traditionally he has been held up as a model statesman, interested in the promotion of culture and the arts. It is noted that he left his wife in order to live with the hetaira Aspasia. But on closer examination it appears that Pericles was a fairly absolute ruler for a quarter of a century, that he was more interested in war and conquest than anything else, and that Aspasia was a madam of a house that trained whores and not merely a hetaira (an "elegant prostitute"). Aristophanes joked that it was Aspasia who induced Pericles to start the war with Sparta (Aristophanes, 1925, pp. 526–534), but his jokes often concealed a bitter truth.

In short, the cultural achievements for which Greece has so justly been admired had little to do with Pericles; he was a warlord, out to gain control over the rest of the world, and he chose an attractive prostitute for sexual pleasure, not for intellectual companionship.

When we turn to an examination of love in such a society, we must know more about the position of women. Here there is little question about the Greek system: Greek society was first and foremost a male society, and women had few rights. In a famous speech Demosthenes summed up the situation by saying: "Mistresses we keep for our pleasure, concubines for daily attendance upon our persons, and wives to bear us legitimate children and be our housekeepers" (cited in Hunt, 1959, p. 25). Further, Greek literature is full of disparaging remarks about women. Pericles's remarks about widows of men is quoted above. The poet Palladas summed up marriage in two sentences: "Marriage brings a man only two happy days: the day he takes his bride to bed, and the day he lays her in her grave" (cited in Hunt, 1959, p. 26).

The anger and hatred toward women come out quite clearly in the literature. Women are there primarily for sexual purposes. Since the Greek male had female slaves, concubines, and prostitutes (and no shame was attached to being with prostitutes), he had a very free sexual life and little use for his wife other than to provide him a home base for his operations and legitimate children. When someone said to Sophocles that Euripides was a woman hater, he replied: "Yes, in his tragedies, but in bed he is very fond of them" (cited in Licht, 1932, p. 71). Yet they really saw no good solution; the comic writer Susarion of Megara says: "To marry and not marry are both equally bad."

Aristophanes says in *Lysistrata*:
  Chorus of Men: How clever is Euripides! There is no
        poet wiser: he says indeed that women are the
        worst of living creatures. . . .
  Chorus of Men: and he never came home again, such was his hate,
        all women he found
        so nasty and we
        quite wisely agree. . . .
  Chorus of Men: No wild beast is more impossible than
          woman is to fight,
              nor is fire, nor has the panther such unbridled
              appetite!

Chorus of Women: Well you know it, yet you go on
    warring with me without end,
    when you might, you cross-grained creature,
       have me as a trusty friend.
Chorus of Men: Listen: I will never cease from hating
    women till I die!

                    [ARISTOPHANES, 1961, pp. 14, 30, 37, 38]

The life of the woman offered little room for pleasure or meaningful activity. In the sixth century B.C. Solon institutionalized the distinction between good women and whores. He abolished all forms of self-sale and sale of children into slavery except one: the right of a male guardian to sell an unmarried woman who had lost her virginity. Solon regulated the walks, the feasts, the mourning, the trousseaux, and the food and drink of citizen women. He also established state-owned brothels staffed by slaves and made Athens attractive to foreigners who wanted to make money, including artisans, merchants, and prostitutes. Partly as a result of these laws, the woman was always maintained in an inferior role. She was not permitted to receive the education of the boy. At 14 she was married off, with or without her consent. If a husband wanted a divorce all he had to do was send his wife away. When there was a shortage of men, as repeatedly occurred, temporary bigamy was tolerated. Studies of skeletal remains shows that the average adult longevity in classical Greece was 45.0 years for men and 36.2 for women (Angel, 1973). Infant mortality was high; infanticide was also practiced, and female infanticide was more common than male (Pomeroy, 1975, chap. IV).

The position of the wife in ancient Greece was in this way miserable in the extreme. Married at 14 to a man she did not know, she had to bear one child after another, many of whom died. She was secluded from the outside world. Women did not even go to the market for food; shopping was done by slaves. Even today women in rural Greece do not do the shopping (Friedl, 1967). There were certain provisions for protection against excessive maltreatment, but these could hardly have provided her with any happiness. Even sexually she could offer her husband little, since he had female slaves, prostitutes, and concubines available.

In sum, men made war and women made babies. In such a male-dominated world, contempt for women was understandably strong. The man's job was to conquer, to take revenge on his enemies, to extend the borders of the world. In all this the woman was supposed only to satisfy his sexual desires and to provide a secure base for him; she had no rights or pleasures of her own. This would also explain the peculiar Greek custom of depilating or singeing the pubic hair of women: They were turned into little girls again, which they were supposed to be.

It is in the light of this social and psychological situation that an explanation for Greek bisexuality must be sought. The adolescent boy was elevated to the role of the greatest beauty possible. As many writers have noted with astonishment, this desire for the adolescent boy is in all respects similar to the modern admiration of the adolescent girl. But in Greece girls could be had for the asking, and boys could not. Hence male prostitution had to be discouraged, because it deprived the adult man of the feeling of a victory. The Greeks noted, as have all other peoples, that prostitutes, whether male or female, are predatory, conniving creatures who have little use for their customers and would often just as soon cut their throats as fornicate.

Homosexual relationships were quite consciously the pursuit of those of lower status by those of higher status; "beauty" in this sense meant desirability. But why was the boy so desirable?

This would explain the sense of shame with which the seduction of the boy by the older man seems to be carried out (Dover, 1978). The most characteristic configuration of homosexual courtship in vase painting is the "up and down position": One of the older man's hands touches the boy's face, and the other moves toward his genitals. The older man bows his head onto or even below the shoulder of the boy, bends his knees, and thrusts his penis between the boy's thighs, thus treating the boy as if he were a girl (Dover, 1978, pp. 97–98).

Thus by and large Greek society must still be seen as a hate culture. In this hate culture bisexuality served the function of providing the older man with fantasies of strength and rejuvenation as a young man, much as Greek society longed for the heroic deeds described in the Homeric epics.

One final question may be raised: How did the boys feel about being seduced? On this of course we have little data, but if we extrapolate from other cultures we cannot assume that they were happy with their lot. In one romance, written by Xenophon of Ephesus in the third century A.D., a boy is carried off by pirates. He exclaims: "Oh, the unhappy gift of beauty! So long kept I myself chaste, only now to yield in shameful lust to the love of a pirate! What then is left to me to live for, if from a man I must become a harlot? But I will not submit to his desires. I would rather be dead and save my chastity!" (cited in Licht, 1932, p. 446).

ROME

The Roman image of love was pure sexuality: Carpe diem; enjoy the day. Live for the pleasure of the moment. In the *Satyricon*, Petronius expressed it in this way:

> Find me any man who knows
> Nothing of love and naked pleasure.
> What stern moralist would oppose
> Two bodies warming a bed together?
> Father of Truth, old Epicurus
> Gave philosophy a soul
> And taught, his followers assure us,
> Love is Life's sovereign goal.
> [1965, p. 151]

But the unchecked lust for sex was accompanied by an equally un-checked lust for food and violence. The Romans were given to orgies and feasts of extraordinary duration. Suetonius reports of the emperor Claudius (by no means the worst of the 12 Caesars) that he seldom left a dining hall but that he was gorged and sodden; he would then go to bed and sleep with his mouth open—thus allowing a feather to be put down his throat, which would bring up the superfluous food and drink as vomit (1957, p. 206).

In a famous passage in *De Beneficiis* the philosopher Seneca (teacher of the notorious Nero) in the middle of the first century A.D. wrote a description of Roman banqueting: "The food which their stomachs can scarcely retain is fetched from farthest ocean; they vomit that they may eat, they eat that they may vomit, and they do not deign even to digest the feasts for which they ransack the whole world"(Hunt, 1959, p. 84).

But, Suetonius goes on to say (1957), Claudius's cruelty and blood-thirstiness appeared equally in great and small matters. Seneca in the satirical work *The Apocolocyntosis* ridiculed Claudius's uncouth physical appearance and attacked his habit of giving legal judgments without a hearing and ordering the executions of relatives, senators, and knights (Cited in Petronius, 1965).

Suetonius comments that if evidence had to be extracted under tor-ture, or parricide punished, he allowed the law to take its course without delay and in his own presence. Once when an execution had been or-dered at Tibur and the criminals had been tied to their stakes, no executioner could be found to carry it out, so he sent for one from Rome and waited all day for the man to arrive so that he could witness the execution. At gladiatorial shows, whether or not they were staged by him, he ruled that all combatants who fell accidentally should have their throats cut, above all net-fighters, so that he could gaze upon their death agony. When a pair of gladiators mortally wounded each other he sent for their swords and had pocket knives made from them for his personal use (Suetonius, 1957, p. 206).

Claudius was emperor from 41 to 54 A.D., and he was followed by Nero, who is notorious as one of the most sadistic and degenerate rulers in history. But Claudius was not so much better. His violent reactions have been attributed to his suspiciousness and justified by the assertion that he lived in an era when emperors were assassinated and revolts did occur. But we are accustomed to such excuses in hate cultures and need not take them too seriously. The fact is that Rome was as much of a police state as Nazi Germany, reliant on spies and informers, and ruthless in executing anyone who rebelled. Claudius was terrified of being assassinated or poisoned. He never attended a banquet without an escort of javelin-bearing guards, and he insisted on being waited on by soldiers performing the duties of servants. Before entering a sickroom he always had it carefully gone over; pillows and mattresses were prodded and bedclothes shaken out. Later he even required all visitors to be searched when they came to pay him a morning call, excusing no one from the most thorough examination.

He would take instant precautionary vengeance against his supposed enemy once he began to feel at all uneasy, no matter how insignificant the reason. On one occasion a morning caller took Claudius aside and told him "In my dreams last night you were murdered." Shortly thereafter he had the man taken away as if caught in the act, and executed (Suetonius, 1957, pp. 207–208).

Claudius was notoriously absentminded and scatterbrained. After executing his wife Messalina for plotting an insurrection against him he went in to dinner, and presently he asked: "Why is she not here?" (This story also shows his indifference to human feelings.) On several occasions he sent for men to give him advice or throw dice with him; when they did not appear he followed this up with a reproachful message calling them lazy sleepers, quite unaware that he had just sentenced them to death (Suetonius, 1957, p. 209).

In sexual matters, Roman men from the time of Julius Caesar (middle of the first century B.C.) lived a free and easy life. Like the Greeks, they had wives, slaves, mistresses, and prostitutes; however, homosexuality never assumed any central place in their lives. Julius Caesar himself was reported to have had numerous affairs with Roman women and in the provinces. When he came home from the triumph in Gaul a verse was sung:

> Home we bring our bald whoremonger;
> Romans, lock your wives away!
> All the bags of gold you lent him
> Went his Gallic tarts to pay.
> [SUETONIUS, 1957, p. 36]

The emperor who followed him (actually the first emperor), Augustus, was also a womanizer, but there was little scandal attached to his name. Instead, what happened at that time was that Roman women became increasingly free sexually, now that Rome was the ruler of the world. Horace, the poet laureate of the Augustan age (he lived from 65 B.C. to 8 B.C. and was friendly with Augustus), wrote in his *Odes* of the Roman matron:

> *Teeming with sin, our times have sullied first the marriage bed, our offspring, and our homes; sprung from this source, disaster's stream has overflowed the people and the fatherland. . . . The young maiden even now trains herself in coquetry and, impassioned to her finger tips, plans unholy amours. Anon she seeks young paramours at her husband's boards, nor stops to choose on whom she will swiftly bestow illicit joys when lights are banished, but openly when bidden, and not without her husband's knowledge, she rises, be it some peddler summons her, or the captain of some Spanish ship, lavish purchaser of shame. . . . What do the ravages of time not injure? . . . destined soon to produce an off-spring still more wicked. [cited in Lewis & Reinhold, 1966, vol. II, p. 48]*

The situation became so scandalous that Augustus enacted a series of laws, known as the Julian Laws, which for the first time forbade a husband to kill an adulterous wife, but ordered him under pain of severe fines to bring her to court and accuse her. If he did not, her father was required to do so; and if he in turn failed, any right-minded citizen might accuse her, winning part of her property if she were convicted. These laws, passed between 18 B.C. and 9 B.C., were also in part stimulated by the open immorality of Augustus's own daughter, Julia, and later her daughter, also known as Julia. Augustus was beside himself when he learned of the affairs of his daughter and granddaughter, and he exiled both of them. As Seneca recorded the story some decades later in his *Moral Epistles*:

> *Augustus learned that she had been accessible to scores of paramours, that in nocturnal revels she had roamed about the city, that the very Forum and the rostrum from which her father had proposed a law against adultery had been chosen by the daughter for her debaucheries, that she had daily resorted to the statue of Marsyas (a place in the Forum where whores came to offer themselves), and, laying aside the role of adulteress, there sold her favors and sought the right to every indulgence with even unknown paramours. [cited in Hopkins, 1978, pp. 118–119]*

An equally lecherous role was played by Messalina, the third wife of the emperor Claudius. As M. Grant (1975) says, if only one-tenth of the stories that made Messalina a byword for lasciviousness are true, she was "phenomenally oversexed" (M. Grant, 1975, p. 145). It was said that Messalina would slip out at night, when Claudius was asleep (he was 20 years her senior), and serve as a prostitute in a brothel. Eventually, as noted above, Messalina was executed by order of Claudius because she was planning a rebellion against him with her lover.

Eventually, it appeared, the married women of Rome became as free sexually as their husbands. Augustus could not control his own daughter and granddaughter, nor could Claudius control his own wife. The Julian Laws were a total failure. Although there are still arguments about what caused the fall of Rome, the open immorality of the noblest women certainly must have been one factor. As in all the hate cultures described in Chapter 1, the women used sex as a weapon.

We have to consider now what kind of a culture it was that produced such sexual freedom and such extraordinary violence. The Renaissance historians tended to glorify Rome—the grandeur that was Greece and the glory that was Rome. And indeed as builders they were great; there are two bridges standing on the Tiber that were built by the Romans, and the Roman Pantheon still stands, 2000 years old, an architectural masterpiece.

But from a human point of view Rome, especially after the creation of the empire by Julius Caesar, was simply a brutal, ruthless military dictatorship. The Roman record is on the one hand that of the conquest of the known world, on the other that of almost interminable revolts, massacres, and dictatorial bloodthirstiness.

Caesar himself came to power when he deliberately, gratuitously, and illegally launched a major foreign war to satisfy his personal ambitions, and he prosecuted this war with unequaled brutality and treachery. In a single day, he claimed, with some slight (but not severe) exaggeration, he had slaughtered 430,000 Germans (M. Grant, 1975, p. 33). His only desire was to be king, in a country which had not had a king for 500 years and to whose citizenry the very idea of a king was repugnant. His will to win by fair means or foul was described by the poet Lucan in *Pharsalia*:

> Thinking naught done while
>   aught remained to do . . .
> His manhood knew
> No rest—his only shame to lose a fight
> Keen and untamed, where hope or anger called,
> He turned his hand, nor quailed to stain his sword. . . .
> To make a path by havoc was his joy.
> [CITED IN M. GRANT, 1975, pp. 33–34]

Although it is hard to see how Caesar could have killed 430,000 Germans in 1 day with the weapons at his command, his statement is typical of Roman callousness. When Carthage was finally captured in 201 B.C. it was as planned burned to the ground and totally destroyed. When Titus defeated the Jews in A.D. 70 Jerusalem was almost totally obliterated. After the military victory Titus had another 2500 Jews killed fighting wild beasts or each other or being burnt alive (Josephus, 1959, p. 364).

Many conquerors have come and gone since Caesar and the emperors who followed him. Many of them too have slaughtered incredible numbers of innocents, men, women, and children; for the campaign of Hitler, a modern Caesar, we even employ the word *holocaust*. But such merciless murders are surely proof of nothing else than unmitigated hatred, not a sign of "civilization" as the Romans liked to boast.

Although Julius Caesar could also show some clemency on occasion, the Roman principle of terror remained the dominant one until the empire's collapse. Even Augustus, probably the mildest of the lot, had no compunction about killing. When he took Perugia, in one of the civil wars, his only reply to pleas for clemency was: "You must die." According to Suetonius, after capturing the city he chose 300 prisoners of equestrian or senatorial rank and offered them as human sacrifices on the ides of March at the altar of the god Julius (1957, pp. 60–61).

Although the army was the seat of all power, its history remained stormy. Caesar himself had to put down two mutinies. Revolts, mutinies, desertions, pillage of the countryside, massacre, and countermassacre were common all through the history of the Roman empire; how Rome managed to survive so long is a mystery in its own right. There were periods of relative quiet, as in the reign of the Antonines in the second century A.D., but they were rare indeed. The bloody history of the empire is by now well known. In a single year (A.D. 69) there were four emperors, each serving only a few months before he was murdered. The army, particularly the Praetorian guard, made and unmade emperors, at times almost at will.

In retaliation, emperors could never be sure of their crowns or of the loyalty of their subordinates. Legions of spies and informers crowded the palaces and other governmental offices. The situation after a while became so similar to the Hitler period that it may well be called a paranoid society.

In addition, there was the other scourge of Roman civilization—slavery. As Mommsen pointed out 150 years ago, "slavery is not possible without a reign of terror" (1854, p. 31). So the Romans lived in a state of terror as long as they subsisted on slavery, which was as long as the Roman empire lasted. The conditions under which the slaves lived were miserable in the extreme. Mommsen says:

> *The abyss of misery and woe which engulfed this most miserable of all proletariats we leave to be fathomed by those who can bear to gaze into such depths. It is quite possible that, compared with the sufferings of the Roman slaves, the sum of all Negro suffering is but a drop.* [1854, p. 29]

In the early years of the Roman republic (before Julius Caesar) slave conspiracies broke out everywhere. In 1 year (133 B.C.) the Romans executed 150 slaves in Rome, 450 in Minturnae, and 4000 in Sinuessa (Mommsen, 1854, p. 29). Around this time a large slave revolt in Sicily took 3 years to put down. When the slaves were finally conquered, the consul Publius Rupilus ordered all those who came into his hands alive, upwards of 20,000 men, to be crucified (Mommsen, p. 31).

The greatest of all the slave revolts was that of Spartacus, in 73 B.C., who gathered an army of 40,000 exslaves and within 2 years defeated no fewer than four Roman armies. But he was finally cornered, and he and his men were massacred (Mommsen, 1854, p. 230). On the Appian Way 6000 slaves were crucified (*Encyclopaedia Britannica*, 15th ed., vol. 9, p. 404).

It is obviously difficult to get clear estimates of the number of slaves, especially since the practice of manumission became increasingly frequent once the empire was established. Augustus actually passed a law that not more than 100 slaves could be freed at a time in a man's will (Hopkins, 1978, p. 115). By the end of the first century B.C. there were about two million slaves in Italy out of a total population of six million (Hopkins, p. 102). In the imperial period, there are no exact figures, but the number of slaves was augmented by conquests (of which there were many) and breeding, so slavery was always an important aspect of Roman society.

The conditions under which the slaves lived were frequently atrocious. In agriculture slaves would work in chained gangs; in *On Agriculture* Cato recommended that worn-out slaves should be sold (or left to die, it is implied) (cited in Lewis & Reinhold, 1966, vol. I, pp. 441–445). The emperor Augustus recorded in *My Achievements* that during the civil wars he returned 30,000 escaped slaves to their rightful owners for punishment (cited in Lewis & Reinhold, vol. II, p. 117), which was presumably drastic. Macrobius in *Saturnalia* wrote quite simply: "At home we become tyrants and want to exercise power over slaves, constrained not by decency but capacity" (cited in Hopkins, 1978, p. 119). In Spain, according to Diodorus of Sicily, 40,000 slaves worked the silver mines, producing great profits for their masters, but wearing themselves out by their arduous labors and dying young (cited in Hopkins, 1978, p. 119).

Roman literature abounds with examples of incidental cruelty to individual domestic slaves. Augustus ordered that the legs of a slave be broken because he had taken a bribe and revealed the contents of a letter (Suetonius, 1957, p. 91). The physician Galen reported that the emperor Hadrian once in anger stabbed a slave in the eye with a stylus. He later regretted it and asked the slave to choose a gift in compensation (cited in Hopkins, 1978, p. 118). The slave after some hesitation replied that all he wanted was his eye back. In *Moral Letters* Seneca portrayed a master at dinner, surrounded by slaves:

> *The unfortunate slaves are not allowed to move their lips, let alone talk; the birch keeps murmuring down. A cough, a sneeze, a hiccup is rewarded by a flogging, with no exceptions. Any break in the silence is severely punished. They stand at the ready all night, tense and mute.* [cited in Lewis & Reinhold, 1966, vol. II, p. 230]

After the early revolts the Romans were justifiably terrified of their slaves. Their only reaction was, in accordance with their sadistic personalities, that of inflicting horrible punishment, incuding death. They even passed a law, which was carried out, that if a master was killed by one of his own slaves, all the slaves in his household should be tortured and executed.

In A.D. 61 in one notorious case 400 household slaves were executed, though only after a debate in the senate and in the teeth of popular outcry. According to Tacitus, the clinching argument in the senate was:

> . . . *do you believe that a slave made up his mind to kill his master without an ominous phrase escaping him, without one word uttered rashly? Assume however that he kept quiet, that he procured his weapon in an unsuspecting household. Could he pass the watch, carry in his light, and perpetrate his murder without an accomplice? A crime has many antecedent symptoms.*

> *So long as our slaves act as informers, we may live a minority amid their mass, secure while they fear, and finally, if we die, certain of vengeance against the guilty. Our ancestors always suspected slaves. . . .*

> *Now that our households comprise tribes with customs the opposite of our own, with strange cults or none, you will never coerce such a mixture of humanity, except by terror.* [Tacitus, 1977, pp. 333–334]

The horrors of slavery ran parallel to the horrors of the gladiatorial system. In these combats, as is well known, men were forced to fight to the death. According to Grant (1978) the "games" were introduced at the outset of the First Punic War (264–241 B.C.) in order to keep up morale. Although he gives few details, Grant does concede: "The ferocious cruelty of these sports betrays the existence of a powerful streak of sadism in their ancient Roman and Italian character" (p. 101). They continued to be popular, legal, and common until the fifth century A.D., when Honorius abolished them, though in reality they do not seem to have disappeared until the Roman empire disappeared (*Encyclopaedia Britannica*, 15th ed., vol. 4, p. 546).

As time went on, and the power of the empire increased, the games became bloodier and bloodier. Where at first in 264 B.C. only three pairs of slaves fought, by 145 B.C. 90 pairs fought for 3 days (Mannix, 1958, p. 21). At a triumph of the emperor Trajan in the second century A.D. 5000 pairs of gladiators fought (*Enclopaedia Britannica*, 15th ed., vol. 4, p. 564). When the Jews were defeated by Titus in A.D. 70, the emperor celebrated the birthday of his brother in the "grand style," murdering many thousands.

Even Augustus, a relatively moderate emperor, boasted in *My Achievements* that he gave a gladiatorial show three times in his own name and five times in the names of his sons or grandsons; "at these shows, about 10,000 fought." That at least 5000 men must have died in these "shows" evidently did not concern him in the slightest (cited in Lewis & Reinhold, 1966, vol. II, p. 16).

In addition to pitting live men against wild beasts, the public was permitted to release every kind of sadistic impulse against the helpless gladiators. The emperor Nero is reported to have disguised himself, tied naked boys and girls to stakes, and plunged them with his javelins. Others stood outside the gates and taunted the prisoners with their fate. Claudius used to order a wounded gladiator's helmet removed so that he could watch the expression on the man's face while his throat was being cut. Girls were raped by men wearing the skins of wild beasts. Other girls were forced to have intercourse with animals. Men were tied to rotting corpses and left to die. Children were suspended by their legs from the tops of high poles for hyenas to pull down. So many victims were tied to stakes and then cut open that doctors used to attend the games in order to study anatomy (compare Hitler's medical experiments on his prisoners). The list could be continued ad nauseam.

Mommsen, in his descriptions, says:

> The gladiatorial games, which both revealed and fostered the worst demoralization of ancient times, had become so flourishing that a lucrative business was done in the sale of programs for them. This age [that of Julius Caesar] introduced the horrible innovation whereby the life or death of the vanquished gladiator depended not on the law of duel or on the pleasure of the victor, but on the caprice of the onlooking public; and according to its signal the victor either spared or transfixed his prostrate antagonist . . . free men not unfrequently sold themselves to contractors for board and wages as gladiatorial slaves. [The] contract of such a gladiatorial slave was "to let himself be chained, scourged, burnt or killed without opposition, if the laws of the institution should so require." [1854, p. 542]

In spite of his abhorrence of the custom, Mommsen fails to note that free men who sold themselves as gladiators were in effect committing suicide. This alone is a fitting reflection on the total sense of despair that pervaded the lower classes in the grandeur that was Rome.

Nor was there much expression of sympathy for either the slaves or the gladiators. Marcus Aurelius reportedly said that he found the games "monotonous," and he is reckoned among the enlightened emperors. Seneca, the Stoic philosopher who was also Nero's tutor, is almost the only one to have uttered some protest. In *Moral Epistles* he writes:

*I happened to go to one of those shows at the time of the lunch-hour
interludes . . . murder pure and simple. The combatants have nothing
to protect them; every thrust they launch gets home. . . . In the morning men are thrown to the lions and the bears; but it is the spectators
they are thrown to in the lunch hour. [cited in Lewis & Reinhold, 1966,
vol. II, p. 23]*

Finally, it should not be thought that the Roman upper classes were
much more secure than the lower. For them too there was constant civil
war, external war, proscriptions, informers, executions, torture, and
wholesale slaughter from time to time. In the year 69 A.D. there were no
fewer than four emperors; the first three were all assassinated. From the
year A.D. 235, when Severus Alexander was assassinated, to the accession
of Diocletian in A.D. 284, 26 soldier–emperors were proclaimed, all but
one of whom died a violent death, usually at the hands of their own soldiers (Lewis & Reinhold, 1966). Gibbon's evaluation, though penned
more than two centuries ago, is still valid for most of Roman history:
"Rome groaned beneath an unremitting tyranny, which exterminated
the ancient families of the republic, and was fatal to almost every virtue,
and every talent, that arose in that unhappy period" (1963, p. 74).

One episode from their military history reveals how the Romans
treated their own soldiers. In the year A.D. 42 Furius Camillus Scriboni-
nus, the military commander in Dalmatia (today Yugoslavia), revolted
against the emperor. The troops remained loyal to the emperor and
killed the rebellious officers. For this the Dalmatian legions were honored, but "Roman military discipline required the execution of the common soldiers who had murdered their officers" (Starr, 1982).

The Roman empire has to this date been the longest lived in history
(some 500 years). To the question of how it could last so long, and the
allied one of why it fell, innumerable answers have been given. But it is
clear that from an early date it ran on fear: fear of the enemy, fear of
civil war, fear of the ruling classes (including their constant suspicion of
one another), fear of the slaves, fear of the dictators.

The Greek contempt for women was continued in the Roman world.
Finley, one of the leading ancient historians, has written an interesting
essay entitled "The Silent Women of Rome" (1977). He comments
that it is not easy to think of another great civilized state without a
single really important female writer or poet, and he raises the question
of what the women did with their energies.

To begin with, Roman women did not even have full names; until fairly late in Roman history they had only family names. The Romans did not even have a word for *family* in the sense we use it ("I am going out with my family"). The paterfamilias was all-powerful; he need not even be the father of the children. As late as the fourth century A.D. an imperial edict defined his power as that of the right of life and death. Women were thus always under the domination of some man. Soldiers in the legions were not allowed to marry during their service, which was 20 years under Augustus and 25 later on. They were thus virtually unable to have a sustained family life.

Women died young; of those who managed to reach 15, half were dead before 40, and in some classes and areas even before 35 (Finley, 1977, p. 135).

Finley sees two outlets for them: one in religion and the other in egging their men on to greater and greater brutality. There must be something significant, he argues, in the group of ferocious and licentious royal females. The religious rebellion eventually brought the Egyptian cult of Isis, in which women are equal to men, into Rome. The support of men's brutality deprived Rome of the mollifying influence that women have exerted in other cultures (e.g., the comedy of Aristophanes, *Lysistrata*, in which the women refuse to have sex unless the men give up fighting).

But actually Finley's analysis helps to explain the Roman love game. Sex orgies, eating, vomiting, and then eating again; the women participated with relish. Augustus was concerned about the declining morality of Roman matrons, then discovered that his own daughter Julia was among the worst; later her daughter Julia was also disclosed to be extremely promiscuous. Augustus banished Ovid in a vain attempt to halt the tide of sexual licentiousness, but while he could get rid of the poet, he could not get rid of his poetry; and Ovid became known as the poet of adultery.

Ovid's major work, *The Art of Love*, which is still read, was a textbook of intrigue, seduction, hypocrisy, and adultery. Some typical verses are:

> Today Mars is kept so busy fighting abroad
> that Venus has things all her own way in Rome.
> Pretty girls play. Chaste means never asked.
> If you're really smart you do your own asking.
> Those girls that hold up their hands in horror—
> look at them closer—they're praying for a lover. . . .
> . . . Pretty dresses need wearing.

Neglected property falls to rack and ruin.
Your beauty needs exercise. It will soon fade
If you don't take lovers—and one or two aren't enough.
Best have a crowd to fleece, like the grey wolf.
It's a surer way and much less obvious.

Thus, once we probe under the surface, the Roman empire has an entirely different face. Terror, war, despair, murder, treason, and violence were the order of the day for centuries. It was a military dictatorship that prevailed for a long time because of the brutalizing psychology that had nothing but contempt for human life.

In such an atmosphere what could sex be? Certainly not any expression of love. Here again we are confronted with the two meanings of sex: love and hate. Catullus, one of the Roman love poets, began a poem with "I hate and I love" (cited in Petroni, 1968, p. 66). Roman women were notoriously profligate and unfaithful, once the empire was established; and why should they have been any different, if their men were little more than mass murderers? Roman sexuality was thus based on contempt for women, contempt for men, and the terrifying climate of a paranoid hate culture.

CHRISTIANITY

It was in such an atmosphere that there arose the ideal of Christian love: divine, ascetic (particularly nonsexual), and nonviolent.

Roman rule was replaced by Christian rule from the fourth century on. In the peculiar entity of the Holy Roman Empire it remained formally the governing power of Europe until Napoleon dissolved it in 1806 (*Encyclopaedia Britannica,* 15th ed., vol. 5, pp. 99–100). The term *Holy Roman Empire* is one coined by historians to describe this peculiar entity; during its existence it was known as the empire; the emperor was variously defined as the Roman emperor, the august emperor, or simply king of the Romans. It involved, in theory at least, a collaboration between king and pope, which led to endless conflict. Although there were lapses of several centuries, the connection between the Roman empire and Christianity is thus quite direct; as Tillich (1968) observes, the proselytizing drive of Christianity to spread all over the known world was a direct descendant of the Roman empire's wish to conquer the whole known world.

The questions to be raised here, as in other sections, are, first, what kind of society produced Christianity and how Christianity related to the various forms of society that existed in Europe in the centuries since Christ; and, second, how the Christian image of love fit into the various social structures. An allied question is to what extent Christianity mitigated or replaced the hate cultures with which it was surrounded.

It is immediately obvious that the Christian image of love was a direct reaction to Roman sadism and destructive sexuality. Prior to the adoption of Christianity as the official church by the emperor Constantine, the Christians are described as rather quiet people, living in placid communities, members of the Roman empire but not participating in its excesses.

Becaues of the Jewish revolt in A.D. 70 through 73, the Jews were reduced to insignificant numbers and scattered all over the Roman world. From then on gentile Christians were in the majority, and Christianity ceased being a Jewish sect.

The difficulties of the Christians before Constantine's conversion (A.D. 312), which led to numerous persecutions, are typical of the problems that any love philosophy encounters in a hate culture. There was first of all the problem of military service, which violated the commandment not to kill. Second, there was the appearance of all kinds of deviant sects, which raised the eternal question of heresy, which was never banished from the church or satisfactorily resolved. And, third, there was the question of the meaning of love itself, the basic Christian tenet, which has been subjected to endless debate by theologians for two millennia.

Jesus's pronouncements against war and murder are clear and unequivocal. The early Christians would often for this reason refuse military service; many were evidently executed in the persecutions of the first and second centuries (R. Grant, 1970, pp. 226–227). Cadoux (1982) states unequivocally that there is no firm evidence that any Christian served in the Roman army before A.D. 170. Gradually apparently a number came around to obeying the laws of the empire and accepted service in the army. By the time of Marcus Aurelius (A.D. 161), Christians were serving regularly in the army. Marcus Aurelius reported a military victory that he ascribed to the prayers of Christian legionary soldiers (R. Grant, 1970, p. 90). Measures against the Christians were in that period then discontinued, or at least not continued with the same severity.

The first paradox thus arises: The earliest acceptance of Christians by Rome was because Christian prayers had secured a military victory for the Romans. Or, put another way, under pressure of the threat of execution the Christians submitted to ordinary military discipline. It was the equivalent in that day of the World War II slogan: "Praise the Lord and pass the ammunition."

Eventually the acceptance of Christianity as the official religion of the empire began with another military miracle, Constantine's victory at the battle of the Milvian Bridge in Rome in 312 A.D.

From then on the Christians cooperated fully in the army, even though, as Patton once said, military men are essentially "paid killers." By 314 A.D., the Synod of Arles, convened at the emperor's command, decreed that Christians resigning from the army in peacetime were to be excommunicated. Within half a century Athanasius of Alexandria, a church leader himself not averse to violence, held that it was lawful and even praiseworthy to kill enemies in time of war (R. Grant, 1970, p. 273).

The full victory of Christianity in Rome did not occur until the reign of Theodosius I, some half a century after Constantine. His decrees abolishing pagan worship "increased the zeal of Christian reformers to extirpate, without mercy, the root of superstition (Gibbon, 1963, p. 498). Once Christianity had become the established church, it began to search for heroes and heroines in the martyrs and saints, and "religious fiction" (Gibbon, p. 501) began. As Gibbon was to put it with his usual irony, "A superstitious practice, which tended to increase the temptations of fraud and credulity, insensibly extinguished the light of history and of reason in the Christian world" (Gibbon, p. 501).

Once the Christians had power, their theories were put to a more crucial test. How can killing, even if it is in self-defense, and warfare be justified? There have historically been three different attitudes of Christianity to war: practicing pacifism, or waging what was pronounced justified or even holy war. Pacifism seems the only course consonant with the teachings of Christ, but it has rarely been observed.

The justified war was first given a secure theological base by Augustine. In *City of God* he argued that the Christian who fights in a just war is merely doing his Christian duty. For "every victory, even though gained by wicked men, is a result of the first judgment of God, who humbles the vanquished either for the sake of removing or punishing their sins" (1968, p. 461). From such a position it is easy enough to rationalize almost any violent actions.

An even more ingenious rationalization was offered centuries later by Thomas Aquinas. In *Summa Theologica* he argued that an act can have two effects, one of which is intended, while the other is unintended. Moral acts take their species according to what is intended, and not according to what is not intended. Accordingly the act of self-defense may have two effects; one is the saving of one's life, and the other is the slaying of the aggressor. Then to save one's life is lawful, even if an unintended outcome is to kill the other person; it is unlawful only if more than necessary violence is used (cited in *Ramsey*, 1961, pp. 39–40).

Clearly, by such casuistry almost any act of violence can find its theological justification. It is not surprising that after 19 centuries George Bernard Shaw could ask in *Saint Joan*: "Must then a Christ perish in torment in every age to save those that have no imagination?" (1971, epilogue). Nor is it surprising, in terms of our major theses here, that Christianity failed to play any great role in transforming the hate culture of the Romans into a true love culture. Howard (1976) regards Christianity, as he does Islam, as a "warrior-religion."

The concept of a holy war to destroy the infidels who do not believe in Christianity seems even more contradictory than that of a justified war. Yet it has played a major role in the interaction of Christianity with society.

As early as the fourth century A.D. in the reign of Theodosius I, who first outlawed pagan rites entirely, this merely increased the zeal of the Christian reformers to extirpate superstition. Gibbon, with his usualy irony, puts it this way:

> *In Gaul, the holy Martin, Bishop of Tours, marched at the head of his faithful monks to destroy the idols, the temples, and the consecrated trees of his extensive diocese; and in the execution of this arduous task, the prudent reader will judge whether Martin was supported by the aid of miraculous powers or of carnal weapons. [1963, p. 498]*

But the Roman empire was not destined to last much longer. It fell apart in the fifth century, and except for the reign of Charlemagne, Europe remained divided into innumerable small warring principalities in which disorder reigned supreme.

No sooner had Europe regained some semblance of order by the eleventh century than the pope of that day, Urban II, ordered a holy war against the infidels who held sway in Jerusalem and adjacent territory. By this time, somehow, the idea had taken firm root, rarely ever again to be disputed, that a war to defend Christianity was a holy war and sanctioned by God. It is another of the ironies of history that the Council of Clermont, which in 1095 called for the First Crusade, at the same time renewed and generalized the Truce of God, which was designed to limit fratricidal strife in Europe (*Encyclopaedia Britannica*,

15th ed., vol. II, p. 991). This is a familiar tactic in hate culture: The hatred that the citizens of one country feel toward one another is channeled and displaced toward an outside enemy.

Again here, it may be observed that the early church fathers, even before they acquired power, had unhestitatingly delivered over to eternal damnation and torture the greater part of the human species. Some mercy might be shown those born before Christ, but it was unanimously affirmed that those who since the birth of Christ had obstinately persisted in the worship of the demons would burn forever. These rigid sentiments, which had been unknown to the ancient world, appear to have infused a spirit of bitterness into a system of love and harmony. The gloating curses that Tertullian hurled at his enemies are so sadistic that Gibbon breaks off before finishing the quote (1963, p. 236).

The Crusades were little more than an exercise in hatred and destructiveness, however they were rationalized. The war was against the infidels, at first described as "god-hating dogs" (as were also any unpleasant neighbors in the west—Irish, Scots, Germans, in fact, anybody the Christians could hate). Indulgences were decreed by the pope for the crusaders: Anyone who took up the cross cast off all the burdens of the harsh terrestrial existence and could meet death freely and cheerfully, secure in the promise of eternal life (Heer, 1962, p. 133).

The church even introduced the curious right of "commutatio," or commutation. Since the Crusades were dangerous enterprises, in which thousands lost their lives, many were reluctant to go; there were at times even open rebellions against papal representatives who tried to enlist people to join the Crusades. Such persons could instead of going to the east undertake a crusade against heretics closer to home, in France or Spain or other parts of Europe (Heer, 1962, p. 141). The essential element, one might say, was to give the Christian a chance to murder somebody for the sake of God and not risk too much in the effort.

For more than two centuries the papal-inspired war against the infidels went on, with various interruptions, with nothing gained and with enormous loss of life. When Jerusalem was captured in the First Crusade, every inhabitant was put to death. Western sources claimed the slaughter amounted to only 10,000 Muslims; Arab sources put the number at 100,000 (Heer, 1962, p. 135). Little wonder that the Muslims began to call the Franks "Christian dogs" and to respond in kind with massacres of their own when they had the upper hand. The Fourth Crusade, which resulted in the sacking of Constantinople in 1204, was little more than unbridled destructiveness let loose; the crusaders did not even bother to go on to their destination but were satisfied with the loot of Constantinople. Even those who express otherwise some sympathy for the crusaders call the Fourth Crusade an "unmitigated disaster."

Eventual open criticism of the papal crusading policy became common. In Germany anyone taking the cross at Regensburg in the early thirteenth century was killed, and the Cathedral Chapter of Passau preached a little "crusade" against the papal legate who had come on a recruiting mission. In France there even grew up a kind of "counter-crusade," supported at times by the queen, the towns, and broad masses of the people. The poets of southern France described crusaders as fools, criminals, and madmen (which may very well have been quite accurate). One critic protested that Rome had inflicted little damage on Saracens but had massacred scores of Greeks and Latins (Heer, 1962, pp. 141–142).

Many anomalies in the theoretical faith of the Christian were inspired by the bloody Crusades. One of the most curious is the special orders created at that time, for example, the Knights Templar. This was a military order that was a brotherhood of fighting monks, dedicated to the "highest ideals of Christendom": poverty, chastity, and obedience. The contradiction between murder of infidels and devotion to Christ never bothered them. In 1306 Philip IV of France, called "the Fair," had ordered the arrest of every Jew in France (Howarth, 1982, p. 13); 15 months later he arrested every Templar in France, accusing them of being heretics, blasphemers, usurers, traitors, sodomites, and idolators. After the usual torture, some of the leaders "confessed" and were executed; the order was dissolved (Howarth, pp. 13–14).

Once it was realized that the price of murdering infidels in or near Jerusalem was staggeringly high, the church turned its attention to victims closer at hand, the heretics. Between infidels and heretics lies the Spanish Inquisition, which deservedly instills a chill of horror in anyone who even begins to examine its activities (Plaidy, 1969). There is scarcely any more damning indictment of the hate culture of Europe, nor any more convincing evidence that Christianity at the highest levels made this hate culture worse. Spain was the country in which the inquisition reached its greatest power, but it existed in other European countries as well.

No torture was too sadistic for the inquisitors, no murder too impossible. For several centuries the population lived in terror, since the country was infested with informers, whose denunciations, like those in other paranoid societies, were the equivalent of death. Even the dead were not immune to the grisly sadism of the inquisitors; if heresy was "proved" against someone who was dead the body was dug up and committed to the flames.

Conventional historians, who ignore the hatred and destructiveness involved in these actions, have swallowed many of the rationalizations of the church. Thus Parker (1982), reporting that masses of new evidence on the inquisition have appeared and are awaiting evaluation, asserts that "it may be affirmed that the principal concern of the Holy Office was the laity: their chief aim was to inculcate a sense of the correct behavior and the correct beliefs expected of a Christian" (p. 520). Similar apologetics have been offered for every murderous paranoid society.

Most gruesome were the auto-da-fé, in which sentences were read and the condemned burned in public. A large crowd would gather to witness the executions, carried out by the secular arm, since the church "shed no blood." The first auto-da-fé ("act of faith," ironically), took place in Seville in 1481; the last in Mexico in 1850. These public spectacles are reminiscent of the gladiatorial combats of Rome and are probably directly descended from them, since the wish of the Christian church to murder people it did not like was no less extreme than that of the Romans (*Encyclopaedia Britannica*, 15th ed., vol. 1, pp. 669–670).

Before the Reformation, which the Catholic church was unable to conquer, many heretical sects appeared in Europe. While theoretically the church could handle these either by charity (*caritas*) or power (*potestas*), in practice it made every attempt to exterminate them, as usual by the bloodiest means available, and with the rationalization that they were to be turned over to the secular arm for proper "punishment," which almost always meant death and confiscation of property. As usual, Thomas Aquinas had produced the rationalization that the social order was part of a divine plan, so that social revolutionaries could also be denounced as heretics; this was almost always the case, since the church was the prime seat of power.

The most prominent group among the "heretics" was the Cathars, and it is instructive to trace what happened to them. They appeared in western Europe somewhere around the middle of the twelfth century. Their way of life and thought was so radical and fanatical that it came close to reproducing the early church (Heer, 1962, p, 212).

The worship of the Cathars was simple. Prayer, by day and by night, was its essence. There was a ritual feast, celebrated with thanksgivings, blessing and baking of bread, and participation in a communal meal, just as in the early church up to the middle of the third century, when the agape (love feast) was still closely bound up with the Lord's Supper.

They had but one sacrament, the *consolamentum*, conferred by the laying on of hands. They saw in the mass a wicked and foolish perversion of the divine service. Theologically, they denied most of the church's doctrines, holding that the God of the old testament committed homicide because he had burned up Sodom and Gomorrah, and that the host did not differ from ordinary bread. Confirmation and confession they considered as altogether vain and frivolous. Some among them were called "perfect"; others were only believers.

The success of the Cathars was so great that the church became alarmed. As Norman Cohn (1975) has pointed out, the fabrications of the church against the Cathars were very similar or identical to the fabrications of the Romans against the early Christians. It could also be asserted that the persecution of the Cathars, which culminated in the Albigensian Crusade of 1208 to 1223, was similar to the reaction of the Romans in destroying rebellious provinces; it appeared to have nothing to do with Christian love.

Innocent III decreed in 1205 that "action ranks greater than contemplation," and he called for the "extermination" of the heretics. *Exterminare* in the Latin of that day was an ambiguous word, which could mean either exile or extermination, but to his followers it meant only one thing: murder. A crusade was decreed against the Albigensians by Innocent III, who baited his summons with the promise of confiscated Albigensian estates for the nobility and for the king the prospect of extending his rule over the south.

The war against the pure Christians was one of immense savagery and fanaticism. Even the dead were not safe from dishonor, and the worst humiliations were heaped upon women, the much-hated, much-feared, and much-courted women of the south. Urged on by the pope, who wrote that "it will be much harder to annihilate Antichrist's satellites if they have been allowed to unite for a common resistance" (Madaule, 1967, p. 64), the pope's legate Arnaud-Amalric, abbot-general of Citeaux, became the effective leader of the Albigensian Crusade. When Bézières was captured in 1209, the inhabitants were massacred to the last man (Madaule, p. 65), just as the inhabitants of Jerusalem had been massacred by the Christians a few years earlier. At Montségur in 1243, the last stronghold of the Albigensians was overrun, and its inhabitants were massacred as well.

Catharism, however, had spread far, so an inquisition was set up immediately. Between 1231 and 1233 Conrad of Marburg was chief inquisitor in Germany; he left behind a horrendous tale of horror and murder. It is not surprising that Friedrich Heer, surveying this period, states that "the later medieval Inquisition . . . can only be understood in the context of mass and group psychoses" (1962, p. 217).

Without going into excessive detail, a few other instances may be cited of the unbelievable primitive violence set loose by Christianity at various periods and of the calls to violence that have emanated even from its greatest leaders.

The pope Formosus died in 896, possibly from unnatural causes (Cheetham, 1982, p. 75). In view of his unpopularity in Rome he was lucky to escape a worse end. His successor, Boniface VI, died of gout within a fortnight. The short reign of Stephen VI (896–897) was remarkable for a piece of grisly play-acting in which the Holy See, blinded by party fanaticism, lost all sense of religious decency and moderation. It was resolved to hold a trial of the dead pope before a synod acting as a tribunal. The corpse was accordingly exhumed, dressed in pontifical vestments, and seated on the pontifical throne. After a travesty of legal proceedings:

> *Formosus was condemned for uncanonical conduct and struck from the rolls of St. Peter. His body was then stripped of its robes, the fingers of his right hand that had given the pontifical blessing were hacked off, and the remains flung into the Tiber. But within a few months popular sentiment swung violently the other way. Stephen was deposed and throttled without any kind of formality, and what passed for the corpse of Formosus was retrieved from the river and entombed in St. Peter's.* [*Cheetham, 1982, p. 75*]

Nor is the call to violence found only in casual bulls or tracts. In a letter to the *New York Times* of September 24, 1982, a Catholic priest, Rev. Neil Hurley, wrote that he had been finding it difficult for almost 40 years to read the so-called "curse" psalms in the Catholic liturgy and breviary.

This is a sample from Psalm 18, in which David thanks Yahweh for delivering him from his enemies:

> *You have girt me with strength for the fight, bent down my assailants beneath me, made my enemies turn their backs to me; and those who hate me I destroy. . . .*

> *Life to Yahweh! Blessed be my rock! Exalted be the God of my salvation, the God who gives me vengeance and subjects the peoples to me.*

Nor is there any real breathing space of peace in the history of Christianity. From the earliest days to modern times violence and destruction have been concerns with which the church has had to wrestle, nor has it ever found any lasting solution to the problems that have been with it from the very beginning.

Much has been written about the reaction of the Vatican to that most awful horror of modern times, the holocaust. John Morley (1980), a priest and historian at Seton Hall College, sums up as follows:

> *The Pope failed not only the Jews but also members of the Church who suffered brutal treatment from the Germans. Moreover he caused Vatican diplomacy to fail by forcing it to make a mockery of its claims that it was an ideal form of diplomacy dedicated to justice, brotherhood, and other similarly exalted goals, when in practice it made little attempt to work toward any of them.* [p. 209; see also letter of Msgr. J. G. Bailey to New York Times, *November 3, 1982*]

Historians are still arguing about the role of the Roman Catholic church in the extermination of their ancient enemies, the Greek Catholic church, embodied in the Serbians, by the Croatian Fascists during World War II. Cheetham gives the following account:

> *According to one estimate seven hundred thousand persons were slaughtered in a series of massacres which seem never to have disturbed the world's conscience to the same extent as Hitler's parallel attempt to wipe out the Jews of eastern Europe. The Church cannot convincingly deny its deep though indirect implication in this ghastly operation. Local Franciscan friars joined joyfully in it. The Croatian dictator and former terrorist, Pavelic, who initiated it, was an ostentatiously zealous Catholic and his regime was at first hailed with enthusiasm by Archbishop Stepinac of Zagreb. The Orthodox victims were nominally offered a choice between death and conversion to Catholicism, but it appears that remarkably few of them were able to avail themselves of the option. When the Archbishop fully realized what was happening, he changed his tune, thereby incurring the enmity of the dictator. However it was too late to save the Serbs. As for the Pope, he remained silent, although he must have been made aware of the facts by some of the numerous Italian clerics, officials and soldiers then active in Croatia.* [1982, p. 289]

While this topic will be discussed more fully later, it should not be thought that the Protestants were less violent than the Catholics whom they supplanted. For example, Luther's views on freedom of religion were expressed in various writings, including "Of the Jews and Their Lies" (1543), in which his "sincere advice" was to "set fire to their synagogues or schools."

> *I advise that their houses be razed and destroyed. For they pursue in them the same aims as in their synagogues . . . I advise that all their prayer books and Talmudic writings, in which such idolatry, lies, cursing and blasphemy are taught, be taken from them . . . I advise that their rabbis be forbidden to teach henceforth on pain of loss of life and limb.* [1971, pp. 268–269]

Christianity came along to resolve the horrors of the Roman hate culture; to what extent did it succeed? There is little reason to believe that the world in A.D. 1500 was any better off than the world in A.D. 300; in many respects it was worse. Tillich has a crucial point when he maintains that the Roman Catholic church had identified with Rome more than with Catholicism.

The reasons for this failure can be sought primarily in the impossibility of the ideals that Christianity had professed. The doctrine of nonviolence, or turning the other cheek, which the Christians had practiced in the period before Constantine, led to persecution and death. Such martyrdom was too much to ask in the long run. Soon pacifism led to the casuistry of the justified war, and then to the even worse casuistry of the holy war.

Likewise with sexuality: To refrain from all sexual excesses was again too much to ask, and to require the clergy to refrain from sex entirely was an utter impossibility. Lea (1966) has carefully documented the extraordinary battles that the church went through before sacerdotal celibacy was really established at the fourth Lateran Council in 1215 (p. 277). It is essential to note that the main thrust was not that a priest should be chaste, but that he should be unmarried, that is, without any strong ties to other human beings (Lea, p. 296). At one point priests were even enjoined from living with their mothers or sisters. The hypocritical lengths to which licentiousness went in the Middle Ages before the Reformation are too well known to require further proof. It is sufficient to mention here that in 1415 the Council of Constance (Lea, pp. 291–292) tried, condemned, and deposed a pope, including among the charges notorious incest, adultery, defilement, homicide, and atheism, to all of which he confessed without defending himself. When he was later released from prison, his successor, Martin V, appointed him dean of the Sacred College.

The image of love offered by the church was one of unconditional, unquestioning love toward the whole world; this too was utterly impossible. Again the idea was to love God, and to tie the individual to God's image, refraining from all close contacts with fellow mortals; the earth should merely be a way station to heaven. With such a theology little love could be expected, though doubtless there were many individuals throughout the centuries who tried to adhere to its tenets. But in most cases when people tried to follow the doctrines of the church too closely, as with the Albigensians, the church mowed them down.

Yet when all this has been said, certain positive elements still emerged from the Christian experience that have remained part of man's heritage. While the ideal of love was almost impossible, the goal of loving instead of hating was one that everybody could understand. Woman as the Virgin Mary was idealized rather than seen as a sex object. For the first time after antiquity woman came to be seen as a person who should be loved and respected rather than one who would merely be exploited for sex and children. And finally there was the emphasis on the good life conducted according to the highest ethical principles as a way out of the horrors of this world. Even if all these ideals were flouted in the extreme, they still represented a vision of life better than had existed, the kind of life toward which a self-respecting person could aspire.

3

Western Civilization as a Hate Culture

PART 2.   FROM THE MIDDLE AGES TO THE PRESENT

THE TWELFTH CENTURY ON: ROMANTIC LOVE

It is not often that a specific emotional constellation that has strongly influenced the human mind can be traced in its beginnings at least to a particular historical situation. That is the case with romantic love. It began somehow in southern France in the twelfth century, in the court of Eleanor of Aquitaine and her daughter Marie, daughter and granddaughter of William IX, duke of Aquitaine, who was the first of the love lyricists who soon appeared all over Europe. Because it began at a court, it has been called courtly love, but its significance extends far beyond its origins as a courtly game.

Ever since that time, in one form or another, romantic love has been one of the western world's major passions. It has created the concept of a lover by which many men and women have guided their lives. The literary output that it has spawned is enormous and seemingly endless. Yet it has always remained a puzzle.

Dante, one of the great masters of the love lyrics of that period, wrote innumerable love poems. A typical poem from *La Vita Nuova* (*The New Life*) is:

> My lady carries love within her eyes;
> All that she looks on is made pleasanter;
> Upon her path men turn to gaze at her;
> He whom she greeteth feels his heart to rise,
> And droops his troubled visage, full of sighs,
> And of his evil heart is then aware:
> Hate, love, and pride becomes a worshipper.
> O women, help to praise her in somewise.
> Humbleness, and the hope that hopeth well,
> By speech of hers into the mind are brought,
> And who beholds is blessed oftenwhiles.
> The look she hath when she a little smiles
> Cannot be said, nor holden in the thought;
> Tis such a new and gracious miracle.
>   [1977, p. 579]

Because it has persisted through the centuries, romantic love was also the major concern of the patients who sought out Freud and his colleagues since the early part of the century. For that reason it has been subjected to intensive scrutiny, not only in the literary texts but also on the psychoanalytic couch. Freud himself was fond of the quatrain from Shakespeare's *Hamlet*:

> Doubt thou the stars are fire;
> Doubt that the sun doth move;
> Doubt truth to be a liar;
> But never doubt I love.
>   [ACT 2, SCENE 2, LINES 116–119]

The paradox of romantic love is that humankind has striven for it so ceaselessly yet found it so elusive. Without it, life becomes dull, even pointless; yet with it life becomes exciting and conflicted. Analysts have called it a transference, a carryover from childhood, and undoubtedly it is. Yet it is also a way out of childhood, a move to a relationship with a woman or a man, an advance to maturity.

While the historical data are voluminous and relevant, our main concern is with the relationship between romantic love and the pressures of the hate culture. One cannot be properly understood without the other. In the following discussion the connections between the two will be given the fullest consideration.

The first question then must be: What was the world of the twelfth century, in which romantic love was born, like? Primarily, as Marc Bloch (1961) showed, it was a world in which violence was everywhere, and fully rationalized. In fact, it was almost a pure hate culture. The church of course was dominant, but as has been seen, in practice the church was more interested in destroying than in saving souls (Hay, 1971). War, murder, the abuse of power were ever-present threats that affected everyone's life.

It was a society that lived by the code of the vendetta. In the extended kin groups, the first duty of a kinsman was to take revenge, even beyond the grave. No obligation seemed more sacred than the blood feud. Among the Frisians, the very corpse cried out for vengeance; it hung in the house until the day vengeance was accomplished, when at last the kinsmen had the right to bury it. The judicial procedures themselves when they did occur were hardly more than regularized vendettas. In March 1134, after the assassination of the subdean of Orleans, all the relatives of the dead man assembled to receive the homage not only of one of the murderers, his accomplices, and his vassals, but also the "best of his kin," all 240 of them. Thus in every way murder, revenged by murder, engulfed large groups of people and continued mercilessly. In the thirteenth century in Castile it was sufficient, if the murder of the relative of a victim was not to be treated as a crime, for the avenger to have the same great-great-grandfather as the original victim (Bloch, 1961, vol. 1, p. 126).

Moreover, murder extended into the most ordinary affairs of life. Every day, bewailed the Bishop of Worms about 1024:

> *murders in the manner of wild beasts are committed among the de-*
> *pendents of St. Peter's. They attack each other through drunkenness,*
> *through pride, or for no reason at all. In the course of one year thirty-*
> *five serfs of St. Peter's, completely innocent people, have been killed by*
> *other serfs of the church; and the murderers, far from repenting, glory*
> *in their crime.* [cited in Bloch, 1961, vol. 2, pp. 411–412]

With such gore an everyday event, some countermeasures were bound to appear. One of the main attempts was the "peace of God." At first this granted special protection to certain classes of persons or objects.

Later the prohibitions were extended and more clearly defined. The list of forbidden acts became more and more detailed. Then days were set apart when violence was prohibited.

Later other peace movements started. In 1182 a carpenter of Le Puy, guided by visions, founded a peace brotherhood that spread rapidly in all the regions of Languedoc and further. Its emblem was a white hood with a sort of scarf. All blood feuds were expressly prohibited by the group. If one of its members committed a murder, the brother of the dead man would give the murderer the kiss of peace (Bloch, vol. 2, p. 416).

But such private efforts were not to the liking of the authorities. They preferred to learn to control the violence with their own troops. Eventually, as control was extended over larger areas of the countries, and as the central powers became better organized, the reign of terror was reduced. But the process took centuries; and it is still going on.

What was set up was a strong ambivalence in the mind of the individual, as well as in the social order—violence alternating with peace. Romantic love is clearly part of the effort to subdue the violence. Thus part of the code of the "gentleman" involved the refusal to inflict harm on a woman; even more emphatically the man was supposed to adopt a protective attitude toward the woman, in which his own safety was secondary to her welfare.

One main achievement of courtly love in the early days was to elevate the woman to the place of a "lady." Man was given a new task, the chivalrous one of serving the cause of the lady in whatever she needed.

In the twentieth century we still find the unhappy lover putting his lady on a pedestal and worshiping her from afar. And in almost exactly the same way this idealization involves a repression of considerable anger and violence. Analytically this results from the worship of the mother, keeping the man a little boy attached to her. In his inner life he still suffers the same kind of ambivalence—loving alternating with anger and the wish to be violent—only now it has become an internal rather than an external struggle.

Looked at from another point of view, romantic love can be seen as the first step in women's liberation. Agreed, it goes too far in idealizing the woman. But this idealization arises from the previous wish to destroy her, just as historically the woman was always despised as an inferior creature and condemned to a life of isolation and subservience.

Even in this perspective it brought a new role for men: loving instead of killing. For the violence of the Middle Ages still continues in one form or another. In the seventeenth century there were only 7 years in which a war did not take place (Clark, 1953). The terrible conflagrations that have convulsed the world have been analyzed more in terms of their technological features (McNeill, 1982) than in terms of their human cost. Humanity urgently needs the ideal of love to overcome its inner despair and hatred.

It was only to be expected that the idealization of the woman involved in making her an unapproachable lady would soon alternate with a denigration that made her a witch. And this is exactly what happened. Beginning in the fifteenth century, a witchcraft fury swept over Europe lasting almost two centuries that led to the judicial murder by a psychotic clergy of hundreds of thousands of helpless persons, very largely women.

The explanation of the witchcraft persecution has always baffled historians, largely because of their difficulties in understanding abnormal psychology. Actually the essentials of the explanation were already given by Ernest Jones in 1931 in his book *On the Nightmare*; later accounts are merely elaborations of his central thesis.

What is important here is the close relationship of the witch to the lady: the bad woman and the good woman, the bad mother and the good mother. And both are connected with the severe conflicts about life and sexuality that pervaded the atmosphere in those troubled times. Socially one of the grimmest findings is that somewhere between half a million and nine million were murdered in the witch trials of the sixteenth and seventeenth centuries.

Much has been written about the psychology of the witches, describing them as hysterics, or at times psychotic. Much has also been adduced for the presence of economic motives in witch persecution, since the property of the accused (and always condemned) was confiscated. But the most essential element seems to have been the dementia of the church. For undoubtedly the whole witchcraft delusion was created and developed by the fathers of the church.

If we get away from the scene and try to view the whole episode as a human tragedy, the most striking factor of course is that the church in the fourteenth century was in a virtual state of civil war. There was a papacy at Rome, and one at Avignon, and the partisans of each literally fought one another to the death. But the leaders of the church were all men, and men who whatever they did were intensely guilty about their sexual feelings toward women.

And so the sexual feelings were projected to the women, who were made to take the blame for the terrible lives the church fathers were forced to lead. The bible of the witch persecutors was the *Malleus mal-*

leficarum, published by two Dominican monks in 1487, 3 years after the pope had issued a bull directing attention to the widespread existence of demonological practices, and the "harm" being done by numerous witches.

The title of the book is already suggestive: the witches' hammer with which to strike witches. As in so many other instances, the church was ordering judicial murders. Perhaps it did not realize the scale on which they would eventually be carried out—or perhaps it did and was, like any man castrated for life, simply vengeful. The *Malleus* devotes four chapters to a detailed consideration of impotence and how the witches brought it about, laying special stress on the fact that witches cannot interfere with any other natural human function. Through the evil spell, they argued, love between a given man and woman could be destroyed, barrenness of women and sterility of men induced, the embryo destroyed, and miscarriages effected. The evil spell could castrate men about to get married; this fear was so widespread in the fifteenth and sixteenth centuries that it became customary to carry out marriages in private (Jones, 1931, p. 193). Ladurie (1981) confirms that in France fear of castration by the aiguillette was so widespread in the period 1550–1600 that almost all marriages were performed in secret (1981, p. 87).

The kernel of the accusations against the witch was always that she had had intercourse with the devil; everything else was an embellishment (Jones, 1931, p. 199). Simple enough to understand: The castrated clergy, in impotent rage, took to burning the women who refused their favors. In exactly the same way, a psychotic patient of mine, rejected by a girl, dreamed of sending her an envelope which if opened by her would explode in her face and kill her.

The sharp split between the good woman (the lady) and the bad woman (the witch), accompanied by the severest kinds of sexual repression, is one of the main features of schizophrenia. Increasingly historians are coming to understand that we are dealing in these ages with overt madness; what happened lends itself to no other explanation. But the mad ones were those in power, the clergy, and they had the power to wreak their vengeance on the women. Then again, as has been pointed out, it was an age in which vengeance was one of the main motifs in life in all classes.

Thus love and hatred of the woman lived side by side in the mind of the man, just as they do today. But the conflict is less severe, the power to hurt the woman has been curbed, and psychoanalytic psychology offers a reasonable explanation of the whole phenomenon. And socially, the fact that the Catholic church has never repudiated the whole delusional system (belief in exorcism is still extant) is noteworthy (Jones, 1931, pp. 235–236). In an apologetic history of the Catholic church (Bokenkotter, 1979) the whole matter is deftly ignored.

The choice between being a lady and being a witch that was in effect offered to the woman led to terrible conflicts in her as well. She possessed magical properties in the eyes of men; either they were "bewitched" by her, or they were tormented by her, sometimes into a state of insanity (man goes "mad with desire"). The conflict persists in the most eminent of men. Thus Mary Gedo (1982) has shown how the life of Picasso was dominated by his extreme ambivalence about women, which was traced back to a cold, domineering mother and the birth of a sister when he was 3 years old.

The man split his image of the woman into the virgin and the prostitute; the woman in return made herself into either a virgin or a prostitute. Such was the first great dilemma that resulted from the doctrine of romantic love. Yet love also showed a way out by emphasizing the gratifications that man and woman can give one another. But this way out took centuries even to formulate. In the meantime the hate culture flourished, and men and women suffered. Changes in men's minds come slowly. The split could only be overcome gradually; the emergence of a more rational outlook on love took a long time. In fact, the struggle is still going on, but there are new weapons available today, particularly modern psychology (of the psychoanalytic variety), so there is a better chance of getting out of the conflict.

In contrast to the standard Christian love, romantic love brought two real people together in a loving relationship, even if it was only temporary and filled with an aura of exaggerated fantasy. For traditionally the church had taught that man is to relate only to God, in fact discouraging any close human relationships. This was the rationale behind the celibacy of the priest. In reality this attitude emphasized the other world, viewing this life merely as a passage to eternity, because of the despair brought on by the horrors of the hate culture. There was really no way out in this life (as there had been no way out in the Roman empire), so get to heaven as fast as you can. Other people can only get in the way.

One of the major outcomes of the Reformation was a change in the attitude to marriage. Priestly celibacy, monasticism, withdrawal were out; ministers were now encouraged to marry. Likewise with the ordinary person: Marriage was now seen as one of the major avenues to happiness. It was no longer the Pauline injunction: "Better to marry than to burn," which grudgingly allowed marriage if one could not tolerate the single life; now it was rather: "Come live with me and be my love." In a book *Matrimonial Honor,* by a Puritan preacher Daniel Rogers in 1642, a typical sentence reads: "Husbands and wives should be as two sweet friends, bred under one constellation, tempered by an influence from heaven, whereof neither can give any great reason save that mercy and providence first made them so, and then made their match" (cited in Hunt, 1959, p. 218).

Even sexually the Puritans were very broad-minded. Married love, says Rogers, is a sweet compound of spiritual affection and carnal attraction, and this blend of the two is the vital spirit and heart blood of wedlock. Thus was born the ideal of married bliss that has dominated the thinking of the western world ever since.

Actually it is surprising, and a commentary on centuries of a hate culture, that this ideal took so long to appear. For it is one that has been found at all times and in all places (Petroni, 1968); one could justifiably say that it is an essential ingredient of human existence, and when it is denied, or absent, there is something drastically wrong with the society.

Some typical examples from various cultures can be examined here. A Chinese poem by Li Po (701–762 A.D.):

> While our horses stood still I accosted her
> Wondering if she had come from Heaven above,
> And so to Velvet Inn invited her
> To drink, to sing and lightly talk of love.
> Sipping the wine behind her scented fan,
> Her face was like the moon through cloud-laced net.
> Alas, to have met, have loved, but never won
> Is sad—far sadder than never to have met!
> [MARTIN & BECHETT, 1968, p. 21]

The quatrain from the *Rubaiyyat* of Omar Khayyam (c. 1050—1123):

> A book of verses underneath the bough
> A jug of wine, a loaf of bread—and thou
> Beside me singing in the wilderness—
> Oh wilderness were Paradise enow.
> [VERSE 11]

An Egyptian poem translated by Ezra Pound:

> Nothing, nothing can keep me from my love
> Standing on the other shore

Not even old crocodile
There on the sandbank between us
Can keep us apart.
I go in spite of him
I walk upon the waves
Her love flows back across the water
Turning waves to solid earth
For me to walk on.

[POUND & STOCK, 1962, p. 9]

Shakespeare highlights the rescue from depression that is found in love (what I refer to as refuge love) in Sonnet 29:

When, in disgrace with fortune and men's eyes,
I all alone beweep my outcast state,
And trouble deaf heaven with my bootless cries,
And look upon myself, and curse my fate,
Wishing me like to one more rich in hope,
Featured like him, like him with friends possessed,
Desiring this man's art and that man's scope,
With what I most enjoy contented least,
Yet, in this state, myself almost despising,
Happily I think on thee, and then my state,
Like to the lark at break of day arising,
From sullen earth, sings hymns at heaven's gate;
For thy sweet love remembered such wealth brings
That then I scorn to change my state with kings.

And finally a poem of our times by Alice Folus.

Carrie

Carrie, I have watched you grow,
There is no other like you, this I know.
Your hair is a halo around your face
Your angelic features none can erase.
Your eyes sparkle an azure blue
I know there are others who love you too.
You bring sunshine and laughter, wherever you go
I want you to stay, this much I know.
My days are empty when you're not here

I love you very much, Carrie, my dear.
And when you have grown and I am gone
Carrie, I leave you this—my song.

[1977, p. 291]

In more primitive cultures there is sometimes a more explicit celebration of sex and love. Thus Berndt (1976) quotes the following from Arnhemland (northern Australia):

Ejaculating into their vaginas—young girls of the western tribes.
Ejaculating semen, into the young Burara girls . . .
Those Goulburn Island men, with their long penes;
Semen flowing from them into the young girls . . .
For they are always there, moving their buttocks.
They are always there, at the wide expanse of water. . . .
Ejaculating for the young girls of the western clans . . .
From the long penes of men from Goulburn Islands . . .

[BERNDT, 1961, p. 60]

These are all poems with one theme and many variations: Love makes people happy, yet it cannot be realized, or something gets in the way, or you have to isolate yourself to get it, and so on. While love (in marriage or out of it) is the ideal, somehow suffering and unrequited love become the rule.

In western civilization we have ascribed this frustration to the prevalent hate culture. In the first chapter a distinction was drawn between love and hate cultures. The differences found in the love experience are explainable only on the basis of an examination of the total culture. As stressed thoughout, the meaning of love will vary widely from one cultural situation to another.

At the point where married bliss became the dominant goal in western civilization, sometime in the seventeenth century (if it can be fixed so precisely at all), Europe was still in the throes of bloody wars and revolutions. Love then became a refuge from the horrors of everyday life. Because it was an escape it was exhilarating beyond measure; because the love couple had to come back to reality it was also full of sorrow and pain. To bring human beings to the point where they could love wholesomely was the goal of many religious leaders; to bring society to the point where it could tolerate more love experiences was the goal of many social reformers. The interlacing of all these threads makes one of the essential motifs in history.

In the seventeenth century love was hampered by many obstacles; not the least among them was the age-old sexual repression that a mere change of religion could not lift overnight. So the struggle for sexual liberation continues to this day.

When courtly love began, in the twelfth century, one of its major delights was the *amor purus*, "pure love," which led people to lie in bed for hours without actually consummating the sex act. Clearly, to elevate such a practice to such a high level implied enormous guilt about sex. And again to overcome this inner guilt requires a titanic struggle, once more still going on.

When Protestantism replaced Catholicism in many European countries, it let in a little fresh sexual air, but not much. Calvin, whose theology enthralled a surprising number, was a somber man whose doctrine of predestination of the elect implied a God who condemned the vast mass of humanity to eternal damnation; in this way he continued the hate culture that had dominated before him. It was a mere changing of the guard, not a real reorganization. The immediate consequence was two centuries (sixteenth and seventeenth) of the most sanguinary wars, in which Catholic murdered Protestant, who retaliated by murdering Catholic. In a real sense these religious wars did not come to an end until the French Revolution, when, as in virtually all leftist revolutions, the church was thrown out in its entirety.

Thereafter the church in general has lost the militancy it once had, not because it lost the will but because it was settled by so many different sects; these divisions had a highly beneficial effect in leading to a separation of church and state, once the new country won independence (Ahlstrom, 1972).

However, the religious fight to control the world is by no means over. Once out of power, the church tries everything to get back into power. Recently the United States has been staggered by the fundamentalist right (Conway & Siegelman, 1982). As these investigators show, the fundamentalist right comprises all the classic elements of total propaganda: a mammoth mass communications network, a tightly coordinated political machine, a fiercely independent educational system. Its expressed objectives: to Christianize the nation, to fill all government positions with Bible-thumping Christians, to gain power, to have fundamentalist beliefs taught as science in the schools, to dictate the meaning of human life, and ultimately to "convert" (read: control) every person on earth, and all this in the name of love. Obviously they have learned nothing from history. In the name of religion, the hate culture rolls on, in much the same way as it rolled on in the past.

The fight to free humankind from its sexual shackles was centered on women after the eighteenth century. The clarion call was sounded by Mary Wollstonecraft with her book *A Vindication of the Rights of Women*, published in 1792, during the French Revolution (not an accident). She argued for an improvement of the lot of women by curbing the existing inequities of marriage, so that women would not be submissive housewives, but equals, capable of friendship with their husbands. Certainly this is not surprising today, but for that time it was radical, especially since all the world knew that she had lived with a man in free love and had had a child out of wedlock.

It was in the nineteenth century that various reform movements began to liberate women, from sexual submissiveness, from domestic tyranny, from fears about their bodies, from being forced to live, in Ibsen's memorable description, in a "doll's house." At the same time many attempts were also being made to reform the hate culture that oppressed the man as much as the woman. It is becoming increasingly clear that hatred, fear, and violence were endemic throughout the recorded history of Europe (Stone, 1982). Three aspects of this liberation can be considered here: freedom of the body, freedom of sexual expression, and freedom from neurosis, that is, freedom of the mind.

Freedom of the body involved an increased understanding of the body, which came about in the nineteenth century. Since Aristotle it had been assumed that the semen was the fructifying influence and that the woman was merely the container that nourished the man's semen into a child. The role of the ovum was not demonstrated until the seventeenth century. That birth involves the union of an egg and a sperm was not explicitly shown until 1854, and then only in the frog. It took almost another 100 years of research and practice before the full process of reproduction in the human was fully elucidated.

In the meantime women were exposed to all kinds of mistreatment at the hands of physicians. It was considered "indelicate" for a physician to examine a woman in the nude, so he had to put his hand under her dress to feel what he could feel. Femininity per se was regarded as a kind of illness, while the center of the illness lay in the womb. Upon the slightest excuse the physician could engage in some inappropriate treatment for the womb, including such barbarous medications as the insertion of leeches into the vagina (Wood, 1983, p. 30). From 1870 to 1920 chlorosis, a form of anemia, was endemic among adolescent girls, many of whom became vegetarians because meat was supposed to inflame the sexual passions, and that was bad (Brumberg, 1982). The list could be continued indefinitely. It suffices to compare the clothes that women wear today with what they wore 100 years ago to see what vast changes have taken place.

The nineteenth century also saw a persistent attempt to flout the sexual taboos that were still the law. In France George Sand became famous as a free woman who took many lovers. Her main message in her numerous novels is that love can overcome all conventional obstacles. Likewise Stendhal in France had many love affairs; on his tomb he wished to have inscribed: "He lived, he wrote, he loved."

While legal penalties were slight in France and other European countries, in America it remained a risky business. Moses Harman knew neither reticence nor revulsion. His daughter, caught living out of wedlock, was jailed for 1½ months; her spouse typically was given a sentence of 2½ months.

Harman had two pet projects. One was to be able to print anything he wanted, and the other was the free love solution which linked evolution with eugenics. In April 1880 he was sent to jail for 5 years for printing shocking material (Ditzion, 1969, pp. 195–200). Harman was a true martyr; when he died Eugene Debs wrote of him:

> *Harman's life was a continuous round of poverty, privation and persecution. . . . He was a purist in the most rational sense of that term, and the sexual ignorance and slavery of his age appealed to all his boundless sympathies and stirred to their depths all the vast energies of his splendid intellect and his sturdy manhood. He was an apostle of freedom and light, a warrior in the cause of human regeneration, but all his methods were the methods of sweetness, gentleness and peace. [Ditzion, p. 199]*

This eulogy to Harman would be equally appropriate for thousands or millions of others who through the ages have tried to reform the hate culture. But the hate culture maintains itself by force, so that it will take and often has taken centuries to effect reasonable changes.

With Freud's demonstration that rejection of the body and sexual repression lead to actual illness, often of the most serious kind, a giant step forward was taken in women's and human liberation. The twentieth century has, in fact, despite the most strenuous denials by its opponents, been dominated by psychoanalytic thought (Fine, 1981).

Freud gave an entirely new turn to the age-old hunger for romantic love. He was able to show that it frequently presents a transference from childhood, the idealization of a woman who resembles or is made to resemble the mother of childhood. For the first time he demonstrated that sexual difficulties were due to childhood fixations, that love was just as often a neurotic as a normal manifestation, and that the love life of the individual could only be understood in the light of the variety of childhood experiences.

But Freud too was struggling against a hate culture. His ideas were misunderstood, scorned, and at times even threatened with police action (Jones, 1953–1957). Paradoxically, when the current women's liberation movement started with the publication of Betty Friedan's book *The Feminine Mystique* (1963), Freud was taken as a primary target, though his attackers misconstrued the entire humanitarian cast to his thought and ignored completely the fact that he was the one who showed that if women do not have sexual gratification in their lives they fall ill (the same is of course true of men) (Howell & Bayes, 1981; Mitchell, 1974).

Hunt calls the twentieth century "by love obsessed" (1959, p. 341). No more so than other centuries. There is, however, a novel element in that a wide array of scientific discoveries has shown that much of the unhappiness in the world stems from the lack of love. And this love can now for the first time be properly understood from a scientific point of view.

One of the major problems encountered has been the confusion of love with sex. If the nineteenth century epitomized sexless love, the twentieth century has glorified loveless sex. And neither one has grasped the role that love plays in the life of the individual who has to make his or her way in a hate culture.

This brief, necessarily all-too-condensed discussion of the development of romantic love from its beginnings in the court of Eleanor of Aquitaine to the present has highlighted several salient features of the love problem. Humankind seeks love and has always sought it. Romantic love as it started was one version of the search. It had to be done under the most peculiar circumstances and in accordance with a variety of special rules. It has functioned mainly as an escape valve from the terrible pressures of the surrounding civilization and for the most part still functions that way. Cuber and Harroff (1965), in what is probably still the best in-depth study of middle- and upper-class marriage, found that by far the most common marriage is what they call the utilitarian, in which love plays a minor role, if it plays any at all. What the modern human being is struggling with is still the wish to combine love and marriage in a gratifying life situation. Such an accomplishment would represent a major break in the hate culture. But, as scarcely needs any statistical proof, it is still a distant ideal. Yet it is an ideal that makes sense and that gives meaning and value to many individuals' lives.

THE SIXTEENTH CENTURY TO THE PRESENT: SOCIAL AND RELIGIOUS REFORM MOVEMENTS

That society is full of evil and hatred is not new. In 1828, the lecturer at the opening session of the Doctrine de Saint-Simon, in a commentary that echoes through the ages, said:

> *Viewed as a whole, society today presents the spectacle of two warring camps. In one are entrenched the few remaining defenders of the religious and political organization of the Middle Ages; in the other, drawn up under the rather inappropriate name of* partisans of the new ideas, *are all those who either cooperated in or applauded the overthrow of the ancient edifice. We come to bring peace to these two armies by proclaiming a doctrine which preaches not only its horror of blood but its horror of strife under whatever name it may disguise itself.* Antagonism *between a spiritual and a temporal power, opposition in honor of liberty,* competition *for the greatest good of all—we do not believe in the everlasting need for any of these war machines. We do not allow to civilized humanity any* natural right *which obliges it to tear its own entrails.* [Manuel & Manuel, 1979, p. 620]

To do away with evil without employing the mechanisms of evil—that has been one of the great dreams of humankind. The reasons it has not yet succeeded must be carefully explored.

At first, the effort to reform society took a religious form. As has been seen, there were always severe critics of establishment Christianity, and always they had excellent justification. But the church was too popular. In 1415 Jan Hus was burned at the stake, with the heretics' hat on his head. A century later Martin Luther rebelled. But this time the church was too weak to murder him. With astounding rapidity Luther's doctrines spread throughout Germany. The imperial cities and princes found that for them power, profits, and piety harmonized splendidly. By 1530 Charles V, the emperor, called a diet to clarify the religious situation of the empire. But war to put the heretics down did not erupt until 1546, the year of Luther's death, only to be settled 9 years later, in 1555 with the Peace of Augsburg (Gay & Webb, 1973, p. 145). The ancient order of the Catholic church, which had lasted some twelve centuries, collapsed within less than 10 years after Luther's appearance, when two of the imperial electors came out for him.

Protestantism soon spread all over northern Europe, England, and even into France. But even though the rebellion was against a tyrannical and corrupt series of popes, the rebels in their turn did not do much better.

Luther himself, to whom Erikson has devoted a much-discussed book (1958), was filled with wrath and vengeance. When he was excommunicated, he preached open revolt, even suggesting that it would be entirely in order "to wash our hands in the blood" of cardinals and popes. First he encouraged the peasants by writing: "What do they better deserve than a strong uprising which will sweep them from the earth? And we would smile did it happen" (cited in Erikson, 1958, p. 235). When the peasants in fact did rebel he wrote a pamphlet against them in 1525, and, as Erikson notes, he suggested both public and secret massacres in words that could adorn the police headquarters and concentration camps of our time. Luther himself wrote that the answer for rebels is "a fist that brings blood from the nose." Eventually the peasants were defeated and massacred in a bloody war; Luther had an increased salary as professor and pastor and said nothing.

Luther's severe emotional disturbance has also been extensively discussed; one psychiatrist viewed him as a steadily deteriorating man who in his mid-forties climaxed into a frank psychosis. While this has been questioned, there is no doubt that Luther was a profoundly disturbed man, and it has been cogently argued that his rebellion against the pope was the expression in religious–political terms of his rage at his father.

Once in power, Luther ranted and raved against the Catholics (Levy, 1981, p. 130). Their church was a synagogue of Satan, full of blasphemous lies and terrible idolatry. They must be compelled to worship in Lutheran churches and, if they failed to attend, their very absence was blasphemy and should be met with excommunication and exile. By 1536 he finally endorsed imprisonment and death for Catholic blasphemers to prevent the spread of their contagion. Mercy existed in heaven, said Luther; on earth the sword. His description of the pope fit himself: "Oh, how he bellows, rages, raves and foams, just like one possessed by many thousands of devils" (cited in Levy, 1981, p. 130).

However, he did not limit himself to Catholics. Impartially, if promiscuously, he condemned Anabaptism, Arianism, and Catholicism as blasphemies, Judaism and Islam as well. Any denial of an article of Christian faith as he understood it was blasphemy, as was speaking against the faith.

We can, in fact, be grateful that Luther never did become the pope, as might have been the case at some other epoch. Erikson points out trends in him that may have prepared his nation for the acceptance of a leader like Hitler (Erikson, 1962, p. 109). And certainly the prevalence of Lutheranism in Germany obviously did nothing historically to curb that country's bloodthirsty expansionism.

The Anabaptist movement, which sprouted at around the same time as Lutheranism, was to the established Protestant church what Luther was to Rome. They believed in a simple, straightforward version of Christianity; one of their sects, described in Chapter 1, is the Hutterites, who eventually managed to get to the United States in the 1870s. Like the early Christians, the Anabaptists abjured the use of violence. And, like the early Christians, they were hounded, harassed, persecuted, tortured, and frequently murdered.

But, again like the early Christians, they were too obedient to charismatic or psychotic leaders. In 1533 the Anabaptists had managed to secure control of the German city of Münster. Sympathizers from the Netherlands tried to join them but were judicially murdered. While the city was besieged, the leaders within expelled Catholics and Lutherans, baptized adults (*anabaptism* means "baptism again"), preached community of property, and began to practice polygamy. One leader, John of Leyden, whose sanity is said to have given way, took a total of 16 wives, had one of them executed, and finally had himself crowned king. In 1535 the city was captured, and most of the remaining inhabitants were put to death. Luther, aware of what was going on, said nothing (Levy, 1981, pp. 123–125).

The sixteenth and seventeenth centuries were marked by religious wars of horrible ruthlessness. Indeed, Christianity remained a "warrior religion." In the Thirty Years War (1616—1648), in which religious and political questions were completely intertwined, fierce battles were fought on German territory. Yet even when the Peace of Westphalia was secured, giving Protestants the right to worship as they pleased, Pope Innocent X solemnly condemned the peace as "null, void, invalid, iniquitous, unjust, damnable, reprobate, inane of meaning and effect for all time" (cited in Wedgwood, 1938, p. 526).

In her work Wedgwood states:

The suffering caused by the Thirty Years War was beyond all reckoning. . . . After the expenditure of so much human life to so little purpose, men might have grasped the essential futility of putting the be-

liefs of the mind to the judgment of the sword. Instead, they rejected religion as an object to fight for and found others. [1938, pp. 7, 526]

Our purpose in this chapter is to see to what extent the religious changes of the Reformation affected the hate culture that had been prevalent in Europe for so many centuries. No sooner had men changed their religious beliefs than they turned to the sword to enforce their convictions. The conclusion is clear: Religion had little effect on the hatreds that continued to seethe in men's minds. In the next chapter religious beliefs will be discussed in more detail; here it is sufficient to note that from a practical point of view the hate culture marched on.

As Wedgwood observes, after the seventeenth century Christians no longer fought bitter wars with one another to wipe out heresy or blasphemy. A certain amount of tolerance came into being, especially after the settlement of the United States, where for the most part religious battles were quite mild or absent. Yet, even here, as Tracy (1980) shows in her study of Jonathan Edwards, there remained in many religious leaders, as in Edwards, a strong wish for unlimited power.

While religion has lost much of its force in the modern world (actually much of the world has by now given up reliance on organized religion), it remains an essential part of western culture. To what extent has the peaceful message of Christ and Christianity modified the violent hatreds found all over? There is little reason to believe that it has had or has much effect. What has happened is that religion has lost the power that it once had, so it prefers to stay in its own corner, with little involvement in the burning issues of everyday life. There are of course innumerable exceptions to this statement, and there is no question that religion has enriched and continues to enrich the lives of millions of people. But the belief that it is a vital force that can change the world, a belief that persisted from the Roman empire to the French Revolution, is virtually gone.

Instead, humanity has tried to change the hate culture by movements of social, economic, and political reform. It is to a consideration of these that we now turn.

Once the religious wars came to an end, Europe was convulsed by violent revolutions that turned the old social order completely topsy-turvy. It is of course obvious that the revolutionaries were looking for a new world, a utopia of their own. In almost all cases, they did create a new world, but there is little reason to believe that the new one was so much better than the old; many times it seemed worse. In effect, humankind was seeking to establish a love culture. Where the medium of religion had failed, now the medium of a political dethronement was to succeed. Our analysis will focus on the causes of the failure to achieve a really permanent change that would lead to a truly superior society.

While it has always been recognized that the social order was awful, it is only recently that historians have come to see, under the influence of psychoanalytic prodding, that the psychological order was equally awful. Human beings, to put it simply, were just plain miserable. Huizinga expressed it as follows:

> At the close of the Middle Ages, a sombre melancholy weighs on people's souls. Whether we read a chronicle, a poem, a sermon, a legal document even, the same impression of immense sadness is produced by them all. It would sometimes seem as if this period had been particularly unhappy, as if it had left behind only the memory of violence, of covetousness and mortal hatred, as if it had known no other enjoyment but that of intemperance, of pride and of cruelty. . . .
>
> We are perhaps inclined to assume without much evidence that, roughly speaking and notwithstanding all calamities, the sum of happiness can have hardly changed from one period to another. But in the fifteenth century . . . it was fashionable . . . to condemn the times or to despise them. [1956, p. 150]

Whatever its slogans, every revolution is based on the hope that the misery of the common mass of humanity, which Huizinga describes so tellingly, will be relieved by a change in the political system. By now there is certainly abundant evidence to question this assumption.

The problem that has emerged, unforeseen by the original instigators of the upheaval, is that after a while, as the phrase about the French Revolution goes, the revolution begins to eat its own children. Initially there is enormous enthusiasm, lives are sacrificed, the old order is turned over. Then, again as in the French Revolution, as the *ancien regime* disappears, the revolutionaries begin to quarrel among themselves. A reign of terror is instituted, of varying degrees of severity. Eventually a strongman takes over, and we are back where we started. The bottles are new; the wine is old.

In the French Revolution the first terror started in September 1792, some 3 years after the storming of the Bastille. The commune silenced the opposition press, closed the tollgates, and by repeated house visits seized a number of refractory priests and aristocratic notables. Frightened by invasion and civil war, the masses sought out scapegoats, particularly the old nobility and the priests, who had refused to take an oath of allegiance to the new state. They stormed the prisons, killing about half of the 2600 persons imprisoned (Lefebvre, 1962, p. 243).

The second, more serious terror, in 1794, took place after the execution of the king and queen. Suspects of all kinds were summarily arrested, on any kind of denunciation, and summarily executed. One historian estimates that 35,000 executions took place in this period (Gay & Webb, 1973, p. 494). Countless people lived in constant fear of death. Senseless sadistic acts were an everyday occurrence. For instance, one woman was charged with the crime of having wept at the execution of her husband. She was consequently condemned to sit several hours under the suspended blade, which shed upon her, drop by drop, the blood of the corpse hanging above her on the scaffold, before she was released by death from her agony (Hibbert, 1981, pp. 227–228). At Nantes, 2000 people were towed out in barges into the middle of the Loire and drowned in wholesale and indiscriminate murder (Gay & Webb, p. 493).

In May 1793 Robespierre put the new revolutionary principles very simply: "There are now only two parties in France, the people and the enemies of the people" (cited in Gay & Webb, 1973, p. 487). Thus the revolution, begun with the greatest of hopes of human liberation, ended in tragedy and despair. Gay and Webb put it this way:

> *Thus baldly summarized, the Terror seems to discredit the whole Revolution as a nightmarish orgy of madmen, a sadistic riot in the name of humanity. Robespierre and his associates seem like so many modern Caligulas, wishing that the French people had but one neck.* [p. 493]

Eventually a dictator, Napoleon, put an end to civil disorder. Under his command French armies conquered most of Europe, because at first the people saw them as liberators who would free them from their *ancien regime*. Eventually it appeared that Napoleon was a bloody tyrant himself, and after some 25 years of almost continuous warfare Europe found itself at peace. Many French historians have since viewed the revolution as a failure and sought to uncover the causes of the failure. Whatever the political events were, psychologically, the despair of the masses, which Huizinga described, remained untouched and again and again and again the French rebelled against their overlords.

While the terror of the French Revolution has been blamed on the foreign invasions that the other kings of Europe undertook to save their own skins (and in fact they did save the monarchical system until World War I toppled it once and for all), Mexico in its revolution from 1910 to 1920 had no such fear. In retaliation for Pancho Villa's raid on a small town in New Mexico, the United States did send an expeditionary force under Pershing to find and capture Villa, but no real invasion was ever considered.

Ruiz (1980) has interpreted the Mexican revolution as a civil war among rival generals, almost all of whom came from the middle classes, and envisaged no real social revolution; the only exception was Zapata, who was ambushed and shot by his fellow generals. The civil war lasted some 10 years, costing the lives of several million people, with devastating effects on the economy. In 1923 Mexico was virtually bankrupt (Ruiz, 1980, p. 40). Today, after more than 60 years of one-party rule, the same situation exists. Perhaps Ruiz is right in his insistence that we should speak of a Mexican rebellion, not a Mexican revolution.

The Russian Revolution, which started in 1917, has been studied most intensively of all. Thousands of persons who lived through it have described the course of events, so that while much remains unknown because of the secrecy of the government, the essential outlines are reasonably well understood. Besançon (1981) has attributed the rise of the Gulag to Lenin's narrow outlook on life, which was accompanied by an insistence that only violence could succeed and maintain the benefits of the revolution. The paranoid society created by Stalin has often been described. That much has changed since his day is questionable, though the worst of the excesses of Stalin's time would appear to be gone, perhaps because none of his successors were as paranoid as he.

However, as time has passed and the sense of prosperity for the ruling class at least has increased, the society seems to have become more corrupt. It is odd to find communist ideologues offer the criticism of the system that people have too little incentive to get ahead, the same criticism that "reactionary" capitalists have been offering from time immemorial. Recently some new material has appeared showing that large-scale corruption has crept into the system (Simis, 1982); Andropov in his first speech made a fairly direct reference to this as one of the Soviet Union's most burdensome problems. Many have raised serious questions about the management of the Soviet economy; capitalism seems to have its uses, after all.

Again here the assumption was that the liquidation of private property would remedy the hostility and despair of the lower classes. Freud had already questioned this assumption in *Civilization and Its Discontents* (1930), when he asked against whom the hostility of the regime would be directed once the old order had been liquidated. He wrote this before the horrendous purges of the 1930s; obviously his insight was a correct one. The human toll of the revolution remains staggering (Antonov-Ovseyenko, 1981), while its concrete results are questionable. Marxism has become just another system in which one group oppresses another.

Two Swedish journalists, Carola Hansson and Karin Liden, have recently described the plight of the Soviet woman as in many ways worse than that of her counterpart in capitalistic countries. She must be both homemaker and career woman; she does not earn enough; facilities for taking care of the children are inadequate; sexual frustration is widespread, especially since sex education is not present. All this after more than 60 years of wholesale slaughter and sacrifice to produce a "utopian" world (Hansson & Liden, 1983).

Outside Europe, the Chinese experience is again similar. The brutal dictatorship of Mao, who obviously visualized himself as a modern Confucius and wanted the Chinese to listen to his every word as they had listened to Confucius through the ages, did not pass with his death. His own wife has been implicated in charges of counterrevolution; whether these charges are fabricated or true we have no way of knowing. Lifton (1969) has made a careful study of the brainwashing process of the Chinese. It is a system of thought reform with the possibility of execution always in the background and occasionally carried out. Again Chinese Marxism has become just another system, with vast possibilities and vast problems.

Apart from large-scale revolutions, many attempts have been made throughout the centuries to reform minds and institutions on a smaller scale. The nineteenth century, when warfare in Europe diminished considerably after Napoleon's defeat in 1815, was notable for the numerous schemes of perfectionism in small communities that were proposed and adopted by enterprising individuals. Europe, however, was too full of hostile states and warring individuals to try out many of these schemes on its own soil. Instead, they were exported to America, the land of "infinite possibilities."

One of the most interesting, notable, and successful experiments of this kind was the Oneida Community, founded by John Humphrey Noyes in 1869 at Oneida, New York. In it are combined all of the social problems that plagued America and the rest of the world then, together with proposed solutions. Noyes was a most unusual man. He came of hardy, wealthy, and respectable New England stock (Ditzion, 1969, pp. 220–226), related to the leading circles in American society. His father had been a congressional representative from Vermont, and his mother was the aunt of President Rutherford B. Hayes.

At first Noyes studied law, but in the excitement of the revivalist movement of the 1830s he left law to enter the ministry. After a short time his license to preach was rescinded because of his unorthodox tendencies. He then looked around for a mold that would contain a religion of biblical simplicity. In the course of his searching he touched upon almost every issue that was agitating America at that time: religion, sexuality, free love, abolition, eugenics, property and its uses and abuses, communism (in the nineteenth-century sense of sharing everything; this was before Marx), and violence. In effect he was looking for a way to establish a love culture, in opposition to the prevailing hate culture.

The community developed out of a Society of Inquiry, established by Noyes and some of his disciples at Putney, Vermont, in 1841. As new recruits arrived, the society turned into a socialized religious community. America at that time was full of idealized communistic groups that were trying to find heaven on earth; most of them had, like Noyes's group, strong religious emphasis. The most original features of Oneida were the doctrine of complex marriage, according to which every man had the right to have sex with every woman in the community, so that all were married to all, and a special committee that decreed the most promising prospective parents, with all agreeing not to have children except under the aegis of this committee(this was called stirpiculture). Noyes had argued emphatically for the notion that the amative function of sex (love) should be carefully distinguished from its procreative function (childbearing).

According to one study in 1921, sickness, disease, and early death were much less common among the residents of Oneida's children's house than elsewhere in the nation. Out of the 58 live births during the stirpiculture period (1869 on) only 6 had died by 1921, when the age range of these eugenic babies was from 42 to 52. The calculated norm for a comparable group in the country was 45 deaths (Ditzion, 1969, p. 225).

In 1847, at a time when revivalist belief was at its zenith, Noyes proclaimed that the spirit of Christ had earlier returned to earth and had now entered into his group at Putney. This proclamation, together with the practice of complex marriage, aroused so much antagonism in the surrounding group that they left Putney to found a new community at Oneida, New York.

For the next 30 years Oneida flourished. The community, numbering about 200, earned a precarious existence farming and logging until the arrival of a new member who gave the community a steel trap that he had invented. Manufacture and sale of Oneida traps, which were considered the best in the land, became the basis for a thriving group of industrial enterprises that included silverware, embroidery, silks, and canned fruit.

The community was organized into 48 departments that carried on the various activities of the settlement, and these activities were supervised by 21 committees. The women worked along with the men; for practical reasons they cut their hair short and wore trousers or short-skirted tunics (one of the consistent aspects of the women's liberation movement has been to change their manner of dress). Though marriage was complex, the Perfectionists (this is what they called themselves; the same name was taken by the Cathars in the twelfth century) denied the charge of free love (obviously a sop to all the rabid critics who were denouncing them en masse). Children remained with their mothers until they could walk but were then placed in a common nursery.

One central feature of the community was the custom of holding criticism sessions, or cures, a practice that Noyes had discovered in his seminary days. They were attended by the entire community at first and later, as the community grew, they were conducted before committees presided over by Noyes.

For those subjected to criticism it was a nerve-racking ordeal; thus Noyes was one of the earliest group therapists as well. The criticism sessions were also a shaming technique that enforced social control and was a highly successful device for promoting community cohesion.

In Oneida as well hostility mounted in the surrounding communities. In 1879 Noyes advised the group to abandon the system. Noyes and a few adherents went to Canada, where he died in 1886. The remaining members set up a stock company that persisted as a commercial enterprise.

It has been widely argued that the community was an extremely happy one under the guidance of Noyes; there is little evidence on this score, except that open enmities and crime were apparently absent for the 30 years that Noyes dominated. It received widespread interest and recognition, with varying reactions, of course. George Bernard Shaw commented that the question of what sort of men they should breed was settled at once by the desirability of breeding another Noyes (cited in Ditzion, 1969, p. 225) (oddly enough, four of his five legal children died in infancy, while nothing is known of any of the others he might have bred).

In any case this attempt at utopia was clearly completely dependent on one man. Once he had gone, the idealism of the community evaporated, and it returned to a state just like that of the surrounding area.

If it was indeed a love culture, as it might well have been, it lasted only one generation. Similar experiences were noted by Noyes himself in his classic work *History of American Socialisms*. History has repeatedly shown that one of the major disadvantages of small-scale utopias or love cultures is that they tend to be dominated by one strong personality and to fall apart when that personality moves on. (A fuller discussion of intentional love communities and their dynamics will be found in Chapter 8.)

On the other hand, large-scale attempts at reform of social inequities suffer from other disadvantages. Slavery, one of humankind's worst scourges, persisted into the nineteenth century. It was justified and rationalized in many, many different ways (Davis, 1965; Lovejoy, 1981), though essentially it is a form of penal servitude (Sellin, 1976), or worse, of social death (Paterson, 1982). Even though the United States was the outstanding democratic society of the nineteenth century, its slavocracy in the south was the only group that went to war to preserve the "peculiar" institution.

Yet when the war was won by the antislavery forces, and slavery was legally abolished, the efforts to give blacks real freedom were crushed by a combination of bigotry, corruption, and indifference. In 1865 the northern states had so many laws limiting the lives of the blacks that it could not afford to offer the southern blacks true liberation (McPherson, 1982). Reconstruction went on for about 10 years, but then it was abandoned and the blacks were forced back into a position that was almost as bad as slavery. There was no hesitation in using force to preserve the union, but when it came to using force to protect the blacks the post–Civil War governments were noticeably hesitant. Grant, the victorious general, cared little about what happened afterwards; his reputation was made. In his autobiography he did not even discuss his presidential years. A not untypical instance was the massacre at Colfax in upstate Louisiana, where on April 13, 1873, a clash between black militia and armed whites left 2 white men and an estimated 70 black men dead, half of the latter killed in cold blood after they had surrendered. Although the perpetrators were known to the government, and some efforts were even made to indict them, Grant cared nothing about the whole affair, and eventually they were freed on a technicality (McPherson, 1982, p. 592). Gradually terror and violence, embodied particularly in the murderous Ku Klux Klan, enveloped the whole south. It has taken more than a century to free the south of its most hateful elements, and to this day the plight of blacks throughout the country remains horrible.

The consequences of the abolition of slavery are but one of innumerable examples that show that when the underlying hate culture is not changed, the consequences of reform are nullified or rendered meaningless. Slavery was only one manifestation of the hate culture; today we look upon all the "arguments" in its justification as hypocritical rhetoric (McPherson, 1982).

The situation is similar with other social reform efforts. In women's liberation, the Soviet Union has been held up as the shining example of how free women can be (Lapidus, 1978), yet after 60 years, and the loss of millions of lives, women still suffer enormously. Lapidus (1978), in her careful review of the situation, writes:

> *Thus, as Soviet experience suggested from the very beginning, there was a critical distinction between mobilization and liberation. The fact that women were perceived as a major economic and political resource was compatible with a degree of exploitation. It may be said that in the Soviet context these terms tended to be extremely unfavorable to women. [p. 338]*

THE EIGHTEENTH CENTURY ON: THE MAKING OF THE MODERN FAMILY

The family is as old as recorded history. In fact, the nineteenth-century idea that humankind initially lived in communally organized societies has been discarded; as Margaret Mead once observed, communes can be found, but sooner or later the family enters in. Yet in spite of this universality of the family, the idea that it is through a happy family that men and women (and children) will find a major source of happiness is relatively new.

Even monogamy, we are surprised to learn, is a relatively new phenomenon historically. Malinowski (1963) states:

> *Monogamy as the unique and exclusive form of marriage, in the sense that bigamy is regarded as a grave criminal offense and a sin as well as a sacrilege, is very rare indeed. Such an exclusive ideal and such a rigid legal view of marriage is perhaps not to be found outside the modern, relatively recent development of Western culture. It is not implied in Christian doctrine even. Apart from such isolated phenomena as the recent church of Latter Day Saints (Mormons) and the heretical sect of Anabaptists (sixteenth century), polygamy was legally practiced and accepted by the Church in the Middle Ages, and it occurs sporadically as a legal institution accepted by the Church and State as recently as the middle of the seventeenth century. . . .*

Monogamy as pattern and prototype of human marriage, on the other hand, is universal. The whole institution, in its sexual, parental, economic, legal and religious aspects, is founded on the fact that the real function of marriage—sexual union, production and care of children, and the cooperation which it implies—requires essentially two people, and two people only, and that in the overwhelming majority of cases two people only are united in order to fulfill these facts. [Encyclopaedia Britannica, 14th ed., vol. 14, pp. 940–959]

This quotation allows us to place the developments of the past three centuries in better perspective. Marriage has always existed, but the effort to make the monogamous family the ideal route to happiness has been one of modern man's ways of overcoming the hate culture. And since it has been a push against the hate culture, rather than a spontaneous development on its own, it has naturally run into numerous obstacles.

Stone (1979) and others have maintained that there was a spread of revulsion against cruelty in Europe throughout the eighteenth century, attached to the progressive ideas of the Enlightenment. On paper one might agree with this, but there are so many exceptions that it becomes a dubious generalization. The wholesale slaughters of colonial peoples, especially in the nineteenth century (mention need be made only of Asia and Africa in this context), suggest that mass murder was merely displaced to "colored" peoples—and there were in fact innumerable arguments that these people were somehow not entirely human, so that to kill them was less of a misdeed. For example, not long after Engels wrote his *History of the Working Class in England* (1845), part of the nineteenth-century campaign that did lead to some amelioration of the state of workers in England, in India the Sepoy Mutiny of 1857–1859 was repressed with ferocious bloodiness; when the British retook Delhi the population was driven out into the open and thousands were murdered (*Encyclopaedia Britannica*, 15th ed., vol. 9, p. 407). In the United States in 1857, the Supreme Court officially declared the black person to be not a human being but a piece of property. In a clear contradiction to the Declaration of Independence and the Constitution, the Supreme Court held that a black could not be a citizen of the United States (Morrison, 1972, vol. 2, p. 363).

In the Crimean War some half a million men died, though the causes of the war remain obscure. Most of them died from disease (Gay & Webb, 1973, p. 747). Likewise, when Napoleon sent 33,000 troops to

Santo Domingo in 1802 to put down the rebellion by Toussaint L'Ouverture, almost all died of disease (McNeill, 1976, p. 266). So cruelty was not eradicated in the eighteenth century; it merely took different forms (Foucault, 1979).

Still, the idea was there, and ideas have a way of becoming weapons. When the French Revolution began in 1789, the numerous petitions submitted to the government were summed up as follows: "Let penalties be regulated and proportioned to the offenses, let the death sentence be passed only on those convicted of murder and let the tortures that revolt humanity be abolished" (Foucault, 1979, p. 73). In the present section we shall examine particularly how these noble intentions were applied to the family.

Historians have only recently turned to the effort to evaluate the intimate lives and feelings of other centuries. While the evidence is never very clear (Stone, 1979; Shorter, 1975; De Mause, 1974), what does emerge is that in the middle of the eighteenth century, let us say, there was little love found between husband and wife. As Shorter says: "On the farm, man and wife got along in quiet hostility and withdrawal" (p. 33). In 1748, the little weekly paper of the small Prussian town of Halle attempted a statistical estimate: Scarcely 10 marriages in 1000 were happy ones, while in all the others "the spouses cursed and bemoaned their choices" (Shorter, pp. 51–58). We are even surprised to learn that for the most part wives did not share their meals with their husbands, standing behind them often and acting as servants. Contempt for women was so strong that it was held that the loss of a stable animal grieved the peasant more than the loss of his wife; the first may only be recouped with money; the second can be replaced with another, who will bring with her some money and furniture and who, instead of impoverishing the household, will increase its wealth (Shorter, p. 7).

There is general agreement that after the French Revolution things began to change. In the nineteenth century the concept of a love or companionate marriage became a widespread ideal throughout Europe and the United States. But this time the image of the woman had turned the other way: She was the embodiment of goodness, of virtue, of loveliness, and of all that was finest in humankind. *Angel in the House* was the title of the best-seller by Coventry Patmore, a Victorian poet, whose book sold more than a quarter of a million copies in his lifetime, though it is all but forgotten now (Hunt, 1959, p. 326).

While there were no doubt many more happy marriages in this period, there were so many problems connected with it that the image of pure, unsullied domestic bliss came under severe attack until it was finally shattered by Sigmund Freud. Nineteenth-century marriage repressed sex, blocked spontaneity, enforced a cruel regimen on children, and was often honored more in the breach than in the observance. Man was still master of the house, woman his devoted slave. In many countries women still had almost no legal rights; they could not work, so that they had the choice only of being housewives or prostitutes (and prostitution flourished on an enormous scale).

Under the stinging impact of both psychoanalytic and Marxist thought, the twentieth century has for the first time seen determined, self-conscious effort to make the family the center of happy living. This involves three questions: (1) the love of man and woman; (2) the love of parents for the children; and (3) the love of children for the parents.

Since the love image of the nineteenth century was based on the repression of sex in the marriage bed, the twentieth, especially since World War I, has witnessed widespread transformations in sexual conduct and beliefs. This has occurred primarily in the western democratic countries but has extended to virtually the entire world.

Sexual freedom has been pursued in many different ways. Clothes have been reduced to the point of virtual nudity, and actual nudity in some situations, such as topless or nude beaches. Many have protested against men's impotence and lack of desire. Homosexuality has come out of the closet. In children masturbation is regarded as a virtue rather than as a sin, provided that they do not do it too openly.

Innumerable books are available that instruct the uninitiated in all possible aspects of sex, such as Comfort's *The Joy of Sex* (1972), which has become an international best-seller. Sex therapists abound, to help those who limit themselves to their sexual disabilities. Analysts and other therapists are available to help with the broader bases of living that led to the sexual problems in the first place. Women have come out of their dolls' houses into the wider world, enjoying virtually every privilege formerly reserved to men; there is even a woman member of the Supreme Court.

And yet with all this sexual freedom the discontent seems as great as ever. In the first place, venereal diseases, including gonorrhea and syphilis and the more recently encountered herpes, have become epidemic. Second, sex is often practiced as a mechanical exercise, without any great feeling of affection for the partner. "Swinging" is out in the open as well as homosexuality; after a while it too becomes a ritualized procedure that leaves most of the participants frustrated (Bartell, 1971). And in the third place, and most important, the role of aggression in sexuality is almost completely ignored.

Freud's thesis, simple enough to verbalize, so hard to realize, is that love is the union of tender and sexual feelings for the opposite sex. This is the hallmark of genitality, equated with maturity. To achieve such a union in marriage is the model ideal, really the first time in history that such an ideal has even been formulated. Yet the number of happy marriages continues to be minuscule, even if it is probably somewhat larger than the Prussian newspaper's finding in 1748 of 10 in 1000.

The reason for the difficulty is again that the sexual revolution has been carried out against the backdrop of a hate culture, without consideration of the overwhelming impact of that backdrop. The psychoanalytic approach is to reduce the hostility first, after which the sexual gratification can form a solid basis for love. In the reverse, when sexual liberation proceeds without consideration of the hostility, the result is only a different outlet for the hostility.

Furthermore, the reform of marriage to include sexual gratification as one of the desiderata is not as easy as it seemed in 1900. Inevitably the questions of fidelity and jealousy come into the picture. Biologically, the sexual appetite is not limited to one mate. The fanatical effort to impose such a restriction has had disastrous consequences. No culture before ours has ever tried to impose such a severe limitation, especially on men. But women too have come out of the closet, released their sexual appetites, and likewise often feel frustrated when they have to confine themselves to one man. This becomes obvious enough when the man is impotent, or sexually inadequate in other ways, but it is true even when the man is as competent as Don Juan. Yet the extension of sexuality to other partners is fraught with perils. Again the underlying hostility must be overcome before a real solution is feasible.

Attempts to reform marriage center generally around the laws of divorce. Rheinstein (1972) has shown that from World War II on, accelerating particularly in the 1960s, divorce has been liberalized throughout the world. The problem has a long history. Thus in 2470 B.C. Urukagina, ruler of Lagash, tried to abolish the custom of simply walking out on a distasteful marriage so as to avoid the fee of a formal divorce (Rheinstein, 1972, p. 408). After reviewing all of the recent changes in divorce laws Rheinstein concludes: "Experienced observers have long known what we have laboriously tried in this book to prove, namely, that a strict statute of law of divorce is not an effective means to prevent or even to reduce the incidence of marriage breakdown" (p. 406).

Using the language of the present book, Rheinstein is saying that the hate culture cannot be transformed into a love culture by any series of legal enactments, no matter how wisely or judiciously framed.

A paradox emerges here. Most Americans (Veroff, Douvan, & Kulka, 1981) see marriage as a desirable way of life (85% in 1976), yet there is at the same time an increase in tolerance of those people who choose not to get married. The Michigan Survey of the Mental Health of Americans of 1976 concludes:

> *Thus we see that the more educated in our society are more sensitive to issues of interpersonal accommodation in marriage, and thus more able to enhance the quality of their marriages. The less educated may be in double jeopardy in their marriages. Their lack of education often bars them from the jobs and money which can contribute to marital well-being and also often bars them from the interpersonal psychological perspective that seems to enhance married life. [cited in Veroff, Douvan, & Kulka, p. 193]*

The Michigan survey is based on a comparison of attitudes of Americans between 1957 and 1976. We shall present the more detailed argument later that what we have been going through is a psychotherapeutic revolution stimulated by psychoanalysis in which it is recognized that a change from a hate culture to a love culture has to be accomplished by internal means rather than external legal or police enactments.

In the care of children a similar pattern is found. In the nineteenth century various legal changes were introduced to prevent the abuse of children by parents or others. By the twentieth century it became clear that all of these legal enactments did little to change the realities. In his ground-breaking work De Mause (1974) accumulated an enormous wealth of information about how badly children had been mistreated throughout history, information which had been completely ignored by conventional historians. De Mause wrote: "The history of childhood is a nightmare from which we have only recently begun to awaken. The further back in history one goes, the lower the level of child care, and the more likely children are to be killed, abandoned, beaten, terrorized and sexually abused" (p. 1).

It is surprising to find that prior to World War II there was hardly any reliable information about what actually happened to children. Again spurred on by the psychoanalytic findings relating to the importance of children, and the horrors of World War II, longitudinal studies of children's development were instituted in many different countries. In the United States Gesell's work, at Yale, the Berkeley group, and the Fels studies are the best known; there are many others. In the 1950s, a great longitudinal project was established in Paris covering many European countries (Thomae, Coerper, & Hagen, 1954; Kotaskova, 1982). The findings are still being published and digested. They already confirm what had been found clinically: that children are exposed to enormous abuse and neglect, which turns them into bitter, hating adults. Again recourse was had to the external solution of legal enactments. Between 1962 and 1967 "battered child" statutes were enacted in every state in the union. Yet the rising tide of crime, violence, and misery obviously has not been stemmed in the slightest. Erikson (1968) comments: "Rapid technological change makes it impossible for any traditional way of being older to become so institutionalized that the younger generation can step right into it, or, indeed, resist it in revolutionary fashion" (p. 38).

Once more the problem comes back to the hate culture, and once more it becomes obvious that legal or other external reform has little if any effect without some inner change. With regard to the attitudes of children toward parents, similar conclusions emerge. Intergenerational problems are all-pervasive and have in fact existed throughout history. The Roman father's absolute right over his children's lives, including the right to have them killed, did not make for a better society. As previously mentioned, in the first century A.D. the emperor Augustus could not control his daughter Julia's promiscuity, and he passed a law to curb similar action in other women, besides banishing Julia (the Julian Laws). He was immediately confronted with the disobedience of Julia's daughter Julia. In our own day parents have the right to put their children in jail if they disobey, or to get PINS (persons in need of supervision) rights, while children or their representatives have the right to get TPR orders (termination of parental rights). All of these are useless without a change in the moral and emotional climate in which families live.

Thus while the modern family has emerged as an ideal, valuable to many, of a way to happiness and a love culture, the realities are entirely different from the ideal. The hate culture that has dominated western civilization for 2500 years cannot be changed by simple manipulation, and cannot be changed overnight.

CONCLUSION

This all-too-cursory survey of some aspects of the history of western culture has been presented in order to make the point that what we have

been living through for several thousand years has been a hate culture. Men have always recognized the horrors of this hate culture and have resorted to a variety of mechanisms to get past it. While it cannot be argued that all of these have been useless, it can also scarcely be proved that the sum total of human happiness has risen to any appreciable degree.

What I have tried to do is take some of the dominant ideals of different epochs, all of them attempts at reform, and see how they fared in the prevalent hate culture. The Greeks sought a way out in homosexuality, limited very largely to that of the adult man for the pubescent boy. The Romans sought it in a savage totalitarianism coupled with completely promiscuous sexuality. The Christians sought it in a theology of denial, nonviolence, nonsexuality, and other worldliness. As long as they were a powerless minority they behaved fairly decently; once they acquired power they differed in no respect from the surrounding rulers.

The courtly love of the twelfth century offered another solution, this time based on the idealization of women. It was soon followed by its opposite, the debasement of women, and the judicial murder of hundreds of thousands (or millions, who knows?) of innocent women by a psychotic clergy. The Protestant reformation did away with the barbarous hypocrisy and excess of Roman Catholicism but effected no real change in the prevailing hate culture. As in the early days of Christianity, enclaves of pure and simple Christians (e.g., the Anabaptists) arose that were horribly persecuted by the newly established churches of Lutherans, Calvinists, and others. The only thing that seems to have prevented the Protestants from duplicating the vicious brutality of the church of the Middle Ages was that they lacked the power. It may be noted in passing that one of the wisest of all measures adopted by the American founding fathers was to separate church from state.

Once the church was deprived of its power, various social reform movements came into existence. On the one hand these included total revolutions, such as the French, the Russian, and the Chinese. Wholesale slaughter accompanied the early years of all of these revolutions; whether what followed is really better has always been questionable. On the other hand there were innumerable efforts to reform obvious social evils, such as slavery, the oppression of women, child labor, and the like.

In all cases great social changes were brought about, but the underlying hate culture did not change.

Finally in the modern world there has been a consistent attempt on the part of many to find happiness through a happy family. This too has been an ideal, far distant from the realities of everyday living.

Thus the hate culture continues to predominate. We shall argue later that the only real solution is a consistent attempt to change the hate culture into a love culture by means of education and psychotherapy. At present it is sufficient to call attention to the real nature of the problem.

4

Religious Images of Love

The subtitle of William James's classic work *The Varieties of Religious Experience* (1902) is *A Study of Human Nature*. Religion is indeed universal, both in the sense of existing in all cultures and in the sense of embracing a wide variety of human experiences. Our concern in this chapter is not to give a full account of religion but instead to examine what it has or has not contributed to a better understanding and practice of love. Religion will be neither glorified nor denigrated; the attempt will be made to place it in its proper human light.

The word *religion* derives from the Latin *religare*, meaning "to bind fast." Thus socially as well as etymologically religion is a way of uniting humankind in a common way of life and a common series of experiences. While no universally valid definition of religion can be found, generally one finds: (1) a belief in God; (2) some charismatic figure who was the founder; (3) a holy book handed down from antiquity; (4) a requirement of obedience to God and his dictates, whatever they might be for that religion; (5) to a greater or lesser extent some sense of otherworldliness; and (6) an eternal alternation of spiritual excitement and dry ritual.

Primitive people, as Radin (1924) showed a long time ago, preoccupied themselves with the same problems that concerned people in later epochs: birth, death, the nature of the universe, why we are here, how to conduct ourselves in life, the control of sexuality and violence, and the like. Yet, with all the answers offered, as Bertrand Russell observed (1912, p. 565), since the French Revolution, religion, and philosophy as well, with which it has always been closely allied, have assumed decreasing importance in people's lives. In fact, the search of the past two centuries may be seen as a manifestation of the distress caused by the lack of religion and the hope that a new one will be found.

The famous Danish historian of religion of the early part of the century, Vilhelm Gronbech, expressed the dilemma beautifully:

> We, the children of the nineteenth century, are a generation without a religion and therefore we have but a single thought: how can we find a god and a devil, a heaven and a hell—all those things which made earlier times great? We know that the old is dead and gone, and that no attempts at resuscitation can give him back the power and the glory. We can date his departure around the year 1770. He died when men found it necessary to prove his existence; he was buried when they discovered that there was nothing by which his existence was disproved. A god who does not make himself noticed lies dead in his grave; and the gods never rise again after the reins of the world have once slipped from their hands. [1964, p. 16]

In terms of the thesis of this book, the thousands of years that preceded the French Revolution produced innumerable religions, but no love culture. It was against this fact that people rebelled and are still rebelling. What effect religion really had or does have is a matter for empirical inquiry.

In order to focus the inquiry and make it manageable, we shall concentrate on five of the great religions: Christianity, Islam, Buddhism, Confucianism, and Judaism. In each case we shall proceed to look at the founder and his book, the attitude to love, the attitude to the family, the feelings about women, the attitude to violence, and the reaction to other religions. Since Christianity has already been considered in fair detail in the previous two chapters we shall leave it for last.

ISLAM

Islam is the most absolute of all current religions. It still sees the universe running its predestined course, determined by the will of Allah, who not only guides the world at large but also predestines the fate of each and every human being. The name *Islam* indicates that the overriding duty it imposes upon humankind is to obey God; it is derived from the verb *aslama*, which means "to submit, to surrender oneself wholly, to give oneself in total commitment" (Patai, 1973, p. 147).

The world for the Moslem is ruled by the will of God as expressed in the *Koran*, the book written by the prophet Muhammad. Since Muhammad is less of a shadowy figure (although much about him is unknown) than the founders of other religious (e.g., Moses or Jesus), his life is worth exploring. The following account is extracted from the presumably impartial description in the entry on Muhammad in the *Encyclopaedia Britannica* (15th ed.).

Muhammad was born in Mecca about A.D. 570 after the death of his father. Because the climate of Mecca was considered to be unhealthful, he was given as an infant to a wet nurse from a nomadic tribe and spent some time in the desert. When he was 6 his mother died; when he was 8 his grandfather died. He then came under the care of his uncle.

About 595, when he was 25, a rich woman, Khadijah, who met him on a trading journey, offered marriage, and he accepted; she was then 40. She bore him 6 children, 2 sons (both of whom died) and 4 daughters. Until she died in 619 (when he was 49), he took no other wife. Thereafter he took nine wives, all for political reasons, and one Christian concubine.

Muhammad's life was spent in building up his religious beliefs and his political empire. About 610 he heard a voice saying to him: "You are the messenger of God." The religious beliefs were written down in the *Koran*, apparently an unsystematic series of utterances by him, often in states of trance (cf. Zinberg, 1977). Gradually he acquired followers, but they seem to have been just as interested in his political ambitions as in his religious beliefs, or more so.

Much of his life was spent in warfare against the surrounding Arabs, especially the Meccans. Like most generals he was quite merciless to his enemies. Thus after the siege of Medina, when reports reached him that the Jews were against him, he had the men all savagely executed and sold the women and children as slaves. He also connived in the assassinations of other supposed enemies.

Although a king in all but name when he died in 632, he left no arrangements for a successor. By the time of his death his community had become the dominant power on the Arabian peninsula (Mortimer, 1982, p. 34). Within 20 years after that it had overthrown the Persian empire and conquered all the Asiatic territories of the Roman empire except modern Turkey. Some 100 years after his death a mighty empire stretched from the Punjab to the Pyrenees and from Samarkand to the Sahara.

Those who regard Muhammad as a great man seem to base this view on his establishment of a mighty empire. In doing so they underplay his religious message, idealizing him as they would any of the innumerable conquerors of history. Since Muhammad's aim was to conquer, the Moslem world has rightly been described by one recent author (Mortimer, 1982) as one based on "faith and power."

Looked at as a human being, Muhammad, orphaned early in life, and poverty-stricken for a long time, appears to be a grandiose opportunist who married for money or political favors and devoted most of his energies to conquest. Deprived of a living father or other male guardian early in life, he sought to become an absolute ruler whom everybody would obey. It is not surprising that the whole history of Islam has centered so strongly on rebellion and disunity. Like the Roman emperors, the caliphs (Muhammad's successors) were all faced with the problem of how to enforce the absolute obedience that they demanded of their subjects. They decreed, for religious reasons, that obedience was an absolute duty, even to an unjust ruler (Mortimer, 1984, p. 37), but the discontent and fragmentation remained, an obvious aspect of the Arab world today. Islam has been described as a warrior religion. Its vicissitudes make sense more in terms of warrior behavior than in terms of theological speculation (Ashtor, 1976).

The Moslem world today in many ways models itself on Muhammad's personal life more than on anything else. It preaches *jihad* ("holy struggle," or "holy warfare"), in which heaven is promised to a warrior who dies in battle. Absolute obedience to an all-powerful God and his representatives on earth is demanded.

Women are subordinate; men are all-important. But even within the male world there is a hierarchy. If all men are equal before God, that equality is reached only in heaven, not on earth.

With regard to the major topics raised, the answers are fairly clear. Love is certainly not one of the major virtues promoted by Islam; obedience is the watchword everywhere. Obedience, devotion, sacrifice, domination—but no love. In fact, quite the opposite; violence is prescribed. In the current regime in Iran, of the Ayatollah Khomeini, the world has again been apprised of the brutal practices sanctioned by

Islam: death for the slightest offence, proscription of unauthorized sex, heedless sacrifice of men in battle, as long as it is for a good "cause," floggings, beheadings, stonings, and the like. The round of executions continues and has claimed many top leaders, including the former prime minister Gotbzadeh. What is most important is not even the violence, which is found in most revolutions, but its total justification.

The education of the Arab boy prepares him for this life of hierarchical domination and justifiable violence. It is harsh indeed once the man's world is reached, just as Muhammad's early life must have been very harsh.

In his earliest years the boy is pampered, caressed, and loved by the mother, even to the widespread practice of fondling his genitals (Patai, 1973, p. 34). Other female figures around the home also serve the boy's needs in every way they can, in marked contrast to the way in which they treat little girls.

Then the transition to the man's world is even more difficult. He has to learn to fulfill his father's wishes, to obey his commands, and to be subservient to him. Obviously such a marked change elicits considerable rebellion, which is severely punished. Among the most tradition-bound Bedouin tribes, he is even cut by saber or dagger, which is supposed to harden him for his future life. But even among the more lenient families painful physical punishment is widespread. In the men's world he also learns that age differences are of the utmost importance. He learns who his other superiors are: all men older than he, including even a brother or a cousin who is his senior by only a year or so. Then again he learns that he can treat younger boys as his inferiors, although not quite as inferior as the women.

The totally cruel subjection of women is one of the most outstanding features of the Moslem world, one that makes the women especially resentful of the freer role of the woman in the west. An Egyptian physician, Nawal el Saadawi (1980), has given a vivid description of the mistreatment to which the girl is subjected as she grows up. Female infanticide was common in Muhammad's day and continued until fairly recently (de Mause, 1974). Almost equally barbarous is the practice of circumcising girls, which is still a common procedure in many Arab countries. Usually it occurs when the girl is 7 or 8. On the scene appears the local midwife, or *daya*, as a rule without any warning. Two women members of the family grasp the child's thighs and pull them apart to expose the external genitals and to prevent her from struggling—as Dr. Saadawi says, like trussing a chicken before it is slaughtered. A sharp razor in the hands of the *daya* then cuts off the clitoris. (Saadawi, 1980).

Dr. Saadawi relates that during her service in rural areas she was often called upon to treat complications arising from this primitive operation. Very often even the life of the girl was in danger. Infection was common. Naturally the psychological trauma cut deep. The stated purpose of the circumcision is to deprive the woman of sexual pleasure, a purpose in which it no doubt succeeds. Sexual frigidity is thus a frequent occurrence; it would be hard to see how it could be otherwise.

In spite of its obvious savagery, this custom is still widespread. Dr. Saadawi reports research on a sample of 160 Egyptian girls and women that showed that 97.5% of uneducated families still practiced it, while 66.2% of educated families did so (1980, p. 34).

With such an attitude toward the girl, it cannot be expected that the Moslem family is a very happy one. Men have it their way with women, but the women are as a rule frigid (Saadawi), merely submitting to brute force. Among men there is a perpetual quarrel, as T. E. Lawrence discovered more than half a century ago when he tried to unite the Arabs into one state. Patai (1974) describes the disease of "conferentiasis," which is endemic among Arab rulers: Whenever there is a problem they call a conference, but they cannot agree on what to do.

With regard to other religions, Islam is clearly intensely antagonistic. The only brake on their *jihad* is the fact that their power is so limited. It is surprising in fact that the Moslem world has been so feeble militarily; the weakness can best be explained by the inherent unhappiness of the population. Regrettably they have a built-in mechanism to prevent modernization and change, since anyone who is opposed to the traditional religious practices is exposed to assassination (itself an Arab word).

Nevertheless, the Moslem lives in a modern world, so that outside influences reach him or her willy-nilly. Socialism, women's liberation, abandonment of violence, and other democratic currents manage to find a way into every Moslem country, even if they have not yet advanced very far.

In summary, in terms of the major thesis of this book, the Moslem world would certainly not qualify as conducive to a love culture.

BUDDHISM

Just as Buddhism is an entirely different kind of religion from Muhammadanism, the life of the Buddha stands in marked contrast to that of Muhammad. *Buddha* means "the enlightened one." His real name was

Siddhartha Gautama. He lived in India from 563 to 483 B.C. Accounts of his life were not recorded until centuries later, so that much of what is known is reconstruction. Still, the outlines of both the reality and the myths seem clear enough.

In the traditional account (*Encyclopaedia Britannica,* 15th ed., vol. 2, p. 342), he was the son of the rulers of the kingdom of the Sakyas, thus a member of the warrior or ruling caste. He married at the age of 16 and lived in luxury and comfort. The turning point in his life came at 29, when he realized that humans are subject to old age, sickness, and death; in short, that human life is suffering. He resolved on renunciation. He gave up the princely life and became a wandering ascetic, leaving his wife and son behind. With one teacher he attained the high mystical state of "no-thing" and with another was taught to attain the sphere of "neither perception nor non-perception." Unsatisfied, he continued his search for the truth.

He was joined by five ascetics at a grove near Uruvela, where he practiced severe austerity and extreme mortification for nearly 6 years. When he fainted away in weakness, he abandoned the ascetic life to seek his own path to enlightenment.

This he accomplished while sitting cross-legged under a banyan tree (about 528 B.C.). Once enlightened he resolved to teach other men the road to follow. Within a short time after his death his teachings began to be disseminated throughout India, later throughout all of Asia. Eventually Buddhism became the dominant religion of many of the Asian peoples, though it ceased to play much of a role in India proper.

Certain details of his reactions on the day of his realization that life is filled with suffering and his reunuciation of his princely life are important. It was also the day on which his son was born. On hearing the news he pronounced his son's name, Rahula, which means "bond." While driving his chariot, he was confronted successively by a very sick man, a very old man, a corpse, and then a holy man who stirred in him the desire to live the ascetic life and strive for spiritual enlightenment.

Also on that day, a woman named Kisagotami (Ling, 1968, p. 94–95) saw Gautama's beauty and glory and was filled with joy and delight. Upon hearing her sing, he thought: "When the fire of passion is cooled, the heart is happy; when the fire of illusion, pride, false views and all the lusts and pains are extinguished it is happy" (Ling, 1968, p. 95). In gratitude for the lesson she had taught him he sent her a costly necklace. She thought he was in love with her. But a few hours later, in the dead of the night, awakening to the sight of the dancers who had been entertaining him and were now asleep in all kinds of disgusting and uns emly postures, he renounced the life of sensual pleasures and took the crucial step of leaving his home to set out in search of spiritual peace.

To a psychoanalyst the story has a curious ring. On the day when his happy marriage is blessed by the birth of a son to whom he feels a strong bond (the son is actually supposed to have become a follower of his), he discovers sickness and death and is attracted to another woman. The conflict clearly centers around his attainment of manhood, which must have produced a great deal of guilt in him. In this state of guilt he then renounces everything that most men hold dear, wanders all over the country, fasting, at one point till he nearly dies, and then finally attains the 4 noble truths and the eightfold path which should lead to enlightenment.

And what are these truths? (1) Suffering comes from desire; (2) the solution is to give up desire by asceticism and meditation; (3) nothing is permanent—the self is only transient (the traditional Indian view); and (4) to give up the self, to have no desire, to lose oneself (one's self) in a feeling of oneness with the universe—this is the highest good.

The life of the Buddha thus poses a curious contradiction, which is found in the lives of many contemporary Buddhists as well. Just when he has succeeded in finding all that ordinary life has to offer, he abandons it, seeks suffering, renunciation, weariness, homelessness—in short, a completely detached way of life.

In a modern compilation of Buddhist scriptures, the Japanese Buddhist Yamabe (1934) called his philosophy "homeless brothers" and wrote:

> *A man who wishes to become my disciple must be willing to give up all direct relations with his family, with the social life of the world and all dependence upon wealth. A man who has given up all such relations for the sake of the Dharma (Buddhism) and has no abiding place for either his body or his mind has become my disciple and is to be called a homeless brother.* [Goddard, 1966, p. 625]

Again the question may be raised: Why should a man turn himself into a homeless brother? All of modern psychology would be agreed that such a way of life must inevitably become a source of intense suffering. And any study of Buddhist communities shows that the vast majority are always seeking enlightenment and never finding it. The "truly enlightened one" becomes an object of worship because such a one is so rare.

Obviously pure Buddhism is a hard path to follow. Consequently there have been many deviations, importations, and variations. In its pristine form there is no God, no afterlife, no supernatural sanctions. But India is the home of beliefs in reincarnation, fate (karma), sacred animals, and the like, and often enough these beliefs have been commingled with Buddhism. In Mahayana Buddhism the sacred has its special place in the heavenly realm where dwell the bodhisattvas, the superhuman spiritual beings who are said to exert their influence to help poor struggling mortals. In directing their attention to this supramundane heavenly community the Mahayanists showed themselves correspondingly less concerned with the ordering of life on earth. Drekmeier (1972) speculated that Buddhism can be seen as the expression of a desire to withdraw from the difficult situation in an increasingly disordered society and to seek refuge in a primeval state of undifferentiated being. Its prime appeal lies in withdrawal from the world. In the years since World War II many westerners have been attracted to Buddhism; analysis often reveals renunciation to be the major motif. Again, or as usual, society is in a highly disordered state, and retreat is one solution, available to many religions, not only Buddhism; the difference is largely that in Buddhism the retreat is the most essential element.

One of the few empirical studies of how Buddhism really works out in practice is Spiro's book, *Buddhism and Society* (1970), subtitled *A Great Tradition and Its Burmese Vicissitudes*. Spiro confined himself largely to Buddhism as practiced in Burma. Several relevant conclusions emerge from his work. First of all, and most important, is that the Burmese generally take the more commonsense view that the way to handle suffering is to satisfy the craving, not to deny it. Thus, as with Christianity, theory was in one realm, practice in another. As one of his informants said to him: "If you are so pious that you would never tell a lie, you should put on the yellow robe and retire from the world. If you want to remain in the world, you must be prepared to tell a lie, despite the precept" (p. 450).

Monasticism is a highly esteemed way of life in Burma. According to Spiro, about 10% of the male population become monks, but a much larger percentage of the men enter monasteries for short periods of time and then leave. His interpretation is that the high regard in which monasticism is held results from a projection of the ideal of renunciation to the monk, so that they do not have to practice it.

It is generally agreed that while monks are frequently vain, narcissistic, and unattractive in other ways, one rule to which they do adhere is that of sexual abstinence. In fact, as with Buddha himself, perhaps a majority of monks already have wives and children when they join the order. Although they must obtain their wives' consent, entering the monastery means abandoning their families. Often they are left destitute with no one to provide for them.

In a "blind" analysis of Rorschach protocols of monks, Steele (cited in Spiro, 1970, p. 343) found that they were characterized by, among other things, latent homosexuality and an above-average fear of female and mother figures. He thus argues that when men enter the monastery and renounce sex, they are willing to pay this price because at least for many of them celibacy is attractive.

In terms of the general questions raised about religion, with regard to love Buddhism takes a somewhat negative position. It is certainly generally nonviolent, especially in comparison, say, with the Moslems. But the goal of a happy love relationship with another human being would mean involvement for them, hence desire and suffering.

While the Buddhist cultures are by and large nonviolent, there are plenty of exceptions. Spiro reports that there is constant bickering and quarreling among the monks, and constant resentment of them by the laity, who make remarks such as: "Today there are no real monks. They are all corrupt, greedy, impious. . . . They are not monks. They carry guns and knives" (Spiro, 1970, p. 375). "I will no longer give alms food to the monks. In this area there are only three pious monks. All the rest are rogues" (Spiro, p. 376).

When U Nu was premier (he had also been head of the United Nations), in 1962 he pushed through a bill establishing Buddhism as the state religion of Burma. In the debate this led to violence and threats of violence, when monks went so far as to overturn automobiles of the military police and to burn and seize mosques (Spiro, 1970, p. 386). However, violence in general seems to be rather muted, especially in comparison with other cultures.

The role of women is not high in Burma. Evidently monasticism is one major device by which ungratified men get away from women. One Burmese saying is that "a male dog is nobler than a female human" (Spiro, 1970, p. 422). The similarity to the American slang work for a hostile woman, *bitch*, is striking. In a questionnaire on what they would like most, a large percentage of women mentioned the desire to be reborn a male. "Maleness pervades all the responses of the female respondents" (Spiro, p. 823).

Again, with such attitudes the role of the family in providing happiness for the individual cannot be great. The family creates suffering, so there are various devices for getting out of it.

With regard to other religions, Buddhism seems to be indifferent.

The emphasis is on finding nirvana; what others do, they do not care.

Here too then we find that the core of Buddhism lies in Buddha's life and the wish to imitate it. This wish can almost never be gratified, yet the longing is there, as is the search.

CONFUCIANISM

Confucianism, which dominated the psychology of the Chinese for 2500 years (until the present Communist revolution, actually), derived from Confucius, who lived from 551 to 479 B.C. (Latourette, 1962, p. 54). He was born in a small state, of an aged father and young mother. His father died during his infancy and he was reared in poverty by his mother. He early showed a talent for ceremonies and the learning of the past. For years, according to tradition, he held office in his native state, eventually rising to the highest position open to a subject, but in middle age he retired to private life, ostensibly as a protest against the unworthy conduct of his prince. During the next few years he traveled from state to state with a group of his disciples, hoping vainly that some ruler would adopt his principles. In his old age he returned to his birthplace, and he died there after some years spent in study and teaching.

Latourette describes him as follows:

> *Dignified, courteous, conscientious, high-minded, studious; modest but self-confident; a lover of antiquity, of books, of ceremonial and of music; thoughtful, affable, but frank in rebuking what he deemed wrong in men in high and low position; calm, serenely trusting in an overruling Providence—all these are terms which immediately come to mind as descriptive of the man pictured in the discourses transmitted by his faithful disciples. [1962, p. 54]*

Confucius left a number of books, which, together with those of his disciples, are 13 in number. For centuries every candidate for office had to master these 13 books and take an examination in them. The Chinese were thus the first to have a civil service theoretically based on learning rather than on patronage.

Of the books of Confucius, *The Sayings* (1955) is still read and still speaks to the modern mind. It consists of a number of wise sayings about all the important events in life. For example:

The Master rarely spoke of profit; his attachment was to fate and to Manhood-at-its-best. [p. 60]

The Master recognized four prohibitions: Do not be swayed by personal opinion; recognize no inescapable necessity; do not be stubborn; do not be self-centered.

When Yen Hui died the Master wept for him bitterly, and a follower remarked, "You are weeping too bitterly." "Not too bitterly. If I didn't weep bitterly for such a man, for whom would I weep bitterly?" [p. 60]

Consider your job of prime importance; put the reward in second place—wouldn't this be Excellence in its exalted form? To war against one's own bad points and not against those of others—wouldn't this be amelioration of services? In a moment's outburst of anger to forget oneself and one's family—wouldn't this be utter confusion? [p. 71]

The two cardinal principles of Confucian philosophy are *jen*, usually translated as "kindness," "goodness," or "human-heartedness," and *li*, usually translated as "order" or "rites." Around these are built prescriptions for the management of the major human relationships: husband and wife, parents and children, ruler and subject, friends. Thus on paper at least it sounds like a naturalistic philosophy or religion, devoid of supernatural trappings, which seeks to find in the harmonious relationships among human beings the secret to human happiness. Its advocates contend that it was eminently successful in regulating Chinese lives; its critics maintain that its prescriptions lend themselves to a ritualistic formulation that takes all the spontaneity out of life.

It has been argued that Confucianism is really an ethical system, not a religion. This takes too narrow a view of religion; the same criticism has been made of Buddhism. It also skirts the real questions of whether ethical principles do have to be tied up with a supernatural system, as in Christianity and Muhammadanism, and, if it is so tied up, whether a supernatural religion leads to a higher ethical level than a naturalistic one. As will be discussed in more detail later, the claim that humankind will not abandon its propensities for violence and instinctual gratification unless it fears the wrath of the gods has little empirical support.

One of his followers, Mo Ti (or Mo Tzu), argued that there is a supreme being, and that humankind finds its highest good in conforming to the will of this supreme being. Since heaven loves people, favoring righteousness and hating iniquity, people ought to love one another and be righteous in life. People should indeed love all their fellows as they would their own blood brothers or sisters. His critics argued that this principle of universal love, by denying the duty of special affection for one's kin, would dissolve the family and so destroy society.

Even though Confucianism seems so eminently sensible, and a perfect guide to a well-organized society, it would be impossible to maintain that China has found a happier resolution of the human dilemma than the west. Any history of China portrays despots, changes of dynasty, wars with losses of millions of lives, slavery (though much less than in the west—Gernet, 1982), prostitution, concubinage, and other evils too numerous to mention. China has a long tradition of placing a high value on history, but the history refers mainly to the change of dynasties, and very little to the lives of ordinary people.

Among contemporary Confucians and Chinese sages (outside Mao's China), Lin Yutang has acquired considerable renown. His major book, *The Importance of Living* (1937), has been reprinted many times, remaining enormously popular. He presents his own version of the Confucian philosophy, emphasizing that life is for living, that earth is the only heaven, that celibacy is a freak of civilization, and the like. He was the son of a Chinese Presbyterian minister, and he left Christianity for paganism of the Confucian variety. Yet in his old age (at 62) he unexpectedly returned to Christianity; evidently all was not perfect in his Confucian paradise.

Another interesting man of the present century is Liang Shu-Ming, whose biographer Guy Alitto calls him "the last Confucian."

Liang played many roles in the history of contemporary China. Alitto contrasts his life and thought with that of Mao-Tse Tung, with whom he was on intimate terms for many years. After early participation in the revolutionary movement that overthrew the ancient empire, Liang became China's leading Buddhist scholar. This led to a spiritual crisis in which he experienced a deep depression and eventually attempted suicide. In this part of his life his renunciation of women, in accordance with Buddhist teaching, was paramount.

Instead of forming a normal family life, as was required of a good Chinese son, he threw himself into the revolutionary activities associated with the switch from empire to republic. Soon he was disillusioned. He wrote:

> *I gradually realized that the facts were not at all in accord with my ideals. This was my feeling toward "revolution," "politics" and "great men." I now saw low-class dealings; and ruthless, cruel and violent things. Before this (while I was) at home or at school, I had encountered*

none of these things. This filled me with a disgust and loathing for life.
[Alitto, 1979, p. 48]

In 1922, after his spiritual crisis of the period 1911–1916, and after his father's suicide in 1918, Liang Shu-Ming publicly committed himself to Confucianism and immediately set about changing his life-style from that of a pious Buddhist to that of a pious Confucian. The major change obviously was that he would have to marry. The girl was not particularly attractive, intelligent, or warm, and because she was of aristocratic birth she had never learned to cook or keep house. Nor was he especially attracted to her; he was, he said, marrying out of love of virtue, not out of sexual desire. "I led my bride to pay obeisance before my father's picture and wept" (Alitto, 1979, p. 75).

The heart of Liang's argument with Mao-Tse-Tung was the different emphases on human betterment versus economic change. Liang argued that Mao's reforms would destroy good relations and damage friendships. Liang argues: "Friendly feeling is the thing most capable of energizing vital activity" (Alitto, p. 217). Obviously Mao's philosophy was the exact reverse. When Liang was asked to contribute to the "Criticize Confucius" campaign of the late 1970s he refused, saying that he was already 83, and that nothing they did to him would matter any more. The wise sayings of Confucius had finally been replaced by the thoughts of Chairman Mao.

With regard to the major topics discussed for all religions, love for the Confucian seems to be primarily a feeling of kindliness, not an intense passion. Violence is eschewed. Women are part of life's pleasures; although nothing is known about Confucious's own sex life, he obviously did not urge celibacy or renunciation.

Above all, the family was the center of the universe and of happiness for Confucius. Filial duty he preached over and over. He urged an inner attitude of devotion and tranquility, though many others have claimed that the family as he described it was a myth, and that instead it was full of the intense quarreling, dutiful obedience, and stultifying formalization that is found in so many other religions. Confucianism seems indifferent to converts; it has never been given to proselytizing for its way of life.

JUDAISM

Like the other three religions discussed, Judaism is dominated by one book, the Old Testament, and by one man, Moses, who supposedly is responsible for at least the first part of the book. However, the figure of Moses is shadowy in the extreme. The story of his life resembles the life stories of many other heroes (cf. Rank, 1909).

Moses was an Egyptian. Supposedly he was picked out of the water by the Pharaoh's daughter, but why she should do that is never made clear. As in other myths, when he grows up he defies his father figure, the pharaoh, and by various magical means rescues his people, the Hebrews, from Egyptian slavery.

Before Moses there was also a Hebrew people; its patriarchs were Abraham, Isaac, and Jacob. God promises Abraham a great future if he will only obey him. Yahweh says to Abraham:

> *Leave your country, your family and your father's house for a land I will show you. I will make you a great nation; I will bless you and make your name so famous that it will be used as a blessing. I will bless those who bless you; I will curse those who slight you. All the tribes of the earth shall bless themselves by you.* [Gen. 12:1–3]

In this form the god is the same as that of Muhammad, and the promise is the same: Absolute obedience will yield you greatness and a marvelous future. Abraham is willing to sacrifice his son Isaac because God demands it of him, but at the last minute a reprieve is granted.

Then along came Moses, who redeemed the promise of God and did in fact help to make Israel a great nation. He defeated the mighty Egyptians, rulers of the universe at that time, then led his people into Canaan under the leadership of Joshua. Moses himself disappears under mysterious circumstances; his leadership is then taken over by historical figures. Whether Moses actually existed is a question with which scholars are still wrestling; his name, which means "is born" in Egyptian, does not appear in any other ancient source apart from the Bible (*Encyclopaedia Britannica*, 15th ed., vol. 7, pp. 45–46).

Although the Jews have been revered as the people who introduced one spiritual god, instead of the idols common at that time, the real meaning of this innovation is open to question. For this god was a very angry one, and in the earlier centuries of the Hebrew epoch he spent his time creating military victories for them. For Yahweh intervened directly in battle, leaving nothing to spirituality; one is reminded that when Constantine in the Roman era won the battle of the Milvian Bridge he ascribed his victory to the Christian god and became a Christian. Yahweh assured Joshua: "Do not be afraid of these men; I have delivered them into your power" (Josh. 10:8). And in fact Yahweh caused huge hailstones to fall from heaven, killing the enemy by the thousands. As Morris Cohen (1964) has pointed out, the Mosaic law commands the Israelites, whenever attacking a city, to kill all the males and all females who had known men. The religious force of this is shown when Saul is cursed and his whole dynasty destroyed for leaving one prisoner, King Agag, alive. The last line of Psalm 137 is: "Happy shall be he that taketh and dasheth thy little ones against the rock."

Furthermore, in the period of the kings, the Jews were anything but loving. Constant warfare went on. King David, in the well-known story, saw Bathsheba in the nude taking a sunbath, so he sent her husband to die at the front in order to have her. Solomon allegedly had 1000 wives, and hundreds of concubines, like any Oriental sultan; he dazzles us with his splendor but does not impress us with his loving nature.

It is only after the Jews have been defeated in battle and sent into exile that the god stops being such a bloodthirsty military genius. From here on in the Jewish religion undergoes marked changes. Now their desire is to return to their own country, obtain freedom from oppression, and maintain their unity as a people. Yet in biblical times there were always prophets admonishing them that if they did not mend their ways God would hurl even greater woes upon them, from which it can be assumed that they were not the most obedient of people. Once they regained at least part of Palestine, under Roman rule, they were not particularly different from the other client states of the Roman empire. Their main crime in the eyes of the Romans was that they would not worship the Roman gods as directed, but they certainly were not especially noted at the time for their exceptional piety or saintliness.

Once Rome had destroyed Judea, in a frightful massacre at Jerusalem that for that time was just as bad as if not worse than the holocaust in our time, the Jews were scattered far and wide. Then history condemned them to an eternal wandering, for there were few places where they could stay with any degree of permanence; paradoxically, it was then in the Muhammadan states that they enjoyed greater freedom than in the Christian.

In these centuries Jews were again exposed to wholesale massacres, and innumerable paranoid rulers whose sadism never seemed to stop for long. They were accused of sacrificing Christian children to get their blood at Passover; in more modern times, they were accused of concocting the *Protocols of the Elders of Zion* in an attempt to conquer the world (Henry Ford believed in this fabrication).

Under these circumstances the religion had to adapt. Faced by such fearsome threats, the Jews were always confronted with the alternatives of assimilation or isolation, when assimilation was permitted. The religion had to preserve the unity of the group; hence it emphasized obeying the ritual to the last drop. Learned rabbis compiled one commentary after another to explain how the Jew should behave in every aspect of his or her daily life.

After the French Revolution Jews were released from their ghettos and allowed to assimilate with the population in most parts of the world. An unknown number did. It is actually this period, after the French Revolution, that produced the great Jewish intellectuals: Freud, Einstein, Marx (whose father had been baptized before Marx was born in order to be eligible for a state position). Thus the release of the Jewish intellect was a concomitant of the abandonment of traditional Jewish practices. Various reform movements were instituted.

Once Israel was reestablished as an independent state, the role of religion changed again. On the whole Israel is reported to be an irreligious country. Its strength lies in the determination of its inhabitants to avoid the persecution that they would experience in other countries. Its extraordinary accomplishments are of course a tribute to Jewish intelligence, but they have little or nothing to do with Jewish religion.

The claim is often made that the Jews are ethically superior to other groups because of their holy book and their history. Konvitz (1980) claims that the essential American idea is the emphasis on liberty and justice for all, and that this is also the essential Jewish idea. Such claims are open to serious question. The Jews for centuries have had to react to severe oppression, only too often by outright murder. Hence their cry for liberty and justice is inevitable.

But within the religion, the emphasis has been on absolute obedience to the law. A noted analyst who had been brought up as an orthodox Jew once related that whenever he ate ham or pork he would almost gag, so strong were the early prohibitions about food. To this day there are many Jewish families who will expel an erring son or daughter who marries out of the faith. The expulsion is marked by actually sitting shiva— the rite for the dead. Marrying out of the faith destroys the unity of the people; it deserves to be punished by death. There is no great ethical principle here; only self-protection.

In terms of the major questions posed, traditionally the Jewish doctrine places no overwhelming emphasis on love. Violence is avoided because Jews have rarely been in a position to fight back. Within-group violence, with bickering and terrible quarrels, as anyone knows who has been brought up in a Jewish household, is an everyday occurrence.

Women are considered inferior creatures. The menstruating woman is taboo for the Orthodox Jew, and she must cleanse herself in a ritual bath after her period. The boy thanks God every day that he has been born a man and not a woman. In many temples men and women are actually physically separated.

The family is stressed above all other social institutions; this too maintains the unity of the people. There are no special monastic orders. It is everybody's duty to marry and raise a family; if one fails to do so for any reason, it is shameful.

Finally, with regard to other religions, Judaism assumes an air of great superiority. Jews are the people of the Book, of the one God, of ethical precepts that are more spiritual than any other religion. While all these statements are dubious, they are widely believed. Thus grandiose notions of fate and profound feelings of guilt among modern Jews are both quite common. Perhaps for practical reasons, Judaism has never been a proselytizing religion.

CHRISTIANITY

Finally, we come to Christianity, which is specifically the religion of love. So much has been written about the realities of Christianity in the previous chapter that only certain points will be examined in more detail here: the personality of Jesus, the nature of love, and the conditions that affect its presence or absence.

Jesus, though the central figure of Christianity, remains a shadowy figure. One authority after another has wirtten an exposition of what Jesus really taught [e.g., Woods, 1953; Kung, 1968; Harnack, 1900; Tillich, 1968; Troeltsch, 1912; Yerkes (on Hegel's views), 1983; Pfister, 1948; Ahlstrom, 1973; Washington, 1969 (on the black churches); Nygren, 1932–1939]. That there are so many expositions merely shows that what Jesus taught is highly unclear. Christians still ask: What is this thing called love?

An eminent historian of the ancient world, Michael Grant, has recently attempted to sift out the real Jesus the man from the various accounts given of him in the four gospels bearing the names of Matthew, Mark, Luke, and John, though these were certainly not their real authors. The gospels themselves did not reach their final form until 35 to 65 years after Jesus's death.

Grant (1977) looks at the gospels with a historian's eye, treating them in exactly the same way he would any other works of ancient literature capable of yielding historical information. The picture of Jesus that emerges is in some respects a new and unfamiliar one. There was no "gentle Jesus, meek and mild," nor was Jesus a political revolutionary, as is often claimed. Jesus, although readily touched to compassion and anger by the sufferings he witnessed, ruthlessly subordinated his every act and thought to the success of his great mission. His admonishments to turn the other cheek, love thy neighbor, welcome sinners, and render unto Caesar what is Caesar's did not so much indicate a love of peace, a sentimental affection for humanity, or a respect for the imperial government as they did a desire to deal quickly with what he considered to be matters that were subordinate and secondary to the main issue, thus enabling his disciples to concentrate wholly on the dawning and imminent realization of the Kingdom of God.

Jesus's mission to the Jews in Galilee, followed by his very brief ministry in Jerusalem, was a complete failure, as he evidently knew and admitted. Grant ends his book with an explanation of the strange course of events by which this failure was converted, after Jesus's death, into triumph.

Palestine was a client state of Rome, but Rome did not handle it well. As a result, in the highly charged atmosphere of that day many independent Jewish spokesmen for popular longings and aspirations arose all the time. One such preacher who appeared in the late twenties was John the Baptist. Jesus, whose early life is virtually unknown, was one of those who came to listen to him. John had preached the Kingdom of God, in accordance with the Jewish tradition of the Messiah. Herod Antipas had had him executed on suspicion of revolutionary aims; nevertheless Jesus followed in his footsteps.

What made Jesus unique was his conviction that the Kingdom of God had already started happening by his agency and under his guidance. The New Testament is virtually a commentary on this one single concept. It was also a carrying out of Old Testament prophecy. The Jews revered their ancient holy books with an all-engrossing, literal-minded reverence that made such connection seem inevitable. This Jewish attitude was fully, consistently, and perseveringly maintained by the early Christians, whose New Testament deliberately presented the career of Jesus as a mass of detailed fulfillments of what the Torah, the prophets, and the Psalms had foretold.

Jesus then fully and urgently participated in the current belief that the end of the world as we know it—the coming of the Kingdom of God—was imminent. But what was much more original, indeed the most original of all his beliefs, was the combination of this idea with the further conviction that the kingdom had already begun to arrive. It was true that the Jewish doctrine of the imminent Kingdom of God had long alternated with a belief that the kingdom was in another sense eternal and that all that needed to happen in the future was for it to be brought to practical effectiveness upon earth. Thus he said: "If it is by the Spirit of God that I drive out the devils, then be sure the Kingdom of God has already come upon you" (Matt. 12:28).

Later, Christian doctrine held that Jesus would come again. But there is no reliable evidence that this is what Jesus believed. The kingdom was here; nothing else counted. Thus when one of his disciples said to him: "Lord, let me go and bury my father first," Jesus replied: "Follow me, and leave the dead to bury the dead" (Matt. 18:21–22). Grant's interpretation of the love message of Jesus was that he preached humility because of the ultimate victory that had been achieved. "Blessed are the meek" because "they shall inherit the earth." [Theodor Reik, in his book *Masochism in Modern Man* (1941), sees this as the essence of masochism: victory through defeat.]

According to Grant, the message of love derived from Jesus by the later Christians misses the point that his major aim was to rescue the Jews from the dominion of the Romans and proclaim to them that the Kingdom of God had already arrived. Eventually, he hoped and believed that the kingdom would become available to every one. But that was beyond his immediate purpose and life work. He was a Jew preaching to his fellow Jews.

It is in this sense that he renounced his family. When his mother and brothers arrived, asking to see him, he sent them a message saying: "Who is my mother? Who are my brothers?" And looking around at those who were sitting in the circle about him he said, "Here are my mother and brothers. Anyone who does the will of God, that person is my brother and sister and mother" (Matt. 18:21–22).

With this interpretation (with which most Christian theologians would probably disagree), the historical events in later centuries become clearer. The message of Jesus was to institute the Kingdom of God immediately—in fact, it had already arrived. For many centuries this was a common belief; even today the Seventh Day Adventists warn their fellow religionists to be ready, since the Second Coming could occur at any time, and they must be cleansed of their sins. Pure Christianity meant and means renunciation of this world, and initiation into another world, the Kingdom of God.

This would also fit in with the thesis of Schneidau (1976) that the Bible is a subversive book. (It may be noted that in the contemporary Soviet Union it is almost impossible to buy a copy of the Bible and that in the south before the Civil War, slaves were not permitted to read the Bible.) Schneidau says: "In philosophic terms, what the Bible offers culture is neither an ecclesiastical structure nor a moral code, but an unceasing critique of itself" (p. 16).

Looked at as a human being, Jesus was a man with grandiose notions about himself, in that he saw himself as God's representative on earth who had brought with him the Kingdom of God. Furthermore, he was a man with no fear, anger, or sexuality. Analytically, we would say he was an impossible ego ideal. Yet analytically we also know that many people identify with Jesus. The result is invariably an overwhelming sense of guilt. Whether the real man Jesus had such a sense of guilt that he was covering up with his grandiose ideas we have no way of knowing; quite possibly. But once more millions of Christians through the ages have identified with Jesus as they conceived him, sometimes with beneficial and sometimes with disastrous consequences.

The love extracted from his message by Grant and others is primarily a love of God rather than of his fellows. And throughout history there has been a strong tendency to relegate the love of one's fellows to a secondary role; the love of God always comes first, which has also done serious damage to ordinary human relationships.

Yet, the question still arises: What is meant by love of God? And what is meant by God's love of humanity? Nygren (1932–1939) has an exhaustive discussion of the topic. He distinguishes agape (the usual word for love in the New Testament), eros, and nomos. According to him agape is the distinctively Christian contribution. Eros is the love of something beautiful. Nomos is the Jewish idea of obeying the law.

He gives the main features of agape as the following: (1) It is spontaneous and unmotivated; (2) it is indifferent to value (unlike eros); (3) it is creative; and (4) it is the initiator of fellowship with God. In fact, he argues, there is no way at all from humanity's side that leads to God. Thus God's love is unconditional, universal, absolute, and only within his power. Psychologically, we have another impossible ideal. It need hardly be added that every one of the above attributes has led to endless disputation within the Christian church.

If human realities are again brought into play, this image of God's love must be related to love, hate, and fear, the three basic human emotions. The Christian abhorrence of sexuality has already been amply documented; no more need be said here. With regard to violence, the impossible dilemma into which Christianity falls has again been noted. If one turns the other cheek, one will be killed. If one looks for a just war, one has to twist the meaning of words in some hypocritical fashion (as St. Thomas Aquinas did). If one looks for a holy war one moves beyond the pale of Christianity altogether (even though it has always been done). With regard to fear, again one simply relies on God; there is little evidence that this has ever reduced fear, or if it has, only in a magical way (Wilson, 1973). Thus again the Christian theory of divine love is confronted by inescapable realities that render it humanly impossible.

The discrepancy between the ideal and the reality was nowhere more beautifully expressed than by Oskar Pfister, the Protestant minister who became a lay analyst and close personal friend of Freud's (*Christianity and Fear*, 1948). Pfister felt that he was practicing the psychiatry employed with so much genius by Jesus. Yet as he studied the history and practice of Christianity he was appalled by what he found. He wrote:

> *Murder, arson and cruelty were practised more savagely than by wild beasts—all this in the name of Him who died for love on the Cross in order to confirm his death His message of love. . . .*
>
> *I learned how inevitably a neurosis affected the Christianity of pious Christians until the latter assumed strikingly neurotic traits. I understood that a loss of love which customarily occurs in non-religious compulsion-neurotics must, inevitably, in the religious, be accompanied by a great over-emphasis of dogma . . . with the result that frequently, and perhaps in most cases, Christianity ceased to be a religion of love and became a religion of fear. . . . The neurosis of individuals leads to a neurotic malformation of their Christian faith, and in certain circumstances must do so inevitably; and when this process is applied to the masses it necessarily affects entire Churches, the Protestant as well as the Catholic. . . . The removal of neurotic traits from religion is effected in principle in the same way as the cure of non-religious neurotics, i.e., mainly by the restoration of love and its elevation to be the dominant factor in life. [pp. 22–24]*

CONCLUSION

After this necessarily brief review, it cannot be maintained that religion leads humanity to a higher ethical place in which love replaces hatred. Some of the most loving religions seem to be those without a god figure (e.g., Buddhism and Confucianism); some of the most hateful those with what is in principle a loving god.

Nor does anthropological research bear out the notion that religion is indispensable to ethical living. In terms of one of the major theses of this book, love cultures versus hate cultures, some of the most loving cultures have been those without religion of the supernatural variety; some of the most hateful the most religious (Douglas, 1966). In order to produce a love culture, we must search for the positive loving elements in the structure of society; whether it has a religion, of the traditional or nontraditional variety, seems to be a matter of indifference.

5

Can Animals Love?

In the nineteenth century, when Darwin revolutionized the world of biology, humans were suddenly brought closer to animals. In the twentieth century, when Freud revolutionized the world of psychology, animals were brought closer to humans. Today we see a broad continuum in the evolutionary scale, so that very little that is found in the human being is completely absent in other animals; the differences are more of degree than of kind.

Since about 1950, a series of striking studies and observations has demonstrated the capacities of animals in many different areas that had thought to be reserved for humans, including attachment, community organization, at times rudimentary families, touching, caring, communication, awareness of the world—and love. Love can be defined here most simply, as Harlow (1974) defines it, as affectional ties. What affectional ties are to be found in animals? Virtually all, especially in the primates, who are closest to humans on the evolutionary ladder.

The first classic experiment that demonstrated the significance of the love life among monkeys was the work of the Harlows, Harry and Margaret, in the 1950s. The Harlows distinguished at least five affectional systems in monkeys: (1) the affection of the infant for the mother—the infant–mother affectional system; (2) the affectional relationships between infants or between juveniles—the infant–infant or peer affectional system; (3) the affectional relationship between adolescent and adult males and females—the heterosexual affectional system; (4) the affection of the mother for her infant—the mother–infant affectional system; and (5) the affection of adult males for infants and juveniles—the father–infant affectional system. Since their pioneering work, much research has shown the ubiquity of these affectional systems among a large group of animals, especially primates, but including others as well (Harlow, 1974).

ATTACHMENT AND SEPARATION

In the early 1960s, reports began trickling back from Tanganyika of a young woman named Goodall who was making a sustained and courageous effort to make contact with the chimpanzees. Up to then, the dominant mode of investigation of animals had been the laboratory situation, guided by the stimulus–response paradigm of Pavlov, Spence, and most recently Skinner. To study animals in the wild, in their natural habitat, required a degree of devotion, patience, and even foolhardiness that very few researchers were then willing to undertake. Goodall was one of the first; others have followed. The results have provided extraordinary insights into the complexities of animal life.

Of Goodall's work, David Hamburg wrote in the preface to her book:

Once in a generation, there occurs a piece of research that changes man's view of himself. The reader of this book has the privilege of sharing such an experience. . . .

The picture of chimpanzee life that emerges is fascinating. Here is a highly intelligent, intensely social creature capable of close and enduring attachments, yet nothing that looks like human love, capable of rich communication through gestures, postures, facial expressions, and sounds, yet nothing quite like human language. This is a creature who not only uses tools effectively but also makes tools with considerable foresight; a creature who does a little sharing of food, though much less than man; a creature gifted in the arts of bluff and intimidation, highly excitable and aggressive, capable of using weapons, yet engaging in no activity comparable to human warfare; a creature who frequently hunts and kills small animals of other species in an organized, cooperative way, and seems to have some zest for the process of hunting, killing, and eating the prey; a creature whose repertoire of acts in aggression, deference, reassurance and greeting bear uncanny similarities to human acts in similar situations. [Van Lawick-Goodall, 1971, pp. xv–xvii]

The first biological basis in chimpanzee society is the tie between mother and infant. During the first 4 months, the infant clings to the mother in the ventral position and only very occasionally is seen apart from her, usually then sitting beside her. Should the infant be more than a couple of feet from her, she pulls it back; and should she observe a predator approach she hugs it more closely. According to Goodall, mother–infant ties may persist well into adult life and may then form the main link in a group comprising a female with infant and older child, adolescent, and a young mature animal.

In general, however, unlike other primates, chimpanzees do not keep close together in stable social groups (Van Lawick-Goodall, 1971, p. 20). Instead, the individuals belonging to what is believed to be a single social group of from 60 to 80 animals break into an ever-changing variety of temporary subgroups. Each subgroup can comprise animals of any age, sex, or number, but two kinds of subgroups are especially common, one a party of several males together and the other a party of several females with infants.

As with humans, the separation from the mother is a gradual one. Between the ages of about 6 and 18 months, the infant more often travels jockey fashion on the mother's back than on belly, and the time it spends not actually clinging to the mother increases. By the end of the period it is out of physical contact with her for as much as 25% of the day—usually playing with age-mates; but it is never out of its mother's sight. Not infrequently it breaks off play to run back to her to sit on her lap or beside her (compare the rapprochement phase in the human toddler). When mother is about to move off, she signals her intention by reaching out to touch the infant, gesturing to it, or when it is up in a tree, tapping softly on the trunk. The infant at once obeys and assumes the carrying position.

The next 18 months, until the age of 3 years, see increasing activity away from mother and play with companions; in this period the young chimpanzee is out of physical contact with mother for as much as 75 to 90% of the day. Nevertheless, it continues to be transported by her, jockey fashion unless she is moving fast, and it still sleeps with her.

During the next 4 years, until puberty is reached at the age of about 7, the small chimpanzee becomes independent of its mother for feeding, transport, and sleeping. It spends much time playing with age-mates and sometimes also with infants or with adolescents. As it gets older, it may leave its mother and join a nursery group of up to a dozen juveniles and adolescents who are moving about in company with one or two mature females; nevertheless, there are times when it is still likely to return to its mother to move about with her.

Adolescence extends from about 7 years to 11 years, and during this phase animals of both sexes often associate with mature males. Even so, some of them at least spend days back with their mothers and siblings. Throughout the years of increasing independence, according to Van Lawick-Goodall, the initiative for departure and return lies with the young animal. She saw no sign of a mother discouraging or rejecting one of her offspring.

Goodall adds a number of interesting details about each stage of development, which can be briefly summarized here. Most of these could only have come to light with the actual observation of the community.

Mothers have an infant only once every 3½ to 5 years. As a result, the appearance of a mother with a brand-new baby often stimulates much excitement among the other chimps. In one case, a dominating male began to display, and the entire group went into confusion—all the adult males leaping around and swaying branches, the mother and other females and youngsters rushing out of the way and screaming. It looked for all the world like a wild greeting ceremony for the new baby, though in reality it was undoubtedly provoked by a sense of frustrated curiosity. The mother stubbornly refused to let anybody else get close enough to examine the baby properly.

What happens when the chimp mother dies, as occurs occasionally? Two surprising events. First of all, the role of the mother is taken over by some other chimp, in one case a brother. And second, the infant goes into mourning; in one instance the infant actually died, apparently of grief.

While birth is a basic biological phenomenon, the next stage, that of play, which starts when the chimp is able to act somewhat independently of the mother, is less easy to explain. Young chimps often play by themselves when no playmates are available, swinging about in a tree, jumping continually over the same gap onto the same springy branch, somersaulting or gamboling on the ground. Mostly, however, they like to play with each other, chasing around a tree trunk, leaping one after the other through the treetops, dangling, each by one hand, while they spar and hit at each other, playfully biting or hitting or tickling each other as they wrestle on the ground. Whatever the biological function of this play, it does serve to make the growing youngsters familiar with their environment. They learn during play which type of branch is safe to jump onto and which will break, and they practice gymnastic skills, such as leaping down from one branch and catching another far below, which when they are older will serve them in good stead, during an aggressive encounter with a higher-ranking individual in the treetops, for instance. It also offers the young chimp the opportunity to become familiar with other youngsters. As with human youngsters, the play is so enjoyable that many mothers have great difficulty persuading their offspring to leave a game when they themselves are ready to move on.

At this stage, the major difference between young males and young females is in what Van Lawick-Goodall calls "the precocious sexual development of the male infant." From a very early age, the male shows great interest in the swellings of females. One young chimp struggled to reach a female in this state almost before he could walk. Once he did get to her, he made repeated attempts to mount her as she reclined on the ground. Between the ages of 1 and 4 or 5 years, male infants spend a great deal of time, when a pink female is in the group, hurrying up to her, mounting her, and making all the movements shown by an adult male during mating.

During the young chimps' fourth year, the very tolerant atmosphere in which up to this time they have been nurtured gradually begins to change. Play sessions become rougher and wilder, and older chimps are quick to threaten younger ones if they behave incautiously. This is the time too when most youngsters are actually weaned physiologically, and weaning can be a very trying business, lasting in some cases more than a year. For many, the transition from infancy to the juvenile age may be a particularly unhappy time.

In the juvenile period, the value of play with other youngsters becomes apparent as part of the transition from mother to the outside world, again just like humans. One youngster who had no playmates became increasingly lethargic and began to show strange idiosyncrasies such as putting one foot in the opposite groin, sometimes for long intervals, or senselessly fiddling with pieces of bark. Almost certainly because of her lack of chimp playmates, she even formed a friendship with a baboon, a most rare event. It is fairly common for young chimps and young baboons to play together, but the games usually consist of wild chasing around, either on the ground or through the trees, or sparring when each hits out quickly toward the other and then draws away. Such games often end with aggressive behavior from one or the other. Gentle friendships are extremely unusual.

At this stage, the chimp mother may quite often have another baby, which arouses considerable sibling rivalry. The older sib has to learn that it is now up to him or her to keep an eye on the mother, not the other way around as in the past. If he or she does become accidentally separated, usually the young chimp is very upset. By this time, the mother also seems to have less interest in the first child, and she will not make any loud call to indicate her whereabouts to the child.

Again just as with humans, adolescence may be a difficult and frustrating time for the chimp. Possibly, it is worse for the male in both species. The male chimp becomes physically mature at puberty, when he is between 7 and 8 years old, but he still is nowhere near being full grown—he weighs about 40 pounds as compared to the 100 pounds of the fully grown male. One of the most stabilizing relationships for the adolescent may well be that with the mother. Each tries to assist the other when attacked, even though there may be little that they can do.

In his dealings with the higher-ranking males, the adolescent male must be cautious, because now, more than when he was a mere juvenile, an act of insubordination tends to bring severe retribution. In spite of the attacks, the adolescent perseveres in his contacts with the older males, perhaps because they "make up" so quickly. One peculiar bit of behavior is that nearly all adolescent males at times spend long periods—hours or even days—completely out of sight and often out of earshot of other chimps.

The female chimp also becomes adolescent at about 7. She is fascinated by infants. Not only does she frequently carry an infant short distances, play with it, and groom it, but she also shows concern for its welfare. By about 9, she develops a swelling that attracts mature males; then her sex life begins. One Van Lawick-Goodall describes as a "chimpanzee nymphomaniac." [However, the psychologist Maurice Temerlin (1975), who brought up a chimpanzee in his home, also describes her as a nymphomaniac when she developed sexually.]

It is in adult relationships that the most marked differences are found between chimps and humans. For the family group of the chimp excludes the male, so that males have to fend for themselves. In spite of this, Van Lawick-Goodall never observed anything that could be regarded as homosexuality in chimps. Sex is over and done with, and there is no lasting relationship. With regard to our main topic, she says:

Although such relationships may be shadowy forerunners of human love affairs, I cannot conceive of chimpanzees developing emotions, one for the other, comparable in any way to the tenderness, the protectiveness, the tolerance and spiritual exhilaration that are the hallmarks of human love in its truest and deepest sense. [1971, p. 194]

In the wild, the chimp is exposed to predators of all kinds, which creates special problems. It has been hypothesized that the social grouping is a defense, built up through evolution, against these predators.

With regard to death, the chimp shows some slight reactions but little that resembles the human rituals. In one case, one of two male friends died, and for almost 6 months his friend would come back to the place where they had been accustomed to be together and would sit in one tree or another, staring around, waiting, listening. However, this extreme was rarely observed.

I have cited the work of Van Lawick-Goodall in such detail because of the light it throws on the precursors of the love relationship in the human. It is clear that the chimp, like the human, begins with a long period of attachment to the mother, and up to adolescence goes through similar stages of peer play, heterosexual mating, and parenting. There the similarity ends, and the cycle begins all over again in the chimp. Still, the physical basis is there, deriving from the need for attachment. What is lacking is the much fuller psychological elaboration of the love experience in the human, which again shows that love is just as much a psychological reaction as it is a physical one, if not more so.

The evidence for the loss attached to separation almost all comes from the mother–child relationship. In the chimpanzees, permanent monogamy in the adult is not found. But the family structure among the higher apes (as well as animals in general) varies widely, for unknown reasons. According to Portmann(1961), one male chimpanzee can suffice for 12 to 15 females and their progeny, one male gorilla for four females on average, and eight to 10 immature young gorillas; the east Asian orangutan also lives in such a large polygamous society.

Yet the gibbons are organized in monogamous families of father, mother, and up to four offspring from babies to adolescents of about 6 to 8 years at the oldest. The family has a territory that remains very stable and is defended against other gibbon families; through living together and long familiarity with each other, they form a very firmly established unit (Portmann, 1961, p. 71). Many other variations are found: harems (long-tailed monkeys and baboons); polygamous families, together with separate hordes of males (spider monkeys); a clan system in which the males lead by turns and the females belong to all males (howling monkeys).

That the apes should come so close to human forms is less surprising than that monogamy should prevail among many lower forms of animal life (Wickler, 1972). Permanent monogamy is referred to as pair-bonding. Pair-bonding can last well into old age, when the animals are no longer capable of reproducing. It may also happen that one partner dies and the other mates again with a much younger new partner, or that one partner becomes seriously ill. The old or sick animal stops all court-ship and sexual activity and the young or healthy partner is often over-whelmed with sexual offers from other members of its species who have not yet mated. Nevertheless, it quite often adheres to its mate, which shows clearly that the pair-bond is not based on the sexual activity be-tween the partners. Thus, pair-bonding is independent of reproduction and can even come into conflict with it.

Occasionally, there are even reports that some animals do fall in love, just like humans. In a remarkable experiment, Beach (1976) investi-gated the preferential attractiveness and attractedness in beagle dogs. When young, these dogs participated in an experiment. The males were tethered to posts widely separated around the edge of a field. Females in heat were then let loose, and each had sex with one of the male dogs. The animals did not meet together again for 7 years, at which time Beach repeated the experiment. To his surprise, the bitches showed an extraordinary tendency to return to exactly the same mate.

A strange situation is observed in the Eurasian tree sparrow (*Passer montanus*) (Wickler 1972, p. 97). The pairs are, as a rule, lifelong part-ners and have three broods a year. However, it is seldom that a pair is lucky enough to rear young birds together for 2 consecutive years. Nor-mally, one of the two will lose its life one way or another and the sur-vivor has to mate again. The partners are faithful to each other, particu-larly the females, who refuse the advances of every other male even when their own partner is ill or wounded. The males, by contrast, al-though they do not leave their female either, will sometimes take care of widowed neighbors, for widows blatantly prefer males whom they al-ready know to total strangers.

The explanation of these and similar anomalies in terms of evolution-ary selection omits the mechanism by which such selections could be presumed to have taken place. We only cite it here to show that there is a sufficient basis in the biological world for the later evolution of love in human beings.

Together with attachment naturally go the depression and sorrow that accompany loss (Scott & Senay, 1973, p. 7). All of these studies involve the separation of the infant from its mother. On puppies, the data show, without exception, that all puppies give the reaction of distress vocalization to separation. While the rate varies, the reaction appears reliably in all breeds and all individual dogs (Scott & Senay, p. 7).

One of the most interesting results was that the effects produced by separation will overcome the effects produced by hunger. Confirmation of this was obtained in experiments that involve prolonged separation. One of the characteristics of the separated puppies is that they do not eat as well as control puppies and consequently do not gain weight rapidly (Scott & Senay, 1973, p. 8).

Scott and Senay justifiably conclude that the separation–depression reaction is a basic biological constellation.

COMMUNITY FORMATION

Even at the lowest evolutionary level, organisms do not remain entirely alone. As Frings and Frings (1977, p. 38) say, the tendency to aggregate is apparently an inherent property of living creatures. In tissue cultures, cells from the same animal aggregate and exclude cells from other species. The slime molds are often thought of as part animal and part plant and therefore not entirely either. For part of their lives the slime molds are amoebalike creatures crawling among fallen leaves on the forest floor. When the time comes for reproduction, however, they fuse into a multicellular mass. At that time, one individual starts to puff out a particular chemical, called acrasin, which attracts other individuals of the same species to fuse into the mass. Specific identification seems to come about through the rhythm of puffing of the acrasin.

Thus, even at this low level there is a strong tendency to aggregation, similar to the sexual drive at higher evolutionary levels.

No doubt the most extraordinary social system seen among insects is that of the ant (*Encyclopaedia Britannica*, 15th ed., vol. 1, p. 304). There are about 8000 species of ant, but all are social in habit. In spite of their minuscule size (0.08 to 1 inch) they live together in organized colonies.

There are generally three classes, or castes: queens, males, and workers. Some species live in the nests of other species as parasites; that is, the larvae are given food and nourishment by the host workers.

Most ants live in nests, which may be located in the ground or under a rock or built above ground and made of twigs, sand, or gravel. Carpenter ants live in old logs and timbers. Some species live in trees or in the hollow stems of weeds. Tailor, or weaver, ants, found in the tropics of Africa, make nests of leaves and similar material, held together with silk secreted by the larvae. *Dolichoderus* glues together bits of animal feces for its nest. Army ants, found in tropical America, are nomadic and do not build permanent nests. They travel in columns, eating insects and other invertebrates along the way. Periodically the colony rests for several days while the queen lays her eggs. As the colony travels, the growing larvae are carried along. Habits of the African driver ant are similar.

The life cycle of the ant has four stages—egg, larva, pupa, and adult—and spans a period of 8 to 10 weeks. The queen spends her life laying eggs. The workers are females and do the work of the nest; the larger ones, the soldiers, defend the colony. At certain times of the year, many species produce winged males and queens. They fly into the air, where they mate. The male dies soon afterward, and the fertilized queen establishes a new nest.

The food the ants eat consists of both plants and animal substances. Some even eat the eggs and larvae of other ants or those of their own species.

The social behavior of the ants, along with that of the honeybees, is the most complex in the insect world. Slave-making ants, which include many species, have a variety of methods for "enslaving" the ants of other species. The queen *Bothriomyrmex decapitans* of Africa, for example, allows herself to be dragged by *Tapinoma* ants into their nest. She then bites off the head of the *Tapinoma* queen and begins laying her own eggs, which are cared for by the "enslaved" *Tapinoma* workers.

THE SOCIOSEXUAL MATRIX

There are two biological bases for the formation of animal communities: one is sexual; the other is social. Of these, the first has always been known; understanding of the second has only come in fairly recent years.

Beach (1977) has an excellent summary of cross-species comparisons of sexuality. There are widely distributed similarities, some of which clearly extend to homo sapiens as well. The theoretical significance or explanatory value of shared patterns of response cannot be assessed until the causal mechanisms have been analyzed for each species. When this is done, some shared patterns prove to arise from different origins and to subserve different functions. Nevertheless, there are others that reflect humanity's evolutionary heritage and genetic relationship to all mammals, especially to other primates.

The further analysis of sexual behavior in animals is broken down into various categories (Beach, 1977, chap. 11):

1. *Appetitive Behavior.* Pursuit and attempts to copulate are two types of male appetitive behavior that often take more elaborate forms termed "courtship," even though courtship is not a masculine prerogative. Appetitive behavior is just as much a female as a male function and is heavily dependent upon ovarian hormones in most species of mammals. The sexual "presentation" responses of female apes and monkeys are obviously proceptive and consist of adopting the copulatory position directly in front of the male while exposing the vaginal area.

Masculine appetitive activities include various forms of bodily contact with the female, the most universal of which involves touching, manipulating, and licking the external vagina. This serves a dual function, common to all forms of appetitive activity in both sexes, namely to stimulate sexually the individual performing the behavior and simultaneously to stimulate the partner.

2. *Consummatory Behavior.* Consummatory responses comprise the species-specific copulatory pattern that for most mammals is relatively stereotyped and unremarkable. The principal male acts are mounting, thrusting, inserting the erect penis, and ejaculating. The essential female acts are assumption of the mating posture, which facilitates the male's achievement of intromission, plus maintenance of this position until intravaginal ejaculation has occurred. After the male has mounted, the female may adjust the position of the vulva so as to compensate for any misdirection of his preinsertion thrusting movements. In most species, these simple activities comprise all of the female's receptive behavior.

For nearly all terrestrial quadrupeds, including monkeys, coitus invariably occurs tergo ("doggie position"), and this is the normal position for apes as well; but several variations do occur.

3. *Postconsummatory Behavior.* In all mammals that have been carefully studied, males become temporarily impotent following ejaculation and show no appetitive responses to females for an additional period of time after the physical ability to copulate has been regained. These refractory phases vary according to age, species, and individual. Female mammals, in general, are sexually receptive as long as they are physiologically in estrus and during this period are capable of many more matings than the male of their species. Nevertheless, there is evidence

that female animals who have just finished copulating with a potent male experience a temporary period of reduced proceptivity. Whether or not climax occurs is unknown, although some observers believe that it does take place in female monkeys.

4. *The Social Setting.* Even though the hormonal and physiological determinants are so powerful, animals usually mate in a social environment composed of other individuals whose relationships to both members of the pair can directly or indirectly affect their sexual interaction. For instance, the dominant bitch in a dog pack may interfere when males attempt to mate with another female, and subordinate talapoin monkeys never approach an estrus female if the dominant male is nearby but copulate with her promptly if he is removed.

In species without a complex social structure, such as the guinea pig or rat, males copulate and beget offspring as soon as their testes produce mature sperm, but the Anubis baboon has very few opportunities to inseminate adult females until several years after he becomes fertile. He not only must attain his full growth but must also achieve a social position high enough to permit access to receptive females. In other primate species, mating privileges are reserved for a few dominant males, and these are the same individuals who control excessive in-group aggression or act in concert to repel predators against the group.

Examination of the complete spectrum of mammalian patterns reveals differences that range from apparently indiscriminate copulation in some species to long-term monogamous mateships in others. The sexual habits of many animals bear a functional relationship to other behavior patterns that also are essential to the effectiveness or biologic success of the species. For example, pair-bonding is often found in species in which the male participates in care and rearing of the young. If the parental role is solely the female's responsibility, mating between males and females does not necessitate protracted precopulatory courtship or formation of a close and enduring heterosexual relationship.

5. *Homosexual Behavior.* Homosexual activities are fairly common in various mammals. They must be analyzed in terms of three variables: (1) the genetic sex of the two individuals (XX or XY); (2) the sex of the behavior pattern displayed by each participant; and (3) the sex of the stimulus pattern to which the individual is reacting.

For example, when they are sexually aroused, male animals of some species will mount inanimate objects, and semen for artificial insemination is collected while bulls or stallions are mounted on wooden dummies that do not remotely resemble a cow or mare. The principle of stimulus–response complementarity emerges: There is a high probability that occurrence of the feminine stimulus pattern will be correlated with the execution of masculine rather than feminine coital responses; nevertheless, there is always an imbalance due to sex-linked prepotency in motor patterns and stimulus sensitivity. Thus, what appears to be homosexual behavior is primarily the release of sexual tensions against objects that in some way resemble the sexual partner, or even simply the release of sexual tensions against any available object.

6. *Masturbation.* All male mammals nose, lick, mouth, or otherwise manipulate their own genitalia under various conditions, and particularly just after or between episodes of mating behavior. Captive monkeys and chimpanzees masturbate manually and orally, often inducing ejaculation in the process. Masturbation is reported to be much less frequent in female than in male animals. Captive monkeys and apes occasionally insert foreign objects into their vaginas and move them rhythmically to and fro; however, this activity appears to be infrequent.

Summary. The age-old idea that there is an inherent drive to physical contact is amply borne out by the studies of animals. There are differences from humans only in degree. Above all, however, animals only mate at certain periods (estrus) when impregnation is likely to occur; herein lies the major difference from humans. Apart from these periods, animals are largely indifferent to sexuality.

COMMUNITY LIVING

Common sense as expressed in language has always acknowledged the importance of community living for animals. We speak of a gaggle of geese, a pride of lions, a herd of cattle, a flock of sheep, and so on. The numerous words, almost one for each animal species, provide recognition that animals like to congregate and live in groups. It is only recently that scientists have come to study this phenomenon more closely. Each animal group has had one or two devoted students who have spent long periods of time with them in the wild, learning their ways of life and answering many hitherto unanswered questions about them. Moss (1982) has an excellent summary of much of this recent work, and our account is drawn from her book, *Portraits in the Wild.*

As Moss points out, it was not until about 20 years ago that anyone thought seriously about watching these animals in the wild. The risks are naturally formidable, injury and even death among them. Some animals, such as the elephant, have been studied by at least 30 scientists; others, such as the hyena, really intensively by only one. The animal studies that she describes were carried out in east Africa; nowhere on earth are so many kinds of life found coexisting in one great ecosystem.

Not surprisingly, every animal species carefully investigated turned out to have its own individuality, much of which was unknown before the animals were observed in their natural habitat.

The first to study the elephant carefully was the Scotsman Ian Douglas-Hamilton, who undertook in 1965 a pioneering 4½-year study of the Manyara elephants. In order to get the amount of data necessary to describe social organization, individual animals have to be recognized. He went about photographing every elephant he could find; this was somewhat hazardous, since some of the elephants could charge him, or threaten to do so. In time, however, they got used to him, and he learned to identify each individual. The combination of ear patterns, veins, and tusks shown in the photographs was more than enough to guarantee accurate identification. The important finding is that no two elephants are alike.

He found (after 15,000 observations) that the basic social structure of the Manyara elephants is the stable cow–calf family unit. The elephants divided into groups, which remained stable over a period of years, except for births, deaths, and the departure of the young males. In Manyara, the mean size of a family unit is nine to 10 members, and the range is from two to 24.

In the normal course of a day, the members of a family unit act as a coordinated body. While eating, drinking, and moving around, the cows and calves will almost always be within 50 yards of the matriarch, and most of the time much closer than that. If they are in thick bush, they keep in contact with each other by their acute sense of smell and by a strange rumbling noise with which they call to one another. If there is danger, the members quickly bunch together and present a united front, the matriarch usually taking the most prominent position, while the calves squeeze in behind and underneath the big females. Then they all stand with heads up, ears spread out, and trunks up in the air smelling the wind. If it is warranted, the cow may charge or the whole group may come—a huge gray mass of anger, even the littlest calves shaking their heads and trumpeting. Enemies seeing this tend to run.

By the end of his study, Douglas-Hamilton had recorded 48 separate family units using the Lake Manyara National Park. He even discovered a higher level of social organization above the family unit. Two or more family units often had a special bond with one another so that the members were probably related; he called this relationship a "kin group." For instance, in one kin group there were three separate family units, which were in close association with each other most of the time.

He even discovered how these family and kin units are formed. There is a hierarchy within each family unit based on age and size, with the largest and oldest females as the highest-ranking and the youngest and smallest females the lowest-ranking adults. This rank order is not clearly seen except at a limited resource, such as a water hole, but then the bigger females have priority and the smaller females are pushed aside until the larger females finish. In some of the groups, particularly those with the largest matriarchs, subgroups led by younger females sometimes form. While still maintaining a close association with the family unit, the subgroup gradually begins to move at a slight distance from the main group, and eventually over a period of several years the distance increases and the group becomes an independent family within the kin group.

Males are brought up by the mother until puberty, which varies but in Manyara occurred at about 12 years. As they approach puberty they begin sexual roughhousing, perhaps as a result of which they are expelled from the family group and forced on their own. Males form loose groups and "pal" around together, but the bonds do not seem to be very strong. When the female is in estrus, which lasts about 4 days, males approach and have intercourse, which lasts about 1 minute; in one case a cow was seen to continue eating during intercourse.

Elephants seem to be affectionate animals. Mothers touch and help their calves. For the first 6 months, one gets an image of the mother elephant constantly watching and fussing over her baby, but then it is on its own. Most of the elephant's time is spent in eating. It must consume 300 pounds of food a day and may drink from 30 to 50 gallons of water. It is estimated that the elephant spends 16 hours a day eating.

A marked contrast to the elephant is seen in the lion, a predator who must hunt and kill in order to live. Most lions live in prides consisting of males, females, and cubs, and each pride sticks to a fairly well-defined range. Some lions (only a small percentage, however) live a nomadic life, roaming singly, in pairs, or in small groups, with no fixed territories. The size of a pride varies from area to area and even within one area. The largest pride in one area had 37 members, the smallest four. But the pride does not act as a close-knit unit. The groups may change composition from day to day. Females seem to form companionships, but it is not known how or why.

The fully adult lionesses remain with the pride for their whole lifetime, which may be over 20 years. Because the pride is a closed system, all the females within a pride are related to each other. Over a 7-year period in one area the number of females in a pride remained fairly stable, no matter how many cubs were born or died, and no matter how many males were associated with the pride. The females also seem to exercise the leadership in the pride. They are usually the first to get up and make a move, and they initiate and make 85 to 90% of all hunts and kills.

Lionesses are reputed to be very poor mothers. In one pride they were able to produce 26 cubs over a 2-year period but could raise only two.

In spite of their reputation, male lions spend a great deal of time, sometimes 20 out of 24 hours, resting. Aside from maintaining the integrity of the pride area, a male's main goal is to mate with the females. As the observer drily remarks, "once a male has accesses to lionesses, he fulfills this role admirably" (Moss, 1982, p. 245). In one case, one lion mated 157 times in 55 hours; in the first 24 hours he mated 86 times (74 times with one female and 12 with another); during the second 24-hour period he mated 62 times, and in the remaining 7 hours, nine more times. During this time, he mated every 21 minutes on the average, with a breathing space as short as 1 minute, or as long as 110, and he did not eat.

No easy generalizations about the social life of the animals can be made. By and large they are much less aggressive than had been thought from previous work. The life cycle of each animal takes a different course, to which it is perforce required to adapt its life-style. But in all cases the animal has its own individualized sociosexual matrix to which it adheres.

COMMUNICATION

When Darwin elucidated the processes of natural selection, Spencer coined the term "survival of the fittest," which caught on very quickly, especially in the form of "social Darwinism," whereby the rich and successful found a justification for their wealth and success. In the animal world this survival of the fittest, however, is only one aspect of the total situation, and in fact it has more or less been discarded by biologists (Mayr, 1982) because of its tautological nature. It soon became apparent that there were other factors involved; some of these have already been discussed in this chapter. Another is the capacity for communication.

Cooperation, it would seem, is as much a law of nature as competition. The whole environment is organized into one ecosystem, the disturbance of any part of which may and often does affect the whole; we are beginning to experience the effects of such disturbances on a global scale now. Communication among animals serves the biological purpose of maintaining this ecosystem.

However, a difficulty arises in the meaning of the term *communication*. There is signaling going on all over the animal kingdom in the form of noises, postures, smells, tastes, heat reactions, and so on. When these signals become a more or less conscious form of communication is a thorny question; the difficulty even extends to the use of language by human beings. Since signaling is easily described, while communication is an inference, the emphasis here will be on external behavior; what intrapsychic events can be inferred will be left to the individual case.

Simple aggregations, in which individuals of the same species form groups at approximately the same spot, are found throughout the animal kingdom. These aggregations have biological value; when the time comes for reproduction, even when the animal cannot move, the adults are so close that they can easily exchange sperm and eggs.

Again, the lowly ant provides a remarkable example of the early development of the capacity for communication (Frings & Frings, 1977, p. 63). The colonies of ants, even though they number thousands of individuals, depend upon a few scouts to find food. The scouts then recruit the workers in the colony, all permanently immature females like themselves, to collect the food.

A scout often finds food at some distance from the nest and so must not only proclaim her find but must also indicate where the food is. Generally, the scout discloses the discovery by agitatedly running around, waving her antennae. The agitation gradually spreads, and the ants gather around and stroke the excited scout. In many species, the scout then leads the alerted ants to the food, a very simple type of communication. In other species, however, the scout, during her trip back to the nest, has deposited a series of odorous droplets to form an odor-trail. The recruits follow the trail and thus reach the food, although the scout remains in the nest. As more and more ants join the procession to and from the food source, they add to the odor-trail, and it becomes more and more distinct.

The elaborately complicated communication of honeybees to their hive-mates that there is a source of food in the distance was first described by the German scientist Karl von Frisch in 1947 (Frisch, 1965). This is done by what is called a "waggle" dance, which indicates both the direction and the distance of a food source and constitutes for the colony of bees an extraordinarily efficient method of harvesting as rapidly as possible a new and abundant source of food. The dance is performed only when a worker has discovered, or is foraging at, a particularly rich source of supply. Each performance of the dance on the comb results in a number of other bees setting out and finding that particular food source (Hinde, 1972, p. 133). If the supply is still rich when the newcomers reach it, they also dance on the combs, and so a large band of foraging workers is quickly recruited for work at a rich source of supply. As soon as the source begins to fail, the returning workers cease to dance, although they themselves continue exploiting that source as long as an appreciable yield is obtained. So the whole mechanism serves not only to direct new foragers to food supplies that have been discovered by fellow members of the colony but also to get them there in approximately the right numbers to exploit the food supply properly.

In the case of birds, the most vocal animals apart from humans, their distinctive songs have been extensively studied (Thorpe, 1972, pp. 153–176). Successful social organization often requires a capacity for mutual recognition, at some distance, between mates and also between parents and offspring. In birds in which the young are cared for in a nest, individual recognition is unimportant, but in the numerous varieties in which the young move about and may scatter after hatching, individual recognition is often crucial to the maintenance of life. Without individual recognition, the feeding of the young, at least as soon as they become mobile, could be a very wasteful process. Hordes of young would be competing for food from each individual adult as it returned to the colony, with the result that the strongest, the most fortunate, or the quickest would obtain ample food and many others would starve. Again, it is important that the parent should bring food, for example, fish, of the right size for young of a given age. Later still in the life cycle, when the young are nearly ready to fly or are flying, it may be necessary for them to follow a particular parent rather than accompany anonymously a flock of adults.

It is not surprising then that birds, which are so highly mobile, should have developed song patterns distinctive for each subspecies. For instance, Tschanz (1968), summarizing nearly 10 years of work, pioneered in the demonstration that young guillemots (Uria) learn to react selectively to the calls of their parents and that, during the first few days of life, the parents similarly recognize their own young. There is even some evidence that the young, while still within the egg, may learn to recognize some aspects of the sounds produced by adults. With the common tern (*Sterna hirundo*), Stevenson et al. (1970) have demonstrated that the young bird, at 4 days of age, while quite unresponsive to the playback of calls of other members of the colony, responds immediately on being played the returning call of one of its own parents, its response being a sudden, alert "cheeping," turning, and walking toward the loudspeaker.

The ethologists (Lorenz, Tinbergen, and their school) have provided a new and much more sophisticated clarification of the concept of instinct than any hitherto available. In fact, the standard biological texts are so heavily involved with the newly discovered mechanisms of heredity (DNA, RNA, genes, chromosomes, etc.) that they have virtually ignored the topic of instinct (cf. Mayr, 1982).

Lorenz (1981) and Tinbergen (1951) discovered that animals respond selectively to external stimuli (in German, *Umwelt*—"surrounding world"). It is by no means an image of the whole object or situation that is innately "known" to the animal, but instead a number of independently effective, very simple stimulus configurations whose releasing functions, obeying the law of heterogeneous summation, add up to a qualitatively unitary effect. For this reason they abandoned the original term *Schema* and decided to call the neural organization available for responding to these stimuli the *innate releasing mechanism* (IRM) [in German, *angeborener Auslösemechanismus* (AAM)].

The IRM is defined exclusively by its function. It is obvious that in organisms differing with regard to the complexity of their nervous organization as well as to the levels of integration attained by their cognitive faculties and their behavior, very different demands are put upon the selectivity of their responses to external stimulus configurations. It is equally obvious that very different physiological mechanisms have evolved to cope with these demands.

Lorenz cites many examples, one of which is the classic case described by his predecessor Jakob von Uezkuell (1909), the stinging response of the common tick (*Ixodes rhizinus*). The female of this species, after the last molt, can wait a very long time before finding a final host, any mammal. The IRM responding selectively to this host object consists of a reaction to only two key stimuli: first, a body temperature of roughly 37°C, and second, the smell of butyric acid. Furthermore, finding the proper object is helped by the tick's sitting patiently on low branches and allowing itself to drop down, when these are shaken, so that there is a good chance of its falling onto an animal moving below (the releaser). The probability of all these conditions being fulfilled by anything but a mammal is negligible (Lorenz, 1981, p. 156). In general, the question of how and when the function of selecting is performed by the IRM must be separately investigated for every single instance.

Examples from animals in the wild that can be explained only by the operation of IRMs and their releasers may be seen in this account from Klingel (cited in Moss, 1982) of the behavior of zebras. The zebras use contact calls when trying to find each other. These calls sound something like the combination of a donkey braying and dog barking. Individual zebra voices vary tremendously and can be distinguished even by humans. The contact call is also used by stallions when they want to get in touch with other stallions. One stallion calls and waits for an answer. Then the two stallions continue calling back and forth until they meet and greet. Aside from the contact call, the zebra makes a number of other noises (1) A two-syllable alarm call is made when danger—a predator or a human on foot—is approaching. All neighboring zebras react immediately to this call by standing still and looking intently in the direction of the danger. (2) A loud snort is made when zebras are about to move into a more dangerous area—for example, thick bush or a water hole. (3) A long, drawn-out snort is a sign of contentment. (4) A short, high-pitched squeal is uttered by a stallion when bitten or threatened in a fight. This is probably an expression of pain or fear. (5) A long, drawn-out wailing call is uttered by foals in distress. This call is highly disturbing to other members of the group (Moss, 1982, pp. 88–126).

Until she reaches estrus the young zebra foal maintains a very close relationship with her mother and other members of the group. The young females leave the group under very abrupt and violent circumstances. When a young mare is 13 to 15 months old and reaches estrus for the first time, she adopts a typical posture that has the immediate effect of attracting every stallion in the vicinity. She stands with legs apart and tail lifted, and it is the visual effect of this position that is the key. The estrus secretions also play a part, but probably not until the stallion has been attracted by the stance. When the young mare takes the estrus stance, the mature stallions in the area converge on the family group and try to abduct her. The family stallion reacts to this situation by desperately attempting to fight the stallions off. But other stallions chase the group until they manage to separate the young mare and drive her away. In the end, the family stallion has to give up from sheer exhaustion. In one case, the Klingels saw 18 stallions fighting over the possession of one mare; the numbers alone make it almost impossible for the family stallion to keep the young female. (Among humans, this would be similar to the "gang-bang," known as the *loteria* in Spanish.)

Once a mare becomes a permanent member of a group, mating behavior within the family is relatively simple. When one of the mares comes into estrus, the family stallion becomes interested in her dung and urine. He defecates on her dung and sprays urine on the spot where she has urinated. After the stallion determines that the mare is in estrus, he begins to pursue her, and from an anthropomorphic point of view, the older mares appear to be taken for granted. Courtship behavior of any duration occurs only between the stallion and his young, newly adopted mares. The stallion is very attentive to the young mare when she comes into estrus, grooming her on the neck, shoulders, flank, and rump before trying to mount her. For the first few days of estrus, she keeps moving away when he tries to mount, and he keeps following her, grooming her and trying again. At the height of estrus, on the third or fourth day, she allows copulation, which lasts from 1 to 4 minutes.

In the normal course of events, young stallions leave their family groups between the ages of 1 and 3 to join bachelor groups. It is interesting that certain bachelor groups consist of mostly adult animals, and new additions to these are also adult, while other groups consist mainly of younger animals, joined by other young animals. The animals in the bachelor groups, especially in those made up of young animals, are very high-spirited and playful. Their running games turn into races, with the whole group of them galloping across the plains at full speed. They indulge in mock fights and playful greeting ceremonies. In the play fights, all the elements of true fights are present but are not carried out with the same intensity. They neck-wrestle, wheel around, bite at each other from standing and sitting positions, rear up on their hind legs, and chase each other. The play fights do not become serious, although they sometimes appear to be quite intense. When they are over, the partners often rest with heads on each other's backs in a friendly manner.

The zebra is one of the most loving of animals. There is a mutual concern for members within a group, and at times there is actual assistance. Time and again the Klingels saw wounded, sick, or old animals being cared for by the other members of its group. Mares and foals remain within the group when they are sick and within it are often able to recover from what appear to be incurable wounds and injuries.

Zebras have a remarkable technique for dealing with danger, which highlights once more the value of the group (group mind in humans). When an enemy is spotted, the zebras react by forming a semicircle, facing the predator, and watch it intently, heads raised and ears alertly pointed forward. The semicircle and the posture of the zebras attract the attention of the other zebras in the area(and other animals as well), who are then also aware that there is a predator nearby. If the predator moves closer, the zebras move away, keeping a distance of about 100 yards, which is their flight distance, when they can outrun the predator. If they are forced to flee when the predator gets too close, the stallion of the group remains behind, acting as a rear guard. He turns and threatens the pursuers, biting and striking at them, and is often successful in warding them off, allowing the mares and foals to get away first. Still, their alertness and group cooperation are not enough to keep all the predators at bay, and large numbers of zebras are killed by predators every year. Lions have to live, too.

SOCIAL HIERARCHIES

In sharp contrast to the popular image of the animal as a lone predator (the "lone wolf"), the reality is that most animals live in groups. To maintain the cohesiveness of these groups, there has evolved a pattern of *dominance* and *submission* in every species, which is quite remarkable. This pattern was first discovered in chickens and has for that reason been called the "pecking order" ever since. How this pecking order is communicated within the group remains a mystery, yet it is an observable fact of social life throughout the animal world. Within each group it is so well established that some authors have even thought that a genetic factor is operative, since the dominance position seems to be passed on in some cases to the offspring.

Dominance or submission can easily be determined by observing the stances of the two animals involved. For instance, among cows (Houpt & Wolski, 1982), the dominant cow, when threatening the submissive one, will stand with its feet drawn well under and with its head down, but perpendicular to the ground. The ears will be turned back, with the inner surface pointing down and back. The submissive cow also stands with lowered head, but its head is parallel to the ground and its ears are turned so that the inner surface points to the side. Aggression is expressed by bunting or striking the opponent with the head. For the most part, however, aggression is unnecessary, since the submissive animal gets to "know its place."

When adult animals that have never been penned together are brought together for the first time, intense aggressive encounters may occur for several days until each animal has established its position in what generally turns out to be a hierarchy of dominant–submissive relationships. In this type of social grouping there is an alpha animal, which is seldom challenged by subordinates, a beta, or second-ranked, animal, which is only challenged by the alpha animal, and so on. Within this organization, the type of aggressive encounter changes once the rank of each animal has been determined. No longer are an attack and susequent fight needed for an alpha animal to establish its rights over a beta animal. Now a direct stare, or the threat of a charge, will generally serve to deter the beta animal from further confrontation. In this way, the assertion of dominance has been turned into a ritualized aggression, where the threat is experienced as so great that its fulfillment is no longer needed.

While biologists on the whole have been content with the explanation of natural selection for these hierarchies, the variety of social groupings and their maintenance is so great that such an explanation seems singularly inadequate. It is only when animals are observed in their natural habitats that the extraordinary variations in social order that have evolved come to the fore.

For example, Kruuk (cited in Moss, 1982, pp. 297–328), in his studies of hyenas in the Ngorongoro Crater in east Africa, found that the hyena population is divided into eight "clans," each consisting of males, females and cubs, and numbering anywhere from 10 to 100 animals. Each clan occupies a range of approximately 8 square miles. The ranges of the clans cover most of the crater floor and border on each other, forming a kind of mosaic. The borders are defined in the hyenas' minds and not necessarily by natural boundaries; how they do this is again a mystery.

Most of the clan's activities are carried out within its own range, although members will cross over into other ranges at times. However, hyenas cannot move freely from area to area, for the ranges are held in a strictly territorial way; that is, they are defended from intrusion by members of other clans.

If a stranger is detected within another clan's range, it will be viciously chased and even attacked. As soon as it is out of its own territory, a hyena's whole manner becomes defensive and wary, and as a result it is even more easily seen to be a stranger. The territorial system can also be seen at work during hunting. A pack of hyenas in the full heat of a chase will sometimes stop dead in their tracks when their quarry runs across the border into a neighboring clan's range. On other occasions they may not stop; then, if they make the kill on foreign territory, and the clan's owners are aware of it, a dispute over the carcass will invariably take place. If the kill takes place far into the other territory, then the invaders will almost always give way to the owners, even if the invaders outnumber the owners.

An entirely different kind of social arrangement was uncovered by

Sugiyama (1967) among the langur in southern India. Here single adult males maintained a harem of adult females with infant and juvenile offspring. There were also bands of adult males and adolescent males in the area who had no access to females. These bands of males would on occasion rush toward and aggressively attack a harem leader, either killing him or chasing him from his female consorts. Typically, the dominant male from the unisex group then chased off his male comrades who had assisted him in the coup d'etat and took charge of the female harem for his exclusive possession. The most bizarre aspect of this accession of power occurred when the new leader, with no interference from the adult females in the harem, then selectively attacked and killed the male offspring of the former overlord—female infants and juveniles were spared. Through some biological mechanism, the adult females then came into estrus and were impregnated by the new leader even when the change in succession did not coincide with the usual breeding season.

Another startling variation in social behavior was noted by Menzel (1974) in experiments with chimpanzees. He reports the following: Taking a group of chimpanzees, he first locked them inside a release cage from which they would not see what was going on in the enclosure. Next, an experimenter entered the field and hid a test object at a randomly designated location, never using the same location over a series of trials. Then one previously selected member of the group was taken from the release cage, carried over to the object, shown the object, and returned to the group. The experimenter left the field, ascended the observation tower, and pulled a cable that opened the release cage door and turned the animals loose to respond as they chose. With this delayed response procedure the group as a whole had no cues as to what object (if any) was out there or where it was, other than cues provided by the leader's memory and behavior (control tests were of course done to verify that variables such as odor or inadvertent behavior on the part of the observers were not sufficient to explain group performance). If no animal was given the information, the group very seldom went to the object directly or responded differentially according to the nature of the object.

The results were clear-cut. Any individual was capable of rallying the whole group to respond in fairly organized fashion to objects about which he alone knew. Ordinarily, the informed animal led the group to the hidden object, and if they were slow to follow he used a variety of devices, including visual glances, grimacing, extending a hand toward a companion, tapping the companion on the shoulder and presenting his back, and so on to recruit a following. He very seldom set off to the object alone, and in this sense performance was clearly a cooperative performance; that is, the leader was as dependent on the group for getting to the object as they were dependent on him for knowing where to go.

Not only did the group continue to travel together as a cohesive unit on the basis of cues from a single leader, but also the animals who had been provided with no cues seemed to know approximately where the object was, and what sort of object it was, long before the leader reached the spot where it had been hidden. Thus, if the leader had been shown food, for example, other animals often ran ahead of him, glanced back periodically, as if to determine his trajectory, and then dove for any likely-looking hiding place that lay ahead on this path and searched it manually in exactly the same fashion as they searched around a leader if he had missed a food pile by a few feet.

Menzel considers whether experiences of this kind deserve the name *communication*. He feels that the very question reveals a human chauvinism that equates real communication with what we think people do. He states:

> On the basis of many such tests, I would hypothesize that the discrimination of negative (caution or aggression-inducing) from positive classes of objects was based principally on cues such as the leader's piloerection, vocalization, locomotor deceleration and increase in caution as he approached and stared at a particular locus, and tendency to circle the locus or approach it from overhead via some vertical structure. [Menzel, 1974, pp. 111–113]

While this explanation certainly has merit, what he does not consider is why the group should choose to follow the leader at all. Communication, of whatever kind, seems to serve the function of social cohesiveness, but why the group chose to act as a group at all is not clarified. We would assume that it represents another aspect of an inborn social drive.

CHIMPANZEES LEARN LANGUAGE

In the area of communication, by far the most startling development of recent years has been the demonstration that chimpanzees can learn language. Not spoken language; that was tried for years without success, which led to the common belief that only human beings have language.

Then in 1966 came the breakthrough. Allen and Beatrice Gardner, of the University of Nevada in Reno, had the brilliant inspiration that it might be possible to communicate with a chimpanzee through gestures instead of spoken words. They acquired a 1-year-old infant female chimpanzee, naming her Washoe after the county in which they lived. Washoe was given the same kind of attention, playthings, games, and loving care provided for human infants.

The experiment worked. Using American Sign Language, ordinarily used only by deaf people, the Gardners did manage to teach Washoe the rudiments of a human language. By the time she left them, 3½ years later, Washoe had learned to express 132 words. The Gardners estimated that Washoe understood about three times as many signs as she could express. (The material here is drawn from Terrace, 1979).

At about the same time, David Premack (1983), a psychologist at the University of California at Santa Barbara, invented an artificial language of plastic chips and a radically new method for studying the linguistic potential of a chimpanzee. Neither the form nor the color of the plastic chips provided any clue to their meaning. The teaching strategy was simple. Premack and Sarah sat across from each other, Sarah in her cage and the teacher at the other end of the table separating them. To teach Sarah the name of a food, her teacher would exchange that food for the appropriate plastic chip. Again a similar capacity was displayed by the chimp.

Still a third method was adopted by Duane Rumbaugh and colleagues at the Yerkes Primate Center in Atlanta, Georgia. Their chimp was a 2-year-old named Lana. The language they taught her was called "Yerkish." It was taught in much the same way as the others, by rewarding her for learning, but Lana learned to communicate by pressing the appropriate keys on a computer teletypewriter.

A number of other successful experiments have followed. The Gardners have taught American Sign Language to at least four other infant chimps; Roger Fouts, one of their students, trained another five (Terrace, 1979, p. 25). Premack has taught three other chimpanzees to communicate in his language of plastic chips, while Rumbaugh has trained four others to learn Yerkish. And in 1979 Francine Patterson, a graduate student at Stanford University, published a paper describing her success in teaching American Sign Language to an infant gorilla named Koko (Terrace, p. 25).

The most elaborate of all the teaching experiments was the one carried out by Herbert Terrace, a professor of psychology at Columbia University. He used almost 100 paid students and volunteers to train a 2-week-old male infant he called Nim Chimpsky (after the linguist Noam Chomsky) (Terrace, 1979). Again Nim learned the language with comporative ease. Terrace and his group also took a close look at the emotional life of the infant chimp and found it in many essential respects similar to that of a child. Further, he was also able to show that Nim retained the memory of the language for at least a year, as well as his memories and fondness for his main teacher. As Terrace says, if so much has already been done, what else will come out about the intellectual capacities of the chimp remains unpredictable. An exciting new frontier has been opened up; where else it will lead no one can tell.

IS AGGRESSION INSTINCTUAL?

The question of whether aggression is instinctual is obviously relevant to the topic of this book. It has been hotly debated for centuries, with no simple answer in sight. Certainly, whether instinctual or not, aggression is a powerful drive in both humans and animals. Rather than call it innate or acquired, what can be done now is to specify the conditions under which it is most likely to appear.

The outstanding advocate of the notion that aggression is largely instinctual is the noted ethologist Konrad Lorenz (1963). Lorenz argues that aggression has survival value. He distinguishes three functions that aggression serves in the evolutionary scheme: the balanced distribution of animals of the same species over the available environment, selection of the strongest by rival fights, and defense of the young. Yet there is also much more; it plays according to him an indispensable part in the great complex of drives, it is a strong driving power behind much motivation, it lies behind behavior patterns that outwardly have nothing to do with aggression and even appear to be its very opposite, while in the most intimate bonds between living creatures a certain amount of aggression is found.

Many biologists and anthropologists have been highly critical of the arguments put forth by Lorenz and his students (e.g., Eibl-Eibesfeldt, 1979). It has been pointed out that the argument of natural selection, which is undoubtedly an essential aspect of Darwinian evolution, has been done to death by Lorenz. Every activity of any animal group is explained by him as part of the survival value inherent in the evolutionary process. Yet, as he freely admits, there is just as much cooperation, bonding, social cohesiveness, and even rudimentary love feelings in animal groups as the opposite. If aggression is innate, so is love. If everything has survival value, then love and cooperation are as important as hatred and destructiveness.

The argument really proceeds from two traditional beliefs that have been taken for granted in spite of their demonstrable incorrectness. It has been assumed (1) that primitive people are more aggressive than civilized; and (2) that animals are more aggressive than humans. Neither of these stands up to closer scrutiny. The argument of this book is rather that there are love cultures and hate cultures among primitive humans as well as among civilized and that there appear to be both love and hate among animals as well as among humans. Human beings, however, contain within themselves the capacity to overcome their aggressive drives by suitable cultural and educational measures.

Perhaps the most crucial point to be made in this chapter is that among animals there is always some special reason for the aggression, except for the few species where aggression seems to run wild (e.g., certain kinds of rats; Lorenz, 1963, Chap. 10). Ashley Montagu (1976, pp. 14–15) lists the following as the forms of aggression among animals and the stimuli that provoke it:

1. Predatory aggression: evoked by the presence of a natural object of prey.
2. Antipredatory aggression: evoked by the presence of a predator.
3. Territorial aggression: defense of an area against an intruder.
4. Dominance aggression: evoked by a challenge to the animal's rank or desire for an object.
5. Maternal aggression: evoked by the proximity of some threatening agent to the young of the particular female.
6. Weaning aggression: evoked by the increasing independence of the young, when the parents will threaten or even gently attack their offspring.
7. Parental disciplinary aggression: evoked by a variety of stimuli such as unwelcome suckling, rough or overextended play, wandering, and the like.
8. Sexual aggression: evoked by females for the purpose of mating or the establishment of a prolonged union.
9. Sex-related aggression: evoked by the same stimuli that produce sexual behavior.
10. Intermale aggression: evoked by the presence of a male competitor of the same species.
11. Fear-induced aggression: evoked by confinement or cornering

and inability to escape or the presence of some threatening agent.

12. Irritable aggression: evoked by the presence of any attackable organism or object.

13. Instrumental aggression: any changes in the evironment as a consequence of the above types of aggression that increase the probability that aggressive behavior will occur in similar situations.

It will be noted that in all of these cases aggression is *evoked*; it is not spontaneous. Jane Goodall (1968) gives a similar list for the aggression that she observed among the chimpanzees. Thus aggression, if it is to be regarded as an instinct on a par with sexuality, should be viewed as a *reactive instinct* (Fine, 1975), which serves entirely different functions from the more spontaneous sexual instinct, which is the biological basis of love.

The sociobiological argument has been that "cultural evolution copies biological evolution at a higher level of the 'developmental spiral' " (Eibl-Eibesfeldt, 1979, p. 122). This argument represents an oversimplification. It has already been seen how nature has created a wide variety of adaptive measures to cope with aggression, sex, and other genetically based drives. Humans have taken a long step beyond the animal pattern, in that, as Marx once put it, man makes his own history, but he makes it from where he stands and how he sees it, not from where others stand or how others see it.

Thus, to begin with, the parallels between humans and animals are only parallels, not copies of the same pattern. And, even though the similarities have been stressed in this chapter, there are obviously also vast differences, especially in the command which humans exercise over their environment, both external and internal. Furthermore, even among animals, as Kortlandt has put it: "The goal of fighting in many species is not so much fighting in itself but rather to establish a social organization which makes fighting superfluous" (cited in Montagu, 1976, p. 86).

SUMMARY: LOVE IN ANIMALS

Our review of the behavior patterns of animals has shown that there are many built-in structures that serve the purpose of love in the broadest sense. Here it is pertinent to begin the discussion of this "broad sense," especially since I have hitherto avoided a categorical definition of love.

Basically, love involves affectionate contact between two animals (or humans). Such contact includes touching, grooming, playfulness, pair-bonding, group cohesiveness, intense personal attachments, sexuality, and many other forms of closeness. With the exception of intense personal attachments, all of these are found in rudimentary form in most, if not all animal species. Natural selection and survival of the fittest are nice slogans. But they do not make it clear that there is an enormously powerful drive toward loving interaction. At the lowest level this is sexual, but it soon goes well beyond that. Aggression exists, but so does loving, fighting but also peaceful cooperation, isolation but also communication.

A major distinction drawn throughout this book is that between love cultures and hate cultures. Looked at from the broad, objective point of view most animal species seem to have evolved into primitive love cultures, in which aggression has been tamed, ritualized, and forced into certain fairly well-defined channels. What is lacking is the elaborate psychological development of the biological drive into art, social living, religion, and the numerous other forms of cultural structures that are the characteristics of humans.

In other words, the major difference between animals and humans is culture, based on the far more extensive brain capacity of humans and hence their far more extensive psychological capacities. This is true of both love and hate. If no animal species has ever been found that commits genocide for the deliberate purpose of exterminating some other animal species or group, then equally no animal "culture" possesses such complicated devices as love poetry, or a Taj Mahal built by an emperor to commemorate the beauty of his beloved queen.

Two of the traditional assumptions about animal and human nature have to be discarded: Animals are not per se more aggressive than humans, and primitives are not per se more aggressive than civilized peoples. The differences lie in the capacity for control, rather than in the strength of the drives as such. Furthermore, both nature (the animal world) and history (the human world) have created an almost infinite variety of social structures. Just why this should be so is not readily apparent, nor are the mechanisms entirely as clear as some would have us believe.

One further conclusion to be drawn from this material is important. What is basic is the love culture, in which the predominant feeling among individuals is one of warmth and affection, rather than coldness and hatred. It could justifiably be said that these love cultures are often found among animals; that in fact, in the process of taming the aggression and perpetuating the species, there is an innate phylogenetic drive toward the establishment of such love cultures.

In much thinking about animals, especially under the influence of the behavioristic tradition in American psychology, there is the gratuitous assumption that animals do not have feelings; the difficulties involved in discussing feelings in humans are multiplied a thousandfold when animals are under investigation. The data introduced in this chapter (and much other material) cast serious doubt on this assumption. Since the initial behavioristic approach has been under attack on many scores for a number of years, it is time to take a new look at the question of whether animals feel, and in particular of whether they can love or not. To the average psychologist altruism requires some special explanation (Macaulay & Berkowitz, 1970), while aggression does not.

If love is looked at from the point of view of the analytic ideal, it becomes clear that many animal species, especially at the higher evolutionary levels, experience love feelings in various degrees. The friendly feeling as such, which is at the heart of love, is so obvious that it requires no special emphasis, nor does the overwhelming importance of sex, except that in all animals outside of the human beings sex is a periodic drive, stimulated by the capacity to reproduce at certain times of the month or year.

That animals have pleasure again needs no particular stress. If the human being is a pleasure-seeking animal, so too animals; more so, in fact, since they have less control over their pleasures and less capacity to delay them.

Reason enters the picture, again especially at the higher levels. The most dramatic demonstration of the animal's capacity to reason is no doubt the success achieved by the Gardners, Premack, Rumbaugh, and others in teaching the American Sign Language, or its equivalent, to chimpanzees. The chimpanzees (Terrace, 1979, has a summary) can not only learn to communicate on an intelligent level, but they also retain a large number of signs or units and seem in every respect to be quite well aware of what they are doing. If they have not yet mastered the intricates of $E = mc^2$, neither have many humans. In other words, the reasoning capacity of the animal has to be evaluated in terms of its natural endowment, but this is true in all areas (Breland & Breland, 1966).

While animals rarely display the nuclear family structure that is virtually universal among humans, they do congregate in groups which, given their native abilities, become the equivalent of a family. Mother–child care among primates is seen everywhere, with the consequent feelings of loss and deprivation when this basic biological pair is disrupted for any reason. And it is quite remarkable that among some species families with characteristics quite similar to those seen in humans are found; though rare, this in itself is significant.

There is likewise a definite social structure found among animals. The "lone wolf" image is a myth. Animals need one another as much as humans do. The extraordinary mechanisms developed in the patterns of dominance and submission have been extensively studied and documented in all animal species. If each species is different, that does not alter the fact that animal societies move toward some kind of natural order. And in this natural order every individual seems to be able to find some kind of niche.

There is by now no doubt that animals can communicate with one another (Hinde, 1972). Again such communication is limited by the basic capacities of the animal. But that is also true of humans.

Many studies have shown that animals at times do demonstrate creative capacities. Again, this is obscured by the fact that their creative abilities do not result in any lasting monuments. But they are by no means the mechanical toys that they have been supposed to be in the past.

As far as work is concerned, animals do the work necessary to sustain their lives and habitats. Once more, this work is at such a rudimentary level that it has been overlooked. Yet much human work is likewise at a rudimentary level.

Finally, since Pavlov and his co-workers it has been known that dogs and other animals can become "neurotic" or even "psychotic." These neuroses and psychoses are externally induced, but there is really no reason to believe that the same is not true of humans. What differs is that in the human there is a more or less elaborate internal reorganization of the original reinforcement, leading to the numerous bizarre manifestations that are so puzzling, while in the animal the symptom remains closer to the original reinforcement.

Thus within the limits of their biological endowment, animals pursue various aspects of the analytic ideal. No doubt it is true that all of this has somehow evolved in the course of the millennia; that explains how it might have come about (see Mayr, 1982, for a trenchant criticism of this simplistic argument), but it does not clarify what is going on now. Consequently we can say that animals do love.

Since Darwin, the animal world has been viewed as the biological substratum with which to understand the human. If animals can display various rudimentary forms of love, in every aspect of the analytic ideal, a base is then provided for comprehending the phylogenetic roots of the human capacity to love. The major differences seem to lie in the far greater capacity of the human being to elaborate his or her world psychologically.

A further caveat is necessary here. All too often the concept of "love" is used in a mystical or semimystical sense. If instead it is viewed as a natural feeling found in varying degrees throughout the animal kingdom it becomes much more comprehensible.

6

The Child in the Family:
Loving Comes from Being Loved

The overwhelming significance of love in the life of the child has been recognized comparatively recently. It was not until after World War II that John Bowlby, the well-known British psychoanalyst, was commissioned by the United Nations to write a book on the indispensability of maternal love. The expression *TLC* ("tender loving care") has become part of the general vocabulary.

Three major points can be made here, to be further documented throughout this chapter. First of all, a child that is loved learns to love others. Second, any interruption in the loving process, or frustration of it, leaves the child dependent and vulnerable. The earlier the frustration comes, the worse it is for the child. And third, all human societies are arranged in families. Love has to be provided within the family environment. When there is a loving family, it becomes the prototype of the love culture.

A comparison of humans with animals serves to highlight several other significant motifs. While animals do sometimes form families, with father, mother, and children, that is the rare exception. The rule is

162

rather a group of mothers and infants, with the fathers off to one side, either as nomads, or in male groups, or as protectors of the species. Loving care by the father, in other words, is for all practical purposes a human invention. Finally, while the psychological ties between animals, such as the mother–child pair, may be quite strong in infancy, they tend to be dissipated as time goes on. Although chimpanzees have come to seem more human than ever, they lack the capacity to form lifelong ties of affection. So while a primitive love culture may be found in many animal species, a true love culture, with marked ties of affection and recognition, is only to be found in humans.

It may be asserted that ideally a human community can be a love culture, even if it rarely occurs. In such a culture the individual can live out his or her life as a series of loving experiences, moving from mother to father to peers and ultimately forming an independent family with similar ties of caring affection. Such a love culture creates an analytic ideal (cf. Chapter 10). Neurosis can best be defined as distance from this analytic ideal. Because of the greater complexity of the human psyche, with its greater capacity for variation from prescribed behavior, humans in general are more neurotic (broadly including psychotic) than animals. Freud's hunch that a careful comparison of children, dreamers, psychotics, and primitives would yield enormous insights into human nature has been amply confirmed.

In order to focus the discussion and marshal the evidence for the main thesis that loving comes from being loved, the major relationships at different stages of the individual's life will be considered in turn.

PREGNANCY

While the physiology of pregnancy and birth in animals and that in humans are similar (Mitchell, 1981), the psychological differences are enormous. For example, among giraffes, the bull seeks out the female by testing her urine; if it is not that of an estrus female, he goes on until he finds one, when he has intercourse. Pregnancy is usually uneventful. When it is time to give birth the mother giraffe leaves the herd and goes to a secluded spot to have her calf. During birth the mother remains standing; the calf is dropped head first 5½ feet to the ground and from all reports lands with a thud. It survives its rather precipitous descent into life, for it is soon on its feet, standing close to 6 feet and weighing about 150 pounds. After 15 minutes the calf manages to stand up without the help of the mother and thereafter has an independent existence.

The mother and calf remain in close contact for 3 or 4 days. In these early days the mother spends a good deal of time nosing and licking the calf. There is a special ritual in which the mother bends down and licks the calf and the calf then licks the mother. While the newborn calf is suckling, the mother bends and licks its rump. While the calves nibble at food within a few days after birth, they continue to suckle until they are around 1 year of age. However, the mortality rate for the newborns is high; one investigator found that 50% of the calves died within 3 months after birth; another found that 73% died. Similar observations (with some species differences, of course) have been made for other animals (Moss, 1982, pp. 51–53).

By contrast, the human female approaches sex and pregnancy with all kinds of psychological conflicts. Analytic authors who have written on the subject (Bibring, 1961; Deutsch, 1945; Benedek, 1970, etc.) are all in agreement that pregnancy represents a true crisis in the life of the woman.

To begin with, pregnancy represents the first decisive affirmation of the woman's femininity, that aspect of living in which she differs most markedly from the man. Hence how it is reacted to depends on the woman's sense of herself as a woman. The women's liberation movement has made us more conscious than ever before of the deep-seated conflicts that go along with just being a woman (though it tends to ignore the equally deep-seated conflicts that go along with just being a man (cf. Fine, 1984). Whether she follows the traditional role of wife and mother or the modern role of career woman and/or mother, the woman is filled with deep ambivalence about herself. The myth that the woman in less complex societies does not have such ambivalence has long since been exploded for just what it is—a myth. Thus Hoch-Smith and Spring (1978) have shown that among the Yoruba the woman is faced with the same dichotomy that existed in Europe in medieval times—good woman or bad woman. There is a widespread belief in witches who are commonly thought to interfere with reproduction (Hoch-Smith & Spring, p. 251). Impotence is said to be common among Yoruba males, who believe that it is the work of witches. A witch may steal the penis of a man and have intercourse with it, with herself or with another woman, or she may visit men at night and tamper with their testicles. Also, she can stop the flow of menstrual blood in a woman, since all women are interconnected, and she may obstruct the passage of a child from a womb or cause barrenness in a woman. Obviously the Yoruba culture, like ours, is a hate culture, so that the projection of men's hostilities to women need not come as a surprise.

The social circumstances under which the woman becomes pregnant obviously are of prime importance, as are the related problems of contraception and abortion. Unwise social restrictions (such as the present antiabortion campaign) can produce extreme distress in the woman who is faced with a choice of two impossible alternatives.

Apart from social pressures, which vary with the culture, intrapsychic factors play a significant part. In the classical Freudian interpretation of the girl's wish for a child, the little girl wishes to have a penis, and then when that wish is denied she turns to father to give her a baby. As an adult woman, the child comes to symbolize the penis that she longed for but could never get. If that is the case, she may feel deliriously happy during pregnancy, only to experience a serious estrangement from her husband after the baby is born—once she has the penis (baby) she no longer has any use for the man. This is a pattern seen unfortunately too often.

Childhood fantasies about birth also come into play. The little girl who is kept ignorant of the facts of life may fantasize oral impregnation and birth through the anus; she also may have great difficulty separating the anus from the vagina in her mind, so that the vagina always remains a "dirty smelly hole" for her. Sex may become distasteful or repulsive. The whole 9 months of pregnancy may become a period of torture for her.

Perhaps most crucial is the girl's identification with her mother during the course of her life. If this is positive, then pregnancy and childbirth are experienced as wonderful events; if it is negative, the girl will foresee the same kinds of battles between herself and her child that she went through with her mother in the course of growing up. On top of this, the mother in our social structure has been the main authority figure who forbade pregnancy until it was socially acceptable; this inevitably arouses a certain amount of antagonism in the young woman. Suddenly this antagonism has to be transformed into a total transformation of the self-image; obviously the psychological changes justify calling this a period of crisis.

Physiological factors naturally play a role as well. Evidently animals have a much easier time getting and remaining pregnant than humans. The myth that women in primitive cultures simply drop the baby in the field and then continue their work is just that—a myth. In all cultures, the birth process is a traumatic one, with unknown dangers and occasional deaths. Accordingly, abortion is a prominent consideration for all women (Devereux, 1954). Devereux has collected both the anthropological data and the psychoanalytically available fantasies and concludes:

Were anthropologists to draw up a complete list of all known types of cultural behavior, this list would overlap, point by point, with a similarly complete list of impulses, wishes, fantasies, etc. obtained by psychoanalysis in a clinical setting, thus demonstrating by identical means and simultaneously, the psychic unity of mankind. . . . [pp. vii–viii]

Thus, all told, while motherhood is of course a biological phenomenon, the social, psychological, and physiological aspects of pregnancy weigh so heavily that the woman is bound to develop a highly ambivalent feeling about her child. Her body goes through extraordinary changes, her relationship to her husband is transformed, her self-image is revolutionized.

On top of that, the exceedingly high infant mortality that prevailed throughout most of human history also impresses itself on the pregnant woman. For example, in the United States infant mortality had fallen from about 100 per 1000 live births around 1915 to about 20 per 1000 live births in 1965 (Erhardt & Berlin, 1974, p. 209). By contrast, in the seventeenth century between a quarter and a third of all children in England were dead before they were 15. The natural reaction to such a high percentage of death is to restrain one's emotions (Stone, 1979, pp. 56–57).

It is not surprising then that the ideal of a happy marriage, in which the child is given full care and attention, should not really have taken root until comparatively recently. Even Freud had only an imperfect understanding of the role of good mothering (and parenting in general) for the emotional well-being of the individual. Modern information about the first year of life began to accumulate largely in the 1940s, after Freud had died. In the first book that stated the current position clearly, Margaret Ribble's *The Rights of Infants* (1943), she wrote:

It is difficult to draw a clear line between the infant's physical and psychological needs, for the very act of making him more comfortable physically, if done by a kindly hand, may at the same time stimulate his sense of aliveness and his consciousness of personal contacts. Certainly we know now that the capacity for mature emotional relationships in adult life is a direct outgrowth of the parental care, more specifically the mothering, which an infant receives. . . . Social impulses are part of our primary equipment; emotional hunger is an urge as definite and compelling as the need for food. When we deny an infant fulfillment of these needs, we stifle his emotional and social life. [p. 13]

It was Ribble who introduced the term "tender loving care," which has been the guideline for all child care ever since. In the ensuing years, the research findings of which will be summarized here, her position has been amply confirmed. Briefly, the capacity to love comes from being loved in a happy family.

MOTHERHOOD

Loving involves a simple feeling of affection as well as attention to the child's needs. Unlike animals such as the giraffe, which is ready to walk 15 minutes after birth, humans go through a long period of helplessness before they can act independently. In the years since Ribble's book so much information has accumulated about the child's innate developmental processes that the practice of psychology has taken on an entirely new dimension. Ideally it should be geared to parent effectiveness training or education, rather than therapy, but in a hate culture such as ours most parents still resent any intrusion into the privacy of their homes ("mother knows best").

Considerable attention has been devoted to the question of whether there is such a thing as a maternal instinct at all. In part this question has been stimulated by the natural wish of women to escape from the drudgery of bearing many children, a considerable percentage of whom died young in the not too-distant past; in part it has resulted from the psychological observations of the terrible cruelty that parents can display toward their children and not infrequently do display.

The most recent and publicized discussion of this topic is the book by the French philosopher Elisabeth Badinter, *Mother Love: Myth and Reality* (1981). Her argument is that the maternal instinct is a myth because no universal and absolute conduct on the part of the mother has emerged.

> *How then can one avoid concluding, even if it seems cruel, that mother love is only a feeling and, as such, essentially conditional, contingent on many different factors? Mother love cannot be taken for granted. When it exists, it is an additional advantage, an extra something thrown into the bargain struck by the lucky ones among us.* [p. 327]

At the same time she concludes that "an indomitable determination among women to share the universe and children with men has been born. And the will of these women will doubtlessly change the future of humankind (p. 330).

Similar arguments have been put forth by others, especially among the present feminists. But they rest on a misunderstanding of the meaning of instinct. Biologists today prefer to talk of genetic endowment rather than instinct (Mayr, 1982). For a clarification of instinct we have to turn to the ethologists, who have shown that the concept of *innate releasing mechanisms* (IRM—Lorenz & Tinbergen) makes more sense than the older term *instinct*. These IRMs are certainly present in women, just as they are in mammals of all species. How they will be expressed, however, is a function of the culture in which the person lives (Dobzhansky, 1973).

Badinter quotes a statement of Lt. Lenoir of the Paris police in 1780 that of the 21,000 babies born in Paris each year only 1000 were being breast-fed by their mothers. Another 1000 newborns, the children of the wealthy, were breast-fed by live-in wet nurses, while the rest were taken from their mothers and sent to wet nurses outside Paris. The mortality among infants sent to wet nurses outside Paris was distressingly high, as has always been the case when infants were sent away to wet nurses. In 1612 Jacques Guillimeau described how the child at nurse might be "stifled, overlaid, be let fall, and so come to an untimely death; or else may be devoured, spoiled, or disfigured by some wild beast, wolf or dog, and then the nurse fearing to be punished for her negligence, may take another child into the place of it" (cited in de Mause, 1974, p. 35). Yet sending the child out continued in England and America until the eighteenth century, until the nineteenth century in France, and until the twentieth in Germany.

Thus what Badinter is referring to is part of a wider picture of maternal hostility toward children, which includes actual infanticide, beating, neglect, and many other forms of abuse, besides sending the infant away for several years to be wet-nursed by a stranger (de Mause, 1974). This is simply one aspect of the hate culture, to which we have been making reference all along. But it would be a mistake to isolate this maternal hostility from the other forms of hatred that were prevalent throughout the ages. Mothers hated children, children hated mothers, men hated women, women hated men, while each generation in one form or another repeated the hatreds with which they had been brought up. It is only in modern times that we have become aware of this enormous weight of hatred that is found in the world and some have been encouraged to do what they could to alleviate it.

Objectively, what is seen most often on the part of the mother is a sharp ambivalence toward the child, which is understandable in the light of her previous life experiences and the various cruelties to which the girl in her upbringing is exposed. Roheim, in his (1932) field work among Australian tribes (the Aranda and the Lutjari), found that women would abort in order to feed the fetus to their starving children, while small children were also killed in order to feed them to their older siblings (Devereux, 1955, p. 19). On the other hand, the next child would be treated with extraordinary warmth and attention. What Roheim found was the extreme of ambivalence; the mothers seemed to view the infants as part of themselves, thus feeling free to do with them as they pleased.

A similar ambivalence is found in the analysis of any mother. In this sense Badinter is right in believing that pure mother love is a myth, but that does not contradict the proposition that the woman is endowed genetically with the capacity to love her offspring. Nor does it contradict the obvious observation that there are loving mothers and hateful mothers, and all kinds of mixtures in between. The reason that the discovery of maternal destructiveness (Rheingold, 1964) comes as such a shock is that the child is taught to deny this hostility all its life, or to rationalize it in some way ("spare the rod and spoil the child"). Until the advent of modern psychology it was almost universally denied that parents could have anything to do with the emotional disturbances seen in their children; "bad" children were just "bad" seeds and had to be beaten brutally to have the "badness" knocked out of them. Such an attitude is characteristic of a hate culture.

Another important caveat that has been raised against psychoanalytic theory is that childhood is not "all that important." Good children will come through no matter what you do; bad children will fall by the wayside. There is by now almost universal agreement that the earliest experiences are of great importance for the future of the individual, though it is sometimes possible for favorable events later in life to undo harm inflicted early.

While exact proof is of course not available, there is ample evidence that poor mothering in infancy (the first year of life) will result in abnormalities ranging from serious neurotic or psychotic disturbances to outright death. Further, there is considerable reason to believe that the incidence of inadequate mothering is extremely high. Statistics vary with the investigator (cf. Dohrenwend & Dohrenwend, 1980). But more broadly and more correctly Judge David Bazelon, a member of the congressionally appointed Joint Commission on the Mental Health of Children (1970), noted that although this nation is aware of the problem, it does not support funds to treat and care for these children because it has really given up on them. The Joint Commission titled its report *Crisis in Child Mental Health*. We need not belabor the point that inadequate and cruel treatment of children is the way in which the hate culture perpetuates itself.

When Margaret Ribble wrote her book *The Rights of Infants* it seemed easy enough to describe what poor mothering is. The child was seen as having an innate physiological growth pattern, and it was the parents' job to see that this pattern was allowed to develop in proper sequence. Failure to do so made the woman a poor mother. Further, the needs of the child were conceptualized in a rather simplistic way: food, shelter, warmth, love, and so on. In this sense love consisted of giving the child what he or she needed, with no regard for the parental personality.

This picture has changed in a number of important ways. First of all, much more information has accumulated about the development of children, and it is now realized that they play a highly active role in their own development. Mother and child interacting is the major key, not merely an active mother taking care of a passive child. Second, the personality of the mother plays a significant role; again researchers are studying the interaction between mother (later father and others) and child, not merely the unfolding of innate capacities in the child. And finally cross-cultural studies have shown that the pressures and cooperation offered by the wider society likewise affect the individual family. "No man is to himself an island entire," as John Donne put it, and no family is either. Thus there is not only interaction between mother and child but also the wider interaction between the family and the broader culture.

In particular, the older concept of primary autism or primary narcissism in the first 2 months of life has had to be abandoned. It has been shown (Chiland, 1982) that imitation begins during the infant's first week of life. If the mother, or another adult, sticks out her tongue, the child begins to stick out his or her tongue. If the mother stops sticking out her tongue and bats her eyelashes, the baby bats his or her eyelashes. If she opens or closes her mouth the baby does the same thing. Moreover the baby synchronizes its movements with her and seeks to take pleasure in these games of reciprocal imitation (Chiland, p. 373).

Other findings likewise attest to the activity of the neonate from birth onward (and before birth too in certain respects). As early as the age of 12 hours, newborn babies who hear recordings of spoken English, isolated vocal sounds, regular beating noises, and spoken Chinese do not react to isolated vocal sounds or to beating noises but move themselves synchronically with the structure of English and Chinese speech coming from a recording or from a living person. At birth babies turn their heads toward a clicking sound, especially one coming from a human voice. They are sensitive to the smell of colostrum and as early as the end of the first week of life (day 6) they distinguish between a compress that has been in contact with their mother's breast and one that has been in contact with the breast of another nursing woman (MacFarlane, 1975). At the age of 2 weeks, babies recognize the face of the mother: They look at it more than at the face of a stranger through a kind of window placed above the crib. When the voice of the mother or of a stranger is produced by a loudspeaker, babies have a "gaze aversion" and turn away their heads if voice and face do not match (Carpenter, 1975). The list of novel discoveries about the so-called "narcissistic" period is endless; the reader is referred to the literature for more details (Stratton, 1982; Lichtenberg, 1983).

If the infant is not a tabula rasa, parenting becomes more difficult. Prematures and minimally brain-damaged infants seem to be less able to compensate in disorganized, depriving environments than do well-equipped neonates, creating additional burdens for the parents. Quiet, nondemanding infants do not elicit necessary mothering from already overstressed parents and are selected by their neonatal behavior for kwashiorkor and marasmus in poverty-ridden cultures such as are found in Guatemala and Mexico (Brazelton, 1980). Hyperkinetic, hypersensitive neonates may press a mother and father into a kind of desperation and produce child-rearing responses from them that reinforce the problems of the children so that they grow up in an overreactive, hostile environment. Most often, parents are unconsciously aware of mild disorganization and in their efforts to compensate they either press such children or overprotect them. In either case the message to them is that they are inadequate and unable to compete in the society around them. This in turn reacts upon the parents, and a vicious cycle is set up.

Brazelton (1979) describes four clear stages of development in the interactive model:

1. The infant achieves homeostatic control over input and output systems.

2. Within this controlled system he or she can begin to attend to and use the social cues to prolong his or her status of attention to accept and incorporate more complex trains of messages.

3. Within such an entrained or mutual reciprocal feedback system he or she and the parent begin to press the limits of his or her capacity to take in and respond to information and to withdraw

to recover in a homeostatic system. The mother–infant "games" described by Stern (1974) are elegant examples of the real value of this phase as a system for affective and cognitive experience at 3 and 4 months.

4. (This phase is perhaps the real test of attachment.) Within the dyad or triad the baby is allowed to demonstrate and incorporate a sense of his or her own autonomy. This goal of competence harks back to the first stage and completes at a more complex level of awareness the full circle of feedback to self-competence in dealing with inner and outer feedback systems.

The net result of this concept of enormously increased complexity in the first few months is that just as the image of the autistic phase has to go by the board, the image of the "ordinary devoted mother" who used to fill the pages of the analytic journals a generation ago also goes by the board. Instead we now see introduced the notion of a mother–child attunement (Beebe & Sloate, 1928).

However, the ordinary mother is not the ideal pictured in child psychology textbooks. She is a human being with her own needs, desires, complexes, and neurotic conflicts. As we saw before, she begins with an ambivalent attitude to the child of varying degrees. Post partum depression ("afterbirth blues") is an almost universal phenomenon. Hence, she will react by paying attention to some of the child's needs, ignoring others, and even punishing ones she doesn't like.

As the Papouseks (1982) point out, the biological roots of human parental behavior have remained almost a terra incognita. The old cliche of a maternal instinct has long since been discarded. Studies of animals, for instance, have elucidated the alternating roles of endocrine and psychological factors in the regulation of maternal behavior in rats (Rosenblatt, 1975). Even the notion that only females have the capacity to take care of the young has to be questioned (Ridley, 1978). Animal male parents share parenting in manifold ways and different proportions, including complete role reversal. For example, in the *Jacanidae*, a female defends a harem of males, the male emu incubating the eggs of one or several females and caring alone for the young. Among the *osteoglossidae* (fish), the male mouthbroods the eggs. The variety of behaviors such as nest building, territory defending, brooding, prosocial care for the progeny, and so on is rich. Just as we are beginning to investigate the role of the human father in more detail, the role of the animal father is coming under increased scrutiny.

There are innumerable investigations of mothers in the literature, and various "normal" and "neurotic" types have been described. Perhaps best known is the work by Sylvia Brody (*Patterns of Mothering*, 1956). Based on a sample of 29 mothers in a midwestern setting, she enumerated four types: (1) those conspicuous for their ability to accommodate to the needs of their infants; (2) those conspicuous for their conscious willingness to accommodate to their infants; (3) those conspicuous for their lack of spontaneity and their intentions to be efficient above all else; and (4) those conspicuously active but also erratic in their attentiveness, efficiency, and sensitivity. But as she herself points out, her typology, which demonstrates a surprising diversity of behavior in a very small sample, is based on only one kind of behavior: feeding. Important though that is, investigation of other types of behavior could conceivably (as she notes) lead to entirely different results. Further, mothers competent in one area could easily be incompetent in another, as common observation shows.

Judith Kestenberg (1975) described the following kinds of mothers commonly encountered in guidance clinics: (1) openly aggressive; (2) anxious; (3) genuinely anxious; (4) distant. Frieda Fromm-Reichman popularized Sullivan's concept of the schizophrenogenic mother, which in itself has given rise to a considerable literature. Still others have offered other classifications. That there is no consistent and universally acceptable classification is the most important observation to be made here. Even among animals all of whom look alike to the human, careful scrutiny will reveal that they are all different (Moss, 1982). Babies are so different, mothers so varied, that only a typology of mother–child interaction would make sense in the present state of our knowledge. But such a typology is as yet not to be found.

In all animals, human as well, the newborn infant is at the most vulnerable time of life. With humans, the worst types of destructiveness become visible only later on, since if practiced early, the infant will simply die. Nevertheless, it is worth noting that up to recently in most cultures, a large percentage of infants did die. Many died from natural causes, because medicine could not cope with the common illnesses. But many others died because of maternal anger, which manifested itself in infanticide, total neglect, shifting the baby to wet-nurses, and the like (de Mause, 1974).

Ours is a culture in which infant mortality is comparatively low (though much higher among the lower socioeconomic classes). The anger of the mother (and of the father) tends to become observable only as the child gets older. Put simply, the demands of the child are more than many mothers can bear.

Our topic is love. What does all this tell us about maternal love? It is not an instinct in the old sense; rather, it provides the woman with an opportunity to have a warm, loving relationship with another human being. This, to begin with, involves a friendly feeling toward the infant. But it also involves an awareness of the infant's needs; Brody described the best mothers as those who had the ability to adapt to their infants' needs, as distinguished from other mothers who merely accommodated to their needs. This ability, it must now be recognized, requires a fairly healthy psyche of one's own, and the willingness to learn what the child really needs. For example, studies have shown that when mothers and infants spend time gazing into one another's eyes, it is beneficial to the infant. Is it not also beneficial to the mother?

Thus appears a third aspect of love, the capacity to enjoy the other person. Put aphoristically, a good mother is a woman who enjoys her child. If the child is sick, she will tend to it devotedly, but if the child is well, she will also take pleasure in it (with the "mothering games," e.g.). A healthy interaction in all states is the basic desideratum.

What of the father in all this? There are many women who are seemingly devoted mothers but at the cost of excluding the man. Traditionally, in fact, this has been the rule rather than the exception, and in the population at large it is still probably the rule: Women take care of the children, men work. To many women, whose sexual difficulties or other conflicts with men are too severe, a child will be a golden opportunity. With these women the problems appear only when the child is ready to move on to a new stage in which the mother will be less important, such as school, or later on, adolescent dating. ["Mothers have to be there to be left" (Furman, 1982).]

In seeking to clarify what we mean by a loving mother, then, the total family situation cannot be ruled out, as has been the case so often in the past. For instance, recently there has been a flurry of excitement about the suggestion of the French obstetrician Leboyer that right after birth the infant should be put on the mother's stomach and allowed to rest there for a while. This is known as "extra contact," abbreviated E.C. This suggestion has been tried, and by now a number of studies have appeared about E.C. babies. In general, they seem to thrive and do well, better than babies who do not have the E.C. But it seems likely that they do well because of their parents' love for them, not because of the E.C. Svejda, Pannabeccker, and Emde (1982) question the generality of the effect and recommend that the bonding model be discontinued as a misleading metaphor.

Thus the heart of maternal love would appear to be in reciprocity.

Brazelton and his colleagues (1974) found that the interdependency of rhythms seemed to be at the root of attachment as well as communication. They were studying seemingly "normal" infants. When the balance was sympathetic to the needs of each member of the dyad, there was a sense of rhythmic interaction that an observer assessed as positive. When the balance was not equalized, and one member was out of phase with the other, there seemed to be a "negative" quality in the entire interaction. At the periods of new acquisition (e.g., at 8 and 12 weeks), when the infant was out of phase, the mother reflected the stress she felt in not being able to communicate. As she readjusted or waited for the infant's readjustment, subsequent weeks reflected the reestablishment of a kind of synchrony between them. Each new thrust of activity in the growing infant requires a new period of interactional adjustment with the caretaking environment to reach stable coordination on the basis of new changes. And this remains one of the essential ingredients of love throughout life.

Summary: Comments on Mother Love

The research, especially in the past 25 years, now permits a more careful definition of mother love, which then forms the basis for love attractions throughout the rest of life. Its main ingredients are:

1. A friendly feeling.
2. Mutual reciprocity between mother and infant. Mother and child seem to be "in synchrony," particularly with regard to the infant's biological rhythms.
3. Adequate physical contact.
4. The ability to accommodate to the other person's needs. This is obviously, at this stage of the development, more true of the mother than of the infant. The loving infant, however, does have a growing capacity to accommodate to what the mother wants.
5. Mutual enjoyment.
6. A loving family in a loving culture. That is, the mother–infant love must be evaluated in the light of the surrounding culture, including the mother's relationship to father, to other siblings, and to the surrounding culture.

The degree of longing with which love is often confused depends on many different factors. The devotion of a 40-year-old primipara to her newborn infant is often extraordinarily intense, but that does not show that she is more loving, merely that she has been more deprived. Contrariwise the seeming indifference of an 18-year-old mother of two may reflect the young mother's grasp of the situation as well as her feeling that she is in good control.

All of these factors can be seen to be operative in animals as well. What is lacking there is the degree of flexibility, together with the psychological elaboration of the situation, which is so characteristic of humans.

In the subsequent discussion this ideal interaction between mother and child will be followed in the course of its normal and pathological development. It is already possible, on this basis, to describe a developmental line for love, similar to other developmental lines (cf. Anna Freud, 1965). From this theoretical position it is already clear that ideally the individual can move from one love relationship to another throughout the course of life.

THE TODDLER: 1 TO 3 YEARS

After the mother, the next important person in the child's life is the father. In part this is due to the diminishing need of the child for the mother, in part to the fact that stimulating human beings are the most important prerequisite for the optimal emotional and cognitive growth of the child. Because of the conventional family structure and attitudes, in which the father goes out to work while the mother stays home and takes care of the children, this obvious fact has been overlooked.

Herzog (1982), summarizing findings on children brought up without fathers, especially because of divorce, found that a striking feature of these children's productions at all developmental stages is the predominance of aggressive themes and content. A second striking feature is the predominance of aggressive motives in boys thus bereft between the ages of 18 and 60 months. Later on (between 60 and 84 months of age) little girls begin to be represented in equal numbers. These observations led him to the hypothesis that a specific role is played by the male parent in the modulation of aggressive-drive fantasy in the young child, and that the father's absence at this time may have specific and long-range consequences. A second hypothesis is that little boys are more vulnerable or at least feel more vulnerable to disruptions in the control of aggressive drives and fantasy than are their female counterparts, at least until the age of 5 years. Little boys therefore suffer more when family disruption leads to father loss.

Finally Herzog introduces the concept of "father hunger," a valuable idea. While he tries to tie up father hunger with the aggressive drives, it is obviously connected with the adequate development of the sexual drives as well.

In the previous section it was argued that Mahler's conceptualization of primary autism has to be given up in the light of more recent research. The first year of life should be viewed as a period when a love relationship with the mother is established.

For the second period, that of the toddler, Mahler's (1975) main novel contribution is that of the rapprochement crisis. Here the child moves back and forth between mother and the outside world until self- and object-constancy are established. This too seems to be an erroneous oversimplification. What the child does is move from mother to father, and the primary task of the toddler period is the establishment and consolidation of a second love relationship, that with father. The other developmental aspects of this period are subordinate to the father hunger.

As with the mother, the awareness of the father's role has led to renewed investigation and novel discoveries among monkeys and apes. In a summary of the more recent literature, Redican and Taub (1981) state that the range of behaviors toward immature conspecifics by nonhuman primate males is impressive. They have been observed to assist during the births of neonates; to premasticate food for infants; to carry, sleep with, groom, and especially play with young; to defend young virtually without exception; to provide a refuge during periods of high emotional arousal; to interact with young in a quasi-didactic fashion; to promote motor development; to interrupt potentially destructive agonistic interactions among young; and to use infants in triadic interaction with other males. They may ultimately contribute to the infant's welfare less directly by defending a territory, the troop, or the mother from predators or conspecifics, and their frequent role as troop leaders may enhance the likelihood of infant survival in the long run. At the opposite extreme they may also threaten, attack, kill, and eat infants, but the more severe of these behaviors have been relatively rare; moreover we do not know how often such destructive behavior also occurs in females.

Careful observation of fathers and children among the monkeys has led to extraordinary revelations. For example, Burton, in his study of the Barbary macaques, noted the following sequence, which he called "extraordinary":

*On four occasions . . . the lead male was the initiator of the infant's
beginning to walk: he placed the animal on the ground, moving back-
ward away from it to a distance of approximately two feet, lowering his
head, looking at the infant and chattering to it. The infant would return the chatter and make crawling motions toward him. . . . As the
infant approached within six inches to a foot, and if no other animal
except the mother was nearby, the head male would again move away
and repeat the chatter. If other animals began to close in, he would pick
up the infant and move away from the crowd, making a mild gesture to
them.* [1982, p. 35]

There is however one momentous psychological difference between
the human and the monkey: the capacity for introjection. It is here that
the significance of early experience is even more fateful for the human
than for the animal, since the human child introjects his or her early
experiences and gradually becomes increasingly sensitive to the intro-
jected version of reality, eventually in many cases stereotypically responding to the introject rather than to the reality. This becomes the essence
of neurosis and psychosis.

If the first-year experience of mother and child is a good one, then the
infant introjects a good mother. (In the literature Freud's term *object*
has been widely used, and a school of "object relations" has grown up,
but this obscures the fact that the object grows from the realistic actions
of the mother.) The question about when this introjection takes place
fully cannot as yet be answered with precision. Brody and Axelrad estimated that the introjection begins at about 3 months (1970); Schafer
(1968), without mentioning any date, speaks of the "fates of the immortal object." Melanie Klein (1952) virtually assumed that the introjection occurs at birth; Rosalind Gould (1972) found that superego formation could occur at any time between 2 and 6 years; Piaget (1973), drawing parallels between the affective and the cognitive unconscious, saw
the capacity to establish a cognitive and by implication an affective object beginning at around 18 months. While the exact date at which introjection begins is thus open to question, there is no question that it
begins early, increases throughout childhood, and eventually becomes
an "immortal object" that stays with the individual throughout the rest
of life. The psychoanalytic hypothesis is that if the early introjection is
a good one, variously referred to as the "good breast," the "good
mother," or "basic trust," then the individual's road throughout life will
be much smoother. We are extending this hypothesis to assume that all
the introjects (mother, father, siblings, teachers, etc.) must have essentially a loving quality, and that when this occurs, the individual becomes

a loving person. (Brenner in his latest work *Mind in Conflict*, 1983, seems to take a similar position, though he fails to discuss the problem of love and does not specifically tie up the loss of love with the introjection of father and mother.)

It is the introjection of an unloving parent that makes interpersonal loss (object loss) in childhood such a tragedy. Lynch (1977) and Parkes (1972), as well as many others, have stressed the disastrous effects of bereavement at any age. This can be best understood for the growing child as a loss of a person with whom to develop the capacity for love. In infancy such a loss is so severe that the infant may well die (Bowlby, 1969). Later it leads to ego defects of varying degrees of severity (Jones, 1929) so that as Ernest Jones once put it, all emotional disturbance is one variant or another of schizophrenia.

In the process of establishing a love relationship with the father and a good introject of him, the child must undergo many other developmental changes in this period. There is first and foremost the capacity to leave mother for another person, which the mother may facilitate, be neutral to, or interfere with, depending on her own personality dynamics. Similarly the father may accept, be neutral to, or reject the child at this age. A little later the conflicting loyalties to the two parents (the Oedipus complex) come to the fore.

In addition, many biologically determined growth changes take place. There is a change in feeding habits, with ever more complex foods being introduced after the breast or bottle has been given up (notoriously many infants are reluctant to give up the easier mode of feeding). There is the need for toilet training, usually the first strong disciplinary demand made on the child. Under the impact of Freudian psychology, the time of toilet training has in the present generation frequently been extended to somewhere between the ages of 2 and 3, thereby avoiding many of the severe inhibitions that arose from excessively early toilet training, and the whole complex of the anal personality structure, which preoccupied Freud and his colleagues so much.

While toilet training can be handled simply enough by postponing its time of onset, a much more difficult problem arises with sexuality, which interferes with the love relationship throughout childhood, and adulthood as well. The research by Galenson and Roiphe (Galenson, 1980) based on a careful investigation of 35 boys and 35 girls has now definitely established that genital awareness begins for both sexes between 15 and 19 months. In this study the boys took the discovery of the penis in stride, only two of the 35 boys showing any sign of psychological disturbance related to their discovery of the penis. By contrast, all 35 girls showed some degree of disturbance. The eight girls who suffered severe disturbance had all experienced an important threat during the first year, either in relation to their body image or in the attachment to the mother. Thus here the conflict in the first love relationship with the mother directly affects the second love relationship with the father.

In most of the girls a new type of attachment appeared to develop in relation to the father. An erotically tinged and much more intense reaction, dyadic, not triadic, as in the later oedipal relationship, was seen in most of the girls whose development was proceeding well. According to Galenson, in those girls who had undergone an unusually severe early pre-oedipal castration reaction, the erotic shift to the father did not occur. Instead, their hostile ambivalence to the mother became even more marked and was eventually replaced by an intense clinging to the mother along with an increase of the previously abated fear of strangers. This development seems to reflect a split in the underlying mental representation, so that the "good" mother image is retained while the "bad" mother is projected onto strangers. The shift of erotic attachment to the father did not take place in this group of girls. Galenson's work, as well as that of many others, confirms the image of the development of the love relationship that is being outlined in this chapter.

Other physiological changes are important, though less so than the sexual. There is a growth in motility, in communication, and in general in the cognitive and emotional spheres. In all of these, development proceeds most effectively for the child when there is a warm, loving relationship with both parents (Brody & Axelrad, 1978).

In transposing the ideal maternal love relationship to that of the father, a number of changes can be noted, though the overall outline remains unchanged. Physical contact tends to diminish, but the child still needs a considerable amount. The child now develops some ability to accommodate to the needs of the father (and the mother as well), much greater than existed before. In general, social forces begin to interfere more with the family structure, although this interference may not amount to much at this time.

Above all by the age of 3, the child ideally has acquired a feeling of outgoing love toward both parents and the ability to verbalize such feelings. This goes together with a high degree of self-esteem and a considerable tolerance for frustration. The child needs guidance and discipline (Sandler, 1962). He or she tolerates the guidance well out of love for the parents; as Ekstein and Motto (1969) put it, it moves from learning for love to love of learning. Discipline likewise is tolerated, though there is no reason why it should be severe; spanking and child abuse are always serious symptoms of family pathology.

Any disturbance in the ideal scheme leads to an impairment of the love relationship, which should be the primary consideration. The literature has dealt so copiously with these problems that no more need be said here. Instead, what we are suggesting is that these conflicts should be viewed primarily in terms of the development of the love experience, rather than in terms of irrepressible drives, or a faulty self-image (the consequence, not the cause), or genetic factors.

It is in this stage too that the early origins of the division into the adjustment neurosis and the maladjustment neurosis become visible. When the child obeys the commands of the parents mechanically, instead of forming a love relationship, then it seems to be growing up properly but in reality is displaying the preliminary stages of an adjustment neurosis—outer conformity with inner turmoil. More severe disturbances, such as infantile autism, failure to toilet train, inability to sleep, and the like presage a maladjustment neurosis. Bleuler (1978), for example, reports that in *all* his schizophrenic patients the childhood could be characterized only as *horrible*.

THE OEDIPAL PERIOD: 3 TO 6 YEARS

In the oedipal period love takes on a number of new dimensions. First and foremost is the child's awareness that the parents love one another. This is not a new love experience as such for the child; rather it is an aspect of his or her psychological growth that he or she can recognize the capacity of two adults to give love to one another.

On the other hand the incestuous wish that matures at this stage is an extraordinarily powerful emotion. It belongs to those aspects of the mental life that have been called unrememberable and unforgettable. For all human societies live in families, of greater or lesser degree of complexity, and in all these families there are incest taboos, often so stringent that their violation is punishable by death. With rare exceptions as well the incest taboo is universally acknowledged and obeyed.

The incestuous wish leads to one of the essential conflicts in human life. It cannot be repressed and it cannot be gratified. Accordingly, it becomes a powerful inner dynamic that colors the entire love life of the child (and of course later on the adult). The child must do something with it, so he or she tries to repress, or deny, or sublimate, or project, or use some other defense mechanism. Much of the time, if not always under permissive circumstances, the child acts out part of the wish. For instance, the boy will show his penis to mother, or will embrace her, or try to fondle her, or get into bed with her. The girl will display herself to father, or get into bed with him, or go after his penis. Innumerable other variations are found. If the incest taboo is too tightly repressed, a severe malformation of the personality may easily occur. On the other hand, if it is gratified, as happens on rare occasions, the person is infantilized.

The incest wish, even under the best of circumstances, represents the first time in the child's life that there is a direct block of the physical enjoyment that is an essential part of love. Since the child's capacity for control is not yet great, this block can become a severe problem.

However, while sexual intercourse is forbidden, other forms of gratification are not. The mother may fondle the boy, wash him, even play with his penis. (Among the Mangaians, described in Chapter 1, sucking of the little boy's penis by adult women is permitted.) The trouble is that the child does not know how to draw the line; if gratified, he or she wants more, if frustrated, he or she is deeply hurt.

The nuclear family is universal. In a survey of 250 cultures, not a single exception was found (Murdock, 1949). It was either the prevailing form of the family or the basic unit from which more complex familial forms were compounded. Since the incest taboo is also universal, we are dealing here with a fundamental aspect of human nature.

Examples of the incest taboo have also been found among monkeys. Van Lawick-Goodall (1971) reported that in her observations of chimpanzees in their natural habitat she had never observed any sexual intercourse between mother and son. In addition, although the young chimpanzees would "play copulate" with other chimpanzees while growing up together, as soon as the females began to ovulate they would leave the group in which they had been raised and join strange groups so that they bred with unrelated males. Terrace (1979) notes in his study of Nim that once when his keeper and her husband were in bed together with Nim in the middle, when they began to stroke one another, Nim (then about 6 months old) got up and bit the husband on the arm.

The origin of the incest taboo remains an unresolved problem, although there are many speculative theories. Mayr (1970) states that in animal and plant species severe inbreeding leads to "inbreeding depression" manifested by loss of fertility, increased susceptibility to disease, growth anomalies, and metabolic disturbances. "Countless laboratory stocks have been lost owing to inbreeding" (Mayr, 1982, p. 190).

Although the oedipal conflict is so severe in our society that Freud believed that every middle-class child (today we would say every child) goes through a neurosis in this period, its severity still requires some explanation. In healthy families (cf. Lewis, 1977) the problem is as a rule less traumatic.

My own belief, based on analytic experience and reports from the literature, is that the intensity of the oedipal conflict is a reflection of the degree of hostility between mother and father. In a world where 4 out of 10 marriages end in divorce it should not be surprising that there are many more unhappy marriages than happy ones. In such marriages it is only natural that each parent should want the child to take that parent's side. Thus the child comes to favor one parent or the other regardless of the biological impetus. More or less directly, he or she then acts out the hostility of the favored parent toward the partner.

In their extensive investigation of the relationship between adequate parenting and the capacity to learn, Brody and Axelrad (1978), concentrating mainly on the mother but including a number of fathers as well, found a positive correlation between maternal warmth (and paternal warmth) and learning capacity, except for the oedipal period, when the conflicts were so intense that they overshalowed everything else. Still, children from happy families were able to overcome these conflicts. What they emphasize in the disturbed family groups is mainly the parental inability to react to the child's needs adequately. They say:

> *Were we to single out a cardinal contribution to unfavorable development in the child we should with knowing simplification, name neglect. We mean neglect, intentional or not, that appears in seemingly benign forms: in* ignorance—*in an inability to recognize uneasiness, distress, or age-inappropriate behavior in the child; in* intolerance—*in overhasty judgments of the child's motives, leading to erratic or excessive expectations of behavior which are incongruent with the child's capacities; in* disinterest—*in a reluctance to respond or to act on behalf of the child's emotional states, curiosities and other age-adequate needs; in* excessive indulgence—*in a failure to nourish the child's capacity for delay or for frustration tolerance; and in* carelessness—*in a failure to protect the child from excessive stimulations, gratifications and deprivations, from aggressive acts or libidinal seductions, physical or psychic, or from threats of such experiences. [p. 553]*

In terms of the major thesis of this book, the frustration of the oedipal conflict should be seen as a blockage of the child's capacity to love. For it is at this age that the child is really able for the first time to experience emotions of deep love for the parents, who then thwart the child's feelings because of their own conflicts, which manifest themselves under relatively good circumstances as neglect, ignorance, intolerance, disinterest, excessive indulgence, and carelessness. That is, at this point, the various aspects of the love relationship delineated earlier become too difficult to grasp and to carry out—mutual reciprocity, mutual enjoyment, ability to accommodate to the other's needs, and so on. It is also at this age that society intervenes more strongly than before in regulations concerning school attendance, peer contacts, sex play (almost all children experiment with some sex play at around 5 or 6), and other activities that are so attractive to the child. It is not surprising that Freud found the Oedipus complex to be a major root of all neurosis, and even though this root has been pushed back to earliest infancy, the oedipal conflicts remain the most powerful obstacles to growth that the child has as yet encountered.

Throughout this period the child's capacity to love is severely tested. And essentially the same formula holds: The child learns to love by being loved. When this is not the case, which is more the rule than the exception, he learns to hate or to resort to various compromise formations. Again it is in this way that the hate culture continues to perpetuate itself.

LATENCY: 6 YEARS TO PUBERTY

The latency period, which extends roughly from 6 years to puberty, is marked by further challenges to the child's capacity to love. There is first of all the expansion into the outside world, which means that no matter how loving the family of origin may be, the child is now moving out into the hate culture directly. Second there is the importance of peer relationships, which played only a minor role before age 6. And finally there is the whole world of extrafamilial influences, which may influence him or her for good or for evil.

Intrapsychically the great event of the postoedipal period is the formation of a superego, which is really the internalization of the parents. This consolidates previous introjects into one major internal mechanism. It is now the superego that dominates the child's life, regulating his or her self-esteem and sense of worth in much the same manner as the parents did before. Clearly, if the previous stages had resulted in the crystallization of a capacity to love, the superego would be a benign and loving internalization, stimulating the child positively in its search for growth and valuable new experiences in the outside world. Sometimes this is the case in our culture; more often it is not. For if the previous stages result in various compromise formations, many of which are highly neurotic, the superego is alternatively harsh and loving, thereby creating considerable difficulties for the child in dealing with other people. For one characteristic of the superego is that it is projected to others, so that the child is not realistic about his or her assets and liabilities.

> *A boy on starting school was told by his fellow pupils that they were going to tease the girls by pulling their hair. He refused to participate, saying that he loved his mother and did not want to pull anyone's hair. He was ostracized by his group.*

This clinical vignette illustrates the problems facing the boy brought up in a loving family when he is confronted by the outside world. To conform to what the other boys want, he has to learn to hate girls; since he prefers love to hatred he cannot get along with them. It poses a real dilemma, to which there is no completely satisfactory solution (Fine, 1986).

At around the same time as the superego is formed or shortly thereafter children become involved in a love affair with a child of the opposite sex. Sometimes they engage in sex play, such as house or doctor games; sometimes they are just fond of one another. It is a true love experience many times, an overflow of the child's love for the parents. Usually, however, parents discourage the whole affair, making fun of their child, and unable to take it seriously. As a result it fades into oblivion. But it leaves a mark—another disappointment in love.

In general in our culture boys and girls begin to avoid one another in the latency period. It is "sissy" for the boy to play with girls; conversely the girl who plays with boys is a "tomboy." Hence there is a long period of avoidance before the sexual desires of puberty emerge and bring the two sexes back together again.

But there is one type of girl (or boy) that the child cannot discard entirely—the brother or sister. Yehudi Cohen (1966) has shown that in this stage, but especially from the age of 8 on, all cultures have had to adopt measures that keep the two sexes apart. Two devices are available: extrusion from the family and avoidance. Extrusion from the family was practiced in Great Britain for a long time by sending the boy away to public school—what Americans refer to as "private school." The net result was an excessively high incidence of homosexuality and general frustration. British schools were notorious for the enormous amount of aggression that they fostered—in the teachers, in the bullies who abounded in every school, in the younger boys who were bullied. Usually, as in Britain, it is the boy who is sent away. At best, however, this policy of extrusion tears the boy away prematurely from his family, thereby again making it more difficult for him to cultivate his capacity to love. Likewise the girl (as in the instances quoted above by Galenson) remains excessively attached to her mother, or her other sisters. Unable to form an attachment to a boy, she too easily becomes homosexual or frigid or both. It was in an atmosphere of this kind that Freud made his earliest discoveries, linking the peculiarities of the love life to the early frustrations.

In the latency period two vitally important changes affect the growth of love. First of all physical contact becomes excessively restricted. The child is at best preoccupied with the growth of the ego and the consolidation of the superego. Masturbation is forbidden; sexual fantasies are repressed. Hence the child often feels that he or she is not receiving much love: no love received, no capacity to love grows. Second, the wider culture enters in through the agency of the school especially, but also the church and the broadening contacts with the outside world. It is no accident that television programs center so heavily on crime and violence. This is what the boy sees in the world around him, and this is what he has to learn to handle. In the lower socioeconomic classes the transition to the outside occurs earlier than in the more affluent classes; Claude Brown (1965) reports that he was out on the street by 7, stealing and engaging in other petty crimes. At 13 he was shot during a holdup.

Because the growth process is so vital to the child, it is possible to push physical contact into the background for some time. But peer groups form fairly quickly and from about the age of 8 assume increasing importance in the life of the child. The age of secrecy has arrived; children will go through many experiences that they are unable to share with their parents, nor for that matter are most parents competent to grasp how these experiences fit into the emotional life of the child. In the traditional way of growing up (which in spite of all psychological teaching is still the dominant pattern in America—cf. *Middletown's Families*, Caplow et al., 1982), while the family remains the solid pivot of the individual's existence, the emotional distance between parent and child grows greater and greater as the child gets older. In the latency period this gulf widens considerably.

To adjust to the peer groups is essential but by no means easy. Group formation requires a change of identity into a new self that may appear undesirable to the parents in many ways. Yet if the new self is not formed, the child feels isolated, lonely, very often "queer," far away from his or her everyday world. The researchers on Middletown indicate that in this respect little has changed in 50 years: The word *love* is not even included in their index.

In the latency period group formation outside the family becomes a major goal of life, especially from about the age of 8. From then on, until the end of life, the individual will move from one group to another. These groups may be dominated by feelings of hatred, feelings of love, or, as is most usual, a mixture of the two. Very often the group will be cohesive within but hostile toward all outside interference.

Group formation is a social phenomenon, well beyond the control of the individual. Hence, if the larger culture is dominated by hatred, then groups will be formed more for the purpose of fighting than of cooperating. In such an atmosphere love relationships are difficult to maintain.

The school-age child usually does not feel any great longing for a person outside the family. But even within the family there is a growing estrangement from the parents because of outside pressures. Thus, in a national survey, such as that done by General Mills in 1976 and 1977 (Caplow et al., 1982, pp. 314–317), of 1230 intact families with children 6 to 12 years of age, it was found that the families fulfilled the functions of physical maintenance and morale and tension management. But two out of three parents agreed that they had trouble communicating with their children, especially on certain sensitive topics, such as homosexuality, death, sex, their own feelings and shortcomings, family problems, and money. Children's complaints about their parents mirrored some of the complaints parents had about their children.

Socioeconomic differences begin to play a major role as well. Jencks (1979) et al., in their study *Who Gets Ahead,* concluded that family background as a whole explained about 48% of the variance in occupational status and 15 to 35% of the variance in earnings among men aged 25 to 64 in the early 1970s (Jencks et al., 1979, p. 81). These estimates imply that those who do well economically typically owe almost half of their occupational advantage and 55 to 85% of their earnings advantage to family background. The term "culture of poverty" that Oscar Lewis (1970) introduced certainly applies to a considerable segment of the American population. And in this culture of poverty love plays a most minor role. This is the world to which the latency-age child is introduced, and here he or she must sink or swim.

ADOLESCENCE

In adolescence all the love problems that have accumulated through the growing-up period coalesce in several major areas, requiring some kind of solution that will determine the course of the rest of life. The areas that are particularly important are: (1) sexual maturity; (2) the move to adult roles; (3) the release of aggression; (4) liberation from the parents; and (5) normal, healthy adolescence.

Sexuality

It is widely believed, and rightly so, that we have gone through a sexual revolution, especially since the 1960s. Actually, as has been seen in the historical survey, sexual mores have varied from century to century. Today we are in the midst of a reaction against the extreme repressions of the nineteenth century.

A few statistics can indicate the extent of the change. According to Caplow and his co-workers (1982), the rates of premarital sex in 1971 were more than double the 1940s rates for each age category. But the increase during the subsequent 5 years (1971–1976) was nearly as great. By 1976, over half of the unmarried 19-year-old girls in the United States had engaged in intercourse. The liberation of women and the consequent demise of the double standard brought men and women to virtual equality in premarital sexual experience (Caplow et al., p. 168).

Apart from the increase in the frequency of intercourse Caplow and his colleagues (1982, pp. 191–192) sum up the changes since the 1920s as follows:

1. Middletown people in the 1970s were more tolerant of diversity than they were in the 1920s, and this tolerance extended to different codes of sexual morality and varieties of sexual expression.
2. Middletown adolescents, especially females, were more apt to participate in premarital sex than they were in the 1920s, and they became sexually active at an earlier age.
3. Information about human sexuality, including birth control, was far more widely distributed in the seventies.
4. Abortion, the use of contraceptives, and sterilization were more common than they used to be.
5. Pornography was more readily available.

But of course greater sexual freedom has been by no means an unmixed blessing. There has been an alarming increase in venereal disease. Recently a popular journal ran a red page on its front cover stating that herpes has become the number one health menace to the country, with some 20 million sufferers. Abortion may be easy, but that does not make it enjoyable. Even direct sexual problems have not diminished, as attested to by the large number of sex therapists who have entered the picture after the work of Masters and Johnson (1966).

Thus if the situation a century ago could be characterized as a world where the emphasis was on love without sex, today the emphasis is on sex without love. While sexual gratification is an important component of love, sexuality can equally be an expression of hostility. Premarital sexual experience will make it easier to adjust to a partner who is sexually healthy, but harder to adjust to one who is sexually inadequate.

The Move to Adult Roles

Part of the growth process is the advancement to more adult roles in sexuality (marriage), work, and social living. In all of these areas the adolescent runs into a large number of problems. Erikson has coined the term "psychosocial moratorium," a span of years in which no demands are made on the young, at least no really serious demands. Many adolescents (without knowing the term) use the years as a moratorium in which they can avoid the more pressing problems of living. The expression commonly heard today that "it's time to move on" reflects the sense of confusion so prevalent among adolescents.

In terms of the major theses of this book, the adolescent love experience is one of the most crucial. Most often this takes the form of a deep longing for a person of the opposite sex; this longing may be the prelude to a real love experience, it may be a transference to some completely unsuitable person, or may be a mixture of the two.

In the typical adolescent love affair, whether it is to be regarded as true love or not depends just as much on other factors as on the relationship between the boy and girl. If it is mutual, with hostility at a minimum, within the bounds of a loving family, it is one of the supreme delights of life. But with equal frequency, if not more, it is not mutual, results from the repression of hostility (and sexuality as well), and takes place entirely outside the bounds of a loving family. It is this kind of love that has been most thoroughly explored by analysis, and we shall have much to say about it in chapters 7, 8, and 9. For the moment it can be said only that whether such a love is "true" or not can be determined only when all the circumstances have been thoroughly investigated.

The Release of Aggression: "Wild Youth"

Perhaps the most obvious characteristic of adolescence throughout the centuries has been its rebelliousness. "Youth must have its fling." Some 2300 years ago, in his *Rhetoric,* Aristotle wrote:

> *The young are in character prone to desire and ready to carry any desire they may have formed into action. Of bodily desires it is the sexual to which they are most disposed to give way, and in regard to sexual desire they exercise no self-restraint. They are changeful too, and fickle in their desires, which are as transitory as they are vehement; for their wishes are keen without being permanent, like a sick man's fits of hunger and thirst. They are passionate, irascible and apt to be carried away by their impulses. They are the slaves, too, of their passion, as their ambition prevents their ever brooking a slight and renders them indignant at the mere idea of enduring an injury. And while they are fond of honor, they are fonder still of victory; for superiority is the object of youthful desire. . . . Their lives are lived principally in hope, as hope is of the future and memory of the past. Youth is the age when people are most devoted to their friends or relations or companions. . . . If the young commit a fault, it is always on the side of excess and exaggeration. . . . for they carry everything too far, whether it be their love or hatred or anything else. [Cited in Kiell, 1964, pp. 18–19]*

What Aristotle does not mention is that the young are also prone to very serious depressions when their hopes are not fulfilled, or when their loves are unrequited. In fact, at certain ages suicide in adolescence is the prime cause of death. Likewise, drugs, "gang rumbles," senseless fighting, sexual excesses, and the like are obvious to anybody. Many people have some kind of fling in adolescence before they settle down to the more serious business of living.

Of more moment is the high incidence of emotional and psychological disturbances. It is at this age that schizophrenia first becomes a major problem, and schizophrenia still afflicts about 1% of the population at some time in their lives.

Liberation from the Parents

The adolescent for the first time in his or her life is free to leave parents both physically and psychologically. Again how he or she makes use of this freedom depends on the nature of the love relationship with the parents. Ideally the adolescent could merely grow up and identify with either father or mother (as the sex may be), moving on to lead a similar life. This happens, though not too frequently in today's society. More often there is a terrible period of Sturm und Drang with bitter battles with the parents, many of whom are unwilling to let go.

Though much has been made of rebellious youth, there are also large numbers of adolescents who grow up in reasonably healthy families, moving on to establish fairly healthy families of their own. Studies of healthy families (Lewis, Beavers, Gossett, and Phillips, 1976; Beavers, 1977; Westley & Epstein, 1969, among others) indicate that they are characterized by certain features that allow us to describe them as loving and moving closer to the analytic ideal (cf. Chapter 10). Beavers, for instance (Lewis et al., 1976) dealt with five family qualities considered important in the development of capable, adaptive, healthy individuals: (1) power structure; (2) the degree of family individuation; (3) acceptance of separation and loss; (4) perception of reality; and (5) affect (pp. 51–83).

In the power structure, leadership is generally in the hands of the father, with a viable coalition with the mother as the next most powerful person. The children are less powerful, but their contributions are attended to and usually influence family decisions.

Tolerance for individuation is reflected in several more discrete qualities of the family system. Among these are: "I-ness"—the ability of family members to express themselves clearly as feeling, thinking, acting, valuable, and separate individuals and to take responsibility for thoughts, feelings, and actions; respect for the unique experience of another; the ability to hear and respond to others.

The ability to accept separation and loss of loved ones is at the heart of all the skills of healthy families. If parents feel competent as humans, then it is unnecessary for them to blur reality, to live out fantasies, to insist desperately on timelessness and the never-broken bonds between generations.

The myths of healthy families fill in the gaps of observation and provide a matrix of shared meaning. In this way they are reassuringly similar to observers' views of the family members' character structure and the quality of their interaction. They are quick to pick up emotional pain or unusual behavior in each other and approach problems with directness and an expectation that something can be done.

With regard to feeling, the most capable families demonstrate open, direct expression of humor, tenderness, warmth, and hopefulness to a striking degree. Expressions of negative feelings are made in the context of awareness of the other person and with a balancing supportiveness. They are skillful interpersonally; the members work together reasonably well and their interaction appears to elicit pleasure with a resulting positive emotional tone.

Thus healthy families come much closer to the ideal of a love culture than unhealthy ones. How many such healthy families are found in our culture remains a moot point.

Healthy Adolescence

Offer (1981) in his study of adolescents contends that the vast majority of normal adolescents are not in the throes of turmoil. They function well, enjoy good relationships with their families and friends, and accept the values of the larger society. In addition, most report having adapted without undue conflict to the bodily changes and emerging sexuality brought on by puberty. The only notable symptom he saw among the normal adolescents was a situation-specific anxiety that they could handle without undue trauma. There were, however, sex differences noted. Girls felt worse about their bodies, less open to sexual feelings, and less confident about vocational aspirations than did boys (Offer, pp. 116–117).

However the numbers turn out, it is clear enough that at least there are healthy families in which the love relationship is stressed. Ideally, then as before, the adolescent who is loved learns to love; the one who is hated or misused learns to hate and misuse.

CONCLUSION

It is often assumed that love comes upon the person unaware, like a sudden conversion experience. ("Some enchanted evening you will meet a stranger. . . .") Hence many people go through life looking for such a miraculous individual who will revolutionize their entire lives. The result, as will be described in the chapter on clinical observations, is all too commonly severe disappointment.

The data presented in this chapter make two significant points about love. First of all, it must be developed from birth on. The whole education of the child must be geared toward the experience of love, *at every level* of development. In that case life becomes a series of loving experiences, moving from mother to father to siblings to peers to the outside world. This becomes an ideal toward which both the individual and the society can strive.

Instead, sharp discontinuities are what is ordinarily seen. There may be a warm, nurturing experience with the mother, contrasted with a harsh, domineering father whom the child does not know how to handle. Or the whole family environment may be secure and gratifying until the thrust into the outside world, which leaves the child bewildered and helpless. Love must be pursued all along the line, not just as a special deus ex machina that appears at puberty.

In the second place, when this love development is not the case, and love comes upon the person suddenly, it is more often than not a refuge love, a way out of the miseries of ordinary existence. In our own culture this refuge love has been more the norm than the exception, for several thousand years, from the time of the Greeks on. Among simpler peoples, who are less dominated by hatreds and grandiose ambitions of world conquest, that is often not true.

7

Clinical Observations

The psychotherapist studies love more intensively than any other person in one culture, in both its normal and neurotic manifestations. From Freud on, it has been recognized that every neurotic disturbance derives from a disturbance in the love life, even if the symptom seems completely remote from any consideration of love. The appearance is not the reality. To get at the reality of the patient's suffering, the material must sooner or later be correlated with his or her love conflicts, either in the present or in the past.

We still see the erroneous claim that people who go to therapists represent a skewed sample of the population, so that their conflicts cannot be generalized to that of people at large. This claim has been refuted so often that it becomes wearisome to repeat the same old arguments, yet many professionals hold onto their erroneous views. In their survey of American mental health, Veroff, Douvan, and Kulka (1981) have shown that between 1957 and 1976 there was a marked increase in the percentage of those who sought help for some psychological problem (pp. 118–

119). This increase was more noticeable in the better educated and more affluent classes than in the lower classes, but that shows only that the reality problems of the lower classes are so pressing that they can give little thought to inner changes.

As far as the philosophy of psychotherapy goes, the authors state:

> *In these characteristics—isolation, detachment, intellectual/verbal analysis—psychoanalysis represents quintessential science. Its popularity marks the movement of the scientific revolution to the last frontier—the sphere of human behavior and the thickets of the human soul—and represents, above all, a remarkable faith in, and optimism about the power of science. Its emergence as the model of human counsel marks modern sensibility and displaces a religious/moral model.* [Veroff et al., 1981, p. 7]

It goes without saying that the core of the philosophy of living espoused by psychoanalysis is a happy love life (cf. Chapter 10). Thus the notion that love is the central experience of human life is gaining increasing acceptance.

Another question arises here: If ours is a hate culture, how is it that so many people are talking about love? The reply is twofold. First, our hate culture also allows for numerous love experiences; if it were exclusively a hate culture love would be outlawed, as in Aldous Huxley's satiric novel *Brave New World*, or George Orwell's *1984*. Second, the hate culture produces deep tensions that cry out for relief. When such relief is offered by a scientific approach that is based on a clear delineation of the human situation, and a solution that appeals to common sense, some at least will hear. The fate of psychoanalysis in the hate culture is a subject that will be treated later on in its own right (see Chapter 10). Here we wish to sum up some of the observations that have been made and are constantly being confirmed on the various kinds of love that people do have and talk about.

ROMANTIC LOVE

Of all its different forms, love is most often equated with romantic love. In its major thesis that romantic love between man and woman in a marriage is the best guarantee of a happy life, romantic love can be traced back directly to the doctrines of courtly love, even though courtly love specifically limited itself to love outside marriage. Still, the depth and description of the love experience in the twelfth and thirteenth centuries, as in the songs of the troubadours (Valency, 1961), are comparable in every respect to those of the love songs we hear today. Perhaps the major difference is that in courtly love there was a surrounding love culture (the court of love), while romantic love is viewed as a highly individualized experience.

When it is consummated, romantic love leading to marriage certainly provides one of life's supreme enjoyments. Ideally, it represents the culmination of a person's life that has gone from one love experience to another—mother, father, peers, chums, love, and marriage. Yet our clinical observations reveal that such a course of life is quite rare. More often than not, the course of true love "never runs smooth"; it has its ups and downs, its alternation with fights and hatreds, its suffering, its disappointments. It is these realities of the romantic love experience that are encountered most commonly by the therapist—and by writers and others who seek to explore the intricacies of love.

Andreas Capellanus, who wrote *The Art of Courtly Love* in 1180, a book which then became a kind of guide for all lovers, defined love as follows:

> *Love is a certain inborn suffering derived from the sight of and excessive meditation upon the beauty of the opposite sex, which causes each one to wish above all things the embraces of the other and by common desire to carry out all love's precepts in the other's embrace.* [1941, p. 2]

Since then suffering has been one of the principal components of romantic love. Today most people are convinced that if the absence of the partner does not make them suffer, it is not true love; this has been referred to as the "glue" theory of love. Mario Praz, the literary historian, in his book *The Romantic Agony* (1933), has documented in extensive detail the exquisite agonies of the romantic poets of the nineteenth century and their followers. Goethe's classic, *The Sorrows of Young Werther*, which supposedly induced many young men and women frustrated in love to commit suicide, is in this tradition.

The explanation of suffering is preeminently the province of the psychoanalyst. If men and women suffer for love, it is because they repeat the tortures of early childhood, in which their longings for their parents could never be gratified.

The following case is typical of a young woman's unhappy infatuation.

Thelma, a beautiful young unmarried woman of 30, fell in love with a man who had repeatedly spurned her and then moved to Paris. Her plan was to go to see him in Paris, even though she openly admitted that her search was hopeless. He had told her in so many words that if she came to Paris he would not even bother to see her. She accepted the suggestion that she try analysis first.

Thelma was the third of six children of a midwestern businessman. Her childhood was not especially traumatic, but when she reached adolescence she became obsessed with sex. However, she was a devoted churchgoer, so she could not allow herself to indulge in sex, except to pet a little. In church she was a member of the choir. Between religious songs the girls would add dirty lines to the official hymns, which led to much private giggling and amusement. Obviously she did not take religion very seriously, even though she went as demanded by her family.

Unable to indulge in any real sex play, she resorted to excessive eating. She would eat till she almost burst then vomit and eat some more. As a result she became very heavy in her adolescence.

When she became so heavy, her father demanded that she reduce, but his demand took a peculiar form. He kept tabs on her by requiring her to weigh herself on the house scale every morning in the nude in his presence. If she had gained weight he smacked her hard on the behind; if she had lost weight he would pat her on the behind affectionately. Obviously with such a seductive system she lost very little weight, remaining quite heavy.

In order to get away from father, she went to New York to enter the theater. Here she had some moderate success, just enough to sustain her. But the pattern of eating and vomiting continued, and she maintained her virginity. Even though she was quite attractive and received many offers from different men, she could not attach herself to anyone.

Shortly before she was 30 the father had a breakdown and was sent to a mental hospital, where he died. As soon as the news came that he had died, she let herself go. Within a few months she had three different sexual experiences with three different men. It was after these sexual experiences that she developed the infatuation with the man who had gone off to Paris. With him she had never had sex. Clearly he was the idealized father, whom she could never obtain and could never give up.

In the analysis she quickly became highly seductive. At the end of every session she would stretch out her hand to shake the analyst's hand, even though she knew that that was not the usual procedure. She had repeated blatant sexual dreams, such as that of a bull chasing her through the cornfields. Several times she propositioned the analyst quite directly, reassuring him that nobody would know.

Gradually the persistent examination of her feelings for the analyst helped her to see the neurotic nature of her fixation on the man in Paris. She was also able to give up most of the bingeing and vomiting and reduce her figure to more attractive proportions. Because she was in reality so attractive, she eventually was able to meet a more suitable man and make a satisfactory marriage.

This clinical vignette brings out many of the characteristics of romantic love: its seeming unattainability, its connections with frustrated sexuality, its emphasis on suffering, its derivation from an unhappy relationship with the father (or with the mother, for a man). It was such a situation that led Freud to postulate that love is "aim-inhibited" sexuality, but this formulation is only part of the total picure.

Freud, in his papers on men's love lives, provided the analytic explana tion for the suffering. The idealized woman in the love relationship is at bottom the mother, who is always desirable and always unattainable.

In addition, romantic love is often the outcome of a hate culture, like ours, where there are strong sexual taboos, and the man is forced to divide love and sex sharply (as in courtly love—the wife is for marriage, the sweetheart is for love play). In spite of all our sophistication, clinical experience teaches us that this division into the "good" girl who is sexually unapproachable and "bad" woman who is sexually available is still quite common. Typical is the following vignette.

Harvey, a 25-year-old man in his last year of college, fell in love with a rather wild young woman who was in open rebellion against her wealthy family. She worked at odd jobs, managing to make a living somehow, but drifting aimlessly in her life. He, who had always been made to toe the line, found this seeming indifference to life's demands highly attractive. Since he was willing to help her out, she invited him to live with her. They stayed together for about 6 months; then she abruptly kicked him out.

Shortly after that he entered analysis. His childhood had been extremely traumatic. He was the last of 6 children, and his mother had evidently tried to avoid having another child for years before he was born; she called him her "thirteenth abortion." In childhood he slept with an older brother, who used to beat him unmercifully. The mother was the dominant figure in the household; at one point the father was ill and unable to work. She took him to court and had him jailed for nonsupport. After that the father and everybody else were terrified of her.

The major favorable influence in his childhood was one older sister who had managed to get away to Europe, where she had a successful career as an artist. She married well and then came back to this country. Since she was about 15 years older then Harvey, he looked up to her with awe and admiration. She would often take him for rides in the country when he was a little boy, adventures that he enjoyed immensely.

When he was old enough to work, his older brother, who was a waiter, took him into the restaurant, where Harvey worked first as a bus-boy, then as a waiter. While the brother no longer beat him up physically, he did abuse him verbally, bawling him out for every mistake he made, cursing him for the meager tips that came in, and the like. At this point the mother was also extremely bitter toward all her children. She had developed high blood pressure and blamed everybody for her woes. Since Harvey was the only one who was still at home, he had to take the brunt of her constant abuse.

In college he met a friend who invited him to share a low-cost apartment. This was his first chance to get away from home and he seized it, even though his mother blasted him continuously for "deserting" her. To support the apartment he had to go to work and college at the same time. The grind was too much for him, and he dropped out shortly before he was due to graduate. His ambition then was to be an art teacher.

Then he met Nina, the wild young woman with whom he fell in love. She seemed to symbolize everything that he had never had, and on top of that she offered him constant sex. He looked back to the time with her as a paradise and felt crushed when she asked him to leave.

Shortly after the analysis began, Nina called him up to ask to see him. Fantasizing that she wanted to get together with him again, he rushed over. The reality turned out to be entirely different. Nina was pregnant by another man (the one who had replaced Harvey) and wanted to borrow money from Harvey for an abortion (this was in the days before abortion was legal). Though her family was quite wealthy, she would not ask them for money because she did not want them to know. Nor did she want the presumed father of her baby to know; she knew she could "rely" on Harvey. Although he was willing to give her every penny he had (in spite of his poverty), the analyst succeeded in getting him to see the situation as it was: that she was just using him for her own purposes and would discard him again when she no longer had any use for him.

Once he recognized that Nina was just exploiting him, his love for her diminished and then vanished. There followed a long period of experimentation with girls. Since he was a tall, good-looking man, he had no trouble attracting women. It was an agreeable surprise that they found him so desirable, and that they pursued him as much as they did. His pattern then changed: He would have sex with a woman for a while, drop her, and then go on to a new one. This was a natural reaction to his earlier masochistic love for Nina.

He also made progress in his work. It turned out that he was color-blind, so his career as an art teacher became impossible. He finished college and then went on to architecture. Since he was always used to working hard, he made steady progress in this field. Although not sufficiently talented to go off on his own, he worked his way up in the profession. His father had been an architect in his youth, and though he had failed at it, Harvey could now identify with the man whom he had seen experiencing so much suffering and heartache in his life.

In his love life he eventually fell in love with a woman who was unable to have children. It was understandable that Harvey would not be eager to have a family of his own, after what he had seen in his own family. In spite of her disability, he married her and made a satisfactory adjustment in life.

The life of Stendhal (his pen name; his real name was Henri Beyle) is typical of the misery of many romantic lovers. Stendhal founded a school called Beylisme—today we would call it *narcissism*—which still has adherents. Its chief doctrines are: Follow your own inclinations; pursue pleasure wherever you can find it.

Stendhal himself in his personal and in his love life was a most unhappy man. His biographers have constantly described him as a "failure"—a failure as a lover, a failure in his military career, even a failure in his vocation as a writer.

His mother died when he was 7. Henri worshiped her; for a long time afterward he spoke and wrote of her beauty, sensitivity, and intelligence. In 1800 he crossed the Alps to Milan, where he joined the reserve army of Napoleon. He fell in love with a Milanese lady but did not become her lover until 11 years later. In the meantime he had his first sexual experience with a prostitute, from whom he acquired a venereal disease that had to be treated intermittently for the rest of his life. Other unhappy affairs followed. He never had a permanent address or a permanent profession; he had no home, no children, no constant mistress; after 1808 and the marriage of his sister Pauline, who was his chief confidante, he had no family. It is true that his novels have profound insights and can be regarded as great. But his renown as a writer is small compensation for the agony of his life (*Encyclopaedia Britannica,* 15th ed., vol. 17, p. 670).

Another common characteristic of romantic love is the extreme dependency. Here the criterion for love is the wish to be with the other person all the time. An absence of even a few hours is felt as a crushing blow. Usually the woman is the dependent partner in the traditional culture; she literally cannot function without the direction and support of the man. Popular terminology aptly calls her the "clinging vine."

It is obvious that this kind of love represents a reversion to infancy, when mother's love could be demonstrated to the infant only by her presence and by her physical ministrations. It is no accident that in this kind of love baby talk is a particularly prominent feature; the partners often call one another "mommy" and "daddy." Looking is particularly central, as in the infant's constant gazing. One authority on children writes that the mutual gaze of mother and infant resembles that of lovers more than anything else (Lichtenberg, 1981, p. 11); it is also curious and interesting that in Andreas Capellanus's treatise on love he states that blind people are unable to love (no gazing).

Dependency usually goes together with a great deal of submissiveness. In effect the woman says: "I love you so much that I will do anything you say. I will be your willing slave. [The existence of the "slave bracelet" as a piece of jewelry embodies this thought.] In exchange, as my master, you will take full care of me and love me in return."

Frequently the submissiveness increases to the point where the woman is not even able to function in any adequate way. This was the case with the "hysterical" women of the nineteenth century, whom the untrained doctors regarded as hopelessly inept. The sexual roots of this kind of masochism were among Freud's major discoveries.

Charlotte Perkins Gilman, a prominent feminist of the nineteenth century, narrowly escaped the living death that doctors foisted on their patients at that time. Having collapsed with a "nervous disorder," she consulted S. Weir Mitchell, the leading "guru" of that day (the 1890s). Mitchell, like his colleagues, held that women were by nature weak, dependent, and diseased. And women lived up to his beliefs.

Charlotte Gilman was one who tried to escape the vicious cycle. She approached Mitchell for help. When she told him her story, he dismissed it as evidence of "self-conceit" (Ehrenreich & English, 1978, pp. 91–92). He did not want information from his patients; he wanted complete obedience. His prescription for her was: "Live as domestic a life as possible. Have your child with you all the time. . . . Lie down an hour after each meal. Have but two hours' intellectual life a day. And never touch pen, brush or pencil as long as you live" (Ehrenreich & English, p. 92).

She dutifully returned home and for some months attempted to follow Mitchell's orders to the letter. The result, in her words, was: "I came perilously close to losing my mind. The mental agony grew so unbearable that I would sit blankly moving my head from side to side. . . . I would crawl into remote closets and under beds—to hide from the grinding pressure of that distress" (Gilman, 1975, p. 96).

Finally she had a moment of clear vision, when she understood the source of her illness. She did not want to be a wife; she wanted to be a writer and an activist (to be both was unthinkable at that time). So, discarding Mitchell's prescription and divorcing her husband, she took off for California with her baby, her pen, brush, and pencil. But she never forgot Mitchell and his near-lethal "cure." Three years after her recovery she wrote *The Yellow Wallpaper*, a fictionalized account of her own illness and descent into madness. If that story had any influence on Mitchell's method of treatment, she wrote after a long life of accomplishments, "I have not lived in vain." But it remained for Freud to liberate women from such hopeless medical incompetence.

Less fortunate was Alice James, sister of the famous James brothers, William and Henry. She began her career of invalidism at the age of 19. Submissively, she listened to the doctors, who told her that she would either die or recover. Today, we would understand such submissiveness as a neurotic transference love. She remained ill all her life and finally died of cancer at 43; at that that point she was ready to commit suicide (Ehrenreich & English, 1978, p. 94).

The romantic woman makes the man a father figure who will take care of all of her life's problems. How does the man react to such a woman? Three main reactions may be discerned: sadism, idealization, and indifference.

In the sadistic reaction, the man sees the submissive love of the woman as a sign of weakness. When he has strong sadistic impulses, which is often the case, he uses her as a target. The sadism may become physical, so that beatings are the order of the day. This is the background of the "battered wife" syndrome, now acquiring increasing prominence. An extreme example is described by Eugene O'Neill in his play *The Iceman Cometh*, where Hickey, always forgiven by his loving, submissive wife, finally shoots her.

Idealization occurs when the man sees the submissiveness as a sign of maternal caring. To him the wife is primarily a mother substitute; he is the spoiled darling. It is only when the wife begins to defy him that he becomes disturbed; otherwise he sees her as "perfect." Many times he even calls her "mother," or "little mother." Often, the idyll ends when the children arrive, as shown in the following vignette.

Frank, the younger of two children (the older was a girl), adored his mother when he was a child. Father had deserted the family, and mother had to work to support them. She continually repeated cliché phrases, such as "mother knows best," and continually assured him that she was devoting her life to him, rejecting all other men after father had left. His task in life was to grow up quickly, and then support her; in short, she had in effect made him a substitute husband.

As long as he was a child, Frank thought that this arrangement was wonderful. But when the sexual conflicts of puberty came to the fore, he was completely floored. He was unable to study, and his grades took a sharp drop. He could not relate to girls because no one could live up to the standards set by his mother. Somehow he managed to get through school and get a job as a teacher.

In adolescence Frank dated very little; he was being true to mother. Further, her sexual repressiveness carried over to him; since she never went out with men, it was obviously wrong for him to go out with girls. His sex life was confined to heavy masturbation and an occasional encounter with a prostitute.

Then, when he was about 22, he fell in love. The girl was attractive, intelligent, vivacious, witty,—and in love with him. In his eyes she had no faults—a complete idealization. When they tried to have sex before marriage, he could not perform properly, and of course he promptly blamed himself; there could not be anything wrong with her. She did everything that he asked her to do, but he was not adequate. This kind of self-blame can easily be understood in the light of his relationship with his self-sacrificing mother; mother too had no faults, and had devoted her life to her son.

Finally they married. At this point the apparent submissiveness of his wife gradually turned into an increasing bossiness. She dictated where they went, what they ate, what they spent, where they lived, what kind of sex they had, and so on. With all this he was still quite satisfied, as long as she took proper care of him, which she did.

Then a child came. Once that happened, his wife turned away from him almost completely. She devoted herself to the child, demanding that her husband rearrange all his activities to suit the needs of her and the child. Sex began to become less frequent and eventually tapered off to perhaps once a month or every 2 months.

It was at this point that Frank discovered, to his surprise, that his wife was sexually frigid. She was staying away from sex not because of the child but because she did not enjoy sex. He tried therapy and suggested it to her. But she refused because she was "perfect." Eventually the love vanished and the two were divorced.

Finally, many men become completely indifferent to the submissiveness. The woman begins to feel to them like an old shoe that they can put on or discard at will (and she often behaves in kind). Some men find their solace in other women, some in overwork, some in addictions of various kinds. Many become extremely neurotic in their own right.

While the woman is usually the submissive one, in many cases the reverse is true. Somerset Maugham's great novel *Of Human Bondage* is a classic description of such a situation, which is a very close copy of the author's own life. The hero, a medical student with a physical disability, cannot tear himself away from a waitress–prostitute who exploits him in every conceivable way.

In the dating stage, which precedes marriage (relatively late in our culture by anthropological standards), a great deal of animosity is often concealed by both partners. Traditionally, the woman wants marriage, the man wants sex. Remarks about teasing and false promises are everyday currency, so that everybody in the dating situation becomes wary of what the other person is really after.

The belief that all of this animosity, wariness, and at times outright paranoia will suddenly disappear once the two get married is another relic of the age of magic. In fact, it does not disappear. The law courts bear eloquent testimony to the relentless bitterness with which many marriages have been held together over many years.

In this respect the statistics on divorce (currently about 4 divorces for every 10 marriages, but statistics vary) should be considered encouraging rather than the reverse. People get divorced because they still have in mind the ideal of a happy marriage.

Another common outcome of a romantic entanglement is a sadomasochistic love affair. Here after an initial honeymoon a lifelong battle ensues, with the couple unable to separate in spite of the obvious impossibility of the situation. "Heaven has no rage, like love to hatred turned" (Congreve, 1697). The love affair turns into a hate affair, with its unbelievable tenacity. Here is a clinical instance.

Henry and Martha fell madly in love. She revealed to him that she was pregnant by another man, but claimed she loved Henry and wished to marry him. He agreed, on the condition that she give the child away when it was born. This she did. The couple then had five children of their own in quick succession.

After the birth of the last child, fighting broke out in earnest. Henry continually assaulted Martha. On four separate occasions in fact he threw her down to the floor and started to choke her; her life was saved by the neighbors. The ostensible reason for his rage was that she had had a child by another man before she met him—even though he had known this from the very beginning.

After some 10 years of these beatings, Martha withdrew from contact with Henry, but she would not leave him. The couple had little to do with one another, confining their contacts to absolute necessities. Sex disappeared.

At this point, he in turn became very masochistic. He worked at three different jobs, keeping himself busy day and night. He gave her all his money, keeping a small pittance for himself, not even enough to eat; he took some of his meals with his sister. He had no friends, no intimates apart from his sister, and no activities apart from his work. Obviously he was paying penance for his previous assaults on her, just as before she was paying penance for having had a child out of wedlock by another man.

After some 25 years of this incessant battle, the couple finally separated.

It is a psychological puzzle why two people with such intense hatred for one another stay together. In one case a man in such a situation when asked why he did not break up the marriage (the children were grown, the wife was independent) blurted out: "Whom would I hate then?" This is the clue: Psychologically hatred has become the dominant emotion, and the person looks for an outlet for his hatred; if he has no such outlet he feels lost. Such an attitude is quite characteristic of a hate culture. It is reminiscent of the blood feuds that went on for centuries in previous historical epochs. (cf. chapters 2 and 3).

The switch from love to hatred is another proof, if one were needed, that in clinical reality much love is a cover-up or reaction formation for hatred. Once the love feelings have been gratified for a while, the hatred then takes over, on some pretext or other. The sociologist John Cuber has offered an interesting classification of marriages into: (1) conflict-habituated; (2) passive–congenial; (3) devitalized; (4) vital; and (5) total(Cuber & Harroff, 1965, chap. 3). The conflict-habituated marriage (the definition is obvious) is one in which two people live together even though they are motivated by the fiercest of hatreds. In the case of an elderly couple, both in their seventies, each spent much time wishing the other would die first. The movie *Divorce Italian Style*, in which the only way of getting a divorce is by the death (natural or unnatural) of the spouse, provides an amusing instance of this psychology.

I do not wish to give the impression that romantic love always ends in such terrible fiascoes. There are plenty of marriages where the two people love one another, enjoy one another, have a gratifying sex life, and are reasonably happy. But both clinical experience and everyday observation indicate that such marriages are in a strong minority.

MARRIED LOVE

In most cultures there has been an image of a woman and a man living together in wedded bliss. The two lovers are seen as merging into one person. The Bible says: "This is why a man must leave father and mother, and cling to his wife, and the two become one body" (Matt. 19:5). St. Augustine, even though he praises the love of God as the noblest of all human feelings, writes:

> *The supreme human law is love and this law is best respected when men, who both desire and ought to live in harmony, so bind themselves by the bonds of social relationships that no one man monopolizes more than one relationship, and many different relationships are distributed as widely as possible, so that a common social life of the greatest number may best be fostered.* [*Augustine, 426/1958, p. 350*]

Here Augustine may be seen as urging a love culture, but a few pages later sexual guilt enters, and he writes: "The union of male and female is, then, so far as mortal living goes, the seed-bed, so to speak, from which a city must grow; but, while the city of earth needs only human generation, the City of Heaven demands a spiritual regeneration to escape from the taint of the generative act" (426/1958, p. 353).

In the twelfth-century Indian poem of Bhavabhuti the verse reads:

> This state where there is no twoness in responses of
> joy or sorrow,
> Where the heart finds rest, where feeling does not dry
> with age,
> Where concealments fall away in time and the essential
> love is ripened—
> Sacred is this state of human fulfillment, which we find
> once if ever.
>
> (Siegel, 1978, p. vi)

Love—the universal longing to merge two people into one. For several centuries in western culture (and often in many other cultures) there has been the attempt to realize this ideal in marriage. How successful has it been? The answer is that it has not been too successful, though it is still better to marry than to remain alone. Of interest here are those dynamic factors that make marriage succeed and those that make them fail.

Marriage is a step forward in development. Like every such step, it makes enormous demands on the individuals involved. The man must give up his carefree adolescence and go to work; the woman likewise, even though her work may be the home. On the surface the tasks seem simple enough; in reality they are enormously complicated. It is not surprising then to see how many marriages break up and how many couples stay together in mutual misery all their lives, even though the two partners say that they love one another. The question of children will be discussed later. Here I wish to call attention to one of the central conflicts in marital disputes: *regression in the service of the spouse.*

Even though marriage is supposed to be based on love in contemporary society, in contrast to the arranged marriage of former centuries, this freedom is to a considerable extent illusory. As Goode (1982) points out, the western system of formally free courtship also controls where love will appear and how people will respond to it. In this system, falling in love is actually encouraged, and people are likely to view being in love as a necessary part of getting married. But the trouble is that love is a threat to the social order, which likes to see matters well arranged and organized. Again, quoting Goode, "families with a higher social rank grant less freedom in courtship than do families of lower rank. They have more to fear from the disruptive effects of love, have more resources for controlling it, and expend more energy in avoiding some of its consequences" (p. 57). By channeling love or keeping it under some control, the family elders can be freer to make marriage bargains with one another.

The net consequence is that love marriages start with several strikes against them. (This is meant as a clinical observation, not as a plea for a return to the arranged marriage.) When there are conflicts people defend themselves. And the most common defense in marriage is *regression*— falling back to an earlier period of development. I call this "regression in the service of the spouse" because unconsciously the purpose is to please the spouse by being more of a child.

It is necessary here to make some comments on the nature of *defense.* Freud showed that the personality core is made up of anxieties and the defenses against those anxieties. Fenichel (1945) also allowed for defenses against guilt and shame. But neither paid enough attention to the role of the parents in the establishment of these defenses.

The child is primarily concerned with pleasing the parents; ultimately all anxieties can be traced back to the fear of loss of love of the parents, or actual punishment by them. This also involves the major difference between psychoanalytic theories of learning and behavioristic theories. In conventional, or behavioristic, learning theory, there must be some reinforcement for learning to take place. This reinforcement may take various forms; the classic model is the dog that learns to salivate to a bell (Pavlov) and is rewarded with food. Dynamically, however, the dog is responding to a trainer whom it wishes to please; thus conditioning can take place only in socialized animals. It is much this way with the human being. For the child, no reinforcement can possibly be as strong as the love of the parents, nor any punishment as severe as their hatred. Eventually these parent figures are internalized, and the child learns to seek the approval or disapproval of the introject, or internalized, parents.

Every human being struggles to liberate himself or herself from the parents. Few, if any, ever succeed. In fact, it remains moot whether it is even theoretically possible. Certainly the importance of the parents can be diminished considerably and is diminished as the child grows older. But whether it can ever disappear completely is questionable. So the child remains with some ties to the parent for a long time to come.

Marriage involves a situation similar to that of the parental couple. Accordingly, for the woman the man will be a father figure; for the man the woman will be a mother figure. There are only differences of degree. When the attachment to the parents is too great, we speak of *mutual parentification*. Once more, this mutual parentification is so frequent that it is more the rule than the exception.

Perhaps the most common complaint in marriage is that the partner "let himself [or herself] go." The woman cares less and less about her appearance; the man glues himself to the television set and may not even want to talk to his wife. Both of these regressive activities can be understood as a substitution of the parent for the spouse, so that the woman becomes a little girl who does not care about her appearance, while the man becomes a little boy whose main pleasure lies in solitary games.

There are many other forms that the regression can take. In general, two patterns can be distinguished: obedience and defiance. In obedience the child remains a baby in order to please the parent, who is afraid of letting him or her grow up. Very often the regression is rationalized by the mother—the child is too delicate, the outside world is too dangerous, people are picking on the child. In the extreme, regression of this kind may lead to schizophrenia, for which I have therefore suggested the term *infantia prolongata*—prolonged infancy. And indeed it has long been the opinion of some careful observers (Jones, 1929) that all emotional disturbances are merely forms of schizophrenia. This is also phrased as the continuum theory—the differences between the normal and the psychotic are only quantitative, not qualitative.

In the other pattern, defiance, the child simply does the opposite of what the parents want—head banging, refusal to eat or sleep, loss of toilet training after the next child comes (perhaps the most familiar form of regression), and the like. This may continue until adolescence, when perversion or psychopathy becomes the child's prominent characteristic. It too may lead to extremes such as homicide or suicide. In adulthood these two forms of regression, obedience and defiance, may well remain.

Clinical experience reveals the lengths to which regression in the service of the spouse can go. Here are some examples:

Sheldon and Beatrice had been married for some 10 years, with two children. She had literally let herself go and, though only 5 feet tall, weighed about 200 lb. He wanted to be an artist. Unable to sell his pictures, he was reluctant to work at anything else, and he remained dependent on his well-to-do family until very late in life. One of their favorite activities was to display their bowel movements to one another; each time either had a bowel movement, the other was called in to look. This is an obvious continuation of the child's pleasure in showing his or her bowel movement to mother, who beams approvingly because he or she is now doing it in the toilet rather than in his or her pants.

In sex she took great delight in swallowing his semen, but this was more of an oral than a genital gratification. Their sex life was actually a long series of battles, like their life in general. He deliberately masturbated so often that he could not get an erection when the time came for sex. She in turn responded by demanding that he seduce her from the beginning, as though they were having their first date. She would sit on the couch, fully clothed, and make believe that he was being "fresh" by asking for sex. This kind of mock seduction could go on for 3 hours.

The childhood background of both partners was extremely neurotic. Sheldon was the youngest of 3 children of wealthy parents. Born when his mother was in her late thirties, he was spoiled and pampered all through childhood. In one of his dreams, he was coming down a mountain full of breasts; his descent involved stepping from one breast to another. When he reached adolescence, he did not know what kind of work to look for, so he turned to art, in which he had some talent, but not enough to go far. His family lived in a small town, and he moved to New York. He eked out a meager living, but primarily he was supported by his family. Much of his time he would spend roaming around the streets looking for women to pick up; occasionally he would find one. He remained a little boy.

Beatrice was the younger of two children of poor parents. She trained as a dancer, but in such a highly competitive atmosphere as New York she could not get far. Her relationship with mother was a bitter, angry one, in which there were constant battles. Her major release lay in eating, and she became fat at an early age.

Once she hit puberty, Beatrice (like Thelma above) became obsessed with sex. When she began to menstruate she told her father, who advised her never to tell anybody else, but to keep it a secret. At 13 she visited the house of a friend who had a dog. Every day she would go into the bathroom with the dog, and have the dog lick her genitals; the sensations were voluptuous.

Beatrice was caught between her sexual obsessions and her puritanical parents. At 15 she attempted suicide for the first time, swallowing a bottle of Anacin. Shortly thereafter she tried suicide again, this time swallowing aspirin. Neither attempt had much effect, but both brought out the seriously depressive side of her personality.

Like a romantic song, Sheldon and Beatrice met on a subway and promptly fell in love. Since they were both so hungry for it, the love at first came as a great blessing and a great release; he was only 21, and she was only 18. They married quickly and entered upon a period of extremely frequent sex (two or three times a day sometimes). But when the children came, disillusionment set in for both, and they spent their energies blaming each other, ignoring their own roles.

Their marriage is a good example of regression in the service of the spouse: He wanted to be a little boy; she wanted to be a little girl. Instead of working, he went around trying to find women, occasionally painting a picture, and masturbating. Until he was well into his fifties he remained a heavy masturbator. She in turn became increasingly depressed, neglecting the children and sitting around fantasizing about wonderful love affairs, some of which she would get from the movies or from TV. Because both were so frustrated with their lives, they spent a great deal of time quarreling, at times breaking out into physical abuse.

The initial love cooled, then disappeared. The marriage worked out badly. It was possible to observe them over a period of many years; they both deteriorated steadily.

In the following case, the love affair was based on slavish attachment to one another. Actually, neither one ever loved the other very much, but because of their childhood background they stayed together and fought it out all their lives.

Robert and Henrietta were virtually glued to one another. When they first came to therapy, she was so afraid to be alone that she would not let him go out without her, except to work. For 17 years before they consulted an analyst, he had never been out alone. Analysis helped them mature, and they seemingly made a good adjustment. (This case is described as Gloria the Easy "Lay" in Fine, 1979.)

Evidently, though, she remained frightened of being alone. When they were in their late seventies, some 30 years after the analysis had been completed, she called to inquire whether psychotherapy could be combined with lithium. Apparently he was still not permitted to go out alone. Retired from his job, he had little to do, so he fell into a depressive state. Conveniently they found a psychiatrist who diagnosed him as manic-depressive and gave him lithium. In reality he was simply afraid to come in for a consultation, and she refused to allow it. It was enough for her that she had him under control, and enough for him that he had a woman—mother—figure to control him. This mutual regression would presumably continue for the rest of their lives, aided and abetted by professional ineptitude.

In the following case, the initial love feelings also wore off quickly, to be replaced by an almost insatiable sexual hunger on both sides. Since neither could feel really gratified with the other, they tried innumerable other partners before they finally settled down to some semblance of normal living. In the meantime, both went through a terrible amount of suffering.

Sheila and Frank were both "swingers." For 10 years she traveled back and forth between the Catskills and Florida, taking numerous lovers. He in turn supported her in her "vacations" because he too was free to have any number of affairs. There was one small child. The regression here took the form of defiance and reversion to an adolescent pattern.

Frank had gone to therapy for some years for treatment of severe headaches, but the treatment seems to have done him little good in the larger aspects of his life, though the headaches did clear up. He made his adjustment by having one affair after another.

Sheila became troubled by her life only when she fell in love. For the first time she met a man she could not get out of her mind. He was tall, attractive, rich, and avoided all attachments. Thus he was in more senses than one her masculine ego-ideal. When she was a little girl, her parents were divorced. One day the father came and kidnapped her brother; Sheila remained intensely jealous that he had not kidnapped her. So the lover was also the absent father who had come back to her.

Among other symptoms Sheila suffered from intense nightmares in which her son would be taken away from her. She would also fly into terrible rages, screaming at friends and tradespeople at the slightest pretext.

In the analysis it soon became apparent that Sheila was driven by a strong desire for revenge against her father, husband, and other men. The extreme promiscuity satisfied her revenge; she could excite a man, have sex with him, and then leave him, as she had been left by father.

At one point one of her former lovers called her to say that his wife was pregnant, and that he wanted sex. She concocted an elaborate revenge scheme. When her husband was away on a trip she invited the former lover to come and have sex with her in her own marital bed, meanwhile deceiving him with honeyed phrases about how much she really loved him. He fell for the bait. After the first night of bliss, he kept calling her, but she would never see him again, savoring the pleasures of seeing him long for her and suffer. Had she not been in analysis she would have continued this indefinitely. Eventually she stopped, realizing that this vindictiveness was doing her no good.

The analysis had a satisfactory outcome. (The case is more fully described in Fine, 1979, as Sally the Promiscuous Woman.)

In his novel *Of Human Bondage*, Somerset Maugham relates the story of his own regressive attachment to a worthless, indifferent woman. Although they were not married, they might very well have been, and Maugham actually acted out feelings of bitterness and vindictiveness toward the woman whom he did marry.

The hero is Philip Carey. He is drawn to Mildred, the waitress in the ABC Restaurant, because of her indifference. He selects someone who he senses will be cruel to him. He seeks the humiliation of being in bondage to a woman he despises. "He hated himself for loving her. She seemed to be constantly humiliating him and for each snub that he endured he owed her a grudge" (Morgan, pp. 196–199). Mildred is shallow, callous, greedy, unintelligent, and utterly conventional. She goes off with a friend of his, and he gives them the money for the trip. After many vicissitudes, and much suffering, Philip Carey finally marries a wholesome, earthy young woman.

In real life Maugham was much less fortunate. Shortly after the publication of *Of Human Bondage* he discovered that one of his lovers was pregnant. Out of a sense of guilt he married her. It was a marriage of convenience, which eventually made them both miserable. The child born of the union he later tried to disown. At about the same time (he was then in his early forties) he fell in love with a young man, with whom he spent many years in a homosexual liaison. The homosexual affair was a reaction to the long series of disappointments with women. By no stretch of the imagination could Maugham have ever been called a happy man. The homosexual "marriage" to Huxton gave him as little joy as the heterosexual marriage to a woman whom he hated.

In many cases where a marriage is based on a mutual regression, symptoms may develop that bring one or the other partner to therapy. Marital counseling, or some other superficial approach, may at times resolve the symptoms but leave the deeper problems untouched. Regression is such a comfortable state that it is hard to awaken the person to the need to grow up. The therapeutic approach will be discussed more fully in Chapter 11.

PARENTAL LOVE

Paradoxically, the problems connected with parental love have been given serious consideration only in the present century; before then it was usually assumed that the child was either a "good seed" or a "bad" one. The notion that parents play a central role in how their children grow up was almost ignored before Freud.

Ideally, the parent must: (1) love the child; (2) be of assistance in letting him or her grow up; and (3) let go when the child is grown up and ready to assume control of his or her own life. Clinical experience indicates the presence of widespread conflicts in all of these areas.

The question of mother love has already been discussed earlier. In order to love, the mother must have enough inner security in her own person to give comfort and affection to the child. The plain fact is that many mothers have not had that kind of security in themselves and have instead misused and abused the child for their own purposes.

It is this way with father love, too. It has not even been assumed in the traditional family psychology that the father should give his child any great amount of love; rather, in a direct descent from Roman law, the father had powers of life and death over the child and it was his function to make the child obey the laws of society. "Spare the rod and spoil the child" was more than a theoretical maxim; it was a way of life until the twentieth century and for many in the twentieth century it remains a way of life.

However, numerous studies bear out the fact that children are spending more time with their parents and trying to get closer to them, lending support to the notion that among considerable segments of the population there is a move toward the analytic ideal, weak though it may be in many instances (Caplow et al., 1982, p. 143).

But even though fathers are becoming more intimate with their children in intact families, the number of fatherless families is increasing rapidly (Biller, 1982); at present (1983) more than 20% of the children in the United States, totaling more than 10 million, live in fatherless families. Father-absent families are especially common among lower-class blacks, surpassing 50% in some areas. It is estimated that 40 to 50% of children born in the past decade will spend at least part of their childhoods in single-parent families.

The single-parent family creates a double obstacle for the child. On the one hand, the father is absent, so that even under the best of circumstances his love is not entirely reliable; in the worst cases it is completely gone. On the other hand, the mother carries an additional burden that makes her love more fragile than would otherwise be the case. On top of that, when one parent is gone the emotional conflict with the other is intensified. All told, in such families the essential love for the child is threatened on all sides and, in too many cases, it is altogether absent. Thus, the most basic of all requirements, that of a simple feeling of love on the part of the parents for them, is all too often missing. On the other hand, since the longing of the child for the parent is always there, the divorced or conflict-ridden family marks the beginning of unrequited love, which may dog the individual throughout the rest of life.

When the simple love feeling is present, as is probably true in the majority of instances, a total reevaluation of the ability of the parent to understand and/or minister to the needs of the child has taken place (what was referred to as mutual reciprocity earlier). So much has been discovered that a whole new field, that of parent education training, has developed to teach parents about the inner needs of their children as they are growing up.

In the earliest stage, that of roughly the first year, the prime need of the infant is for physical contact together with recognition of his or her (probably biologically determined) bodily rhythms. Here is an instance where these early rhythms were entirely out of line.

Mary (the sister of Henry, described earlier) was the youngest of 4 children; the other 3 were boys. Her mother would be described as an ordinary devoted mother, taking care of the house, shopping, cooking, and always present whenever the children needed anything. But the trouble was that while both parents were devoted, they were also highly neurotic. Her childhood home, as Mary described it, was a horror story.

Before Mary was born, her mother had given birth to another girl, who had died in infancy. No one knew why the infant had died; Mary said that the story around the house was that "her blood ran cold." Obviously disturbed by this loss, the mother would periodically awake Mary at night to ask her: "What is my mother's maiden name?"

The house in which the family lived was a small one, and no one had any real privacy. Mary never had a room of her own as a child; she slept in a small alcove that was closed off by a curtain. The house was still heated with coal, and the coal was stored in the bathtub. Accordingly no one ever had a chance to wash properly. Presumably they would wash in the sink.

When she was 7, Mary was hit by a baseball bat and suffered a fractured skull. This healed, and she went through college satisfactorily (in fact, she later earned a Ph.D.), but she always gave the impression of being slightly brain-damaged.

When Mary was about 10, the father went through an alcoholic period. He would come home drunk, take off most of his clothes, and crawl around the house. No one paid much attention to him. But through this all he continued to support the family. This alcoholic stage passed after a few years, but he was always a detached noncommunicative man.

The children were thrown on their own; the parents provided food, clothing, a home, but little else. When she entered puberty, Mary was sexually approached by all of her brothers; whether she actually ever had intercourse with any of them was never made very clear.

When Mary was about 18, her mother fell off the porch and died. Mary thought that she had committed suicide; others thought it was an accident.

None of the children turned out well; in fact, Mary, thanks to some 20 years of analysis, did better than any of the others. The life of the oldest brother has been described earlier. The middle brother became a gambler. The youngest brother joined the navy. Upon his release he took a menial job and got into a terrible fight with one of his co-workers, in which he was stabbed to death. There was some hint that it was a homosexual affair.

When Mary was about 20, a friend invited her to go across the country on a hitchhiking trip. They went all through the middle west and west. At that time Mary was still a virgin. The two girls were both badly dressed and looked like prostitutes or easy pickups. Many men picked them up, and Mary would let them suck at her breasts but would not allow them to go further.

One time in Texas, several boys picked them up and drove into the hills. Mary's story was that the boy she was with pulled a knife on her and threatened to kill her if she did not have sex with him. She consented, then went to the nearest town and filed a charge of rape. After about a year, the case came to court, and Mary returned to press charges. The boy was found guilty and fined $1, obviously a terrible humiliation for Mary. But her girlfriend had not been raped, so the story never sounded too convincing.

When Mary came back to New York, a friend induced her to go to a therapist, who treated her in a most directive way. He taught her how to walk, how to talk, how to dress, even suggested that she try to find out what a penis looked like. At this suggestion she went home and asked one of her brothers to show her his penis.

After 2 years the directive therapist no longer knew what to do and dropped her. She then went into analysis, at which she persisted for many years, achieving substantial improvement.

When Mary entered analysis, she was still so infantile that she went to work wearing two slips, instead of a slip and a dress. When she had a bowel movement, she liked to play with her feces at times ("it feels good"). Alternately she would be promiscuous and then supervirginal. For instance, she would go to a bar and pick up a man, take him home, and have sex with him. The next night she would have another date, insist on absolutely "correct" behavior, and when the young man would take her to her door, ask to come in, or ask for a goodnight kiss, she would say: "What kind of a woman do you think I am?" In the midst of all this she was also obsessed with being raped. Whenever she walked along the street, she was sure that she was being followed by a man who was going to rape her. At one time she even became so afraid of a man in the elevator in the analyst's building that she got out at the wrong floor in order to evade him.

It was obvious that Mary's behavior, as well as that of her brothers, resulted from seriously inadequate parenting in the earliest years of life. Yet on the surface everyone would have said that the family was almost a model of propriety and togetherness.

One of the earliest significant resistances in the analysis was that Mary could not start the session. She would lie on the couch, silent, for 10 or 15 minutes, until the analyst would prod her, asking why she was unable to begin. This continued for about a year.

There were other serious resistances that appeared. At one time, when she was looking for a job, the company referred her for a psychiatric interview. The psychiatrist came back with a diagnosis of chronic schizophrenia, largely because she had difficulty talking to him.

As indicated, in the long run this analysis turned out exceptionally well. She was able to get over her infantile traits for the most part, marry, raise two children, and even earn a doctorate. Thus the pathology of her childhood could be overcome, but only by long-term analysis.

Physical contact has to be supplied in doses that are neither too small nor too great. Traditionally, the principle applied has been to "let the baby cry it out"; it is only since World War II, roughly, that this has changed. There has been a strong move, especially among those influenced by analytical thought, toward more contact all along the line— delivery without drugs, rooming-in for the newborn, extra contact with the mother, breast-feeding, holding, stimulation, and so on. Breast-feeding has even acquired some of the stature of a reform movement through the organization La Leche League.

Breast-feeding is the traditional and ideal form of infant nutrition, usually capable of meeting a child's nutritional needs for its first 4 to 6 months of life (Berg, 1973, p. 89). Even after the essential introduction of supplemental foods, human milk can serve as an important continuing source of a child's nutritional well-being. From the sixth to the twelfth month it can supply up to three-quarters of a child's protein needs and a significant portion for some months beyond.

Yet surprisingly, breast-feeding has declined markedly in the developing countries. For most infants in these countries prolonged breast-feeding is necessary to growth and quite often survival, as it represents the only easily observable source of protein of good quality containing all the essential amino acids.

In spite of these dietary observations, and in defiance of all common sense, women in the less developed countries have found it more desirable to imitate their more affluent counterparts and give up breast-feeding to preserve their figures, or to have more mobility, or for other reasons unconnected with the child's welfare. Berg reports that in 1949, 95% of Chilean mothers breast-fed their children beyond the first year; by 1969 only 6% did so, and only 20% of the infants were nursed for as long as 2 months. In Singapore, between 1951 and 1960 there was a decrease from 71 to 42% of children in low-income families breast-fed at least 3 months. Other figures where obtained were comparable with these. Thus, for reasons purely of social prestige mothers in these countries deprived their infants of an essential constituent of love (Berg, 1973, p. 9.)

In the area of physical contact, several serendipitous findings from Harlow's (1974) studies of rhesus monkeys are striking. Some of his subjects were reared in individual wire mesh cages, in a condition that he calls "partial social deprivation" (p. 95). When these monkeys reached reproductive maturity, heterosexual tests revealed that the secretory subsystem was undamaged. Deprived males achieved penile erection and masturbated, sometimes to ejaculation, with normal frequency. Females masturbated with normal low frequency, although orgasm then (as well as now) is not a measurable response in female monkeys.

What he calls the "romantic subsystem," however, was severely affected by the partial social deprivation. The need for sheer social proximity was depressed below normal levels and the component of sex role behavior in the romantic subsystem was also damaged, particularly in males. Although deprived females quickly learned to suppress threat and aggression against feral males, deprived males never developed inhibition of their brutal aggression. The deprived males were sexually aroused by their feral partners, but even when they succeeded in recognizing the female's sex-role postures and solicitations, their only response was puzzlement or aimless groping, sometimes of their own bodies.

The mechanical sex subsystem was damaged but not totally destroyed in deprived females, who displayed the sexual presentation posture with normal frequency but were unable to support the male adequately when he mounted. Although limited, the partial mechanical support led to the discovery that a major deficit in the romantic subsystem of deprived females was their nonacceptance of heterosexual contact and their basic mistrust of heterosexual contact when it did occur. In general, the effects were far more severe in the deprived males. Harlow cites Beach (1947) as stating that the greater effect of experimental factors in males than in females has been confirmed in a variety of test situations with many different species, ranging from rodents to carnivores to primates (1974, p. 96).

Harlow's findings with monkeys dovetail beautifully with the clinical findings on humans. Freud postulated that sexual disturbances in human adults can be traced back to peculiarities in their early lives; this has been confirmed by a number of generations of clinicians. The need of the infant for warm, close contact with the mother (or a substitute) is amply confirmed. Many theoreticians speak of separation anxiety (e.g., Bowlby; Ainsworth) but the opposite should be stressed even more: the need for contact. Montagu (1971) has offered extensive evidence that the human being is a "touching animal," and if his or her need to touch is denied or thwarted, the consequences can be serious. The need for contact is often covered over by a seemingly "good" mother who does everything for her child. Here is a clinical example.

Dudley, the only son of 2 immigrant parents, was breast-fed for a while, until the mother developed some difficulty with her breasts that led the physicians to amputate one of them. Thereafter the mother remained extremely solicitous about the boy but rarely had any physical contact with him. She was an illiterate woman with few interests in her life, so mother and child on the surface at least remained very close. To all appearances she seemed like the "ordinary devoted mother" of which the literature speaks in such glowing terms.

The lack of contact led to a gradual withdrawal on Dudley's part. Since mother needed him to be with her, he obediently remained at her side, avoiding play with other boys and outside activities as much as possible. He was gifted in many areas, including drawing and mechanical activities. For a while he would pursue these, but then he would give them up in order to get back to mother. The father was a clothing salesman who paid little attention to his son.

When Dudley entered college, he complained that the physics teacher was "picking on" him. Mother, ever eager to have him at her side, encouraged him to drop out of college and stay home, which he did.

On top of that, the father was caught up in the toils of the great depression. There was no longer any need for his kind of door-to-door salesmanship; the big firms had so many men they would not hire him, so he gave up when he was about 50. Thereafter he spent all his time at home. Instead the mother went to work to support the family (this was in the 1930s when welfare scarcely existed).

Dudley did much the same thing with his father that he had done with mother. He stayed home, tinkered with one thing or another, and increasingly drew back from any kind of emotional or physical contact with anybody. In a desperate attempt to get out of this environment, at one point he ran away from home (he was then in his early twenties). In one of the local parks he collapsed, was found by the police, and was taken to Bellevue (the main psychiatric hospital in New York City).

After a few days there, he was released to a private hospital, where he received electroshock treatment and a few sessions of psychotherapy, but he refused further treatment. The psychiatrist who treated him felt that his case was hopeless. He returned home.

When his father died, he stayed with mother, who continued to support him. His time was spent doing virtually nothing beyond caring for his immediate physical needs. There was no contact with any other human being. The army rejected him as a typical schizophrenic.

Mother and son lived on like that for a number of years, neither one overtly dissatisfied with the arrangement. When the mother was urged to send the young man to psychiatric treatment, she refused, saying that his only trouble was that he "lacked ambition."

When the mother died, the son lived on alone for only a short while. He spent his time in this period visiting the places in the city where his mother had worked.

Eventually he could no longer take care of himself, and was hospitalized. He died at 48 of malignant hypertension. When he died, the psychiatrist at the hospital in charge of his case said: "He's better off dead."

In the light of the extensive new knowledge of the interaction between mother and child in the first year of life, the need of the mother to be much more familiar with the child's development looms larger all the time. A child develops from being talked to; learns to smile from being smiled at; acquires liveliness, motility, and action from being played with. In all of these areas, if the child's needs are not met, he or she feels unloved. No wonder then that the universal cry heard by the practicing clinician is: "Nobody ever loved me."

It is primarily in these areas that psychodynamically oriented psychologists have alerted the population to the complex development of the child, and the need of the mother (later father) to pay careful attention to this development. Actually, following upon the classical Freudian discoveries a revolution in child rearing has occurred in this century. Some of the main points can be briefly outlined.

The literature frequently refers to the "ordinary devoted mother." Certainly such mothers exist in abundance; perhaps they are the majority. But mothers tend to bring their children up in the ways in which they were brought up, and unless their attention is directed to the newer psychological findings they will ignore them.

In toilet training, up to about 1940, mothers were advised to toilet train their children as soon as they could sit up. This led to generations of anal compulsives and innumerable bowel and other toilet problems. Today the consensus is that if the child is trained somewhere between 2 and 3 years of age on the basis of identification with the parent rather than compulsion or punishment the emotional outcome is much more satisfactory. Yet innumerable exceptions are found; here as so commonly elsewhere the mothers who listen to the child guidance experts are those least in need of advice.

Josef was the son of 2 Polish-born immigrant parents. In line with her own upbringing, the mother taught the child that if he did not move his bowels three times a day he could be considered constipated. He tried his mightiest but rarely succeeded. Until he went off to college, where he learned the facts of life, Josef was convinced that he was constipated.

Josef was an only child. His father was a farmer who had been a machine gunner in the Austrian army during World War I. There was little contact between father and son in childhood. Later in his life the parents became enamored of some evangelists and would spend much of their time listening to sermons on the radio. Although urged by his father to listen to them, Josef consistently refused.

The most positive influence in the family was an uncle, the mother's brother, who had become a millionaire after immigrating to this country. This uncle was held up by the mother as a model of behavior, which Josef bitterly resented. However, his success did evidently stimulate the boy to make more of his life.

Another paradoxical event in his childhood came from his mother's peculiar concern with sex. When he was about 10, she began to tell him about bad women and what they could do to him if he let himself go. She would provide him with lurid descriptions of prostitutes, dance-hall girls, burlesque shows, and the like (where she got this information was unclear). He obediently promised to be a good boy but in the meantime absorbed the message that there were many sexual women in the world.

The family lived on a farm, but Josef was bright, and he was able to move out into the world when he went off to college. This proved to be an enormously liberating experience for him. He did brilliantly, eventually becoming a college professor. Although he bogged down in two unhappy marriages (as might have been anticipated), in the long run through therapeutic help he was able to make a sensible life for himself.

If this case is compared with that of Dudley there are two notable differences: First of all, his mother inadvertently taught him a lot about sex, which stimulated him immensely. And second, the mother was willing to let him go into the outside world, where he was able to discover an entirely new kind of life. The moral is again that the quality of the relationship between parents and children is much more important than the surface manifestations. A second moral is that children will often do better if removed from their parents at an appropriate point in their lives.

The attitude toward childhood masturbation has likewise gone through a complete about-face. One hundred years ago every conceivable illness from pimples to insanity was ascribed to excessive masturbation (which meant simply masturbation, since any kind of "self-abuse" was considered immoral and harmful). Throughout history both the Jewish and Christian churches have condemned masturbation as either unnatural or harmful. As late as 1940 the United States Naval Academy at Annapolis ruled that a candidate "shall be rejected by the examining surgeon for . . . evidence of . . . masturbation" (Kinsey, Pomeroy, & Martin, 1948, p. 513).

Spitz (1952), in a bibliographic investigation, showed that up to about 1940, masturbation was treated as an illness in textbooks of pediatrics. Clitoridectomy was extensively employed in many countries. Startling therapeutic measures were used by a peculiar medical organization that existed in the United States until 1925, specializing in various surgical procedures on clitoris, prepuce, and rectum. The persecution of the masturbating child was sadistic, often in the extreme; the consequent feeling of being unloved was inevitable.

Kinsey et al. (1948) shocked the country when they reported that 92% of the male population was involved in masturbation which leads to orgasm (p. 499), with a higher percentage among the better-educated group. However, Kinsey et al. held on to the cultural prejudices in his evaluation of the frequency of childhood masturbation, about which he obtained no direct information. They wrote:

> However extensive the incidental touching of genitalia may be, specific masturbation is quite rare among younger boys. Of course, there are cases of infants under a year of age who have learned the advantage of specific manipulation, sometimes as a result of being so manipulated by older persons; and there are some boys who masturbate quite specifically and with some frequency from the age of two or three. But most young boys, in attempting masturbation, engage in such desultory motions and so quickly cease their efforts that no satisfaction is obtained and they are, therefore, not interested in trying again. When an older person provides the more specific sort of manipulation which is usual among adults, the same child may be much aroused, and in a high proportion of the cases may be brought to actual orgasm. [p. 501]

At another point, in contradiction to what they say above, Kinsey et al. state: "Freud and the psychoanalysts contend that all tactile stimulation and response are basically sexual, and there seems considerable justification for this thesis, in view of the tactile origin of so much of the mammalian stimulation" (1948, p. 163).

Subsequently, more careful direct observation of children has shown that children begin to masturbate as soon as they can reach their genitals, that they enjoy what they are doing, and that they are prevented from continuing only by the forbidding attitude of the parents (Galenson, 1980). Boys begin to masturbate at about 7 or 8 months of age, as soon as they can reach the penis, girls a little later. Thus once more unless the parents take an enlightened view of the child's sexual development, which begins with masturbation, the child will feel unloved.

> When Tommy came to analysis, he was 30 years old, living on welfare, and spending most of his time in his room drinking tea and listening to records. His background was one of strict Catholicism, and he had been taught that masturbation is a mortal sin. Tommy was terrified of touching his penis with his hands. He did, as a result of some previous therapy, manage to masturbate by rubbing his penis against the bed. It took another year of analysis before he felt secure enough to masturbate with his hand. Naturally, with such an attitude he was terrified of girls and lived a solitary, cheerless existence.

In the area of discipline another marked change has occurred. Since the 1960s there has been an increased concern with physical violence in the home, hitherto a taboo subject (Gil, 1970; Martin, 1978; Gelles, Steinmetz, & Straus, 1981). While statistics are hard to come by with great precision, Gelles et al. estimate that in 1975 violent actions against a child victim by their parents were quite common; in that year, according to their findings, between 1.4 and 1.9 million children were vulnerable to physical injury (p. 64). A man's home can no longer be considered his castle, and laws against violence in the family have been enacted in almost all states.

One of the central theses of this book is that a hate culture tends to perpetuate itself by the hostile emotional climate of the family in which the child is brought up. While many would agree with this, others argue that absolute proof is lacking. Still, even though there is no crucial experiment proving it, there is a mass of evidence available pointing in that direction. One of the most recent efforts is that of Werner and Smith (1982), who have been conducting a study of every child born on Kauai in Hawaii in the year 1955. Their conclusions are devastating.

Of the entire cohort, some 20% were high risk and succumbed in the sense of delinquency, mental illness, or other evidence of behavioral disturbance, 10% were low risk but encountered enough stress to show maladaptation, 10% were high risk but emerged as the resilient group, and the rest were not high risk and did reasonably well (Weiner & Smith, 1982, p. 257). Because of the coping capacity of the resilient group, they argue: "All give us a glimpse of the universality of the enduring forces that allow the human species to overcome adversity" (p. 155).

This topic will be considered in more detail in Chapter 10. Here it will suffice to say that based on their study at least 30% of the population is markedly disturbed; the rest I would prefer to call an "adjustment neurotic group" rather than simply resilient. At any rate, while statistics vary depending on the intensity of the search, it is again shown here that inadequate parenting produces a feeling of being unloved and perpetuates the hate culture.

As the child grows up, it moves to the outside world. When this occurs (school-age period) the parents may react in all kinds of neurotic ways. Quite common is the parent who just holds on too long, unable to tolerate the "empty nest" that would result when the child leaves. Naturally this wish to hold onto the child is rationalized in a variety of ways—the child is sick, or too delicate to tolerate the slings and arrows of the outside world, or people pick on the child, and so on. Usually this conflict comes to the fore in adolescence, when the child for the first time is really free to leave the home, but it may appear sooner.

The family constellation in these cases usually involves an overprotective mother and distant or cruel father, with few or no siblings to take up the slack. In turn, the child may react by becoming too submissive, unwilling to leave the home, or too defiant, leaving home too soon. Here is an example combining the two reactions.

> Gloria was the third of 6 children, 5 girls and 1 boy. Father was a manufacturer, in comfortable circumstances. Mother was a housewife, taking care of the children. Outwardly the marriage seemed to be a traditional one.
>
> The father, however, took an unusual sexual interest in his daughters. It was rumored (and believed by Gloria) that he had sex with the oldest, who later became a prostitute and died at an early age. Another sister became a kept woman and eventually committed suicide. But Gloria he left alone, leading her to act out her desire for father with other men.
>
> The first memory she had of anything sexual occurred with her music teacher when she was 5. He took out his penis and asked her to play with it. "Innocently" she did what she was asked and then told her mother about it. The teacher was immediately dismissed, but Gloria had to conceal her pleasure at the sexual seduction.
>
> Since she was much younger than several of her sisters, there were brothers-in-law who were much older. One of them began to play with her sexually when she was about 10. He would put her up on a sideboard, take down her pants, and lick her vagina. Somehow the father discovered what was going on, and he kicked the young man out of the house.
>
> At this time the father went into an alcoholic period. He would sit at the table drinking and throwing knives around the room. Since he was

half drunk and angry (no one ever knew quite what he was so angry about), the children were terrified.

When she was about 13, Gloria began to act out on her own. With a girl friend at first she engaged in mutual masturbation, in which each would try to put her breast into the other girl's vagina.

From this it was a short step to picking up men, which she began to do when she was about 14. She and two of her girlfriends would march up and down the street, picking up any men who asked for their favors. Indiscriminately she would have sex in a hallway, at the man's place, or anywhere else he would take her. She took no precautions, ignorant of both contraception and the dangers of venereal disease. She realized that she was being completely defiant of father and mother and lived in constant dread that father would discover what she was doing and punish her unmercifully. Twice she contracted gonorrhea, three times she became pregnant and had abortions. School was a nightmare because she spent her days worrying whether she was pregnant or sick. However, her native endowment was good, so that in spite of her extreme anxiety she was eventually able to become a teacher.

After years of this indiscriminate kind of sexual activity, she met a man who fell in love with her and asked to marry her. She gladly agreed.

At this point her behavior underwent a complete change from total promiscuity to total propriety. Had he been a more forceful individual she would have submitted to his every wish (as she had done earlier); but since he was in reality a very frightened, mousy kind of man (like his father, he had once attempted suicide), she was the boss of the family. She made all the decisions, never let him out of her sight, and dominated the home completely.

One son was born to the couple. When he was about 8 years old he developed a symptom of excessive urination, for which he was taken to a physician. No physical abnormalities were found, but she was advised (foolishly) to watch his penis carefully to see how it grew. This advice needed no reemphasis; from then on, the major interest of her life was her son's penis. In her own sex life, while she was reasonably active, she was also quite disinterested, submitting to her husband because he wanted it. She did not have orgasms; instead she insisted on extensive anal play.

The combination of defiance and submissiveness led to interminable quarrels; the couple were truly "conflict habituated." Time after time they would decide to get a divorce, seek out a lawyer, draw up papers, then change their minds at the last minute.

Both partners went into therapy, with some improvement in their feelings about themselves. Gloria's lifelong anxiety diminished considerably, and she was able to pursue other interests such as music and art. Her husband's sexual performance improved and he felt much better about himself. The son, who entered therapy later with an unsatisfactory outcome, bogged down in psychosomatic symptoms.

In the area of sexuality, with which love among adults is most closely identified, the greatest conflicts occur when the parents impose excessive restrictions on their children. Here there has again been a revolutionary change within the past few generations, a change that is well documented. Kinsey in 1953 had reported that in a limited sample of grade-school females 18% were having intercourse by age 15 as against 1% of the college and graduate groups. Between the ages of 16 and 20, 38% of the grade-school group and 32% of the high school group were having intercourse as against 17 to 19% of the college-educated groups (Kinsey, 1953, p. 295). The Middletown study of the 1970s mentioned earlier documented the enormous change that had taken place in 20 years.

In this connection the figures on overt homosexual activity should be noted. According to Kinsey et al., at 30 years of age (1953, p. 450) 10% of the grade-school sample, 18% of the high school sample, and 33% of the graduate group recognized that they had been erotically aroused by other females. On the other hand, in a study some 20 years later, Sorensen (1973) reported that current homosexual behavior among adolescents is minimal: 2% of all boys and virtually no girls had had a homosexual experience during the preceding month. It would make sense that the increasing availability of heterosexual intercourse and/or petting would reduce the incidence of homosexual contacts. Sorensen comments: "The visibility of homosexuality, as well as the tolerance that young people have for other people's homosexual experiences, perhaps mistakenly persuades many people that there is far more homosexuality among young people than there really is" (1973, p. 293).

On the other hand, while overt sexuality has increased enormously, the more important question is whether love is on the rise or not. For sex can have both a constructive meaning of love or a destructive meaning of hostility. Here there can again be little doubt: Sex per se does not guarantee love at all. A popular magazine recently ran a special feature (*Self*, 1983) on America's number one emotional illness: romantic malnutrition. Everybody longs for love; few find it.

As Goode (1982) has pointed out, societies everywhere are concerned that the love feelings will upset the social order and therefore use a variety of means to control them. The same is true for our own society. While the conquest of the extreme sexual repression of the nineteenth century is on the whole for the good, no one could really argue that it has produced or will produce a love culture without much more attention to the emotional reactions that inevitably attach themselves to such an intimate experience.

FILIAL LOVE

"Honor thy father and mother" is one of the Ten Commandments. Nor can there be any question that it is a good commandment. Brought up in an atmosphere of love, warmth, and understanding, the child reaches maturity in the most appropriate way possible. As in Rudolf Ekstein and Rocco Motto's excellent book, *From Learning for Love to Love of Learning* (1969), the child first learns to love his or her parents, then acquires pleasure in imitating their activities and identifying with them.

Yet in practice it is unusual to see a child grow up in such an atmosphere. More commonly, obedience, discipline, and conformity are impressed on the child, who then comes to see "doing the right thing" as the greatest goal in life. As in animal societies, there is in the education of the child usually an alternation between submission and defiance. The submissive child is seen as "good" as a rule; the defiant child as "bad." Clinical experience shows that such a view looks at the child from the vantage point of the parents or the authority figures. In reality, the "good" child is not so good, nor is the "bad" child so bad. There are important underlying dynamic factors at play in both.

Some submission to authority is of course essential in any social order. But when it is carried too far its effects can be seriously damaging to the individual. In terms of the interactive process that we have been describing all along, what happens is that the submissive child gives in to the parental wishes, forgetting his or her own. "Mother knows best" becomes the motto of these families.

In the 1950s a number of social philosophers, such as Erich Fromm, David Riesman, and William Whyte, called attention to the overemphasis on conformity in American culture. Riesman (1969), following Fromm, coined the terms *other-directed* and *inner-directed*. Whyte (1956), in a well-known book of the same title, spoke of the "organization man." Both authors, and numerous others, described the excessive reliance on parents and authority that these descriptions implied.

Riesman saw the other-directed man emerging in recent years in large metropolitan centers yet similar to the American as seen more than a century ago by de Tocqueville. The American is said to be shallower, freer with his money, friendlier, more uncertain of himself and his values, more demanding of approval than the European. The parents of these people are increasingly in doubt as to how to bring up their children. They turn to their contemporaries for advice, or even turn to the children. Yet they cannot help but show their children how little they depend on themselves and how much on others. Whatever they may seem to be teaching the child in terms of content, they are passing on to him or her their own contagious, highly diffuse anxiety. They reinforce this teaching by giving the child approval when he or she makes good but taking all the credit for themselves.

Whyte, in his description of the organization man (or, rather, his caricature of it), writes as follows:

Be loyal to the company and the company will be loyal to you. After all, if you do a good job for the organization, it is only good sense for the organization to be good to you, because that will be best for everybody. There are a bunch of real people around here. Tell them what you think and they will respect you for it. They don't want a man to fret and stew about his work. It won't happen to me. A man who gets ulcers probably shouldn't be in business anyway. [1956, p. 129]

So much for the outside. How does it look from the inside? Here are several clinical vignettes:

Susie was known as "Sugar" in her childhood. She did everything that was expected of her: She was quiet, well behaved, never loud, good in school, outwardly friendly. She was the model obedient child who loved her parents dearly.

Her problems came to a head when she reached puberty. Then she discovered that in the adult world where everybody was talking about sex, she was terrified. Her father professed to be an authority on the Bible (in reality he was a businessman who knew little about it) and would give her long lectures on the topic. Sometimes at night he would lie in bed, asking her to hold his hand, while he lectured her. It was her feeling that at such times he was masturbating under the covers.

It was not surprising that with such a background she remained a virgin until she was 27.

Unable to tolerate her frustrations any longer, she sought out a psychiatrist. With his help she managed to move away from home, establishing a life of her own. Her father could not see why she was moving and accused her of "crucifying" him. Mother, who did nothing with her time, drifted away from life more and more and seemed to become openly psychotic in her later years.

Susie went into business and did well. She could take orders and do what she was told, even though inwardly she was in total rebellion, seething with anger at her incompetent superiors.

Eventually, after years of long-term therapy, she was able to marry and find work that was congenial to her.

John, the only child of Irish parents, was obedient in the extreme. At the age of 8 he identified with Jesus Christ and vowed to live a life like his; for a while he even entertained the idea of becoming a priest. He was brought up as a strict Catholic.

Several sexual episodes came to light in the early stages of the analysis. One memory broke through from the age of 4: He woke up one morning to find that his father's penis was between his legs. (Whether this was an actual event or a fantasy could never be determined.) Another—this time a clear-cut—memory was that he used to play with the genitals of the family dog; in particular he liked to stroke the dog's penis to the point of erection.

In school John did not do too well, undoubtedly because of the anxieties aroused by his sexual fantasies. He had to go to a second-rate school and finished without any specific skills.

During World War II John became attached to the Naval Command, where he learned a new skill in radar work and was decorated for his efforts. This accomplishment served to bolster his sense of self-esteem but did not diminish his anxieties in any way.

In the meantime father had given up or lost his job, and it never became clear how the family lived after that. Somehow father managed to make some money; the parents never asked John for help.

At the end of the war John was still a virgin, true to his Catholic beliefs and early identification with Jesus. In desperation he married a woman who was somewhat malformed and could not have children. With her he was extremely unhappy, unable to live with her and unable to extricate himself from the dilemma. He clung to the belief that divorce was wrong.

When he was about 35, he met another woman, who attracted him very much and was quite sexual. He was eager to marry her, but full of guilt. In despair he went to his mother and asked for her permission to leave his miserable marriage (he did not tell her about the other woman). Mother agreed.

The second marriage was a happy one, but he remained quite anxious. When the war ended, he attached himself to one of the Fortune 500 companies, eventually reaching a post of some importance there. In the second marriage there were 3 children.

Through it all John was always anxious. He consulted one neurologist after another, all of whom assured him that there was nothing wrong with him, and all of whom prescribed sedatives such as phenobarbital (this was in the days before tranquilizers). One device used to control his anxiety was to move around, and he actually moved to eight different cities before he settled down for good.

In analysis he made an immediate and strong positive transference. Every session he announced that he was feeling better. One of his pet fantasies was that he would march up and down in front of the analyst's office with a signboard, urging everybody to go to the analyst for help. And indeed his anxieties steadily diminished.

But while he could improve externally, the guilt instilled in his childhood took a long time to eradicate. One particular form that it took was a reluctance to move ahead in his firm. He complained that the only people to reach the top positions were those who worked night and day, including taking work home over the weekend, which he was reluctant to do.

Eventually the analysis aroused in him a desire to help his fellow men (similar to the earlier wish to become a priest). He retired from his firm, at a generous pension for which the firm was famous. Though over 60, he went back to school, and he spent the rest of his life as a social worker. The guilt about his life retreated but never entirely disappeared.

Both of these examples, and numerous others that could be cited, demonstrate the intense, excruciating anxiety that affects the conforming, other-directed, organization person, an anxiety that rarely appears on the surface. What surfaces more often is alcoholism, or sexual adventurism, or psychosomatic symptoms of one kind or another.

In the years since the 1950s, so much has been written about the submissive, other-directed individual and psychotherapy has expanded to such a large extent that many persons have sought out therapists to help them understand and overcome their inner fears, which continue to plague them regardless of how much success they have. This has led, among some segments of the population at least, to large-scale changes in values, attitudes, and life-styles. The authors of *The Inner American* (Veroff, Douvan, & Kulka, 1981) describe it as follows:

> *Between 1957 and 1976, our culture underwent what can reasonably be described as a psychological revolution. The establishment of the Joint Commission which sponsored* Americans View Their Mental Health *was in itself a signal and symptom of the shift toward a psychological orientation in our culture. A congressional committee took on itself the task of assessing the psychological health and well-being of the American people! This act as well as the programs and policies launched in the wake of the commission's extensive series of studies and reports revealed, among other findings, a faith in mental-health services, a belief that psychological well-being could be reasonably assessed, and that psy-*

chological technology (i.e., mental-health service) properly applied, could increase well-being. This sanguine assertion by Congress may not have initiated the "therapeutic age," but it certainly signaled the fact that this new era was abroad in our world. . . .

Child raising, which had always been permissive in America compared to Europe, took a new turn. . . . Women were attracted back to full-time work in the home . . . by the prospect of raising perfect children. Impelled by this goal and the advice of child-raising experts, women sought to mold children's attitudes and motives to a degree previously unheard of. Where in earlier times parents sought obedience–compliance from children and left their internal psychological world alone, they now aimed at creating the attitudes and motives that would lead the child to behave properly on the basis of his/her own desires. They invested the child with "potential" and took the goal of socialization to be the realization of that unique potential. [p. 14]

While the authors seem rather sanguine about the success of this inner psychological resolution, the practicing clinician reserves some skepticism in the matter. As has been seen, the hate element in the culture is still strong, and to change a hate culture into a love culture is a formidable understanding. I believe that it can be done, but we must be more conscious of the problems and obstacles that face us in the effort. This topic will be discussed more fully in Chapter 8.

The defiant child is as much a part of our culture as the submissive. Revolution, individualism, and rebellion against authority are all essential parts of the American tradition. Rebellion even seems to be one of the built-in values for many people. One mother of my acquaintance, who did everything theoretically required of a mother, was later told by her daughters reproachfully: "You never gave me anything to rebel against."

Since adolescents have always tended to defy their elders, it is not surprising to find so much disobedience and flouting of authority. Fighting, drugs, indiscriminate sex without love, dropping out of school, and the like are the order of the day, requiring the efforts of thousands of professionals to help the troubled.

In the following case the early childhood attachments to the parents did not result in any symptoms until both of the partners had married and had children of their own.

Sol and Rebecca were both submissive, obedient children who loved their parents and obeyed them implicitly. Neither, however, had any significant inner emotional life, and neither had any gratification in his or her sex life.

Sol became an accountant and tax lawyer. The training requires long hours of work well into the thirties. As long as he was in training, Sol could bury himself in his work, paying little attention to the children, and without any interests outside his work. Since he was highly intelligent and competent, by the time he was 30 he was worth more than a million dollars.

Rebecca was the daughter of two wealthy parents who had likewise made a fortune in their business. She too was obedient to their wishes, never showing any sign of disagreement or rebelliousness.

The couple had two children, a boy and a girl. Once the family came, the problems came and multiplied.

First of all, Rebecca lost her mother when she was in her early thirties. Because of her strong devotion to her mother, Rebecca began to go to mediums and spiritualists who allegedly would bring the mother's voice back from the other world. Since she was wealthy and paid handsomely for the seances, there was never any dearth of spiritualists to do her bidding.

Then Sol fell ill with cardiovascular disease: coronary weakness and high blood pressure. From the age of 35 or so he spent much of his time going from one doctor to another. Convinced that he was going to die at an early age, he made up one will after another. He alternated between including the children and excluding them from his will when they began to defy him, which began early. He finally died at 67.

Neither child turned out well. Both began to rebel in their teens, each in a different way. The boy began to be truant from school, used drugs, and engaged in various pranks to irritate his mother, such as hanging out the window. (The family lived in a large apartment house of 30 stories; they were on the seventeenth floor.) When the mother shrieked about what he was doing he would calmly say: "What are you worried about? I'm holding on." He would not apply himself to any business or occupation, became a homosexual, and drifted through life, supported by his wealthy parents. He refused all efforts to get him into therapy.

The girl began to act out sexually during her adolescence. She went to USO dances (she was then about 18) and picked up soldiers with whom she would have sex. The parents knew nothing about it, even though she was quite indiscriminate. She was fortunate that she never became pregnant or infected with an venereal disease. She did, however, develop a rather severe case of duodenal ulcers, which were not treated properly and left her with lifelong somatic complaints.

In her twenties she went to the country one summer and fell in love with a member of the band, who was twice her age and physically handicapped. Against the vigorous objections of her parents, who threatened to cut her off without a penny (which they did for a while), she married this man. It turned out that he was only out for her money. After two children came, he wanted out, and her father agreed to pay him a substantial amount of money to leave his daughter. The husband never had any interest in the children, both of whom were girls, and he disappeared from sight.

The girl did go to analysis and made more sense out of her life than the boy. But unexpectedly a number of other physical complaints emerged. Although she later made a happier marriage and developed an unexpected artistic ability, the eventual outcome was far from ideal.

LACK OF LOVE

In the twelfth-century chronicle of Salimbene (cited in *Encyclopaedia Britannica*, 15th ed., vol. 8, p. 810), a linguistic experiment of Frederick II is reported. King Frederick wanted to find out what kind of speech and what manner of speech children would have when they grew up, if they spoke to no one beforehand. So he bade foster mothers and nurses to suckle the children, to bathe and wash them, but in no way to prattle or speak with them, for he wanted to know whether they would speak the Hebrew language, which is the oldest, or Greek or Latin or Arabic, or perhaps the language of their parents. But he labored in vain because all the children died. They could not live without petting and joyful faces and loving words.

The story illustrates beautifully the infant's intense need for interaction with mother. Language is not just communication; it is an expression of love. Today, as noted in previous chapters, we have evidence that these expressions of love are found among many animal species, not just humans. But in the human, with its greater capacity for intelligible speech, it is a primary concern.

By now, as stressed earlier, there can be no doubt that the child desperately needs the love and affection of the mother (or a mother substitute) to grow up properly. What if it does not get such love? Then it grows up with a varied assortment of ego disturbances, and above all it grows up without the capacity to love, the most serious of all human disorders. The psychoanalytic position has been nowhere stated more clearly than by Ernest Jones (1929), who wrote:

> *The disorder underlying all mental morbidity can be defined as a failure on the part of the ego to deal in any final manner with certain fundamental intrapsychical conflicts that are the inevitable lot of every human*

being. These conflicts arise from the difficulty in adjusting the claims of the sexual instinct in its earliest stages with those of other psychic forces. . . . The ego . . . is threatened if the conflict in question is not solved, and the ultimate danger menacing it is paralysis of mental functioning. . . . All mental morbidity is therefore a state of schizophrenia, although Professor Bleuler has proposed to reserve this term for the most striking of its forms. What we meet with clinically as mental disorder represents the endless variety of the ways in which the threatened ego struggles for its self-preservation. [p. 373. See also Breggin (1983) for a recent evaluation of the organic position.]

If for "sexual instinct" we substitute the term *love* in the above quotation, Jones's remarks are as pertinent today as they were when they were first made more than 50 years ago.

During World War II considerable experience was accumulated about the reactions of an infant to separation from the mother. The British psychoanalyst John Bowlby has researched and summarized this problem more than any other figure on the contemporary scene (1969–1980). His formulation of the reaction to loss is graphic: protest—despair—detachment. The most pathological is the last—detachment. It is important to realize that it comes only after a long period of frustration; detachment is reached only as a last resort. And these children—and adults—the the hardest of all to reach therapeutically.

Nevertheless, it is essential to note that even the individual who is seemingly most far gone from reality (the schizophrenic) can in some cases be helped therapeutically. As noted earlier, the resiliency of the human being in many life situations can be truly amazing. The theory of such therapy fits in with the theses presented here about love. The infant in childhood has a "horrible" time (Bleuler, 1978), which means he or she receives much hatred and little love. In the later therapeutic situation, the patient receives an extraordinary amount of attention and understanding from the therapist. This gives him or her some of the oneness (Silverman, Lachmann, & Milich, 1982) that he or she failed to receive as a child. With the help of this therapeutic oneness the patient can then resume the growth interrupted by childhood traumas.

The argument about the schizophrenogenic mother can now be rephrased in this form: If the child receives too little love from mother (schizophrenogenic), his or her ego will be weakened, and later traumas may precipitate a psychotic episode, or a totally psychotic life-style. Many mothers act in this unloving way, even though there is a total denial on the surface.

The child's development moves from mother to father to the outside world. In this process love is needed at every stage; hatred impedes growth, love fosters it. When there is a lack of love at any stage, the child incorporates that lack of love, identifies with it, and behaves that way later on in life. These are the people who are "cold," "eccentric," "distant," "unempathic," and the like; they are doing to others what was done to them. What they are called diagnostically is of little importance: They were not loved as children, so they do not know how to love as adults. As mentioned earlier, the experimental demonstration is Harlow's discovery that the monkeys brought up on wire mesh mothers (i.e., not real, live mothers) failed to respond normally when the sexual period arrived. In the human being essentially the same paradigm applies. But it can take many different forms. Here is one clinical vignette:

Helen was the daughter of a sickly mother who died when she was a toddler. She was brought up largely by grandparents who were in their sixties.

When she was 9 her father remarried and moved out of the country, leaving her with her grandparents. To the ordinary observer, no noticeable disturbance appeared until she went away to college and began to engage in homosexual beatings; that is, she would have other girls beat her and have sex with her.

When she was 20, the homosexuality stopped, as well as the beatings. She met a man who was very congenial, and they married. They had two children, girl twins.

Once the twins were born, her homosexuality was apparently revived, and she felt disturbed. She began to seek out psychiatrists. Her condition worsened.

During World War II, her husband was overseas. When he returned he confessed to her that he had fallen in love with a French woman and wanted a divorce. This shock unnerved her completely, and she had a complete breakdown. The various therapies in vogue at that time were used on her—electric shock, insulin coma (no real psychoanalytic therapy or psychoanalysis). Some 10 psychiatrists were unable to help her.

Then in the course of one hospitalization she met Dr. C., a handsome young psychiatrist who came from her home state; in fact, he was born about 10 miles away from her birthplace. She fell madly in love with this man. He arranged her life and did everything for her. She improved markedly.

What she did not know was that Dr. C. was a drug addict. When confronted with the possibility of a jail sentence, he suddenly left the hospital, terminating her therapy on 3 days' notice.

Still the love experience she had had with Dr. C. helped her through the subsequent crisis. Even when her husband remarried before the divorce papers were filed with her, she kept enough equilibrium to function, and she even wrote a book about her hospital experiences. Eventually, with another therapist, she came back to a reasonably normal life.

In the above case, what carried Helen through the depths of her despair was her love for Dr. C., which persisted even after he had deserted her. Technically we call this "transference," but the love aspect is the major component. As Freud emphasized (1915), the difference between transference love and normal love is only one of degree. Thus, here too, once she found love, which she had missed in the turmoil of her childhood, she was able to move forward again.

RECAPITULATION

Clinical observations have been presented about five commonly experienced varieties of love: romantic, married, parental, filial, and lack of love.

In romantic love, even though the lovers sometimes experience the heights of human bliss, more often terrible suffering is involved. It is rare for romance to last indefinitely, let alone a lifetime. All the poetry, all the stories, all the clinical observations of romantic love highlight the union, and then the separation, with the consequent anguish attendant upon the breakup of the relationship. Much of the suffering, it should be noted, is due to the holdover of infantile wishes.

In married love, again when it goes well it is beautiful, but when it does not it can be awful. A common problem is the regression in the service of the spouse. In this conflict, there is mutual parentification, in which each partner sees the other as a representative of the original parent. Naturally the partner cannot live up to these expectations, and trouble follows.

In parental love, the complexities of the child's development are so great that relatively few parents are able to cope with them. Psychology has clarified many of the problems of children, but parents will more often stick to the way in which they were brought up; those who do listen to the psychologists often need them least.

In filial love, again ideally such love could produce great happiness. But again it is rarely seen. More often there is the expression of defiance or submission, neither of which suffices to lay the basis for a good life.

Finally, there is the most pathological of all, the lack of love. In the extreme this produces the markedly detached individual, who may or may not be overtly schizophrenic, and whose love disappointments are so great that it is extraordinarily difficult to induce him or her to try again. Yet even here, some love at a later stage can at times produce wonders.

All in all, however, our clinical observations tend to confirm the thesis that we are living in a hate culture, in which the predominant feeling among people is one of hatred rather than one of love. The usual statistical studies are inadequate to test this thesis. What is needed is a careful evaluation of the clinical data on an intensive individual basis. The cases presented in this chapter are designed to give some idea of what lies behind the surface appearance of the conventionally "good" family.

8

The Social Control of Love

While love seems to be a private feeling, a closer examination shows that it is invariably subject to a variety of social controls. For love, in the romantic sense, threatens the social order in a number of ways, and so in most of the world love has not been given much institutional support and has been kept under strong controls (Goode, 1982). In terms of our thesis, this could be phrased as follows: The meaning of love varies with the overall culture; its fullest flowering can only be expected to occur in a love culture.

Suggesting that western culture has been a hate culture for several thousand years is scarcely a novelty, though the connections of this underlying hatred with other social institutions have been interpreted in different ways by different thinkers. In fact, the notion of an apocalyptic destruction of the world goes back a long way. The biblical notion of the flood expresses it, as does the legend of the destruction of Atlantis (Friedrich, 1982, p. 20). The image of virtually imminent world destruction is repeated throughout history and stressed in many religions (e.g., the belief in the imminent Second Coming of Christ) and recurs in many pessimistic philosophies. Yet in spite of this overpowering fear millions have throughout the ages made an effort to find love, either in small enclaves separated from the rest of the world or in grand schemes to transform it.

INTENTIONAL LOVE CULTURES

From time immemorial, human beings, disheartened by the victory of evil in the world, have tried to withdraw into groups of their own, where they could practice love and harmony, far from the madding crowd. These communitarian groups have been called intentional love cultures, since whatever their basic philosophy might be, sooner or later it turns out that they are seeking to establish a rule of love, or in our language, a love culture. One such group, the Oneida Community, is discussed in Chapter 3. The study of such groups should cast a most revealing light on the degree to which society does exert control over what seem to be very private feelings at first sight.

The most recent study of American communes is that by Benjamin Zablocki (1980). He examined intensively 120 different communes throughout the country in the period 1965–1978 and reports extensively on his findings in his book *Alienation and Charisma*. He defines a commune as any group of five or more adult individuals (plus children, if any), the majority of whose dyads are not cemented by blood or marriage, who have decided to live together, without compulsion, for an indefinite period of time, primarily for the sake of an ideological goal, focused upon the achievement of community, for which a collective household is deemed essential (p. 7). Although the original ideology may vary widely, upon closer examination it turns out that the commune sample is nearly unanimous in its high regard for only one value: *loving* (p. 196). Half the respondents rank loving as their first or second most important instrumental value, and 90% place it in the top half of their lists of values. "Truly, it can be said that love is the common coin of the entire communitarian movement" (p. 196).

Zablocki, like most observers, was concerned with the stability of the communes that he was studying. In this respect his findings were paradoxical, since he found that love is both the bond and the bane of communal life.

The most powerful single predictor of leaving is defined at the relational level of analysis: the amount of love received from fellow commune members. But by *love* here he refers to the number of times that a person is mentioned by fellow commune members as an object of love; he seems to mean popularity rather than love. The more popular a person is, the less likely he or she is to leave the commune (Zablocki, 1980, p. 128).

But then comes what seems to be the opposite finding: the more love relations existing at any time in a commune as a whole, the more likely it is that the commune will disintegrate, or, if the commune should survive, the higher its annual membership turnover is likely to be (Zablocki, 1980, p. 147). This appears to mean that when many individuals feel strong love relationships for a number of others, the tensions aroused are too great to sustain the social grouping and many people simply leave.

But matters are even more complicated: This very strong relationship between dyadic love and communal instability is almost completely suppressed by the physical presence in the commune of a charismatic leader. Only under direct daily charismatic influence, among the communes in the sample, was it possible for very high densities of dyadic love relationships to coexist with very low membership turnover rates. Yet on the other hand charismatic leaders themselves were just as likely to leave their communes in any given year as ordinary members.

To translate these sociological findings into more ordinary language, especially as they relate to our central examination of intentional love cultures: When the group members like one another, the group stays together, but if there is too much of a demand for intimacy, then the group begins to fall apart. Both of these propositions however are contradicted if there is a strong charismatic leader; then whatever the leader says becomes the law.

•Although the small communes that Zablocki (and others) investigated are made up for the most part of individuals rebelling against an ungratifying society—that is, an unloving family background—it is striking how the composition of the commune becomes increasingly similar to the pattern of the family. When group members like one another, it becomes a happy family (the term is used quite often), but when dyads form with too much intimacy, it becomes incestuous, arousing the same kinds of jealousies and resentments in the others that the pairing off of father and mother arouse in the average child. And overall, if the father is a powerful figure (less often the mother), then the previous attitudes are subordinated to the more imperative wish to bow to the will of the leader.

These findings tend to confirm the thesis that humans sooner or later move toward hierarchically organized groups. History is full of father figures and other leaders who have caused untold destruction. Yet they are obeyed and followed to the death. In the evaluation of any love culture this fact must be given great weight.

The question of who goes into communes, or intentional love cultures, has been extensively investigated. The description given by William James almost 100 years ago (James, 1902) is still largely valid: He felt that psychologically immature individuals were the ones most likely to undergo a conversion to an unorthodox religious group; those who were introverted and pessimistic, with a negative outlook on the world; those who were brooding and steeped in despair. He coined the terms *once-born* and *twice-born:* Those who convert to a new religion or enter a commune are twice-born—they feel a tremendous uplift after wallowing for a shorter or longer period of time in a quagmire of depressions, shiftlessness, and drifting. They have a new family, they have a new goal, they have a new set of values that makes them feel twice-born. What James did not describe, but what has been described by many modern researchers is, that the resurgent feelings of confidence, optimism, and trust do not last indefinitely; for a great many they peter out very quickly and they are in despair all over again. In his study, Zablocki found that communes are typically but not intrinsically unstable. "A great many of them begin life full of hope and enthusiasm, only to perish before being able to celebrate a first birthday" (1980, p. 146). Half of the communes in his sample had disintegrated in little over 2 years, and almost half of those remaining were gone after 4 years. However, this is not the entire picture. Many of the communes reformed and led longer lives. Yet while the statistics are not entirely clear, it seems clear enough that communes do not last indefinitely.

In his examination of the motives for joining an intentional love group, he tended to find that communitarian organization is based upon the attempts by the charismatic to mobilize the alienated. This task is never fully completed, and in many instances it is a losing battle.

In other words, disaffected people who have not been able to find or build a loving family of their own join up with others in the attempt to set up a new kind of loving family. There are the strong ones (charismatic) who take the initiative, the weak ones (alienated) who go along. After a while, in the great majority of cases, the new family falls apart, and for many of the same reasons: jealousies, resentments, power struggles, battles over sexual rights, and so on (Zablocki, 1980, p. 104).

Every love culture, of course, is immediately concerned with the management of sexual relationships. On the current scene many communes have sought not to restrict sexuality but to encourage fuller sexual freedom. Images of sexual utopia in which repression disappears and the communes come to be bound together through mutually harmonious relationships of sexual love are quite common. Sexual repression is often attacked not only as something harmful in itself but also as the linchpin of the entire repressive capitalist system. Wilhelm Reich and Herbert Marcuse are sometimes cited as the charismatic leaders who have pointed the way. Sooner or later these images of total sexual freedom end up in frustration of one kind or another.

According to Zablocki, for at least three centuries there has not been a single year without the formation of a communitarian organization in the United States. Wilson (1973) has depicted numerous millennial movements among tribal and third world peoples. The yearning for love is virtually universal, as is the attempt to establish what has been called an intentional love culture. Usually these have had religious overtones, but many have been unrelated to religion of any kind.

Veysey (1973) describes one nonreligious group in New Mexico, which he visited in 1971, a community of about 30 people who had been together for several years on an isolated ranch in the New Mexico desert. There is a strong charismatic leader, named Ezra, who dominates the community. Ezra describes his philosophy as follows:

> *Earlier groups failed because they didn't integrate the inner with the external. Here we're deliberately combining them in a total new formula for life. Western civilization isn't simply dying. It's dead. We are probing into its ruins to take whatever is useful for the building of the new civilization to replace it. This new civilization will be planetary. The whole earth will be our home. We are no longer Americans, or Westerners, even though as individuals we were once raised in that tradition. We will build a series of centers in various parts of the world to demonstrate the new way of life. This ranch is merely our first training ground.* [Veysey, 1973, p. 279]

In this group, the theater forms a major segment of expected daily activities. In practice the pace accelerates when drama festivals are about to be held. Sometimes the rehearsals go on till past midnight. The dome, barely completed before the festival of August 1971, is an enormous source of group pride, a constantly visible testimonial to their capacity to carry an arduous project through to completion.

This community, according to Veysey seems "neither hip nor straight." Every Sunday evening the group has a special meal known as a feast. At these occasions beer or wine is served, though in such small quantities as to be merely ceremonial. It is drunk to the accompaniment of a long series of toasts.

Ezra's domination of the group is open. One soon realizes that every small practice that makes up the complicated rhythm of the commune's daily life carries the stamp of his considered approval, and that the major outlines are wholly the product of his mind. This entire social order is the tangible enactment of his own vision.

Among other methods, control is exercised by Ezra by sudden angry explosions, usually directed at one person. Calmly in control of himself at one minute, in the next he will be shouting the most hurtful words conceivable in a furious assault upon the ego of some trapped individual.

Ezra's line of approach is that we can survive through intelligence. Shrewdness is the correct response to any overwhelming situation. We should follow it, never allowing ourselves to become fatalistic. But for the others the sudden sharing of hitherto secret fears remains uppermost.

The group life is organized around work more than anything else. In this work, themes of self-punishment and self-correction dominate their attitudes. Laboring day and night as if possessed, often far into the early morning, these people might almost be called, Veysey says, "Do-It-Yourself-Stakhanovites."

Sex is not forbidden, but neither is it encouraged. The one glaring component missing from the group is children. Several children are there, but no provision has been made for them.

The group was formed early in 1967 and thus had existed for 4 years when Veysey visited for 5 weeks in 1971. Ezra conceived of his own idiosyncractic philosophy, which includes concepts of men like Gurdjieff, Buckminster Fuller, and Wilfrid Bion. Bion's book in fact came to seem the most appropriate manual for group living in this community. New members have to pass through an initiation period of about 1 year, after which they agree to be bound by five "inner rules," which are revealed to no outsider.

Characteristically, Ezra's strongest conviction is that the greatest sickness of western civilization is the nuclear family structure. "The triadic form of mother-father-child leads to self-destruction" (Veysey, p. 393). Obviously he wishes to be the father of a new family, but one with few or no small children.

In the fall of 1971, the group began a scheduled drama tour of the east coast, playing to several university audiences in the Boston area. Then they spent three weeks in England. After this trip about a third of the group members defected. Ezra however, is determined to carry on.

Among the earlier intentional love cultures, one that has attracted considerable attention is the Shakers, perhaps because they took a vow of celibacy, allowing the group to die out. They were dedicated to a life of productive labor and perfection. For a while Shaker communities flourished handsomely.

The Shakers derived originally from a small branch of English Quakers who had adopted the French Camisards' ritual practices of shaking, shouting, dancing, whirling, and singing in tongues. The Shaker doctrine was formulated by Ann Lee, an illiterate textile worker of Manchester, who was converted to the "Shaking Quakers" in 1758. After experiencing persecution and imprisonment for participation in noisy worship services, "Mother Ann" had a series of revelations, following which she regarded herself, and was so regarded by her followers, as the female aspect of God's dual nature and the second incarnation of Christ. It was she who established celibacy as the cardinal principle of the sect.

Although often persecuted for pacifism or for bizarre religious beliefs falsely attributed to them, the Shakers won the admiration of the outside world for their model farms and prosperous communities. In exchanges with the outside they were noted for their fair dealing.

The group reached its height in the 1840s, when there was a large-scale interest in communitarian utopias. In 1840 Ralph Waldo Emerson wrote to Carlyle: "We are all a little wild here with numberless projects of social reform. Not a reading man but has a draft of a new community in his waistcoat pocket" (cited in Zablocki, 1980, p. 37). But by 1874 the society was advertising for members; by the late 1960s only a few elderly survivors remained.

Among the non-American communitarian movements several may be described in more detail. There is first of all the Soviet communes, a neglected chapter of history (Wesson, 1963). When the Russian Revolution broke out in 1917, communes were highly regarded as a valuable utopian experiment. They had a long ideological history; as noted earlier, they drew upon innumerable intentional love cultures that had existed in Europe from time immemorial.

At first enthusiasm for the commune idea, or at least the label, seemed to be gaining. The Paris Commune, which had been so closely studied by the Bolshevik leaders, was exalted as a glorious example for the Soviets, and every effort was made to see where it had gone wrong and how its mistakes could be avoided. To build upon the inspiration of her illustrious predecessor, Soviet Russia was sometimes called the Russian Commune, and Petrograd was solemnly baptized as a commune (Wesson, 1963, p. 83). Speakers at the Party Congress of July 1918 proposed that the official title of the government become *Commune*, but this was turned down on the grounds that the word referred to local government. When in the spring of 1919 consumer cooperatives were made obligatory distributors of the scanty rations, they were called consumer communes.

At first the number of communes grew steadily, and they seemed on the march to triumph. In October 1918 it was predicted that they would cover Russia thickly by the following spring, and in February 1919 their expansion still seemed irresistible. The commissariat of agriculture supported the communes strongly in 1918, but decreasingly thereafter. Ten million rubles were assigned for furthering the establishment of communes in July 1918, and another 50 million in July 1918; these sums were enormous by the standards of those times and conditions.

By 1922 there were 1672 communes registered all over Russia. The average commune numbered about 50 until pressure for collectivization began in 1927. The biggest spurt came in 1930, when the communes (together with other forms of collective farms) reached a dimension about six times greater than had been usual when membership was voluntary.

Further, the ideology of the commune was completely equalitarian. One agitator for the communes declared in 1919:

> *Our chldren must be all equal. If some have shoes, then shoes for all. Or if without shoes, then all without shoes. Likewise the fathers and mothers should all be equal: everybody has a suit, or nobody has one. Then nobody will envy anybody, and there will be no quarrels, for quarrels come from envy.* [Wesson, 1963, p. 83]

Later of course the regime found no justification for the commune; it wanted power, not equality. Stalin himself spoke of equalitarianism as the mortal sin of the commune. In the 1959 *History of the Communist Party of the Soviet Union* it was stated flatly that "equalitarian distribution is incompatible with socialism" (Wesson, 1963, p. 228). Eventually of course the communes disappeared. The need for a powerful father figure is again brought out here.

It is one of the ironies of history that the commune idea, once seen as the wave of the future in Russia (though not by the leading Bolsheviks), later became a point of divergence between the Soviet and the Chinese forms of Marxism. And in China too. after Mao's death, the ideal of equalitarianism has been pushed into the background in favor of power and economic progress.

Three other historically documented intentional love cultures are of special interest to us. One is the Saint-Simonians of France in the 1830s, usually regarded as one of the utopian forerunners of Communism; the second is the social movement established by Franz Mesmer before the French Revolution, which combined a utopian scheme with a therapeutic mechanism (similar in that respect to psychoanalysis); and third is the early Christian communities, the first large-scale attempt in the western world to replace violence with love.

Henri Saint-Simon was a nobleman born in Paris in 1760. At first he seemed an unlikely candidate for founder of a love culture: He is depicted as stubborn and self-willed, in a continual bitter conflict with his father, who once had him jailed for his behavior. (The material here draws upon Manuel & Manuel, 1979, chaps. 25, 26.) In 1779, obeying royal orders, he went to fight in the American War of Independence as a line officer. Later in a naval battle of St. Kitts in 1782 he was taken prisoner.

During the French Revolution he rejected his aristocratic heritage and assumed an earthy peasant name. In concert with others, he speculated in the mansions of nobles who had emigrated or been guillotined. The whole group led licentious lives. Once caught, most were executed; but Saint-Simon escaped.

His first work seems to have been published by a Paris bookseller in 1803. By 1805 he was penniless. He then devoted himself increasingly to the development of his philosophical projects. Curious scientific intuitions poured forth in an outburst of disorganized tracts. He became megalomanic, his letters becoming a series of wild ravings about genius, his mission, and the persecutions he endured from his enemies, but somehow he attracted followers, among them Auguste Comte. He raged against the complacent scientists of his day, arguing that science should try to reform the world. He proposed that the medieval priestly and ruling classes be replaced by the scientists and the bourgeois. To these he later added the moralist leaders of the new Christianity. The basic idea was similar to that of many others: Society needed scientists to discover positive laws that in turn could be translated into guides for social action.

What is significant is the primacy that he gave to love. What he was proposing was thus a new love culture. Love was the fluid that coursed through the body social, giving it movement and energy. In his view the ideal of love created an organic, harmonious whole out of society's vital parts. In his last publication he urged the restoration of the primitive brotherly love of the early Christians but argued that the church of his day had betrayed the teachings of Jesus and the apostles. When he died in 1825 he said to his disciples: "The pear is ripe; you must pluck it" (Manuel & Manuel, 1979, p. 614).

No sooner had he died than a movement developed around his ideas, led by Olinde Rodrigues and Barthelemy Enfantin. The latter quickly rose to be the head of the new religion. The new commandment was: "Sanctify yourself in work and pleasure." (The similarity to Freud's image of normal is striking.) They were united in their resolve to establish a new organic order in which the senses would be gratified through the flowering of art, science, and material prosperity. Enfantin also sanctioned promiscuous love relationships.

In 1831 Enfantin solemnly announced that he was founding a new religion. It turned its light on humanity's sexual nature and its relation to the intellect, on the psychic debasement of women, and on the nature of love and God. Enfantin developed a complex theory of love and proposed a new sexual order, based on the realities of human affections, to replace the monogamous marriage that recognized no divorce. Particularly notable is that 60 years before Freud Enfantin and his followers proclaimed that sexual repression is an illness that affects humanity's rational capacities adversely. They also, as did the Freudians in their time, urged that civilization was threatened with total dissolution.

While their ideology of love and humanity as a cure for the mal de siècle evoked a widespread emotional response, the purely religious doctrine of the cult was a dismal failure. Nevertheless, in spite of their excesses, the Saint-Simonians did bequeath to western civilization a solid, relatively systematic body of social thought, changing the very definition of humanity and the understanding of history. World history for them became the study of the general diffusion of love and the contraction of antagonism, and a history of the successive progressions of love replaced the successive advances of mind.

They believed that in order to achieve the proper distribution of capacities profound changes had to be effected in the order of western society: The property system had to be reorganized, and then a new educational system had to be introduced. Since a whole aspect of people's instinctual natures, their capacity to love, had atrophied, a totally reshaped educational system was urgently required to rectify the basic failings of the old order.

One of their basic doctrines was that people must work. At Ménilmontant, a small retreat near Paris, they set up headquarters, and they dressed in special costumes of red, white, and blue. White is the color of love, red that of labor, and blue that of faith. They had public festivals celebrating their faith that were sometimes attended by 10,000 people.

Finally, the government brought them to trial in 1832 on various charges, such as embezzlement and outrages against public morals. The trial was the usual farce, with the judge commenting that "the defense is degenerating into a scandal" (Manuel & Manuel, 1979, p. 637). They were found guilty and sentenced to a year in jail. Because of the advent of the July monarchy they were released after 7½ months, but the movement was dead. Its major historical legacies were its influence on Marx and its emphasis on humanity's all-consuming need to love. But as with so many of the love cultures we have examined, the surrounding hate culture destroyed much of the good that could have been found in the Saint-Simonians, and history marched along on its destructive course.

Mesmer is known to us from the history of psychiatry as the discoverer of hypnosis and a forerunner of Freud's. Less well known is the fact that he also established a social movement in the 1780s that attained a considerable vogue right before the French Revolution and then disappeared. Two of his disciples, Bergasse and Kornmann, in 1782 set up a Society of Universal Harmony to propagate his ideas. The movement began as a revolt against the incompetent medicine of his day, basing itself on hundreds of notarized cures of illnesses. Since so much of illness does have a psychogenic component, and since the purgations and bleedings used at that time by conventional doctors probably did more harm than good, it is understandable that Mesmer's promise of health would attract a wide following. By the spring of 1784 one journal wondered whether mesmerism "soon will be the sole universal medicine" (Darnton, 1970, p. 62). Actually the doctrine soon spread all over Europe, where it persisted until the French Revolution.

The Paris police had submitted a secret report that some mesmerists were mixing radical political ideas in their pseudoscientific discourses. In 1784 accordingly a royal commission was set up to evaluate its theories; they agreed that Mesmer's fluid, which supposedly flowed from the mesmerist to the subject, did not exist. He left France, but the movement continued. An underground current of radicalism ran throughout the mesmerist movement and occasionally erupted in violent political pamphlets. Again the similarities with psychoanalysis in the twentieth century are prominent. (Darnton, 1970).

The origins of Christianity have naturally been studied in extraordinary detail, limited only by the paucity of source material. Like the others, Christianity can be regarded as an intentional love culture within the Roman empire; as noted earlier, its ultimate victory came only with the conversion of Constantine, not because of greater moral force.

Two of the most striking features of Christianity are its hatred of women and its horror of sex. It is clear by now that these two features came after the death of Jesus and through the dissemination of the religion by the early church fathers. In the Roman world Christianity was first well organized by Paul in the first century A.D. (Meeks, 1983).

As in other love cultures, the group had to have love feelings for one another yet avoid excessive intimacy. The first was accomplished by Paul with his admonitions to belong to the group. "Just as a human body, though it is made up of many parts, is a single unit because all these parts, though many, make one body, so it is with Christ. In the one Spirit we were all baptized, Jews as well as Gentiles, slaves as well as citizens, and one Spirit was given to us all to drink" (1 Cor. 12:12–13). To unite the various groups, largely urban and embracing all classes (Grant, 1977; the notion that Christianity appealed only to the lowest classes has since been refuted), Paul traveled nearly 10,000 miles (Meeks, 1983, p. 16). Thus he was the charismatic father figure who united the group.

Typical of the pressures that are used to block expressive intimacy in most intentional love cultures are these songs of the Oneida Community:

> We have built us a dome
> On our beautiful plantation
> And we all have one home
> And one family relation.

But then later a man sings, looking at a woman near him:

> I love you, oh my sister
> But the love of God is better;
> Yes, the love of God is better—
> Oh the love of God is best.

To this she replies:

> I love you oh, my brother,
> But the love of God is better;
> Yes, the love of God is better—
> O the love of God is best.
>   [Nordhoff, 1965, pp. 299–300]

But Paul, unlike Jesus (Pfister, 1924), was horrified by sexuality. The marriage rule he propounded stands under the general rubric "avoid *porneia*," a term used for all sorts of illicit sexual connections. "Yes, it is a good thing for a man not to touch a woman; but since sex is always a danger, let each man have his own wife and each woman her own husband" (1 Cor. 7:1–3). "It is better to marry than to burn" is another of his sayings, indicating that if man could not avoid sex he would do best to marry; thus marriage is not determined by love but by the inability to avoid sexual temptation. "There is something I want to add for the sake of widows and those who are not married; it is a good thing for them to stay as they are, like me, but if they cannot control the sexual urges, they should get married, since it is better to be married than to be tortured" (1 Cor. 7:8–10). Again and again (Meeks, 1983) he speaks of *pornoi* as being the worst of abominators. As Hunt put it:

> *Christianity developed a fanatical fixation about the glory of virginity, the evilness of woman, the foulness of sexual connection, and the spiritual merit of denying the only concerns of Christianity, which also warred against the riches, selfishness, war, usury and cruelty of the Roman world. Yet even these evils were always linked with sexual sin; in Revelation and much other early Christian writing, for instance, the terms "fornication," "lust" and "whoredom" were used symbolically to refer to any and all sins against God.* [1959, p. 104]

In spite of the fulminations of the leaders, Christians in these early centuries (and often in later centuries) held to their sexual ways. Before the persecutions by Diocletian, who preceded Constantine, Eusebius, one of the church fathers, complained bitterly about the internal demoralization of the Christian communities (Burckhardt, 1949, pp. 249–250). A host of unworthy persons had invaded the church, he argued, and even forced their way to the episcopal thrones. Among these evils Eusebius mentions in particular the bitter feuds between bishops and between individual congregations, the hypocrisy and deception, beliefs well nigh atheistic, wicked deeds, and again quarreling, envy, hatred, and the violent rule of the clergy. Thus the fanatically antisexual stance of Christianity was foisted on it by the neurotic leaders of the early centuries and is not inherent in the religion as such, as Pfister never tired of pointing out (1948).

Pagels (1981) has shown how the gnostic movement of the second century was regarded as heretical because it proposed a more equal treatment for women. Shortly after the death of Jesus women held important positions in the church, and at Christian initiation the person presiding ritually announced, "in Christ . . . there is neither male nor female" (Pagels, p. 73). But Paul won the day, with such pronouncements as "Neither was man created for woman, but woman for man" (1 Cor. 11:7–9). In spite of many protests the charismatic leader won out, and this has remained the dominant position in the church to this day. Thus in 1977 Pope Paul VI declared that a woman cannot be a priest "because our Lord was a man" (Pagels, p. 83). The hatred of women and of sexuality, taken over from the early charismatic father figures of the church, has recently once more become one of the most serious sources of rift within the church.

In other words, there are social controls on love, whether spelled out or not, and most of the time they are not. Since the individual is so highly constrained to conform to his or her culture, the detachment and objectivity that would allow him or her to see the culture from a different point of view are extraordinarily difficult to achieve. Instead there is in virtually all cultures either conformity or rebellion, neither of which leads to real love.

Summing up, there have been innumerable intentional love cultures set up throughout history. According to Zablocki (1980), in the United States there has been at least one new one every year for the past 300 years. These cultures thrive if the members love one another but fall apart when the love becomes too intense. And overriding both considerations is the powerful influence of a charismatic father figure (on occasion a mother figure) who demands and receives absolute obedience no matter how arbitrary or irrational the demands may be (cf. the recent mass suicide in Guyana—Layton, 1981).

The problem arises, then, because of the imposition of sudden external controls on adults. What about those cultures where love feelings are woven into the fabric of the society and taught in one way or another to the children from their earliest years? Are there, in other words, true love cultures? To several of these we now turn for more answers.

In a number of publications Turnbull (1978) has described the way of life of the Mbuti, a group of hunter–gatherers who live in the Ituri Forest of northeastern Zaire. In spite of severe environmental problems, they have developed a life-style that is largely nonaggressive and non-violent. As he describes it, this life-style is inculcated into them from birth on. We shall summarize his description here, as given in his chapter in Montagu (1978).

The world to them is conceived of as a sphere, in which we are always normally in the center. But if one's movement in time or space is too violent, too sudden, one can reach the edge of the sphere before it has time to catch up, and that is when a person becomes *wazi-wazi*, or disoriented and unpredictable. Turnbull does not discuss how often that happens.

A child is conceived out of joy, for the sexual act to the Mbuti is a supremely joyous act. By and large the young mother-to-be pursues her normal everyday life without much change right up to the moment of delivery. In the last few months she takes to going off on her own, to her favorite spot in the forest, and singing to the child in her womb. This is the only traditional form of song that can be sung as a solo. Thus the mother treats the child as an individual from 3 or 4 months before birth.

There seem to be few difficulties in delivery (though he never saw a delivery), and even minor problems seem to be rare. The infant emerges easily, helped only by the mother's hands or those of a friend, and is immediately placed at the mother's breast as she lies down. When the umbilical cord is cut, the father and close friends may be invited to see the child, who by then is happily suckling. Surprisingly, he reports that the newborn rarely even cries, although medical science regards this cry as a physiological reaction dictated by the need to get accustomed to breathing outside air.

About 3 days after birth, during which time the mother and one or two close friends stay in her spherical hut, with the child in almost constant contact with mother, the mother emerges and presents the child to the camp. She then hands the child to a few of her closest friends, who hold the infant close to their bodies. After introduction to the hunting camp, the mother takes the child back into her home. As long as the infant does not protest by crying, mother gives him or her the breast and sends the visitors away. The child is thus protected from the very beginning.

But infancy is by no means a time of total protection; it is rather one of controlled experimentation and perpetual learning. Children seem to learn to speak more by listening to their mothers talk with other adults than by direct instruction, with mothers talking to them. Still, the young child's life to date has been devoid of willed violence, physical or mental. More familiar sounds than screams, from a newborn infant, are gurgles of apparent delight at finding that this new world is not all that strange after all.

For the Mbuti there are four major principles of social organization that correspond to the four major areas in which conflict is most likely to occur in their lives: territory, family (or kinship), age and sex. These areas are progressively explored by the growing child, in approximately that order.

Infancy is certainly the time for exploring territory. There is not an inch of the new world that the infant has not explored within the first few weeks of life. And while the child is exploring the relatively familiar confines of the mother's body, in total security, he or she is constantly being introduced to other sensations that will, in future life, also be associated with total security.

Then the child moves on to the *endu,* the dwelling made of forest sticks and leaves. The crawling child will explore the floor of the *endu* just as thoroughly as he or she explored the mother's body. In a matter of weeks the *endu* has been fully explored, all but its upper reaches, and the young child is ready for yet another birth, this time into the sphere of the *apa,* or camp.

At this point the adults begin to make demands on the child, for his or her own good. For at this stage they discipline a child only for getting into a dangerous situation, such as crawling into a fire. Only when the child learns to walk will he or she be disciplined for merely "being a nuisance" to others.

Then at the age of 2, if not before, the child moves on to father. The child is taken to the breast of the father and held there, even encouraged to try and suckle. The child expects milk. But instead of milk at the father's breast the child receives his first solid food. Fathers do slap their children if they hurt themselves, but while such slapping is increasingly frequent, it is never hard nor is it in any sense violent.

From there the child moves on to the *bopi,* a broader territory, where he or she plays with other children. It is in the bopi that the child, from the age of 2 or 3 to 8 or 9, begins to face the conflicts of aggressivity and violence. The socialization here is mainly physical. It consists of games with other children, but these can hardly be called competitive; rather they are pastimes or sports. The only competition encouraged by the Mbuti is an inner competition between the individual and his or her abilities.

Once they begin to climb, they all climb trees. But the idea is never just to get to the top; it is to know more about the tree. A group of up to 10 children climb a sapling. When they reach the top, it bends down until they are all a few feet off the ground. At that point they all jump together, with precision. If one lingers, he or she learns not to do it again because that child gets flung back up and may very well be injured. Thus the child learns by prescription, not proscription, the essence of cooperative, communal life.

Children, united with other children by the bond of age, retain all their trust and confidence in their kinship and territorial bondings; they have been well explored and tested, and while there is more to learn, children can safely take these bondings for granted, return to them at will, and meanwhile, in the seclusion of the *bopi*, explore not only this new form of bonding but also the shared experience of all these other categories and their infinitely complex interrelationships.

Laughter, jokes, and ridicule are vital elements in Mbuti life, and together they constitute a major factor in developing the affective characteristics of adults and in minimizing the disaffective. It is when the child is in the bopi that he or she acquires a nickname, and it is likely to contain an element of playful ridicule. If any child teases another to the point of bringing him or her to tears (a more likely reaction at this point than anger) a new pastime will be improvised that demands that the tearful child play the role of a joyful hero or heroine, and from this pastime the offending name caller will be absolutely excluded.

Not long after (before the child is 4), sex enters the picture. Sex and sexual relationships are important to the Mbuti as a potential source of aggression and as a principle of social organization. Their own naming system and kinship terminology teach them at an early age that gender is relatively unimportant. A boy and girl may well go by the same name.

Then the child (after 4) becomes increasingly conscious of sex differences. Intensive exploration of the bodies of other children then occurs, but neither sex excludes the other. They explore each others' bodies without discrimination and will even imitate the act of copulation with equal lack of discrimination, in the form of dance. At this stage the children hold nothing back from each other.

Around the age of 8 or 9, perhaps as late as 11, boy children enter the *nkumbi*, an initiation ritual, and emerge a mere 3 months later as adults in village (outside the forest) eyes, but as youths in Mbuti eyes. For the girls the transition is more easily marked by their first menstruation. The menarche is hailed with joy by all, for now the girl has the power to become a mother. She will become an adult, and her mate will become her husband, and an adult as well.

Following the *nkumbi* ritual, there are still 6 or 7 years to go in the realm of youth. These years are spent in the exploration of sexuality, and in the development of the rights connected with the hunt. There is no discrimination among the youth, yet not once did the ethnographer come across a case of homosexual intercourse (Turnbull, 1978, p. 196).

In their system of values the following are stressed: security, dependence, interdependence, coordination, cooperation, and the alternation of quiet and disturbance (*ekimi, akami*). These values have been developed and sharpened throughout the entire life span.

The honey season is considered a time for relaxation and enjoyment of the pleasures of life, of which honey is one of the main symbols. Sexual activity among the youths is heightened. But the association of the individual quest for pleasure, however legitimate, with conflict is brought to the fore in the honeybee dance. This season is also the time for the great premarital festival, the *elima*. From this festival only adult males, children, and elders are excluded. This festival involves a ritual conflict between male and female youths, manifested in a battle waged with sticks, large nuts and seeds, and other weapons. In order to gain access to the *elima* house and thus acquire the right to sleep with one of the girls, a male youth or medial adult male has to fight his way through the barrage of fire set up by the adult women. This physical violence (apparently not severe) that they meet in pursuit of their individual sexual desires is a dramatic ritualization of the inherent conflict between their individual and social selves. This ritualized *elima* lasts a month. At the end, the youths themselves, increasingly recognizing the potential of sex as a source of conflict, discuss among themselves their preferences as to when and where to have sexual intercourse with a girl. Parents have little to say about the choice of partner.

It is the adults who are primarily involved in the most dangerous of all areas of conflict, that between the sedentary village farmers outside the forest and the nomadic hunter–gatherers within. The constant mobility of the Mbuti, who change campsites almost every month, helps prevent conflict between Mbuti and villagers. Several other rituals also serve to tame the aggression and violence.

Both male and female adults have been effectively educated from infancy onward to avoid conflict, avert it, divert it, or, when it erupts despite all precautions, resolve it with a minimum of aggressivity, mental or physical. Some conflict arises after the birth of a child, when the woman refuses to have intercourse with her husband for 3 years. Yet devoted affection persists between the marital pair. Once the transition of elderhood is over, the danger of aggressivity is reduced to practically nil.

It may well be that Turnbull has idealized this society. He even maintains that when the Mbuti die, they do so without fear, and the songs that mark such a death are songs that express the same joy in which life itself was conceived (1978, p. 220). It may be that some other anthropologist will some day come along and come to radically different conclusions, as Derek Freeman did with Margaret Mead's observations on Samoa. In the most recent discussion of this controversy (Brady, 1983), anthropologists have generally found Freeman's criticisms of Mead too harsh, though admittedly they have some validity. But for the time being, we have to take Turnbull's description as the most accurate. And what he describes is a culture in which from birth to death there is a careful control of aggressivity and violence, as well as love. It could readily be placed side by side with the cases in Chapter 1 as another example of a love culture. What is significant for this chapter is that the love is not suddenly imposed from without, like the romantic "falling in love" of our own culture, but is nurtured and developed throughout life.

Unlike the Mbuti, the Tahitians have been known to westerners for several centuries. Levy (1973, 1978) has studied them most intensively. The account given here is taken from his works.

All observers have commented on the gentleness and nonviolence of the Tahitians. Forster (1778) wrote about "the Character of the Tahitians . . . their gentleness, their generosity, their affection and friendship, their tenderness, their pity." Ellis (1830) said:

> *They certainly live amongst each other in more harmony than is usual amongst Europeans. During the whole time I was amongst them, I never saw such a thing as a battle; and though they are excellent wrestlers, and in their contests give each other many a hard fall, the contest is no sooner concluded than they are as good friends as ever. [Levy, 1973, pp. 223–224]*

Levy states that when he did his fieldwork there in the early 1960s the impression of gentleness was amply confirmed. What he saw was an extreme lack of angry, hostile behavior. The people, he says, are passive optimists. This common sense, generated by the conditions of socialization, was reinforced by legends, healing practices of spirit doctors, and generally expressed conscious values. A universe so defined is cognitively less frustrating then those cultures that spur their members on to impossible heights (e.g., Don Quixote's impossible dream).

Levy describes several pervasive and multiple influences that make the Tahitians so gentle (Levy, 1973, pp. 213–239):

1.   A number of aspects of community life, including the prevalent institution of adoption that allows mothers to give away babies whom they are not ready for, the fact that patterns of marriage tend to produce relatively comfortable and anxiety-free relations, plus a set of parental orientations about an infant's relative strength and ability to grow because of his or her own internal integrity, tend to produce anxiety-free, warm early relationships between infant and mother. They do not push the child. They feel that they must take adequate care of the child, which is not particularly difficult. Such factors foster in the child a core sense of the elementary adequacy and safety of the world, a sense of basic trust. Young infants are the center of attention, cherished, fussed over, gratified, protected.

2.   As the gratified, relatively anxiety-free child gets older, between the ages of 3 and 5, he or she is taught in various forcibly presented ways the need to accept definite limitations. There is a dramatic and marked diminution of indulgence by the child's caretakers, and he or she is pushed from the center of the household stage. Typically, the child going through a period of parental withdrawal briefly exhibits rage and temper tantrums and begins to look sullen and depressed. At this time, he or she is encouraged to enter the company of other children. The child soon recovers and is in active and happy interaction with his or her peers. Peer play itself is markedly lacking in fights and confrontations.

3.   As the child leaves the infant stage, he or she encounters a situation that becomes most marked about the time of disindulgence in that he or she is managed, controlled, socialized, and educated not primarily by a single adult or pair of adults, but by a whole network of classificatory siblings and parents. The effects of having socialization messages passed on through such a diffuse network are complex, but one of the major effects seems to be a sense that social frustrations are caused not by one or two specific individuals against whom one can rebel, but rather by a whole system against which one is powerless to deal by any external, struggling activity. One gets a sense of resignation. The child learns that the system has its rules to which one must adapt, and he or she adapts.

4.   There are cultural forms against aggression, in the general sense of *aggression* as the changing of the given structure of things, the given situation. Through a number of institutional patterns the child learns that it is difficult to resist or change social reality. For instance, more than half of the homes in the rural community are involved in adop-

tion. This custom of adopting seems to have the meaning that the society as a whole has dominance over individual relationships, and thus individual striving. Likewise, the ritual of superincision for young adolescent males symbolizes the dangers of masculine sexuality and also shows that these dangers can be healed and reintegrated with the help of socially provided resources of nature. Masculinity, striving, and aggression are dangerous, but cooperation with nature and adaptation to society will be protective and successful.

5.   In regard to socialization patterns specifically directed against hostile behavior, there is a clear, dependably repeated set of reactions to children. Small children are permitted and in fact encouraged to exhibit brief, explosive, aggressive behavior in response to clear frustration and annoyance. But prolonged sulking, vengeful continuing hostility, and hostility thought to be unjustified are discouraged in various ways.

6.   Great cultural clarity exists about the nature of hostile aggression. There is a large vocabulary bearing on nuances of hostile action, clear cultural doctrine about which behavioral states are expressions of hostility (including suicide), and a great deal of cultural doctrine about the effects of hostility and what to do about it.

7.   Doctrine about anger states that anything more than a transient verbal expression of anger is wrong, that it is an indication of a lack of self-control and of competence. It is thus a matter for shame.

In sum, the Tahitian grows up with a calm, nonanxious core sense that the world is basically dependable and nonthreatening. But there is also a strong sense that the gratification of one's desires must be limited. This is frustration with the nature of things and thus unavoidable. But if one does try to violate limits, there will be automatic retaliation. Anger is felt to be disruptive to the self and to relationships. It should be expressed verbally with a discussion of its interpersonal causes, in the hope that chronic effects will not result.

Levy also has a fair amount of material on the strength and existence of bonds of love and affection among people. In general, these seem to be strong. Adolescents form in groups that act together; the ties are so strong that in some cases the boys will avoid the sisters of their friends as though they were tabooed.

For marriage there is a sequence of desire, followed by getting used to each other, then love, and finally compassion for the suffering of the other. It is interesting to look at the answer given by an informant Manu as to whether he loved his wife (*vahine*), Tetua. Yes, he did love Tetua.

If not, Manu said, their life could not be going properly. If he loved her and she did not love him, she would go and do as she pleased. But the way it was, she loved him and he loved her, and "when things are like that, life goes properly for a couple" (Levy, 1973, p. 318). Manu goes on to say:

> When you talk about love, it is the sort of thing that you have come to believe with your body, your calculating thoughts, with everything that this is your true woman. . . . You trust and believe in that woman of yours. It is as if she were a parent for your household, for your way of living. That is what it means when Tahitians say here. [*Levy, 1973, p. 318*]

The gendarme who administered Huahine on Tahiti in the early 1960s had worked in Indochina, French Guinea, Algiers, and Morocco. For him the people of Huahine are "lambs." He contrasts them with the people of Morocco, whom he calls "hot-tempered, easily angered, thieves, murderers, rapists" (Levy, 1973, pp. 276–277). What surprises him is the lack of a vengeful spirit. Even though people are occasionally cheated or insulted by a visitor or merchant, they do not seem to show any anger over this, or any need to get even. There is, he says, no serious crime in Huahine, no violence, no "forced" theft. There are only very occasional and minor disturbances connected with drinking, and these are usually easily controlled by a few stern words. The records for Huahine between 1940 and 1962 show only one serious crime, a murder, in 1953. For the period before 1940, there is only one other serious crime known to the older people in Huahine. This took place in 1928 and involved a man who, angry with his wife, beat her and then drowned her.

Thus in both Mbuti and Tahiti we have instances of love cultures. In both, the loving feelings are created by a variety of social controls and institutions. Aggression is not absent, but people are taught how to tame it, control it, or channel it into nondestructive directions, such as festivals, or mock fights. Again, what is significant is that love is not introduced out of the blue but is cultivated by the entire society throughout life.

SOCIAL CONTROL OF FEELINGS

While the intuitive belief is that feelings are private experiences arising from something within the person, more careful investigation reveals that feelings are also, and in many cases essentially, determined by interpersonal events. Hence, it should come as no surprise to learn that love is socially conditioned and controlled as much as any other feelings.

In more recent years social psychologists have conducted many experiments in which the coercive power of the group can easily be demonstrated. Perhaps the best known is the early study by Asch (1952). Asch experimented with perception. He showed a group lines of varying lengths. The subjects were asked to say which of the old lines the new line was most similar to. Four of the subjects were confederates, while a fifth was the real subject being tested. The confederates would insist that the new line was most similar to one of the old ones, from which it was quite different, thus confronting the unknowing subject with a deliberately wrong answer. Many subjects in this dilemma would change their answer to a wrong one in order to "go along with the crowd." Such acquiescence was of course quite unconscious: The subjects did not know that the others were confederates of the experimenter. In fact, according to Asch, the incorrect answer was given by his college student–subjects about 35% of the time (1952, p. 311).

In another study, which was given wide publicity at the time, Milgram (1963) showed that most subjects will obey the experimenter even when they believe that their actions hurt another person. He asked subjects to administer electric shocks to a confederate who was supposed to be learning something; whenever he made a mistake he was to receive a shock. The learner even mentioned that he had a slightly weak heart. In spite of all this, the subjects continued to give electric shocks, dutifully obeying the instructions. More than half of them continued to the end of the scale and administered the most severe shocks, labeled "450 volts."

Another study (Ehrlich, 1973) showed that racial prejudices had remained fairly constant among white Americans over a 40-year period, from 1926 to 1966. The rankings of 28 national and ethnic groups were approximately the same in 1966 as they had been in 1926, ranging from the English as highest to the Indians as lowest. Goodman (1952) observed 103 black and white children intensively for a full year. She concluded that racial awareness was already present in many children at ages 3 and 4, and that 25% of the 4-year-olds were already expressing strongly entrenched race-related values.

Another phenomenon in which feelings are obviously determined by the group situation is that of mass psychogenic illness, particularly hysteria, which has often been observed (Colligan, Pennebaker, & Murphy, 1982). In their summary of various incidents they conclude that the classical outbreak has the following epidemiological characteristics: It involves a small group of segregated young females. It appears, spreads, and subsides rapidly, with a bimodal curve of one group of early affected, most affected, often relapsing cases and frequently a second wave of least affected, not relapsing cases. Symptoms are usually limited in time to 1 day. These are variable, mostly fainting, malaise, and convulsion, with hyperventilation and excitement. Signs are scarce and laboratory values normal except for those associated with hyperventilating. Incubation is notoriously short. Adults are spared, with no secondary attack in household. Transmission is by sight or sound, fostered by reuniting the group. It is brought about by a trivial triggering factor that activates a larger but diffuse group tension relevant to its formation, task, or maintenance. This group process carries important shared unconscious fantasies that are abreacted in the outbreak. When social or controversial issues carry similar fantasies, the outbreak can take on endemic proportions.

Well over a century ago Charles Mackay wrote a book he called *Extraordinary Popular Delusions and the Madness of Crowds*, anticipating the modern view that humanity has been more insane than sane in the course of its history (Fine, 1981). In reference to the Crusades, Mackay writes:

> *Every age has its peculiar folly; some scheme, project or phantasy into which it plunges, spurred on either by the love of gain, the necessity of excitement, or the mere force of imitation. Failing, in these, it has some madness, to which it is goaded by political or religious causes, or both combined. Every one of these causes influenced the Crusades, and conspired to render them the most extraordinary instance upon record of the extent to which popular enthusiasm can be carried.* [1932, p. 354]

In our own more scientific era, anthropologists in particular have been able to demonstrate the underlying unities in the various cultures that they have studied. These unities are maintained by a series of customs, many of which look peculiar to the outsider yet have deep significance for the member of that culture. As Fortes (1977) has phrased it:

> *Custom implies consensus, collective authorization and compulsion. Yet to be of service to the individual, custom, as the example of language shows well, must be at his fingertips, assimilated, appropriated, internalized. Custom transcends the individual, but without custom he cannot be human.* [p. 128]

The gruesome events of the present century have provided further evidence of how a determined collective can not only enforce its ideas on its members but also get them to change their opinions. There is a parallel here between repression in the individual and ideology in the larger society. If the parents forbid a certain type of action, for instance, aggression, or masturbation in childhood, the child will accept it, then eventually come out with the feeling that he or she has no desire for that (aggression, masturbation). In accordance with a principle of psychic economy the simplest solution for the child is to repress the wish, that is, to put it out of the mind altogether so that he or she will not be faced with a constant conflict of wanting something, then finding it forbidden by the parents and being frustrated. This repressive process, never fully complete, forms a major basis of individual psychology.

In the social sphere, if the government forbids some kind of action with enough emphasis and force, a similar process occurs. In modern times this has been dubbed brainwashing, although it has always existed. If the consequences of deviation are severe for the individual, then eventually the principle of psychic economy will induce him or her to abandon the desire leading to the deviation, that is, to conform. The major point is that conformity is enforced (at an unconscious level) in every society through the agency of the superego, which links the family and the larger group (Parsons, 1952).

In totalitarian societies this change of ideology can also be and usually is accompanied by a certain amount of force. Lifton (1969) has provided an excellent description of how that has worked in present-day China. In order to convert the older generation to its way of thinking, the Chinese Communist government undertook an extensive campaign of thought reform. Men and women were incarcerated for longer or briefer periods of time, and during their imprisonment they were exposed to intensive efforts to get them to change their views (brainwashing). However, this brainwashing was not simply verbal; it was also accompanied by occasional executions, with the clear implication that if the prisoner did not undergo a change of mind he or she too might be executed. Galileo (whom incidentally the church has never completely exonerated) could agree and mutter under his breath, *"e pur si muove"* ("and yet it moves itself"), but the Chinese whose thought was being reformed had a harder time.

These considerations apply to the experience of love in our culture. The harsh superego, which forms the link between the family and society, on the one hand permits love under certain circumscribed conditions and on the other forbids many of its expressions. Not surprisingly, as the clinical observations in Chapter 7 indicate, more often than not love starts with great excitement and soon turns to disappointment and frequently hatred. In a hate culture, long-lasting love is taboo, or hedged about with so many conditions that it becomes taboo. As a result, the hate culture perpetuates itself, and even minor reforms become difficult to maintain. Thus, even in the nineteenth century, the heyday of communitarian experiments in the United States, closer examination suggests that they were all beset by constant legal battles (Weisbrod, 1980) related to the distribution of goods and the proper allocation of love resources; these legal battles played a major role in the eventual disappearance of these noble experiments.

At the same time, it would be a serious error to underestimate the positive forces for good in our society. If we were a monolithic hate culture, this book could not be written. There are many ways in which the search for love and the battle against hatred continue. Whether love or hate will win out in the long run is impossible to predict; but at any rate the powers of good continue to play a significant role. There are many hating people, yet there are also many loving people. As the Michigan survey (Veroff et al., 1981) shows, a considerable percentage of the population has been so strongly influenced by psychoanalytic thought that they are consciously striving for a better world in which love can take its rightful place. From another point of view, Gardell and Johansson (1981) have shown how the systematic investigation of work satisfaction has broadened into a larger examination of the quality of life.

THE FAMILY AS THE MODEL LOVE CULTURE

Sociobiologically, the human is distinguished from the primates and other animals in various ways; among the most important are the formation of the family and the permanent significance of the male. Murdock (1949) says, "The nuclear family is a universal human social grouping. Either as the sole prevailing form of the family or as the basic unit from which more complex familial forms are compounded, it exists as a distinct and strongly functional group in every known society" (1949, p. 2).

Ideally, families are held together by ties of love. The term *kith* derives from an old English word meaning "known"; *kith and kin* means "friends and kindred" (Webster's *New Third International Dictionary*, 1969). Thus, the world for humans is basically divided into the family, who are known and loved, and the outsiders, who are unknown, feared, and often hated.

Just what it is that holds families and the larger kinship groups together is a matter of dispute among anthropologists. The most plausible explanation seems to be that of Fortes (1969) and others, who assume a "principle of amity." Fortes says:

> [Kinship] . . . is associated with rules of conduct whose efficacy comes, in the last resort, from a general principle of kinship morality that is rooted in the familial domain and is assumed everywhere to be axiomatically binding. This is the rule of prescriptive altruism which I have referred to as the principle of amity and which Hiatt calls generosity. [p. 354]

Or, as Turner puts it:

> People live together because they are matrilineally related . . . the dogma of kinship asserts that matrilineal kin participate in one another's existence . . . the norms of kinship state that matrilineal kin must at all times help one another, [so] open physical violence between them seldom takes place. [cited in Fortes, p. 239]

With regard to the male role, in the most recent survey of primate field studies, Richard and Schulman state:

> In most primate societies males leave their natal group as they approach maturity while females spend their lives in the group into which they were born. In general, then, females tend to be surrounded by female kin while males do so only to the extent that they migrate into groups already containing male kin. [1982, p. 236]

Thus, there is ample reason, derived from many sources, to assume that the family is the basic human group, that it provides a place for the male, among other purposes, and that it is cemented by ties of love and friendship. So much for a summation of the anthropological data.

To this must be added the observations of the psychoanalysts. It is one thing to observe theoretically that incest is a universal human taboo; it is another to note clinically the vast amount of suffering that such a taboo can inflict on many individuals. The human being grows within the family; then he or she is gradually forced by various maturing abilities and taboos to leave the family. Thus begins the process of separation–individuation which, in Mahler's formulation (1975), has become an important basis of the entire conceptualization of human growth and development.

The conflict may be restated as one of love versus sexuality. The infant must suck at the mother's breast (or its equivalent nowadays) for a while but not too long, for then he or she becomes fixated at an infantile level. The child develops hostility toward siblings but is prevented from carrying this hostility to extremes by murdering them. The child is permitted to excrete freely up to a certain age; then again limitations are placed upon the function, the violation of which would again make him or her more infantile or more asocial.

All human societies have had to find ways to cope with these developmental dilemmas. But they may cope with them in a loving or in a hostile manner. Hostility toward infants has been strong, occasionally leading to infanticide or outright murder. When Freud began his work, the rearing of infants was cruel in the extreme, far more cruel than that found in most primitive societies. It is one of the achievements of psychoanalytic practice and research to have shown that maternal love for the infant is essential for the infant's proper growth. As Freud once put it, it was his fate in history to rediscover the obvious. In terms of the thesis of this book, the hostility toward the infant and child, virtually universal a hundred years ago in western civilization, was the psychosocial basis for the hate culture that has been so obvious a feature of our society for several thousand years. It was always there; it took psychoanalysis to call attention to its damaging features.

Difficulties arise for the individual at every transitional stage, or crucial point of development. There is ample reason that Erikson's famous book *Childhood and Society* (1950), in which he delineates the psychosexual stages through which every human being passes, has been one of the best-sellers of the century and has been translated into almost every known language. Whether the move from one stage to another is accomplished smoothly or with pain and bitterness depends on the degree to which the culture is built on love or on hatred.

In terms of our own culture, which is after all the primary concern, Freud first demonstrated that the family is a hotbed of neurosis. The same position was taken by Marx and Engels in their condemnation of bourgeois morality, and by the Israelites in their formation of the kibbutzim. This led, in the 1920s (as before), to numerous attempts to replace the family by collective institutions. As noted earlier, all these attempts have failed and for the most part have been abandoned, though people keep trying.

Yet even when the family stays together, the conflicts that arise can be enormous. The constantly increasing divorce rate shows how dissatisfied people are with the duty and obedience that were the hallmark of families in former times. In general, a large number of people have accepted the proposition that the family should provide a loving environment and rebelled against the hatred and bitterness that they find instead.

It is only recently that the amount of violence found in the American home has become a focus of attention. The publication of an article by Kempe, Silverman, Steele, Droegemuller, and Silver "The Battered Child Syndrome" in the *Journal of the American Medical Association* in 1962 directed both professionals and lay persons to a hitherto neglected aspect of American society.

Gelles, Steinmetz, and Straus have put together the known data on violence in the family (*Behind Closed Doors*, 1981). The account here is taken from their work.

The historical record demonstrates abuse of extensive and lethal forms of violence by parents. The dictum "spare the rod and spoil the child" was stated and supported in the Bible. The Puritans laws threatening death to the unruly hung over the children's heads, and parents supported their right to whip and punish with biblical quotations.

The historical record continues, though in somewhat attenuated form. Nevertheless the statistics that emerge on the present scene are gory indeed. In 1968 it was estimated that more children under the age of 5 died from parentally inflicted injuries than from tuberculosis, whooping cough, polio, measles, diabetes, rheumatic fever, and appendicitis combined (Gelles et al., 1981, p. 9).

Battered women have also been frequent. The classic "rule of thumb" gave legal justification to common law that sanctioned a husband's striking his wife with a switch, provided the stick was no wider than his thumb. Wives in America have been raped, choked, stabbed, shot, beaten, struck with horse whips, pokers, bats, and bicycle chains, and had their jaws and limbs broken. Yet wife abuse as a social problem did not receive national attention until the mid-1970s. Women have been violent too; many husbands are slain by their wives. The most lethal room in the house for men is the kitchen (Gelles et al., 1981, p. 12). In general, about as many people are murdered by relatives in New York City each year as have been killed in all the disturbances in Northern Ireland from 1969 to 1981 (Gelles et al., 1981, p. 16). In one early study (Gelles, 1974) of ordinary middle-class homes, it was found that 54% of the couples had used physical force on each other at some time.

Psychological abuse is harder to document, but it has been studied as well, most extensively in the families of schizophrenics. Lidz and his associates (1965) were the first to pay careful attention to the pathology in the parents of schizophrenics. He hypothesized that the schizophrenic patient has been "raised amidst irrationality and chronically exposed to intrafamilial communications that distort and deny what should be the obvious interpretation of the environment" (Lidz et al., 1965, p. 305). Since Lidz's work the transmission of irrationality in all families has been given careful consideration.

The common assumption that people raised within a certain family context have the same psychological background is contradicted by these studies. The "consensus Rorschach," in which all members of a family try to agree on a set of responses to the Rorschach cards, is noticeably different in different families. Wynne, Cromwell, and Matthysse (1978) have shown that pseudomutuality is the rule in the families of schizophrenics and that words and experiences have an entirely different meaning for the various members of the family. In effect, the child in a sick family is brought up in a state of emotional isolation, and the number of sick families is large indeed. Even objects in the environment are experienced in a different way in the family (Csikszentmihalyi & Rochberg-Halton, 1981).

Ever since the pioneer study by Rennie and his colleagues (1962; revised edition by Srole & Fischer, 1978) the frequency of mental and emotional disorder in the general population has been a topic of much interest. Rennie's group found an incidence of over 80% disturbed, more than 20% markedly so. Dohrenwend and Dohrenwend (1969), reviewing other studies, found the incidence much lower, but obviously the findings depend on the criteria used.

In one of the most recent epidemiological studies (Werner & Smith, 1982), every child born in Kauai in 1955 was followed up from birth to the threshold of adulthood, a period of 20 years. In general, much disturbance was found, some 90% having emotional difficulties of one kind or another. What is particularly notable in this study is that some 10% of the children were found to be, in their words, "vulnerable but invincible." It was found that these had had much more love and attention in their early lives than those who grew up with various disabilities. (Cf. also pp. 1–39.)

Thus there is ample evidence for the proposition that a warm, loving environment in childhood will produce a warm, loving adult, and that combinations of such warm, loving adults grouped together will form a love culture, while aggregates of families with bitterness, hostility, and revenge will group together to form a hate culture. In such a hate culture the social controls exercised over love militate against it in a powerful manner. It is not surprising then that love is rare, that it frequently starts out with great excitement, then degenerates into hatred and bitterness, and that it is the state of existence that human beings long for more than anything else.

9

Theories
of Love

In the introduction to the book *The Idea of Love*, edited by Robert *Hazo* (1967), Mortimer Adler writes:

> *Of all the ideas so far subjected to dialectical analysis by the Institute [for Philosophical Research] the idea of love proved to be the most difficult—more difficult than the idea of freedom, and much more difficult than the ideas of progress, justice and happiness. One measure of its difficulty is the wide variety of meanings of the term as it is used in the literature on the subject, ranging from the identification of love with sexual desire, at one extreme, to the conception of love, at the other extreme, as purely disinterested benevolence—a supernatural mode of love made possible by Divine help.* [Hazo, 1967, p. xi]

While Freud and the psychoanalysts have not resolved all the mysteries of love, they have certainly come closer, as we shall see, than any other group of thinkers, primarily because psychoanalysts have studied with great intensity the empirical manifestations of love, while others have largely speculated, in the main from their own experience. Before moving on to Freud it will be instructive to see what others before him did say.

The inquiry can begin profitably with a comparison of two symposia, separated by some 2500 years: Plato's dialogue *The Symposium*, and a series of papers by social scientists based on a panel organized by the American Psychological Association in 1970 (Curtin, 1973). This latter covers the entire range of western thought from the culture of the Greeks to the present day. Some remarks about the concept of love in non-western cultures will also be appropriate.

In Plato's *Symposium*, a number of friends are gathered together to have a discussion about love. They begin by dismissing the flute-girl because they want conversation (1927, p. 339); thus it already becomes clear that a homosexual theme may predominate and that the love of women will not be given serious consideration.

One speaker after another then gets up to praise love. Phaedrus states that first in the train of gods he fashioned love (1927, p. 341). Pausanias distinguishes two kinds of love, deriving from the two goddesses Aphrodite (p. 343). One goddess is called heavenly because she was the daughter of Uranus and had no mother; the other is common, born of Zeus and Dione. Common love does good and evil indiscriminately, but the heavenly love is noble and worthy of praise. Eryximachus the physician likewise distinguishes two kinds of love, fair and foul, and states that the best physician is the one who is able to separate fair love from foul, or to convert one into the other.

Aristophanes puts forth the theory that has become most famous. Originally, he says, there were three sexes: man, woman, and a union of the two. Zeus cut this combination of the two in half to make them "more profitable to us." After the division each half perpetually longed to be rejoined with the other. Thus, "desire and pursuit of the whole is called love" (Plato, 1927, p. 357).

Agathon opines that love is the noblest of all feelings. "He whom love touches not walks in darkness" (Plato, 1927, p. 362).

Finally Socrates speaks; presumably his views are the expression of Plato's. Even Socrates, however, does not speak to the topic directly; he relates what he learned of love from a wise woman, Diotima of Mantineia (Plato, 1927, p. 367). After some questioning he arrives at the position that love is love of the everlasting possession of the good. "This is that life above all others which man should live, in the contemplation of beauty absolute" (p. 379). Note here that the Socratic–Platonic view in no way stresses the significance of human relationships. Toward the end Alcibiades arrives, drunk and angry because Socrates had slept with him and refused to have sex. "In vino veritas," he says; then he goes on to praise Socrates as the greatest of men.

The other great luminary of Greek thought, Aristotle, devotes his analysis of love for the most part to friendship. Mutual admiration is presupposed. Of the three friendships he lists, those of utility, pleasure, and virtue, only the last is true friendship. Aristotle's is less abstract than Plato's but still away from women and still largely merely a theoretical statement.

In the 1973 work by American social scientists, most of the participants were psychologists; only two were trained analysts (Dahlberg and Weigert). The paper by Dahlberg is really misplaced, since it is a report on an empirical study of sexual relations between patients and therapists, which has no bearing on the general topic. Thus essentially only one analytic paper was included.

In contrast to the Platonic dialogue, where everybody praises love, in this symposium almost everybody condemns love, usually in the form of romantic love. Lawrence Casler leads off with the statement: "There is no evidence that love is either necessary or sufficient for psychological maturity. Indeed, to the extent that love fosters dependency, it may well be a deterrent to maturity" (Curtin, 1973, p. 18). He goes on to argue (in the face of the overwhelming kind of evidence that has been presented in this book) that "there is simply no good evidence that human infants, or the young of any other species, need to be loved in order to attain an optimal level of development (Curtin, p. 23). He seriously argues that an adult without love can be happy, emotionally fulfilled, and socially useful (Curtin, p. 24). No definitions of these terms or of what he means by maturity are given.

The next paper, by Sidney Greenfield, a social anthropologist, views love as a behavioral syndrome that makes possible the formation of the nuclear family households so vital to the working of the socioeconomic system. He totally ignores the fact that the nuclear family is found in all known human societies (Murdock, 1949). He agrees with Casler that there is something radically wrong with love. In the next paper, also by Greenfield, some sociological consequences of proposed alternatives to love are discussed. He frankly states: "Personally, I have no standards other than my personal biases with which to judge" (Curtin, 1973, p. 54). He deplores what he calls the American tendency to define human worth, dignity, and fulfillment in terms of occupational and professional achievement, yet this is precisely what he himself does.

Two papers by Louis Karmel, a counseling psychologist, follow, in which love is praised as the essence of life. These have more of a religious aura than a psychological consideration of all the factors involved in love. Rogers Wright states flatly that love is neither necessary nor sufficient for the good life, agreeing with Casler.

Annette Brodsky, a feminist therapist, complains that today only women are likely to see their lives as revolving around love. "Present-day Juliets are still taught to overlove" (Curtin, 1973, p. 97). She sees love as a kind of political device designed to keep women in their place. There is of course no discussion whatsoever in her paper of the larger social issues involved in a love and hate culture.

Margaret Horton, a psychologist at a mental health center, discusses alternatives to romantic love. She sees romantic love as destructive (Curtin, p. 113). Proceeding from the mistaken notion that in romantic love one partner must be dominant, she argues for something called epigenetic love (not clearly described).

In the next chapter James K. Cole musters the familiar arguments in favor of homosexual love, even though he admits that "most current knowledge about homosexuality is at best tentative" (Curtin, 1973, p. 127). Albert Ellis continues with a paper on unhealthy love; at least he does point out that there are many healthy or normal aspects of love (Curtin, p. 176). After presenting a case of his rational–emotive therapy, he concludes: "One of the main purposes of effective psychotherapy is to help him to love compellingly but uncompromisingly. A difficult but hardly impossible goal" (Curtin, p. 194). In this respect he essentially agrees with the analytic position, but he leaves out all the analytic data and data related to it.

Shirley Thomas, a professor of Afro-American studies, continues with a paper on the meaning of love in the black experience. She stresses particularly the need to love the black community (Curtin, 1973, p. 209). Edith Weigert, the well-known analyst in her paper argues for love and respect, in accordance with the analytic tradition.

In conclusion there is a light dialogue by Lewis Lieberman, a psychologist, including the following:

He: I know you mean; all that analysis and theorizing is heavy stuff.

She: Yeah, but more than that. I have the feeling that somehow all that technical jargon is inappropriate to the subject. Love is something to sing about, to rhapsodize about, to experience, to live. When you start getting abstract about it, it begins to seem like you're talking about something else. [Austin, 1973, p. 229–230]

This symposium obviously adds nothing of scientific value. Perhaps the best comment is a quotation from Freud in 1915:

Sexual love is undoubtedly one of the chief things in life, and the union of mental and bodily satisfaction in the enjoyment of love is one of its culminating peaks. Apart from a few queer fanatics, all the world knows this and conducts its life accordingly; science alone is too delicate to admit it. [1953–1974, vol. 12, pp. 169–170]

RELIGIOUS VIEWS

All religions have emphasized the importance of love in one form or another, none more so than Christianity. Here we shall examine their theoretical views; the practical realities of the way in which religions have operated have been discussed earlier (chapters 2, 3, and 4), especially in western culture.

Actually religions have varied in the emphasis they have placed on love. The religion of love, more than any other, is Christianity. From the life of Christ to the present day the gospel preaches love.

Yet when it comes to defining more precisely what is meant by Christian love, arguments immediately arise. God is love, and his benevolence extends over the entire earth and to all creatures. Immediately the problem arises: What is the relationship of divine love to human love? And second, is divine love without any self-interest at all, or does it have some connection with self-interest? How is evil possible?

The man who from ancient times dominated the theology of Christianity was St. Augustine (354–430). The purpose and the way of knowledge are expressed in Augustine's words: "I wish to know God and the soul" (cited in P. Tillich, 1968, pp. 111–133). Nothing else, just God and the soul. This means that the soul is the place where God appears to the human being. He wants to know the soul because only there can he know God, and in no other place. This implies, of course, that God is not an object beside other objects. God is seen in the soul. He is in the center of the human being, before the split into subjectivity and objectivity. He is not a strange being whose existence or nonexistence one might discuss. Rather, he is our own a priori; he precedes ourselves in dignity, reality, and logical validity. In him the split between subject and object, and the desire of the subject to know the object, are overcome. God is given to the subject as nearer to itself than it is to itself; i.e., God is more important than the self.

Augustine's idea of love is the power that unites the mystical and ethical elements in his idea of God. Christian theologians have argued at length about the differences between agape, unconditional love, and eros, desire for what is good and beautiful. In Augustine there are both elements.

> *We pursue Him with our love so that when we reach Him we may rest in perfect happiness in Him who is our goal. . . .*
>
> *It is this Good which we are commanded to love with our whole heart, with our whole mind, and with all our strength. It is toward this God that we should be led by those who love us, and toward this God we should lead those whom we love. In this way we fulfill the commandments on which depend the whole Law and the Prophets: "Thou shalt love the Lord Thy God with thy whole heart, and thy whole soul, and with thy whole mind"; and "Thou shalt love thy neighbor as thyself."* [Augustine, 1953, p. 191]

Agape is the element of love in the New Testament sense of the forgiving, personal character of God. Eros represents the longing of all creature for God as the highest good, the desire to be united with it, to fulfill itself by intuiting eternally the divine abundance. The agape element is emphasized when we speak of God moving down to man *in caritas*, of becoming humble in Christ, exercising grace and mercy, participating in the lowest and elevating it to the highest. Eros, on the other side, drives from below to above; it is a longing, striving, being moved by the highest, being grasped by it in its fullness and abundance.

The distinction between agape and eros has created fundamental controversies throughout the history of Christianity. Nygren (1932–1939/1982), a Swedish Protestant theologian, asserted that agape was the highest form of love, while eros was inferior. Tillich on the other hand claimed that if you remove eros you cannot speak of love for God any more (P. Tillich, 1968, p. 115). For Nygren the mixture of eros and agape in Catholic theology represented a profound error, which in his opinion Luther corrected; hence Protestantism stood for a purer form of love than Catholicism.

The problem of evil is another perennial that has plagued Christian theologians. If God is omnipotent and all-benevolent love, how can evil exist? The Manichaean heresy, which Augustine once belonged to, solved this problem in a commonsense way by postulating two Gods, one controlling good, the other controlling evil. However, this was ruled out of court so some other "solution" had to be found. Two others existed. One was that God is all-powerful so humans have no right to question him. And second was Calvin's position (P. Tillich, 1968, p. 226), that God has produced evil people in order to punish them and in order to save others who are evil from their evil nature. No matter how you twist them, both arguments are so ludicrous that sooner or later somebody would have to rebel against them, which is indeed what happened historically.

Another dilemma that dogs the history of Christianity is the revulsion against sexuality. It is difficult, if not impossible, to find some cogent *theological* reason that Christianity should have been so antisexual; the historical and social reasons are plain enough (see Chapter 2). Why should God, who loves everybody, refuse them this simple pleasure? He could place it in a secondary position, but why ascribe so much evil to it?

Tillich, who led a deviant, openly promiscuous sexual life in his day (cf. Hannah Tillich's autobiography, 1974), claimed that Protestant reformers had cleared the way for sexuality. But then:

> *The reformers tried to reestablish the dignity of the sexual, but they succeeded only in a limited way. They never completely followed through on their own principles against the Roman Church. Therefore, anyone who knows anything about the history of moral behavior and the history of ethical theory in Protestantism will see that Christianity has been very uncertain on this point and has produced no satisfactory answer to this question implied in human existence. [P. Tillich, 1968, pp. 127–128]*

All the great religions have been antisexual to one degree or another, but none as much as the Christian. Thus Christianity has stood for the greatest demand for love (unconditional love of God and of all things, experiencing God through oneself) and the greatest repression of sexuality. Freud hypothesized accordingly that the command to love became in many cases a reaction formation against the underlying hatred, and this underlying hatred broke through every once in a while when the repressions were lifted, as in chaotic social conditions.

Finally, it should be mentioned that the command to love everybody, or the golden rule, is psychologically impossible. Thus religion, like philosophy, comes to grief because it makes an impossible demand upon the individual. Hence there are in any religion few saints, while most people remain sinners, obeying the ritual of the law but ignoring its ethical precepts, or toning them down to the point where they cannot readily be perceived.

In other religions quite often very little attention is paid to love.

Books that seek to present the major precepts of various religions often do not even list the term in the index (Konvitz, 1980; Ling, 1968; Nasr, 1966). When a religious leader urges love upon his or her people, it is often in opposition to the mainstream of the religious current, as is the case with Martin Buber, or the Sufis in Islam. Even Gandhi (1957) urged nonviolence rather than active love, and he was so eager to banish sexuality that he cut himself off from his own son when the latter married. Nygren argues that Catholicism stands for eros, Protestantism for agape, and Judaism for nomos (law). Almost all religions seem to stand for law (ritual) more than anything else, while the doctrinal precepts, as in Christianity, are so vague as to be incomprehensible, or so difficult that they cannot be fulfilled.

On the positive side, it could be said however that the order induced by a religion in whatever social structure it happens to be regulates the relationships among its members in a theoretically loving way, while they direct contempt or scorn or hatred for those outside the religion. Even Gandhi once tried to communicate with Hitler because, ignorant as he was of the political situation in Europe in 1936, he knew that Hitler was opposing England, and England was India's enemy. And once Gandhi was assassinated a fierce war broke out that killed several million people (Murphy, 1953). Thus, just as in Christianity, when social turmoil lifts the repressions, hatred breaks through in fearful form.

PHILOSOPHICAL VIEWS

It is a surprise to find that most philosophers have shown little interest in love, pressing their concerns in other directions. However, a number have made some statements about it, which can be briefly reviewed.

Hazo (1967) distinguishes between acquisitive love and benevolent love, the desire to get something from the other and the desire to give something. Philosophers have placed varied emphases on each of these aspects.

Descartes discusses love in two works: *The Passions of the Soul* (Descartes, 1948) and *Letters to Chanut* (Hazo, 1967, p. 111). *Letters to Chanut* focuses exclusively on love, deals directly and at length with the question of what love is, and sets forth the essentials of the theory of love. Most philosophy texts that describe his views, however, pay so little attention to what he says about love that they do not even mention it (cf., e.g., Randall, 1976, which does not even mention the word *love* in the index).

Descartes discusses love in three different ways: as purely intellectual, as passion, and as a combination of elements from both spheres. Intellectual love can exist in the soul apart from the body, whereas the love that is a passion presupposes the body's connection with the soul as well as the soul's ability to love intellectually. For the most part his treatise is armchair philosophy, not derived from the direct study of human beings.

Hume is as usual more pragmatic. His main concept is that of impressions, which include "all our sensations, passions and emotions as they make their first appearance. in the soul" (1896, p. 1). Since love is a passion it is also an impression. He did, however, contribute the idea that love always involves two people. "Our love and hatred are always directed to some sensible being external to us, and when we talk of self-love, 'tis not in a proper sense, nor has the sensation it produces anything in common with that tender emotion, which is excited by a friend or mistress" (p. 329).

For John Locke the passions of love in relation to pleasure and desire are understood as the judgments that what is loved will or can produce delight. For Kant love is a matter of feeling, not of will or volition. Will and duty play the central role in his thought about practical reason; hence love takes a back seat.

Hegel, on the other hand, deals with love more directly; he is important as a forerunner of Freud, since he dominated the German philosophical scene so completely for 100 years after his death. He too stressed the interpersonal character of love: "Love means in general terms the consciousness of my unity with another, so that I am not in selfish isolation but win my self-consciousness only as the renunciation of my independence and through knowing myself as the unity of myself with another and the other with me" (1942, p. 261).

Some philosophers did note the connection between sexuality and love. For Schopenhauer love is completely sexual. It is accompanied by an illusion, which derives from the competing interests of the species and the individual in sexual matters. Similarly, for Vladimir Solovyev, a Russian philosopher of the nineteenth century, the most basic contrast is that between love and egoism. Egoism (what we would call today narcissism) consists in the exclusive acknowledgment of absolute significance for oneself and in the denial of it for others. The only force that can sap egoism at its root, and effectively undermine it, is love, and chiefly sex-love.

It cannot be argued that the summary of philosophical views is very enlightening. In spite of the importance of the topic, philosophers in

general have paid little attention to the nature of love, or to its significance in human life. It is because of this armchair theorizing that the
observations of Freud and other psychologists become so fresh and enlightening.

Like many others, Freud held that poets had throughout the ages
understood love better than any other group of individuals. I hope then
that it will not be considered out of place to quote some love poetry
from various cultures.

Chinese

Tiny drops of sweat are like a hundred fragrant pearls,
The sweet full breasts tremble.
The dew, like a gentle stream,
Reaches the Heart of the Peony.
They taste the joy of love in perfect harmony.
    [CHIN P'ING MEI; DOUGLAS & SLINGER, 1981, P. 46]

Egyptian

I think I'll go home and lie very still,
    feigning terminal illness.
Then the neighbors will all troop over to stare,
    my love, perhaps, among them.
How she'll smile while the specialists
    snarl in their teeth!—
    she perfectly well knows what ails me.
        [FOSTER, 1974, p. 72]

Shakespeare

O mistress mine, where are you roaming?
O stay and hear; your true love's coming,
    That can sing both high and low;
Trip no further, pretty sweeting;
Journeys end in lovers' meeting,
    Every wise man's son doth know.
What is love? 'tis not hereafter;
Present mirth hath present laughter;
    What's to come is still unsure;
In delay there lies no plenty;

> Then come kiss me, sweet and twenty,
> Youth's a stuff will not endure.
> [*Twelfth Night*, Act 2, Scene 3, lines 42–53]

Elizabeth Barrett Browning

> If thou must love me, let it be for nought
> Except for love's sake only. Do not say
> "I love her for her smile . . . her look . . . her way
> Of speaking gently, . . . for a trick of thought
> That falls in well with mine, and certes brought
> A sense of pleasant ease on such a day"—
> For these things in themselves, Beloved, may
> Be changed, or change for thee,—and love, so
>   wrought,
> May be unwrought so. Neither love me for
> Thine own dear pity's wiping my cheeks dry,—
> A creature might forget to weep, who bore
> Thy comfort long, and lose thy love thereby!
> But love me for love's sake, that evermore
> Thou may'st love on, through love's eternity.
> [Sonnet XIV, *Sonnets from the Portuguese*]

Mozart and Beethoven's Views on Love

For Mozart the ideal was Don Giovanni, who wishes to assert his potency as a male by playing with women (p. 29).

For Beethoven it was more the longing for an absent woman. In a notebook for the year 1818 he wrote: "Only love, yes, only love is capable of granting you a happy life. O God, let me find her at last, the woman who may strengthen me in virtue, who is permitted to be mine."

[Singer, 1977, p. 123]

PSYCHOLOGICAL VIEWS

Before the advent of Freud psychologists likewise had little interest in love. William James, in his classic *Principle of Psychology* (1890/1950), identifies love with sex and says: "Of all propensities, the sexual impulses bear on their face the most obvious signs of being instinctive, in the sense of blind, automatic and untaught" (vol. 2, p. 437). Ignoring his own personal shyness, he has a curious footnote in which he says: "To most of us it is even unpleasant to sit down in a chair still warm from occupancy by another person's body. To many, hand-shaking is disagreeable" (vol. 2, p. 430). Parental love he claims is an instinct stronger in woman than in man, at least in the early childhood of its object (vol. 2, p. 439). At another point he ridicules Bain's reduction of sociability and parental love to the pleasures of touch. Bain had written: "Touch is both the alpha and omega of affection. Why should a more lively feeling grow up towards a fellow-being than towards a perennial fountain?" (Cited in James, vol. 2, p. 551).

In this review of philosophical, religious, and psychological views on love prior to Freud, there is little that is illuminating. Even today philosophers talk little of love, while psychologists comment that they can go through year after year of *Psychological Abstracts* and find nothing on love. While the review is somewhat tedious, it can serve to highlight the tremendous revolution in our notions about love and its importance in life that was created by psychoanalysis.

FREUD

In a recent article Leon Altman (1977) wrote:

> *What is love? For most of mankind it has been a sweet mystery whose presence was a miracle, whose absence was a disaster. For philosophers, before and after Plato, love has been the subject of serious disquisition and debate as either madness or the only road to salvation. To poets over the ages, it is reason for ecstasy, dismay, or serious perplexity. Love has its undoubted biology, its possible chemistry, its manifest physiology, and what may be deemed its anatomy. But it had no scientific psychology until Freud began his investigations into the depths of human behavior. [p. 35]*

Altman makes a very good point here: What Freud contributed was a scientific psychology of love, based on careful empirical study of human beings. The statement that Freud's approach was a full scientific one will no doubt be denied or ridiculed by many brought up in the standard academic tradition. Science can best be defined as a system that offers responsible interpretations for the data obtained (Fine, 1983a; Nagel, 1961). In this sense Freud's enormously detailed and careful study of the love lives of human beings is fully scientific, even if the conclusions may be altered in some ways. I cannot take the space to argue this point more fully here; I have done so in other works (Fine, 1981; Fine, 1983a).

Freud's emphasis on love has been improperly understood for several reasons. First of all, he showed that love and sexuality are closely allied, and the argument then shifted to the proper role of sexuality in human affairs. Then, with his change in instinct theory from one based on sexuality to the dual one of eros and thanatos, his earlier theories become confused, and the relationship between love and aggression is still unclear. And finally some of what Freud was describing relates to normal love, some to neurotic love. All of his remarks are descriptive, but some are prescriptive, and he did not bother to discriminate between the two carefully. He often failed to make clear whether he was writing about normal love or about neurotic love. And finally he would change his mind without saying so, and he allowed himself many remarks and observations that have since been questioned. In spite of all these drawbacks, he did pen the greatest tract ever written on love; Hitschmann (1952), for example, counted 133 discussions of love in his works. It is necessary to sift the valuable from the trivial and the dubious. Part of what he wrote (such as the nature of psychosexual development in the *Three Essays*) has become an essential part of all psychology; part is questionable; part is philosophical speculation. Hence what follows is a careful critical review of his views on love.

Even in the earliest analytic paper Breuer made the observation that his patient had never known the emotion of love and had never developed it during the treatment. He also commented on the close connection between being in love and nursing the sick. In the *Studies in Hysteria*, which was written jointly by Freud and Breuer, the issue was always reduced to some problem in the love lives of the women. Both the therapeutic techniques and the theoretical structure have long since been outmoded and now play only a historical role in the growth of psychoanalysis. But what is significant is first the close study of the love lives and second the consistent use of psychology. In fact, in the theoretical section Breuer finds it necessary to apologize for his avoidance of physiology. He writes:

> *In what follows little mention will be made of the brain and none whatever of molecules. Psychical processes will be dealt with in the language of psychology; and, indeed, it cannot possibly be otherwise. . . . Accordingly I may perhaps be forgiven if I make almost exclusive use of psychological terms.* [Freud, 1953–1974, vol. 2, p. 185]

Freud's elaboration of psychoanalytic theory really began in 1900, with the *Interpretation of Dreams*, written after his self-analysis (Fine, 1979; Anzieu, 1975). The next major work was the *Three Essays on Sexuality* (1905), where the whole question of love and sexuality was carefully considered.

The first and most essential observation is that love and sexuality are closely connected. He extended the meaning of sexuality to include loving and liking, on the one hand, and bodily gratifications of all kinds on the other. The whole was summed up in what he called the libido theory (though this in turn went through many changes).

The concept of sexuality was greatly clarified by his demonstration that it does not appear full-blown until puberty, but that it has a long developmental history, going back to birth. This development involves several subsidiary propositions.

1. There are psychosexual stages of development—oral, anal, phallic, and eventually puberty (though these concepts were inserted at various periods, not all at once into the *Three Essays*). At puberty, genital primacy is established, a state in which all the other forms of gratification become subordinated to the main aim of sexual intercourse.

2. Human existence is divided into three main periods: childhood, or infantile sexuality, the latency period (from school age on to puberty), when sexual manifestations are quiescent, and adulthood, when genital primacy takes over.

3. Normal love involves a union of the tender and sexual feelings toward a person of the opposite sex. The prototype is the child sucking at its mother's breast (Freud, 1953–1974, vol. 7, p. 222).

4. At the same time ordinary love is aim-inhibited sexuality. That is, the sexual wishes in childhood are gradually repressed, the tender ones continue and gain the upper hand. This is one of the many places where Freud failed to distinguish clearly between normal and neurotic love.

5. Neurosis derives from fixation on or regression to the psychosexual life of the child. The child is polymorphous perverse; that is, he or she will accept any form of bodily pleasure without guilt until taught that it is wrong. Hence the sexual behavior of the neurotic finds its explanation in this polymorphous perverse disposition. In the *Three Essays* he wrote: "The innumerable peculiarities of the neurotic life of human beings as well as the compulsive character

of the process of falling in love itself are quite unintelligible except by reference back to childhood and as being residual effects of childhood" (1953–1974, vol. 7, p. 229).

6. How determinative childhood is for all future growth is not made entirely clear by Freud. At one point he refers to "psychoneurotics, a numerous class of people and not far removed from the healthy" (1953–1974, vol. 7, p. 231). Likewise he says: "What we describe as a person's 'character' is built up to a considerable extent from the material of sexual excitations and is composed of instincts that have been fixed since childhood" (1953–1974, vol. 7, p. 238).

   But then again he allows for sublimation and other mechanisms that allow the individual to grow. And in the paper on narcissism (1914) he writes: "The development of the ego consists in a departure from primary narcissism and gives rise to a vigorous attempt to recover that state" (1953–1974, vol. 14, p. 100).

   The general impression is that Freud was dubious about the wish of the child to grow and saw growth rather as imposed by external influences. On the other hand, later analysts have questioned this position (Hartmann, Kris, & Loewenstein, 1946). And it is obvious that if no growth were possible, no therapy would be possible. Thus we can say that for Freud childhood tends to be decisive, that the human personality is fairly fully formed by the age of 5, but that there are many exceptions, and much capacity to grow beyond that stage.

   With regard to such questions as romantic love, however, the emphasis on childhood throws an entirely new light on the situation. For the vicissitudes of romantic love, like those of any other love, cannot be properly understood without reference to the childhood circumstances of the individuals. In this way it can be understood why both the Christian emphasis on divine love and the romantic love of the courtly period were doomed to failure, insofar as they did not take into account the nature of childhood and its lasting influences.

7. Freud made no definitive distinction between neurosis and psychosis; indeed, the terms themselves were not in commonly understood use at the time. He always held on to the continuum theory: that there is only a quantitative distinction among the various forms of emotional disturbance. In other works, such as the 1908 paper on *Civilized Sexual Morality*, he extended his findings to

normal people, while in *Totem and Taboo* he widened them to other cultures. Thus in the course of time psychoanalysis became a general psychology, helpful in understanding all people and in all cultures.

Nevertheless, in the course of psychoanalytic treatment a new difficulty arose—the transference, the emotional relationship of the patient to the analyst. Transference, however, though uncovered and isolated by analysis, is actually a universal phenomenon of the human mind: "It decides the success of all medical influence, and in fact dominates the whole of each person's relations to his human environment" (Freud, 1953–1974, vol. 20, p. 42). So transference can be viewed in two different ways in regard to love. First of all love relationships are basically transferences; their success or failure depends on how close to reality the transference lies. Second, in therapy the transferences have to be worked out before any other real change can occur.

This led to a new formula for change in psychoanalysis: working through the transferences and resistances (1914); earlier the goal had been formulated in terms of lifting the amnesias. Later in 1923 in *The Ego and the Id* still another formula was added: that the ego had to replace the id. And finally in his 1937 paper, "Analysis Terminable and Interminable," he changed again, stating that the object of analysis was to establish the most suitable conditions for the functioning of the ego. Thus in the course of time he left the question of normal love up in the air, especially after he added the death instinct, or instinctual hostility, to sexuality as a basic instinct in 1920.

To the important topic of the relationship between transference love and normal love Freud devoted the paper "Observations on Transference Love" in 1915. Here he argues that transference love differs from normal love only in degree, and he goes on to say that "being in love in ordinary life, outside analysis, is also more similar to abnormal than to normal mental phenomena" (1953–1974, vol. 12, p. 168).

Thus love is abnormal, yet it is necessary to love in order not to fall ill. The contradiction can be understood, though not resolved, by examining his changing views of sexuality, and the consequences of his position, especially the social consequences.

Freud's only open statements about the sexual reform of society was in a paper entitled "Civilized Sexual Morality and Modern Nervousness," published in 1908. This was prompted by a book by von Ehrenfels, a prominent professor of philosophy of that day, entitled *Sexual Ethics*, which had appeared a year earlier. Von Ehrenfels had made two main points: First, the prevailing sexual morality of civilization is character-ized by the transference of feminine demands onto the sexual life of the man, with deprecation of any sexual intercourse outside of marriage. Second, this leads to a double standard of moral life, with evil conse-quences for honesty and humanity; and the glorifying of monogamy paralyzes the process of selection, which is the only hope of improving the human constitution, a hope that humanitarianism and hygiene had already reduced to a minimum.

Apparently Freud was in agreement with both of these points. As the title of his paper implies, "civilized" sexual morality is a sham and has primarily one outcome—nervous illness. A tone of considerable moral indignation at the senseless demands made on the modern human being runs throughout the discussion. Freud was particularly impressed by the widespread incidence of impotence in men and of frigidity in women. In order to obtain more precise information about sexual frustration, at a discussion of the Vienna Psychoanalytic Society he even offered to re-vise a questionnaire drawn up by Magnus Hirschfeld and send it around—a kind of forerunner of the Kinsey Report, which never got off the ground (Nunberg & Federn, 1962–1975, vol. 1, p. 376).

Freud's earlier theories in the 1890s easily implied that if the patient changed his or her sexual activity, the neurosis would disappear or im-prove. And in fact in his autobiography he states that that is what he advised in some cases. "If it was possible to put an end to the abuse and allow its place to be taken by normal sexual activity, a striking improve-ment in the condition was the reward" (1953–1974, vol. 20, p. 25). But that was in the 1890s, when the significance of childhood and innate psychosexual development had not yet occurred to him. In the 1900s it was no longer a question of direct sexual activity, but rather of changing the order of society.

Freud was in favor of revolutionary changes, particularly in regard to the sexual code. However, politics was not his favorite and he retreated from social change. At a meeting of the Vienna Psychoanalytic Society the notes state that "Freud personally takes no stand on the efforts at reform" (Nunberg & Federn, vol. 2, pp. 89–90). Then Rank goes on to summarize what Freud meant:

> *The terrifying picture that is painted of libertinage is an exaggeration: we can be sure that all the instincts would continue to exist alongside of liberty. Social need would take care of that. He is not inclined to regard the Caesars as mentally sick. It was their position that drove them to their excesses; we must not give people that unlimited sense of power.*

Actually, the best selection would be achieved by establishing "libertin-age" for one generation; for then the inferior individuals would auto-matically eliminate themselves in sterile indulgences in love. The num-ber of those who are worthwhile and have offspring is too small; hence the state cannot make use of that situation. With regard to hate and love, we have learned from analyses that they not only have a common root but are identical, and that there is not love without an admixture of hatred. One can easily turn into the other through a reversal of affect, a change of sign. [Nunberg & Federn, vol. 2, p. 90]

In other meetings of the society he was also more open than in his published writings. For example, at the meeting on February 12, 1908 (Nunberg & Federn, vol. 1, pp. 306–317) he stated that there are oddi-ties and queerness of people that are substitutes for a neurosis. There are three choices: that of neurosis, that of transgressing the rule (infidel-ity, etc.), and that of virtues and queerness. A large number of people choose this third path. Then he went on to suggest that there should be an academy of love founded where the art of love would be taught (Nunberg & Federn, vol. 1, p. 311).

Publicly, however, his thought took a different and curious turn. If civilization interferes with instinctual gratification, there are obviously two possibilities: Change society, or be frustrated. He took a third step, that of questioning the instinct itself. As early as 1906 he had announced to the Vienna Psychoanalytic Society his intention of writing a book or essay on the love life of the human being. The notion of an academy of love has already been mentioned. After much vacillation he decided that the sexual instinct did not lend itself to gratification, and in 1912 he stated in his writings:

Thus we may perhaps be forced to become reconciled to the idea that it is quite impossible to adjust the claims of the sexual instinct to the demands of civilization; that in consequence of its cultural develop-ment renunciation and suffering, as well as the danger of extinction in the remotest future, cannot be avoided by the human race. [1953–1954, vol. 11, p. 87]

In 1914 he changed the libido theory in a drastic manner by assuming that the ego has a libido as well as sexuality, although he had previously defined libido as sexual desire. He postulated an original ego libido in the neonate, which is living in a state of primary narcissism that provides it with a blissful existence. When the libido has reached a certain level it reaches out for objects (people). This variation on the libido theory makes little sense and has accordingly been the subject of much criticism (cf. Kardiner, Karush, & Ovesey, 1959; Fine, 1984, in press). Then came the greatest change of all in 1920, with the introduction of a primary destructive drive (thanatos). Thereafter, sexual gratification naturally could not be put forward as a valuable social reform because the destructive drives would remain. Finally, with *Civilization and Its Discontents* (1930), he stressed above all the need to curb the aggressive drive, stating, *Homo homini lupus*: "Man is a wolf to man." While he still maintained that love was a foundation of civilization, he no longer seemed to have much interest in it or in the reform of the sexual code. As to love, he thought that when the love relationship is at its height there is no room left for any interest in the environment (1953–1974, vol. 21, pp. 108–109).

Thus there is a long progression from the fearless reformer of 1908 who wanted to set up an academy of love to the disillusioned philosopher of 1930 who could see nothing but destruction tearing civilization apart. Yet even in this disillusionment of 1930 he could urge each person to seek his or her own salvation:

> *The program of becoming happy, which the pleasure principle imposes on us, cannot be fulfilled; yet we must not—indeed, we cannot—give up our efforts to bring it nearer to fulfillment by some means or other. Very different paths may be taken in that direction. . . . By none of these paths can we attain all that we desire. . . . There is no golden rule which applies to everyone: every man must find out for himself in what particular fashion he can be saved.* [1953–1974, vol. 21, p. 83]

Thus, in spite of the greatness of his achievement, Freud left a large number of questions open, unanswered, or treated in a contradictory way. These deficiencies in his theory, plus the very human desire to do better than he did, help to account for the numerous vicissitudes in theory in the history of psychoanalysis.

In his other writings on the topic, Freud contented himself mainly with describing certain neurotic malformations of love. These descriptions of neurotic love are of course quite valuable. Of particular note are the papers on certain kinds of object choices made by men. He called this the "preconditions for loving," or the "necessary conditions for loving." These are men who fall in love with injured women, who are of bad repute sexually (love for a prostitute). Their love is accompanied by a rescue fantasy. He showed that these preconditions derive from the infantile fixation of tender feelings on the mother, the split between the good woman and the bad woman that has been such a hallmark of western history. A second set of preconditions applies to those men who as a defense against incestuous wishes turn to a psychical debasement of the object. Where they love they do not desire and where they desire they cannot love (1953–1974, vol. 11, p. 183). This type of love does much to explain the sexual conflicts that come to the fore in marriage and the need in many men for an extramarital partner. Either one, the wife or the mistress, may be debased, while the other is idealized. Many other neurotic malformations of love were alluded to by Freud and other writers.

The general conclusion is that love is more frequently neurotic than otherwise. This has been misinterpreted to imply that he saw all love as neurotic. Actually, once he refrained from the possibility of social reform, he devoted all his efforts to further scientific advances.

Particular interest of late has been aroused by his differentiation of the characteristic modes of loving of men and of women in their choice of object. Complete object love of the attachment type is, properly speaking, characteristic of the male (1953–1974, vol. 14, p. 88). In contrast, women's love is of the narcissistic type; they wish to be loved. "It is only themselves that such women love with an intensity comparable to that of the man's love for them" (1953–1974, vol. 14, p. 89). These statements have caused endless confusion because he does not distinguish normal from neurotic love. It would have been more correct to describe both of these attitudes as part of the preconditions for loving characteristic of our culture, rather than as characteristic of men and women as such.

Finally, in 1921, in *Group Psychology and the Analysis of the Ego* Freud ventured upon an examination of social psychology by trying to see how the libido theory could throw light on group psychology, a topic that had hitherto been ignored. To begin with, he saw the essence of the group mind as love relationships (or, he says, to use a more neutral term, emotional ties). These considerations obviously are relevant to the question of the social control of love discussed in the previous chapter.

Next he distinguishes two kinds of groups: leaderless and those with leaders. As a prime example of a leaderless group he chooses the church; as a prime example of a group with leaders he discusses the army.

In both kinds of groups each individual is bound by libidinal ties on the one hand to the leader (Christ, the commander in chief) and on the other hand to the other members of the group. When there is a relaxation in the libidinal structure of the group, panic may ensue. In the led group (the army) this panic may ensue when the general in charge loses his head or is removed. On the other hand, when a church dissolves, or the libidinal ties relax, ruthless and hostile impulses toward other people make their appearance that, owing to the equal love of Christ, had previously been held in check. "Fundamentally indeed every religion is in this same way a religion of love for all those whom it embraces; while cruelty and intolerance towards those who do not belong to it are natural to every religion" (1953–1974, vol. 21, p. 98).

A further examination of these libidinal ties reveals that every human relationship is ambivalent. He adds here the dubious comment "perhaps with the solitary exception of the relation of a mother to her son, which is based on narcissism, is not disturbed by subsequent rivalry, and is reinforced by a rudimentary attempt at sexual object-choice" (1953–1974, vol. 21, footnote to p. 101). A new group requires the formation of libidinal ties among the members of the group; the question now is what kind of libidinal ties.

These libidinal ties cannot be sexual. They rest upon identification, which is (for him at that time) the earliest expression of an emotional tie with another person. This fits in very well with the Oedipus complex, the core structure of the personality. Apart from the original emotional tie, identification may result in a regressive way from an abandoned object cathexis, and also from introjection of the object into the ego and from any new perception of a common quality shared with some other person who is not an object of the sexual instinct.

The mutual libidinal tie in a group may now be seen as the relation to the leader. The members seem to be in love with the leader, which Freud summarizes in the formula: The object has been put in place of the ego ideal (the leader is the ego ideal). The significant question about groups then is whether the object is put in the place of the ego (identification) or in the place of the ego ideal (submission to authority). These possibilities are tied up with hypnosis: From being in love (one of his favorite topics) to hypnosis is but a short step. In hypnosis the hypnotist has stepped into the place of the ego ideal. This leads to the formula: A primary group is a number of individuals who have put one and the same object in the place of their ego ideal and have consequently identified themselves with one another in their ego. (These considerations are obviously relevant to the problems of intentional love cultures discussed in a previous chapter.)

Traditionally, the herd instinct was viewed as the tie that kept a group together; animals too get together in groups. But closer examination shows that social feeling is based upon the reversal of what was first a hostile feeling into a positively toned tie in the nature of an identification. This reversal seems to occur under the influence of a common affectionate tie with a person outside the group (the leader). Thus the human being can be said to be a horde animal, not a herd animal.

In the next chapter he goes back to his notion of the primal horde, actually a hypothesis of Darwin's. Then he introduces the important concept of the superego, here still called the ego ideal, which has been so extraordinarily fruitful in later theorizing. Then a group becomes a collection of individuals who have a common superego; or rather, if they have a common superego they stay together, while if they do not they may fall apart.

In the great artificial groups, the church and the army, there is no place for women as sexual objects; that remains outside the group. Hence it seems certain that homosexual love is far more compatible with group ties, even when it takes the shape of uninhibited sexual impulses, which he calls "a remarkable fact, the explanation of which might carry us far" (1953–1974, vol. 21, p. 141).

One final comment is relevant. A neurosis, he says, has the same disintegrating effect upon a group as being in love; this would explain why the deviant becomes the outcast of society. On the other hand it appears that where there are strong groups neuroses may diminish and even temporarily disappear; this thought has been followed up in many ways, including the development of group therapy.

Freud realized that the questions surrounding love cannot be separated from the body of psychoanalytic thought. Since the advent of ego psychology, from the 1940s on, the emphasis has been shifted to ego functions and cognitive aspects of the personality, in contrast to the earlier emphases on love and hate. This has served to obscure the fact that love and hate remain essential to the entire psychoanalytic philosophy. Accordingly, it will be worthwhile to examine some of the later aspects of Freud's thought as well, even though they may not seem at first sight to relate so directly to love as his earlier work.

In the latter part of his life Freud turned his attention to the larger social and philosophical questions raised by psychoanalysis. With regard to moral reform, his attention was first drawn to this question by his opponents, who attacked him as immoral, doing such awful things as attributing sexual feelings to children. This nonsense he simply disregarded.

More significant was the insistent demand by Putnam, a professor of neurology at Harvard who became one of the first American analysts, that psychoanalysis must bring about moral improvement. Freud was not in essential disagreement; all he felt was that this moral improvement should not be undertaken by the analyst. In 1915 he wrote:

> *I quite agree with you that psychoanalysis should find a place among the methods whose aim is to bring about the highest ethical and intellectual development of the individual. Our difference is of a purely practical nature. It is confined to the fact that I do not wish to entrust this further development to the psychoanalyst.* [cited in Putnam, 1971, p. 115]

As to the kind of world in which we live, he had few illusions. At an early stage he discovered that he had, as he put it, "all mankind as my patient." Yet the social scientists were oblivious to the moral rot that was all around them. Although he did not dabble much in psychohistory, he did say in 1915: "The primeval history of mankind is filled with murder. Even today, the history of the world which our children learn at school is essentially a series of murders of people" (1953–1974, vol. 14, p. 292).

Most historians today still have not reached this level of sophistication. For instance, McNeill in his book *The Pursuit of Power* (1982) speaks of the increasing bureaucratization of violence. Yet not a word is said about the fact that this increasing bureaucratization murders increasing millions of people and has created the danger that the world itself may be destroyed. Thus Freud came close to the concept of a hate culture, though he never used that word, perhaps largely because he was preoccupied with the instinctual aspects of hatred rather than its cultural origins. Nevertheless he could see that whole civilizations become hotbeds of pathology, and that psychoanalysis could be a possible corrective. In *Civilization and Its Discontents* he wrote:

> *If the development of civilization has such a far-reaching similarity to the development of the individual . . . may we not be justified in reaching the diagnosis that under the influence of cultural urges, some civilizations, or some epochs of civilization—possibly the whole of mankind—have become "neurotic"? . . . As regards the therapeutic applications of our knowledge, what would be the use of the most correct analysis of social neuroses, since no one possesses authority to impose such a therapy upon the group? But in spite of all these difficulties, we may expect that one day someone will venture to embark upon a pathology of cultural communities.* [1953–1974, vol. 21, p. 144]

Later this pathology of civilization was pursued by many psychoanalysts on a much broader scale. However, to some extent Freud was still rather misled by the Rousseau-inspired notion of the noble savage, since subsequent investigation has shown that every culture has its own kind of pathology. However, there are differences, so that the division into love and hate cultures offered in the present book has considerable empirical justification. Had Freud considered the problem more directly, he would undoubtedly have been in agreement with the position adopted in this book.

The question of what professional group should undertake the task of therapy preoccupied him a great deal in his later life. On this point he was crystal clear: The decisive element in the formation of a good therapist is his or her analytic training, especially his or her personal analysis, not any kind of degree or theoretical courses. His book *The Question of Lay Analysis* in 1926 sounded a clarion call for the training of therapists and reaffirmed his lifelong conviction that medical training was not essential to the psychotherapist. In 1928 he wrote to Pfister:

> *I do not know if you have detected the secret link between the* Lay Analysis *and the* Illusion. *In the former I wish to protect analysis from the doctors and in the latter from the priests. I should like to hand it over to a profession which does not yet exist, the profession of lay curers of souls who need not be doctors and should not be priests.* [*Freud, 1982, p. 122*]

Clearly he felt that a psychoanalyst should be able to teach others how to love.

Slowly he broadened his image of analysis, moving from an emphasis on technique to an awareness of its broader social meaning and the large-scale existence of neurotic disturbances. In 1926 he wrote: "Perhaps once more an American may hit on the idea of spending a little money to get the 'social workers' of his country trained analytically and to turn them into a band of helpers for combating the neuroses of civilization" (1953–1974, vol. 20, p. 250).

To a certain extent this has happened, in that a profession of clinical social work has grown up that does therapy, whereas when Freud wrote the above in 1926 such a profession did not exist. Yet much remains to be done.

Does psychoanalysis carry within itself a philosophy of living that can be offered to the suffering individual or to humanity at large? Technically Freud's answer to this question was no: Psychoanalysis has no special *Weltanschauung*; it is compatible with any *Weltanschauung*. Yet he would easily have grasped the current limitation of psychoanalysis to the free democracies and the severe opposition to psychoanalysis of all totalitarian regimes, whether of the right or of the left. And, like all intellectuals since the French Revolution, he remained profoundly irreligious, castigating religion in his earlier work as an obsessional neurosis, and in his later as an illusion. But Freud looked at *Weltanschauung* in too narrow a sense. Had he broadened his horizons he would certainly have included love as part of the basic philosophy of psychoanalysis.

As to where psychoanalysis stands in the field of the sciences there was never any doubt in Freud's mind: It is psychology. In *The Question of Lay Analysis* (1926) he wrote:

> *I have assumed that is to say that psychoanalysis is not a specialized branch of medicine. I cannot see how it is possible to dispute this. Psychoanalysis is a part of psychology; not of medical psychology in the old sense, not of the psychology of morbid processes, but simply of psychology. It is certainly not the whole of psychology, but its substructure and perhaps even its entire foundation. The possibility of its application to medical purposes must not lead us astray. Electricity and radiology also have their medical application, but the science to which they both belong is none the less physics.* [1953–1974, vol. 22, p. 252]

Thus from first to last Freud regarded himself as a psychologist. He even said in 1926: "I became a doctor through being compelled to deviate from my original purpose; and the triumph of my life lies in my having, after a long and roundabout journey, found my way back to my earliest path" (1953–1974, vol. 20, p. 253). And it should be noted that Freud's works today are still entitled *The Complete Psychological Works of Sigmund Freud.*

In sum, the entire body of Freud's work is an elaborate and profound discussion of the question of love. In the earlier years the emphasis was explicit, and in 1908 he spoke of setting up an academy of love. In the later years (after World War II) his emphasis shifted to hostility, but where hatred is uppermost love recedes into the background; thus here too he was talking about love, though from a different angle.

The main points that Freud made may be summed up as follows:

1. Love makes people happy.
2. Love is intimately connected with sexuality.
3. Neurosis arises from inhibitions in love.

4. Love represents a union of tender and sexual feelings toward a person of the opposite sex, which ideally should be gratified in marriage. But such a union is rare.

5. The instinctual drives admit of no complete gratification; thus some renunciation is unavoidable (though his notion that primitive peoples and lower-class groups live out their sexuality freely and hence do not suffer from neurosis has long since been abandoned).

6. There is a developmental line leading from early primary narcissism to later objective love.

7. Libidinal ties determine the structure of every group; "man is a horde animal." Hence the notion of love cultures and hate cultures could easily be fitted into his theories, though he did not do so.

8. The love life of the contemporary human being is seriously disturbed; civilization is threatened with disintegration by the forces of hostility.

9. Therapy is effective through the working through of the transferences, and transference love differs from normal love only in degree.

OTHER PSYCHOANALYTIC VIEWS

While Freud's views represented an enormous advance, he left many loose ends. The difference between normal and neurotic love was never made very clear. Whether sexuality produced love or love produced sexuality remained ambiguous. The relationship of love to the culture was left unexplored. Various other questions were left unanswered.

Yet surprisingly Freud's gigantic opus on love (since his works may be viewed in that light) was not continued consistently by his followers. A number of commentators have in fact remarked on the paucity of discussions of love among analysts after Freud. Thus the *Journal of the American Psychoanalytic Association*, now the most prestigious English-language psychoanalytic journal, in its 22-year cumulative index published in 1976 lists only 16 entries under *love*; thus, all other analysts together have said less about love than did Freud. No doubt the chaotic situation of the world since 1939 has contributed to the shift from love to hatred in psychoanalytic writings. But it is certainly time to offer a systematic approach to the topic, including Freud's views and everything that has been written since. That will be the goal of the next chapter. In the present chapter I wish to summarize briefly some of the more important papers by other analysts that have appeared.

In 1928 Karen Horney published an interesting paper entitled "The Problem of the Monogamous Ideal." First she expressed some astonishment that no thorough analytic exposition of the problems of marriage had ever been undertaken. Marriage she viewed as the gratification of the oedipal wishes. But this gratification is inevitably accompanied by disillusionment and the incest prohibition (each partner represents psychically the parent to the other). The consequent hostility leads the person involuntarily to seek new love objects. "This is the basic situation which gives rise to the *problem of monogamy*" (p. 323). This problem, she felt, could not really be resolved. "It never has been and never will be possible to find any principle which will solve these conflicts of married life" (p. 323). In principle Freud had agreed with this point of view in 1908, when the work of von Ehrenfels came up, but then he left the topic, apparently as unable to resolve it as Horney was 20 years later.

In 1937 Ernest Jones wrote a short paper entitled "Love and Morality," in which he described the process whereby a moral attitude toward others is substituted for an attitude of love (not further defined). In these people he had always found a strong vein of repressed sadism. Earlier Sandor Ferenczi (1916) had spoken of the common moral attitude as a form of "sphincter morality."

In 1921 J. C. Flugel, one of the early British analysts, published a book entitled *The Psychoanalytic Study of the Family*. His position was essentially that taken by Freud in the *Three Essays* in 1905, that family education should take care not to interfere with the instinctual development of the child, yet some clash was inevitable.

Of the other early analysts the one who wrote most extensively on love was Oskar Pfister, a Swiss minister who became a close friend of Freud's and a lay analyst (1924, 1948). His major work, which he regarded as his literary testament, was *Christianity and Fear* (German ed., 1944). Pfister is notable particularly for his analysis of the terrible hypocritical contradictions inherent in Christianity. "Many readers as well as myself have experienced grief at the monstrous volume of anti-Christianity discoverable in the history of Christianity" (1924, p. 9). He saw the history of Christianity as in reality a neurotic malformation of love, which had developed in accordance with the laws governing the growth of neuroses. His major thesis was that if Christianity is to remain true to the tenets of love propounded by Jesus, Christians would have to be analyzed; otherwise "the pathological malformations of Christianity which hitherto have so wretchedly thwarted the intentions of Jesus" would recur (p. 10).

The relationship between love and sexuality was much debated in the 1920s, partly because of the large-scale release of sexual inhibitions following the carnage of World War I and the Russian Revolution. Among the analysts the most vocal leader of the sexual school was Wilhelm Reich. (It should be remembered that in the 1920s he was still an analyst and had not yet gone over to the absurd orgone doctrine.) In his views he leaned heavily on Freud's 1890s doctrine of the actual neuroses, in which the assumption was that adult sexual frustration leads to anxiety by some unknown biochemical process; this theory had since been discarded by Freud.

Reich maintained that the severity of any kind of psychic disturbance is in direct relation to the severity of the disturbance of genitality (1927, p. 64) and that the prognosis depends directly on the possibility of establishing the capacity for full genital satisfaction. For him the whole process was a physiological one, and he looked forward to verifying one of Freud's early remarks that psychoanalysis would have to be placed on an organic foundation; this foundation was sexuality. By that time Freud had given up his earlier theories, but Reich held on to them.

While his genital theory has as such been discarded, Reich should be given credit for being the first to describe the whole sexual act and some of its psychical components. He anticipated Masters and Johnson by 40 years, depicting the four stages of excitement, plateau, orgasm, and resolution in almost identical terms. (Masters & Johnson, like those who have followed them, have ignored the analytic literature.) Reich also drew an important distinction between orgastic potency and ejaculatory potency in men: Many men can ejaculate but do not experience the full enjoyment attached to ejaculation.

In the 1920s there was still some hesitation among psychoanalysts about whether the physiological reaction as such could create the psychological response; today the issue has been settled by the repeated proof that the same physiological reaction can produce myriad psychological effects. Marie Bonaparte, who was a friend and analysand of Freud's, suffered from frigidity. Although she was in analysis with Freud, she induced a Viennese surgeon by the name of Halban (Bertin, 1982, p. 141) to move the clitoris closer to the vagina by surgical means; evidently this is an easy procedure. Apparently she tried the operation a number of times but never succeeded in overcoming her frigidity. What Freud said about it she does not report. Freud was however quite clear in his evaluation of Reich. In a letter to Lou Andreas-Salome in 1928 he wrote:

> We have here a Dr. Reich, a worthy but impetuous young man, passionately devoted to his hobby-horse, who now salutes in the genital orgasm the antidote to every neurosis. Perhaps he might learn from your analysis of K. to feel some respect for the complicated nature of the psyche. [Freud & Andreas-Salome, 1972]

A significant step forward was taken by Michael Balint with his theory of primary object love (Balint, 1953). In his view Freud's theory of primary narcissism missed many of the significant phenomena of early life. Instead what dominates the infant is primary object love, the longing for the mother. Quoting an important paper of Imre Hermann (1936), he states: (1) The infant of the primates spends the first few months of extrauterine life clinging to its mother's body; and (2) the human infant is forcibly separated from the maternal body much too early. He then describes the earliest phase of life as a passive longing for love using the formula: I shall be loved and satisfied, without being under any obligation to give anything in return (pp. 98–99). This is and remains forever the final goal of all erotic striving. He also cites a paper by Peto (1949), who showed as early as 1937 that reactions of infants to libidinous environmental influences can be demonstrated indisputably as early as the first week of their life and certainly in the first month (a remarkable observation for that period). Then he sums up his position as follows:

1. The phase of object relations, which could be called primary or primitive object love, must occur very early in life.
2. This phase is unavoidable, a necessary stage in mental development. All later object relations can be traced back to it; that is, vestiges and remnants of this primitive phase can be demonstrated in all the later ones.
3. This form of object relation is not limited to any of the erotogenic zones; it is not oral, oral–sucking, anal, genital, and so on, but is something on its own, as are the other forms of love, such as autoerotism, narcissism, and object love.

In my opinion this fact is of paramount importance and I hope that through this strict discrimination it will be possible to disentangle the hopeless confusion brought about by equating both in our theory and in

our terminology the development of instinctual aims with the develop-
ment of instinctual object-relations. [1953, pp. 101–102]

4. The biological basis of the primary object relation is the instinctual interdependence of mother and child; the two are dependent
   on each other but at the same time they are tuned to each other;
   each of them satisfies himself or herself by the other without the
   compulsion of paying regard to the other. Indeed, what is good
   for one is right for the other.

5. This intimate relation is severed by our civilization much too
   early. Consequences of this early severance are, among others, the
   well-known tendency to cling, and the general discontent, the insatiable greed of our children.

6. If the instinctual desire is satisfied in time, the pleasure experience never goes beyond the level of fore-pleasure, that is, the
   tranquil, quiet sense of well-being.

Obviously Balint was far ahead of his time. In a companion piece, his
wife Alice Balint (Balint, 1953) developed the thesis that maternal love
is the almost perfect counterpart to love for the mother. The relation
between mother and child is built upon the interdependence of the reciprocal instinctual aims (Balint, 1975, Chap. 6). With the publication
of Margaret Ribble's book *The Rights of Infants* in 1943, the extensive
exploration of the first year of life, and of the earliest forms of love and
hate, was fully launched; it is still going on.

The question of the basic differences between men and women was
always a topic of psychoanalytic concern. Freud spoke of the equation
of feminity and passivity, as opposed to masculinity and activity. Helene
Deutsch (1944), following his lead, asserted absolutely that "the fundamental identities of 'feminine–passive' and 'masculine–active' assert
themselves in all known cultures and races, in various forms and various
quantitative proportions" (pp. 224–225). Annie Reich in 1940 took
issue with her, in a paper the thesis of which is that extreme submissiveness in women is a masochistic trait, not inborn. Since then, while it is
recognized that there are biological differences, the feeling is general
that the major factor in gender identity is cultural. Considerable changes
in the psychoanalytic theory of women have accordingly taken place
(Blum, 1977). It is noteworthy that the psychology of men has only recently become a matter of interest to analysts (Cath, Gurwitt, & Ross,
1982).

Several authors have speculated that love involves an identification with and a fusion with the other person. Actually this is one of the oldest and most universal of all theories about love; it was proposed by St. Augustine. And in the famous love-death poem *Tristan and Isolde*, she says to him: "We are one life and flesh. . . . You and I, Tristan and Isolde, shall forever remain one and undivided. . . . I am yours . . . you are mine . . . one Tristan and Isolde" (cited in Siegel, 1978, p. 2).

Schopenhauer, who felt that marriages based on love as a rule turn out to be unhappy, wrote:

> *They feel the longing for and actual union and fusing together into a single being, in order to live on only as this, and this longing receives its fulfillment in the child which is produced by them, as that in which the qualities transmitted by them both, fused and united in one being, live on.* [1969, p. 342]

It is surprising that two analysts of such different persuasions as Fenichel and Sullivan should have reported this ancient doctrine of love as the longing to merge. Fenichel writes:

> *It has been mentioned that the full genital climax of an object relationship brings also a kind of regression to its earliest forerunner; it is an incorporation in so far as the feeling of union and a disappearance of the feeling of separateness occurs. Infatuation is characterized by the form this feeling takes: "We are one, but the partner is the more important 'half.'" Overestimation of the sexual partner means simultaneously: "I am participating in my partner's greatness." In this sense, every love is a "narcissistic gratification," a regaining of the lost and projected omnipotence.* [1945, p. 352]

Apart from a few occasional comments, Fenichel, in spite of his vast knowledge of the literature, does not undertake to integrate the analytic theory. What he says about merging should be regarded as the pathology of a love union, not the normal reaction.

Sullivan, in a similar vein, writes:

> *When the satisfaction or security of another person becomes as significant to one as is one's own satisfaction or security, then the state of love exists. So far as I know, under no other circumstances is a state of love present, regardless of the popular usage of the word.* [1939, p. 43]

He also makes the obviously incorrect remark that "the capacity to love in its initial form makes appearance as the mark that one has ceased to be juvenile and has become preadolescent" (p. 42).

Thus many psychoanalysts, in their theorizing, have simply repeated popular notions held through the ages without realizing it. At certain stages in life, love could involve a heightened awareness and appreciation of the other person, but this is a far cry from fusion or merger. The mistake is similar to Freud's, where he does not distinguish clearly between normal and neurotic love. (The term *corrective emotional experience*, first used by Alexander, has been widely misunderstood. What it refers to is the patient's transference distortions, which are analyzed and corrected in the course of therapy.)

An original note was struck by the Peruvian psychiatrist Carlos Alberto Seguin in his book *Love and Psychotherapy* (1965). First he defines psychotherapy as a kind of interpersonal relationship in which, through the medium of corrective emotional experiences, undesirable traits of personality become modified. Next he considers various modes of love: (1) friend to friend; (2) father to son; (3) teacher to pupil; (4) pastor to follower; and (5) lover to lover. Psychotherapeutic love is characterized by being none of these, since none is appropriate to the situation in which a sick person comes for help. Instead what the therapist experiences is a new kind of love, which because it is new Seguin distinguishes with a new name: the psychotherapeutic eros. This psychotherapeutic eros must be free from (1) authority or any tendency to possession; (2) identification; (3) dogma; (4) the imposition of values, rules, or knowledge; and (5) sexual attraction.

In the therapeutic situation, the therapist presents himself or herself with this form of love, which is based on values: the values of the loved person (the patient). This psychotherapeutic eros is characterized by love for the patient, indestructibility. "It is a love in which the supreme possibilities of the spirit are manifested and it is therefore capable of the most pure and satisfactory realizations" (1965, p. 126).

Thus Seguin goes beyond the stance of therapeutic neutrality that is the hallmark of so many analysts. It is a noble idea, though one difficult of realization. What he does not consider adequately is that it imposes demands on the therapist that he or she may not be able to meet, as well as that the transferences of the patient may very well not be able to respond to the love that the doctor offers him or her.

In a widely quoted book, Erich Fromm (*The Art Of Loving*, 1956) stresses that the act of love always implies certain basic elements: care, responsibility, respect, and knowledge. He defines love as "the active concern for the life and growth of that which we love." Such concern however must be accompanied by approval. Thus Fromm is primarily concerned with certain forms of maternal love; he seems to leave pleasure and enjoyment out of his theorizing entirely.

In another popular work, *Love and Will* (1969), Rollo May sees a tendency in society to set love against will. Man's task is to unite love and will. They are not united by automatic biological growth but must be part of our conscious development. This theory skirts virtually all the major questions connected with love.

Heinz Kohut (1971, 1977) devotes the major portion of his two major works to narcissism and has comparatively little to say about love. His psychology of the self has been both idealized and denigrated; a true evaluation of his contributions will have to wait for time.

With regard to love, Kohut's major innovation has been to postulate different developmental lines for love and narcissism. This assumption was first made by Jung, who called it introversion. Kohut has a much more sophisticated version, one more in keeping with subsequent analytic theorizing. However, this is one aspect of his thinking that has received the severest criticism. Thus he says:

> *I believe that the tendency to assume that the grandiose self is the more primitive of the two structures rests on the same prejudice which assigns to object love, without qualification, the supremacy over narcissism. Objectively, however, the original narcissism . . . is a precursor of object love.* [1971, p. 107]

At another point he comments:

> *Here I only repeat what I stated previously . . . namely that it is the improper intrusion of the altruistic value system of Western civilization, and not objective considerations of developmental maturity or adaptive usefulness, which tends to lead to a wish from the side of the therapist to replace the patient's narcissistic position with object love. Stated conversely, in many instances, the reshaping of the narcissistic structures and their integration into the personality must be rated as a more genuine and valid result of therapy than the patient's precarious compliance with demands for a change of his narcissism into object love.* [1971, p. 224]

Thus Kohut is not only describing a psychology of the self and narcissism but is also setting up narcissistic gratification as a desirable goal of therapy, more important in many cases than love. This goes so far against the mainstream psychoanalytic tradition that it has been emphatically rejected by many. In a recent paper Nikolaas Treurniet, in his evaluation of Kohut's self psychology, writes:

> *This paper is an attempt to evaluate critically some theoretical and clini-*
> *cal consequences of the psychoanalytic psychology of the self in its*
> *broad, supraordinate position.*

> *From this either–or position, advocated by Kohut and his followers, self*
> *psychology corrodes some of the most central explanatory concepts of*
> *psychoanalysis—conflict, transference, and resistance. . . . These con-*
> *sequences of the supraordinate self-psychological viewpoint are related*
> *to its overt attack on metapsychology, which is linked to an epistemo-*
> *logical fallacy as a consequence of the exclusive use of empathy and*
> *introspection with grave consequences for our explanatory power, i.e., a*
> *fundamental confusion between the realms of content and of function.*
> *This also implies an obstacle in the systematic study of self-deception*
> *and a threat to psychoanalysis defined as the study of human behavior*
> *considered from the viewpoint of conflict. [1983, p. 98]*

Otto Kernberg has written two recent papers on love, one on immature love (1974a) and the other on mature love (1974b).

In the paper entitled "Barriers to Falling and Remaining in Love" he
describes different stages of love incapacity. The most severe is that of
the narcissistic personality who has never fallen or been in love. (This
was Breuer's observation about Anna O., although at that time the term
narcissistic was not in use.) For these patients the prognosis is grave.

The next stage is seen in those with a narcissistic personality structure
who have a type of sexual promiscuity. These patients, while unstable, at
least struggle to overcome their basic incapacity for establishing object
relations. In male patients of this type there is a devaluation of female
sexuality.

Next on the continuum is the development of very intense love attachments (with primitive idealization) somewhat more enduring than the
transitory involvements of narcissistic patients. These are characteristic
of borderline patients without the typical narcissistic features. This as
well as the previous cases represents a relative freedom of genitality.

Next come patients with a greater capacity for romantic idealization
in the context of genital inhibition. Finally there are patients who have
the capacity to fall in love but cannot change a passionate involvement
into a stable yet passionate love relation.

Finally he suggests a modification of an earlier formulation of Balint's:
The incorporation of pregenital trends in the form of tenderness, a cru-

cial precondition for the capacity of mature falling in love, is a consequence of the integration of part object (absolutely good and absolutely
bad) into total object relations, an integration that implies at least partial resolution of pregenital conflicts over aggression and the reestablishment of the capacity for tolerating ambivalence to love objects.

In the paper on mature love (1974b), Kernberg emphasizes particularly oedipal conflicts as the overriding etiological factors. He agrees with
Lichtenstein (1970) that the concept of genital primacy in the classical
sense can no longer be maintained (p. 217). He agrees with Balint that
genital satisfaction, idealization, tenderness, and a special form of identification—genital identification—are the main components of a true love
relation. In addition he stresses the sense of transcendence that accom-
panies the experience of true love:

> Such an intense double identification during orgasm also represents a
> capacity for transcendence, for entering and becoming one with another
> person in a psychological as well as physical sense, and a reconfirmation
> of emotional closeness, linked to the activation of the ultimately bio-
> logical roots of human attachment. [1974b, p. 223]

Other points he makes are: The full development of oral and body
surface erotism and its integration is needed, together with the development of libidinally and aggressively determined part objects into total
object relations. Internalized object relations transform body surface
erotism into tenderness and need-gratifying relations into object con-
stancy. There must be a capacity to tolerate mourning: The mourning
processes involved in being in love are those of growing up, becoming
independent, and leaving behind the real objects of childhood at a time
when the most intimate and fulfilling kind of love relation with another
human being is established. In this process of separation from the real
objects of the past there is also a confirmation of the good relations with
internalized objects of the past. The final stage is the full integration of
genitality into the love relationship, achieved by resolving oedipal conflicts. All through life a history of having genuinely fallen in love and
remained in love is prognostically favorable.

Though couched in different language, Kernberg's theory does not
differ in its essentials from those propounded earlier, by Balint, for example. He sidesteps the social, cultural, ethical, and moral dilemmas
associated with love that had been such a cause of concern for previous
generations of analysts. In a later paper (Kernberg, 1980) he does pro-
pose the thesis that sexual love in an exclusive love relationship with a

person of the opposite sex that integrates tenderness and eroticism, human depth and common values, is always in open or secret opposition to the surrounding social group. The implications of this thesis for the structure of society are not however explored.

Finally, mention may be made of several interesting papers by Martin Bergmann (1980, 1982). His major concern has been with the intrapsychic characteristics of falling in love, especially in relation to the ego. He suggests that the ability to love one person rests on the capacity of the ego to integrate love impulses coming from many early objects. Children raised by many adults will find it particularly difficult to achieve such an integration. They will need more than one love object or love objects alternating in rapid succession.

To conclude on a lighter note: Levy in his book *Tahitians* (1973) reports that they had a word *here* which seemed to mean "love." When he asked one informant, Manu, to explain, he said: "Yes, if we didn't love each other, our life [together in the household] would not be going properly." Then he went on to say: "First I desire her, then I get used to her, then I begin to feel love for her, and finally when I'm not with her I feel compassion for her and miss her" (p. 317).

CONCLUSION

A review of the numerous views discussed in this chapter indicates that love may best be approached in terms of the analytic ideal. This is an extension of Freud's famous remark that the normal man is the one who can work and love. Enlarging upon this position, we can say that the human being reaches the greatest degree of happiness when he or she can love, enjoy sex, have pleasure, feel yet be guided by reason, be part of a family, have a role in a social order, communicate with his or her fellows, work, has a creative outlet and is free from psychiatric symptomatology. The effectiveness of love can be evaluated by the degree to which a person's life reaches this analytic ideal.

As will be seen, the analytic ideal is attainable, within the limits of their biological endowment, by animals. It is an attitude to life that must be inculcated from birth on. Cultures can be divided into love and hate cultures, as seen in whether the predominant emotions are love or hate. Looked at in this light, western civilization has been a hate culture from the time of the Greeks and still is a hate culture. The Christian emphasis on love has not been borne out in practice. Other religions preach order and serenity but have little to say about love. Clinical observations bear out the view that, whatever symptom the person comes to therapy with, there is always some disturbance in the love life. Character analysis, as contrasted with symptom analysis, attempts to correct this deficiency in the love life; symptom analysis limits itself to one symptom, which is often of minor importance in the framework of the total personality. The implications for therapy are that the person comes in with a neurotic image of love, which is then corrected by the therapeutic process, whereupon he or she can leave with a normal image of love. Such is the ideal; the practice often, as a result of the hate culture, ends in a compromise. Finally, the implications for social change are that we should direct our efforts quite consciously to improving social conditions in which love is possible, rather than to juggling isolated bits and pieces of the social structure. Change must come from the inside as well as from the outside; neither one alone will do.

10

Love and the Analytic Ideal

Since this chapter will present an integrative theory of love, we shall first review the previous material to see what conclusions can be drawn.

First of all a distinction was drawn between love cultures and hate cultures. It is true indeed that these are relative terms; no society has ever been found that has no hatred. Yet there are vast differences between cultures like the Mangaia, who live and love on an island called Peace, and those like the Jivaro, who are "born to die fighting." Within our society, a difference can also be drawn between families dominated by love and families dominated by hatred.

Next an attempt was made to show that western civilization has been a hate culture from the time of the Greeks; that is, the predominant form of relationship among people has always been primarily hatred. It is only the power of this hatred that can explain the course of western history. In general, traditional historians have overlooked this aspect, concentrating instead on the victories and material advancement created by our civilization. It is only recently that one historian after another has presented the data (which were always available) on the evils that have been with us from time immemorial. It was also seen that the numerous attempts to reform society either on a large scale or on a small scale have failed, because of hatred. Nevertheless, the battle must go on, especially now that the means to destroy the entire world have been developed.

Religious images of love were then reviewed. All religions have preached love in one form or another, but no religion has been notable for the practice of love. Rather, an examination of the lives of the founders showed that the identification with the founder is a more potent influence than the abstract ideas he or she presented.

The section on animals raised the question of whether animals can love. The answer was strongly in the affirmative. Darwin's principle of survival of the fittest has long been superseded by the genetics of adaptation. But adaptation also involves a moving toward their fellow creatures that should be called love. Harlow's classic demonstration (1974) that among rhesus monkeys the need for warm motherly love is stronger than the need for eating led him to formulate a cogent theory of the development of love in the monkey. He distinguished five different kinds of interactive, interpersonal love: (1) maternal love; (2) infant love (for the mother); (3) peer or age-mate love; (4) heterosexual love; and (5) paternal love. This may be taken as the biological basis for the development of love in the human.

Chapter 6 took up the question of how the child learns to love. The answer is simple and direct: by being loved. This need for love occurs at every stage in the growth process, and whenever it is interfered with, the capacity for love is adversely affected.

Clinical observations were then brought in to show that the vast mass of people in our society suffer from a variety of disturbances in their love lives. Because of the growing awareness of the lack of love, there is a large and increasing cross-section of the population that seeks out therapy for help with their problems, which confirms Freud's observation that he had all humanity as his patient.

That love, like other feelings, is under social control is the topic of Chapter 8. An examination of intentional love communities showed that the longing for love is universal and that people, if they cannot find it in the wider society, will often attempt to set up a society of their own where they can find it. However, the realities of the hate culture are too strong, causing various interferences with these isolated love cultures, all of which disappear or deteriorate sooner or later.

Theories of love are examined in Chapter 9. The preanalytic views betray a wide variety of opinions, none of which carry any great weight.

The first real philosopher of love was Freud, and his philosophy was based on a careful empirical study of thousands of people called patients. The body of work that he left us, though incomplete, is by far the most extensive and the most profound discussion of love to be found any-where. But he was never clear about the difference between normal and neurotic love, or the difference between normal and neurotic sexuality, or the relationship of love to the hate culture; many other points were omitted. Subsequent analytic authors have added relatively little to Freud's views. It is time for a critical reexamination and integration of the whole subject.

THE ANALYTIC IDEAL

Freud once said that the ability to produce and enjoy is the hallmark of the normal. Ordinarily, this is misquoted as "normality is the ability to work and to love," which nevertheless serves to convey the core of his thinking. I have elaborated this into the concept of the analytic ideal (Fine, 1981). This postulates that the human being achieves the greatest degree of happiness if he or she loves, enjoys sex, has feelings yet is regu-lated by reason, has pleasure, has a role in the social structure, is part of some kind of family, has a strong sense of identity, communicates with his fellow human beings, is creative, works, and is free from psychiatric symptomatology. The love life of the human being must be coordinated with all these other facets of the analytic ideal; it cannot be understood in isolation, as many (including Freud at times) have tried to do.

The kernel of love, which is a universal striving among the higher ani-mals as well as among all people, lies in the reaching out to another person for mutual gratification. It goes through a developmental line throughout life, like all other aspects of the personality, so that its mani-festations differ at different ages. But this reaching out for mutual gratifi-cation is everywhere the essence of it. Ideally, it can be successful. Then life can be a series of loving experiences with different people. As in the monkey, it moves from maternal love to infant love, to peer love, to heterosexual love, to parental love. Its elaboration beyond parenthood leads to a love culture, which is a further development beyond the monkey, who stops at the biological fact of parenthood and does not have the capacity to elaborate a larger culture.

Beyond these developmental factors there are other characteristics of true or ideal love. To begin with, it is a feeling that makes people happy. Poets of all ages and all times have never tired of singing the raptures of love; as Dryden put it: "When beauty fires the blood, how love exalts the mind" (*Cymon and Iphigenie*). Dryden's quote also brings out the physical aspects of love. In all varieties of love the desire for physical contact is present. (That this desire can sometimes not be gratified leads to some of the conflicts noted; this will be discussed later.) The mutuality of love involves a reciprocity in which each will pay attention to and try to satisfy the needs of the other, though in varying ways, depending on the circumstances. Love will color every aspect of the analytic ideal, including work and social cohesiveness. Finally, a group of loving families will band together to form a love culture.

This ideal has been reached only by a few rare individuals, if any. Yet ideals, even when they cannot be reached, serve a significant purpose in that they provide a direction in which people can move.

LOVE AND THE HATE CULTURE

Because of the hate culture, for most people the experiences of love are distorted all along the line. Even psychoanalysts are afraid to state flatly that the human being is a loving creature; among the theoreticians the anthropologist Ashley Montagu is the most prominent advocate of the position that love is deeply rooted biologically. He is right.

Current research (see Chapter 6) has shown that the infant is an active, striving, reaching being, not at all like the old image of the *tabula rasa* who depended entirely on input from the outside to grow (Lichtenberg, 1983). This striving and reaching of the infant should rightly be called love, just as in the animal. The fact that the infant cannot verbalize it or probably even conceptualize it is beside the point; love has to be depicted in different ways in accordance with the level of maturity of the person.

In psychoanalytic theory the dominant view is that the infant attaches himself or herself to mother; this has led to the position that attachment theory is basic (Bowlby, 1969). But *attachment* is a rather neutral term. The evolutionary precursor to the human infant is the monkey that clings to the mother's body for several months after birth. Such clinging is the monkey's form of love. Attachment is the human form. One has but to look at a happy, contented, well-fed infant eat, gurgle, coo, and react to the mother in so many varied ways to realize that instinctually the infant loves the mother. Love is an instinct in the ethological sense, based on a preformed neurological apparatus that responds to an external releaser in positive ways. It is also the *feeling* that the infant has for the mother in the healthy situation.

The human being is also preadapted to internalize the kind of care it gets from the surrounding environment; primarily this has been explored in terms of the mother–child relationship. Currently, these internalized structures are being referred to in terms of object relations theory, as though the idea were something new. The term is, but the idea is not. Psychoanalysis has always been an object relations theory; thus Freud defined the object as the *person* who gratifies the sexual aim (1953–74, vol. 7, pp. 135–136).

Into this early love matrix elements of the hate culture sooner or later intervene to prevent the infant from developing in a healthy manner. Several generations of analysts and analytic researchers have provided voluminous evidence for how much can go wrong in the mother–infant love relationship. Mothers have been categorized as rejecting, possessive, schizophrenogenic, phallic, abusive, and the like. While many in the women's liberation movement in particular have rejected these as "male epithets," unfortunately they conform to clinical reality and to direct observation. Even the classical theory that the girl resents the penis that she longed for but could never get often has much merit to it. The thesis is not that all women behave in this way, but that many do; how many is a matter for statistical research. But in the light of the widespread incidence of emotional disturbance it can realistically be assumed that a considerable percentage do.

For many, love, at every stage in the life span, becomes a refuge from the hatred felt in the outside world. Because it is a refuge it leads in the earliest love relationship, that between mother and child, to excessive possessiveness, jealousy, submissiveness, brutality, narcissistic grandiosity, and many other neurotic reactions.

Nor need this come as a surprise if one reflects on the upbringing of the girl in the traditional manner. She is not given much information about her body, as a result growing up to assume that there is something radically wrong with it. The cosmetics industry profits heavily from the women's derogation of her body, offering palliatives to remedy an internal feeling of insecurity. She is still depreciated and made to feel inferior to the boy. Nowadays many women try to combine a career and a marriage, but the difficulties in this combination are numerous.

It is curious that in these times, when there is so much discussion of sociobiology, the biological facts of motherhood should be so vigorously denied. Ann Dally (1983), a British psychiatrist, titles her book *Invent-*

ing Motherhood: The Consequences of an Ideal. She argues: "During the twentieth century, for the first time in history, the majority of women have had, increasingly, to bring up their children virtually alone" (p. 9). This is a serious distortion of history. If anything, as Shorter (1975), Stone (1979), and many others have shown, there has been a movement *toward* closer family formation in the past three centuries. In this movement, increasing efforts have been made to help the mother bring up her children wtih care, tenderness, and an improved knowledge of their needs; in a sense this is what the whole mental hygiene movement is about. Dally disparages the ideal of motherhood (although she seems to be the happy mother of six) without recognizing that it is the ideal of love applied to the mother–child relationship. What is needed is a reorientation of the family and of the conditions under which mothers bring up children, not a relinquishment of the ideal.

At the same time, in another recent book, Barbara Ehrenreich (1983) contends that it was not women who first rebelled against their sex roles, but men. The male flight from commitment, she argues, began a full 10 years before the feminist revival in the 1960s and has changed not only our social expectations of men, but also the economic prospects for women. In *The Hearts of Men*, she traces the male revolt against the "breadwinner ethic" from its origins in men's complaints about conformity in the 1950s to what has been called the "me" generation of the 1970s.

The attempt to create a loving family, which has been one of the ideals of western civilization since at least the French Revolution, thus encounters resistance from both men and women. For this major reason, we again have to examine the hate culture. In this culture people try to find love, partially succeeding and partially failing. Horney's point (see Chapter 9) that marriage, which is designed to resolve the oedipal conflict, must necessarily fail is correct in a hate culture, but not in a love culture. (It is paradoxical that Horney, who was so biologically oriented in Europe, made a complete about-face when she came to the United States.) Again, in the hate culture love turns into a refuge. In Shakespeare's Sonnet 29, he is despondent about life and his fortunes (quoted in Chapter 3) but then is transformed by love:

> When in disgrace with fortune and men's eyes . . .
> Haply I think on thee . . .
> For thy sweet love remembered such wealth brings
> That then I scorn to change my state with kings.

This expresses the refuge idea beautifully. Courtly love began literally as an escape from the horror and massacres of the everyday world of the eleventh century. Even Freud overlooked this point when he held that two people in love are altogether self-sufficient; people always need a surrounding culture with which to interact. The two people who need only one another are living out a refuge fantasy. Such a refuge fantasy sooner or later turns sour, which helps to explain why romantic love fails so often. Samuel Butler (1912) once said: "To live is like love, all reason is against it, and all healthy instinct for it." Reason turns against love in many people only after they have had one or more disappointments in love; in the hate culture these disappointments are inevitable, though the reactions vary. From the earliest days of analysis (cf. Breuer on Anna O.) it was noted that people who never loved had a poor prognosis in therapy. (Today this point is expressed by saying the patient is too narcissistic, as in Kernberg's and Kohut's formulations.) As Freud put it, people must love in order not to fall ill, but the usual form of love serves mainly the longing for a safe refuge. "A man's home is his castle." This is why Freud in his later years visualized a state of nirvana as the ultimate goal, instead of a state of happy love.

LOVE AND SEXUALITY

Freud had two major theses in his early work about love and sexuality. The two are intimately intertwined: You cannot speak of one without considering the other. Also the adult manifestations of both have a long history going back to earliest childhood; the peculiarities of the person's love life have to be traced back to childhood. Both of these theses have been amply confirmed by subsequent investigation.

On the other hand, neurotic love, whether romantic, parental, filial, religious, or any other kind, is again intertwined with neurotic sexuality. In the hate culture love generally becomes a refuge from the horrors of the outside world; hence most of the love that we see on the current scene is a refuge love. It is intense, passionate, idealizing, exciting, and possessive, more because of fear of losing the loved person than because of the extraordinary qualities that the loved one has.

Normal love, on the other hand, can still be correlated with genital primacy, at all levels. Although the modern tendency among psychoanalysts is to desexualize the theory, thereby creating endless confusion, the arguments that have been offered against Freud's notion of genital primacy do not hold up under closer scrutiny (Bachrach, 1983).

In a symposium on genital primacy held in 1968 it was generally agreed by the participants that the traditional notion of genital primacy, in which the orgastic experience becomes one of the main desiderata of mature living, was outmoded. The evidence given, as is usual in such discussions, was clinical, impressionistic, and questionable. Ross even stated:

> *Here I must introduce another variable—the sex life of the analyst himself, or herself. Analysts are by no means endowed with the capacities for mature behavior on the levels postulated by the theory of genital primacy. To what extent do the limitations of the analysts's own orgastic capacities influence the achievement of genital primacy in their patients?* [1969, p. 272]

The frank admission about his personal preferences casts a revealing light on the argument about genital primacy. Freud's theory was that love represents the union of tender and sexual feelings toward a person of the opposite sex, that this love matures at puberty with the sexual changes, and that love of this kind represents the greatest gratification a human being can experience. Although he vacillated quite a bit about it (as has been seen), there is really no reason to reject this image of genital primacy. It fits in with biology, history, anthropology, and the vast majority of clinical and experimental evidence.

Much has also been written about homosexual love, and the change in the nomenclature of the American Psychiatric Association which appeared in the latest edition of the DSM (*Diagnostic and Statistical Manual*). Gonsiorek echoes the common claim: "There can be no empirical justification for the viewpoint that homosexuality, in and of itself, is a psychiatric illness or related to poor psychological adjustment" (1982, p. 159).

This statement entirely misses the point. Tender feelings between persons of the same sex are perfectly natural. At issue are the compulsive limitation to persons of the same sex and the oftentimes peculiar sexual gyrations executed in homosexual encounters. The evidence is overwhelming that the exclusion of the opposite sex results from severe deprivation in childhood, and that homosexual love is another form of refuge love.

In the parent–child relationship sexuality and tenderness also have to be united. But here the incest taboo, universal and perhaps biologically determined, enters the picture. Sooner or later both parent and child run up against physical desires for the other that are incompatible with ordinary social living.

Looked at first from the point of view of the child, the Oedipus complex in the sense of a sexual desire for the parent of the opposite sex would appear to be universal (Roheim, 1950). It poses the first serious unresolvable dilemma that the child faces in growing up; as Sylvia Brody has shown (1978), even the intellectual achievements of the child are interfered with at this age.

However, the oedipal conflicts are not necessarily as sharp as once was thought. The child can accept his or her wishes, transfer them to another male or female, be allowed some physical contact with the parent, and live on with a minimum of conflict. The suggestion has been put forth earlier that the intensity of the oedipal conflict is more of a reflection of the intense hostility between mother and father than of the biological strength of the drive per se. Theoretically the child can internalize the wish, desexualize it somewhat, be allowed some physical gratification, and move on. On the other hand, if the oedipal conflict is too strong, the consequences for personality growth can be serious or even disastrous.

The physical desires of the parent for the child are likewise a source of conflict in the average family. Even in such a matter as toilet training, if the mother is squeamish or neurotic about her own toilet functions she will have a hard time training the child properly. Many other physical desires appear in the parents as the child is growing up. In the hate culture in which we live these wishes often create enormous conflicts, but these are by no means inevitable. The anthropological evidence, as well as the evidence from more liberated families in our own culture, is overwhelming that the parent can allow himself or herself all kinds of physical contacts with the child without creating any psychological damage.

This brings up a necessary distinction in the discussion of sexuality. It can be either loving or hostile, and the mere observation of sexual behavior, or the mere liberation from sexual taboos, cannot determine which is the case. In a hate culture sexuality is generally hostile. What is seen on the current scene, for example, is men who "make" women to prove their superiority, or women who tease men or seduce them in order to prove how feminine they are.

In the wake of Freud's early theories and the murderous carnage that decimated so much of the world in World War I and World War II, a sexual revolution has indeed occurred. But the value of this sexual revolution cannot be properly estimated until we find out whether the sexuality involved is loving or hostile.

After a brilliant beginning, Freud himself created an enormous amount of befuddlement by his constant changes of mind about the nature and desirability of sexuality. In the 1890s he still believed in the actual neurosis, according to which sexual frustration is transformed into anxiety by some unknown biochemical process. For such a problem the only solution is to have sex. Then came the psychosexual theory in the early 1900s; this made more sense, but the solution to the sexual problem was left open. For the most part analysts believed in a freer sexual life, but Freud, as we have seen, held back from promoting reform. Then he surprisingly came out with the idea that the analyst liberated sexuality only to have the patient renounce gratification of the instinct.

Surely he was not preaching celibacy. But what was he advocating? He never made it clear, so his followers interpreted his teachings in various ways. On paper his main recommendation seemed to be still the renunciation of instinct, but he never specified to what degree. Then came the theory of narcissism, which, as Jones observes (vol. 2, 1953–1957), bewildered everybody when it came out, for how could the ego have a libido if libido is sexual hunger? No sooner had this been digested than Freud proposed the death instinct in 1920, according to which the aim of life is death. Had this come from anybody else it would immediately have been discarded, but it could not be ignored if Freud said it. Eventually it was discarded by the vast majority of analysts. Sexuality was then replaced by the dual instinct theory, sexuality and aggression. Now (1930) he saw civilization threatened with disintegration by the release of aggression; 20 years earlier he had feared that the renunciation of sexuality might lead to the extermination of the human race.

In short, Freud after the early 1900s never could make up his mind what to do about sex. Perhaps it is not unfair to apply Ross's (1969) comments to him, that as he grew older sex became less important, and his views changed accordingly.

In spite of his waverings, analysts recognized that the theory needed amendment, not repudiation. The amendments suggested here are not original, but the course of analytic history has tended to obscure the fundamental significance of sexuality, with the remedies that are suitable to it.

We still need an academy of love, as Freud proposed in 1908. Love does make people happy, and an essential ingredient of love is sexuality. Exactly how much sexuality should be permitted and how much denied is a difficult question to answer; in the course of the century more and more has been permitted. The answer I have suggested lies in the pursuit of the analytic ideal; sex is an essential ingredient, but not the only one.

The matter could be phrased in this way: Sexuality without love is an enjoyable experience, and within certain reasonable limits (such as avoiding disease or not hurting the other person) its pursuits lead to a happier life. Actually this was Freud's position as late as 1915, when he wrote to Putnam: "Sexual morality as defined by society, in its most extreme form that of America, strikes me as very contemptible. I stand for an infinitely freer sexual life, although I myself have made very little use of such freedom. Only so far as I considered myself entitled to . . ." (Cited in Putnam, 1971, p. 73).

Many persons, taking the teachings of analysis seriously, have broadened their sex lives considerably. We have seen childhood sex play, permission to masturbate, innumerable tracts teaching people how to enjoy sex in marriage, extramarital sex, swinging, and many other changes. If done in a loving manner, all are conducive to a healthy, happy life. In 1898, after saying that we are all hypocrites in sexual matters, Freud wrote, "And so here, too, there is enough work left to do for the next hundred years—in which our civilization will have to learn to come to terms with the claims of our sexuality" (1953–1974, vol. 3, p. 278). His prediction may yet come true.

One of the most persistent problems that comes up in every love relationship is that of jealousy. The pathological aspects of jealousy are well known (paranoia, homosexuality, etc.), but the normal degree of possessiveness has yet to be determined. Anthropology teaches us that there are many cultures in which extramarital affairs are freely permitted without any apparent damage to the marriage or the relations between the partners. Biologically, the notion that there should be a lifelong attachment to one person, with never another considered, has no basis. It is true that there are many animal species in which there is lifelong pairing, but this is still more the exception than the rule.

In any case, whatever the situation with animals, in humans extramarital sex has been one of the sore points of our civilization. A woman confronted by an impotent or unexciting husband is still considered "bad" if she "plays around"; the man is still allowed a little more leeway in the popular mind. Legally, infidelity is a serious breach of the marital contract, while regressive sense-dulling fidelity, which is much worse psychologically, is ignored. It is only recently that the lack of sexual desire has been included as an identifiable symptom in the psychiatric diagnostic system.

While sex without love is possible, and often enjoyable, the opposite, love without sex, has created serious havoc. The notion of an all-loving God who rules the universe, which has dominated Christian thought, is a projection of the wish for maternal care of the infant. It is also a psychological impossibility. Because unconditional love without sexuality is such a psychological impossibility, it has led to rebellion and continual violation of its precepts. The Protestant reformers often saw this but then they in their turn instituted repressive sexual measures that were equally bad. As John Donne once put it beautifully: "Love's mysteries in souls do grow, But yet the body is his book" (1966, p. 93).

In the mother–child situation as well, love without physical contact becomes an empty shell. In the first few years, infants do not know that they are loved unless they are fed, bathed, played with, and so on. Later on there is always room for some physical contact, even if it has to lessen as time goes on. There are "kissing" families where everybody kisses everybody else when they see each other; there are distant families where nobody touches. The latter are infinitely worse off. As Ashley Montagu has put it, the human being (like all others) is a touching animal.

LOVE AND HATRED

In a hate culture such as ours, when love does occur it is often intermixed with hatred; the result is the almost universal ambivalence which is found between any two human beings.

The questions of whether and in what sense hostility should be regarded as an instinct have already been discussed before (cf. Chapter 5). What is relevant here is that just as there are love affairs, there are also *hate affairs*.

In the hate affair, two people are glued together, not infrequently for life, even though they hate one another and fight all the time. Often enough the fights are physical, and one party or the other may be injured, sometimes seriously. The question arises: What is the cement that keeps these two people stuck to one another?

Many times in a hate marriage the two parties swear that they love one another. This is of course a kind of refuge love, each side fearful that if he or she leaves, the hatreds on the outside will be much worse.

Hate marriages may very well go along with what I have called *regression in the service of the spouse*. These patterns can be traced back to the childhood conflict with the parents. In childhood regression there are two main variations: obedience and defiance. In obedience the child remains a baby in order to please the parent, who is afraid of letting him or her grow up. Very often the regression may be rationalized by the mother—the child is too delicate, the outside world is too dangerous, people are picking on the child, and so on. In the other variation, that of defiance, the child simply does the opposite of what the parents want—head banging, refusal to eat, loss of toilet training after the next child comes, later on refusal to do school work (or even refusal to go to school).

Marriage in the hate culture generally involves a neurotic compromise that has been called mutual parentification. Symbolically each partner becomes the other's parent. Hence again there is regression, with either obedience or defiance. Much of this is confused with love; thus particularly in the traditional family the wife is excessively obedient, drops all her interests, even friends, and lives for the sake of the husband. Ibsen was the first to caricature this kind of marriage in *The Doll's House*. In *The Iceman Cometh*, Eugene O'Neill describes such a marriage too, in the man he calls Hickey. His wife "loves" him so much that Hickey can do anything he wants—stay out late, run around with other women, and the like. Finally he can't stand it any longer and shoots her. Her murder reveals the true sadomasochistic nature of the marriage.

In this way love in marriage is really a reaction formation against hatred: Hickey hates his wife for being so submissive, she hates him for being so domineering. In a true love match there would be real autonomy, with each one respecting the personality and need of the other—mutual reciprocity.

LOVE, PLEASURE, AND REASON

Love, as everybody knows, is one of the greatest pleasures in life. Yet it still has to be guided by reason. A characteristic of love cultures is that love is a calmer, less tempestuous feeling. As Manu, the Tahitian informant, told the anthropologist (Levy, 1973), first you desire, then you get used to, then you love, and then you miss her when she's not there. It is a slowly growing feeling of attachment, devotion, and eventually love.

By contrast, in the hate culture, where love is a refuge from the world's hatred, the wild infatuation is common. People live with the idea that there is a "Mr. Right" or "Miss Right" and wait for that person to come along. "Some enchanted evening" they will find him or her. At times this one seems like the ideal, at others, another. Then the human being cannot live up to the ideal (for no human really can) and disillusionment takes over. The result is disappointment, depression, often withdrawal from any attempt at a further commitment.

In the mother–child relationship, John Bowlby had occasion during World War II to observe many children who lose their mothers. The sequence of feelings that he noted was protest—despair—detachment. At first the child protests, crying, demanding that mother come back. Then there is a growing sense of despair that she may not return; this may be accompanied by a series of promiscuous efforts to find a substitute. Finally there is a sense of detachment, a feeling that nothing can ever replace the lost object. These people function, but without real feeling about life; inwardly they have given up the fight.

These letdowns explain why romantic love is so often a cause of unhappiness after the first period of excitement. Such ups and downs are especially noticeable in adolescence where the boy or girl may fall in love one week and out the next. Underneath there is a powerful sense of despair, or even inward detachment, which can lead to drugs, promiscuity, suicide (the most common cause of death at certain ages), psychosis, and other serious emotional disturbances.

As will be elaborated more fully in the next chapter, psychotherapy ideally is a way of teaching people how to love. Freud took the development of psychotherapy through four stages: (1) making the unconscious conscious; (2) working through the transferences and resistances; (3) replacing the id by the ego ("where the id was the ego shall be"); and (4) setting up the most suitable conditions for the functioning of the ego. It is this final stage that we are talking about here. Love should be in the ego, in the sense that a rational control of the passions should prevail. In wild infatuations and unrestrained passions, the id is the ruler, with disastrous consequences.

LOVE AND THE FAMILY

So far as is known, all human societies have been based on the family, with the nuclear core father, mother, and child always the center, though it may be extended in various directions. For this structure, as we have seen, there are significant biological reasons. Only the human female does not have a brief rutting season that is the only time she is interested in sex. Only the human male is sufficiently intelligent to wish to maintain a stable, loving existence with a female. And only humans really maintain their relationships with their children once the children are fully grown. These statements are generally true, though many exceptions may be found among animals. It should also be noted that the old notions that human societies were originally promiscuous or completely dominated by the mother (Bachofen) have long since been exploded.

Marriage should be based on love, rather than arranged by the parents. Even though the love marriage is a recent innovation in human history, its significance goes beyond the immediate question of whether the child should choose or whether the parent should; it lies in the philosophy that the love relationship should always be paramount.

What we are sketching here is an ideal family in an ideal society. Naturally much interferes with normal family functioning, but these questions can be set aside for the moment in order to be clear about the ideal.

To have a marriage based on love, there has to be a healthy development toward genital primacy from earliest childhood. This means that both must have gone through the various stages of growth from a loving attachment to mother to father to the outside world. Probably essential is a free period of sexual experimentation in adolescence, since it is psychologically impossible to choose a life partner without some prior experience. This assumes that the dangers of pregnancy, venereal disease, and other illnesses have been overcome. (There are some who are claiming now that the free period of sexual experimentation should begin earlier, in the latency period, as Turnbull describes it among the Mbuti. Conceivably this could be so, but it is too early to be sure about it. Certainly one change that is required is that the harsh sexual frustration commonly practiced in the past must come to an end.)

A marriage for love is not an easy attainment. On the current scene, where so many women prefer to combine a career with marriage and children, many complications set in, but in reality the release of women from total dependency on the man can operate only for the good in the long run. A love match is one in which two autonomous human beings join forces in life, not one in which the major consideration is who will be the boss. This is really a new ideal toward which humankind is striving, yet it is an ideal that is attainable.

Children serve to bring the parents closer; they now have new love objects whom they can share with one another. Here the size of the family and the economic situation of the parents begin to play an important role. It is clear that excessive demands made on the family, whether economic or emotional, are the root cause of much marital disharmony.

It has long since been recognized that parenthood is another stage in development (Anthony & Benedek, 1970). The child becomes another love object who must be nurtured, understood, and loved for the rest of his or her life.

With the abundance of knowledge available in modern psychology, parenthood becomes a kind of education in its own right. Naturally, the child in many respects recapitulates the growth of the parents, as a result of which the parents understand themselves in a new way. Furthermore, the notion that children just somehow manage to grow up has to be abandoned, and with that the parallel notion that the parent just grew up. Often the grandparents are still alive, especially in the child's early years, so that the parents can directly relive their early years with a new understanding. As Benedek (Anthony & Benedek, 1970) points out, parenthood implies continuous adaptation to physiologic and psychological changes within the self in the parent, parallel to and in transaction with changes in the child and his or her expanding world. In a very real sense, then, parenthood becomes a kind of self-therapy going on throughout the life cycle (p. 185).

While children in a love culture bring the parents closer, in a hate culture they drive them apart. Who is the favorite? Who loves whom more? Almost as a rule the parents shift their frustrations to the child, either seeking a refuge love in them that they cannot find in their partner, or blaming them for all the friction that goes on. In a love culture, on the other hand, the child becomes a common bond, another source in which they can release their love feelings.

Many popular books on the market offer an excellent review of the life cycle, with the numerous conflicts that inevitably arise at each stage. Gail Sheehy's work *Passages* (1976) is one of the best, discussing adult crises in a manner superior to that of many technical books, which tend to lose themselves in jargon or arguments comprehensible only to the initiate. In this way a whole and wholly desirable process of parental education is in progress.

The love culture in the larger sense is an abstraction, never really found; an ideal. But within families in our own society it is feasible to point to loving and unloving families, and to characterize them with some precision. Beavers (1977), for example, is one of many who have investigated healthy families. Deploring the overemphasis on pathology, he writes: "We are not unlike energetic and enthusiastic missionaries who encourage others to be good Christians, but have knowledge only of sinners" (p. 123).

Healthy, loving families do not remain isolated; they seek out others with similar ideals and thus move toward a love culture. The problems of the group are then handled with a minimum of friction, although here outside crises, such as illness or economic dislocation, can create new and potentially or actually very serious problems. Nevertheless, here too the analytic ideal need not be considered a distant star.

Once the children grow up, they form new families of their own, and the cycle is repeated. The grandparental stage is a recapitulation of the parental, except that now the inevitable human tragedies of old age, sickness, and death have to be faced realistically.

LOVE AND SOCIETY

How are we to understand the larger society in which humankind lives? This is the problem of anthropology and of sociology that has been much debated but never adequately resolved.

In his standard work on the history of anthropology, Marvin Harris (1968) writes: "During the first half of the twentieth century, anthropology in the United States was characterized by a programmatic avoidance of theoretical syntheses" (p. 250).

Later various theoretical positions were brought to the fore. The major factor in anthropology until his death in 1941 was Franz Boas. Of him his former student Ruth Benedict wrote: "Boas found anthropology a collection of wild guesses and a happy hunting ground for the romantic lover of primitive things; he left it a discipline in which theories could be tested" (Cited in Harris, 1968, p. 253).

Innumerable theories about how to approach society have since been proposed: Among the better known are those relating to shame versus guilt cultures, culture and personality, symbolism, structuralism, cultural materialism, and most recently the etic–emic distinction (outside vs. inside forces). The evolutionary perspective that guided anthropology in the nineteenth century has been given up, with little if anything to take its place. What I am proposing here is that every culture should be examined in the light of the fundamental question of love versus hate, love cultures or hate cultures. To the ordinary common sense, the question of happiness is the major one in evaluating any society, yet anthropologists have sedulously avoided it; thus in the index to his book Harris does not list *love* or *hate* or even *sexuality*. As has been remarked about behavioristic psychology, it is a psychology without content. For instance, Harlow sarcastically observed in his book *Learning to Love* (1974) that the topic of love is virtually absent from *Psychological Ab-*

stracts. With such an attitude anthropology likewise becomes a subject without content. The cognitive factors are highly overstressed and the emotional reactions scarcely touched (cf. Jahoda, 1982).

Freud of course offered a comprehensive understanding of culture. But, as so often, he did not systematize it, he contradicted himself in various ways, and he left out a great deal. In *Totem and Taboo* (1913) he presented his first great synthesis of cultural anthropology as it was then understood, attempting to show, first, that there is a psychic unity of humanity, and, second, that it centers around the vicissitudes of the Oedipus complex, which is universal. His final theory on the primal horde, which took off from Darwin and added to it the actual murder of the father, has mistakenly been attacked as the core of the book, thus ignoring his really vital contributions. But then again in *Civilization and Its Discontents* (1930) he went off on an entirely different tack, this time stigmatizing hostility as the great enemy of civilization and virtually ignoring sexuality and love.

In the realm of cultural theory Freud's two greatest followers were Geza Roheim and Abram Kardiner. Roheim was more extreme, insisting that cultures can be analyzed in much the same way as individuals; he was also the first psychoanalyst to do anthropological fieldwork. He viewed the human being (Roheim, 1950) as a fetalized species, from which he drew six conclusions about human nature: (1) the antisex attitude of all human begins; (2) the search for new objects; (3) regression; (4) ambivalence; (5) the immortality of fathers (all cultures have gerontocracy, the cult of the ancestors and gods), and (6) conservatism (maintenance of the culture). He insisted on the psychic unity of humanity, and he felt that the interpretation of culture in its own terminology is at best a surface interpretation on a preconscious level.

Kardiner, on the other hand, was more interested in the variations among cultures. With his associates he formulated the concept of the basic personality structure of every culture. Although this concept has been attacked, it retains much of its force. To arrive at the definition of any culture, Kardiner (1939) listed a number of key integrational systems: (1) maternal care; (2) induction of affectivity; (3) early disciplines; (4) sexual disciplines; (5) institutionalized sibling attitudes; (6) induction into work; (7) puberty; (8) marriage; (9) character of participation in society; (10) factors that keep the society together; (11) projective systems (religion and folklore); (12) reality systems, derived from empirical or projective sources; (13) arts, crafts, and techniques; and (14) techniques of production. He was reluctant to characterize cultures in broad sweeps in the manner that Ruth Benedict had suggested in her famous book *Patterns of Culture* (1934) (Apollonian–Dionysian and the like).

While much has developed since these seminal writers, the question of how best to approach culture is still a puzzling phenomenon (Jahoda, 1982). In a very real sense the psychoanalyst has become the most profound anthropologist of our own culture, and the general description of the malaise that afflicts the modern human being, as offered by various psychoanalysts, has had profound repercussions.

In the individual analytic situation, the conflict that is most severe is that between love and hate. Those who reach a stage of love are happy; those who bog down in hatred are unhappy. It would even appear that excessive repressed hatred is at the root of all the psychosomatic disturbances, so that just as Freud discovered in the 1890s that excessive sexual repression leads to physical illness, other psychoanalysts since have concluded that excessive hatred leads to physical illness.

Hence the distinction between love and hate cultures, deriving from the observation of our patients, seems highly justified. Even though the facts are hard to come by, it sets up a direction in which the researcher can move. This direction also relates squarely to the key problem of human existence, that of happiness.

The social sciences offer a wealth of data from which to interpret the love and hate functions of any given culture. For our own society, the conclusion that it is a hate culture is indicated by very intensive and exhaustive studies, inspired at first by clinical observations, then extending to the entire society. The thesis that ours has been a hate culture for several thousands years is based on historical evidence. This thesis helps to explain historical events such as the Crusades, the Inquisition, numerous revolutions, and efforts at reform in a manner that is absent from other explanations; the only thing that conventional historians are agreed upon is that on the larger questions that history poses there is always controversy. One major reason for this incessant controversy, in history as well as in all the social sciences, as I have tried to show in *The Psychoanalytic Vision* (Fine, 1981), is that the social scientists have operated with the nineteenth-century image of the human being: that humans are rational, conscious, and subject to the control of powerful external forces. In conformity with this image, the task of the social sciences was viewed as discovering what these external forces are and learning how to manage them.

In sharp contrast to this nineteenth-century image is the discovery of psychoanalysis that in many cases humans are unconscious, irrational, and subject to internal forces over which they can gain control by the processes of education and psychotherapy. It is the clash of these two images that explains much of the intellectual history of the twentieth century.

Several examples may illustrate the problems involved. The book *Human Sexual Behavior* (1971), edited by Donald Marshall and Robert Suggs, presents a number of descriptions of sexual behavior in other cultures. The first is of an Irish folk community, which they call Inis Beag. They describe Inis Beag as one of the most sexually naive of the world's societies; even dancing is severely restricted.

The population of Inis Beag has dropped from a high of 532 persons in 1861 (up 76 from the prefamine census a decade earlier) to 497 in 1881, 483 in 1901, 409 in 1926, 376 in 1956, and 350 in 1958 (when the anthropologists were there), a drop of about 35% in 100 years (Marshall & Suggs, 1971, p. 34). Although there are many reasons for this drop, the primary one seems to be the severe restrictions placed on sexuality; it certainly qualifies as a hate culture. Blanshard states:

> *When all the reasons for flight from Ireland have been mentioned, there still remains a suspicion that Irish young people are leaving their nation largely because it is a poor place to be happy and free. Have the priests created a civilization in which the chief values of youth and love are subordinate to Catholic discipline?* [cited in Marshall & Suggs, 1971, p. 34]

An entirely different situation is described by Harold Schneider among the Turu. (Marshall & Suggs, 1971). The Turu (or Wanyaturu) are a Bantu-speaking people, numbering about 175,000 and inhabiting parts of Tanzania. Their culture centers very strongly around romantic love, though the term *mbuya* means both a romantic relationship between a male and female and a friendship.

Girls are clitoridectomized at 10 years of age and marry directly afterward. Men are circumcised at about the age of 15. (The consequences of these actions are not discussed by the author.)

Information on the *mbuya* relationship was gathered by asking people about their own sex lives and those of others in the village. Most individuals know what is going on between others in the community and are publicly advised on the existence of certain *mbuya* relationships. They show no hesitation in discussing *mbuya,* except that a cuckold is seldom informed of his wife's adventures. *Mbuya* is firmly a part of Turu society, and its effects radiate into many areas of behavior.

The quality of the *mbuya* relationship can best be explained by comparing it to romantic love as it is understood in the west, for partners tend to engage in the same mooning, jealous, and possessive behavior westerners associate with this term. Titillation derived from the furtiveness of the relationship is so great that an effort is made to retain it even after the affair is known to everyone and tacitly appoved by the woman's husband.

Turu men usually seek their mistresses from a limited group of women. By the rules of this covert game of romantic love, the husband cannot charge his wife's lover unless he actually catches him in the act of intercourse with his wife. When the husband succeeds in catching the couple, he is permitted to demand compensation in the amount of two heifers if the relationship is incestuous, six goats if it is not. If the discovered adultery is not incestuous, the cuckold must decide whether he will forbid it or ignore it. If he tries to forbid it, everything works against him, since there too all the world loves a lover.

Marriage tends to be strictly business; love is often outside. One norm prescribes that a woman is not supposed to visit her lover at his home. The whole system in theory demands compliance by a woman with her husband's commands in all areas, including her sexual life.

The anthropologist is not sure how this system of romantic love can be explained, nor even that a defensible explanation is possible. Lest it be thought that the solution is ideal, it should be noted that the Turu have one of the highest rates of assault and murder of any Tanzanian people, and the usual cases of assault are disputes over grazing land and women. Furthermore, the divorce rate is very high.

Whether the Turu are to be considered a love culture or a hate culture is unclear from the report. Only one thing is clear: The anthropologist focused on external behavior; for example, he plotted a clear diagram of all the extant *mbuya* relationships in a small village. But he failed to examine what these relationships meant to the people involved. Is the sexuality tender or hostile? Is the love relationship a refuge from external hostility, or a real feeling of tenderness, or both? These are the questions we try to answer in our own culture by in-depth analysis of the persons involved; without such an in-depth analysis the mystery remains.

It thus becomes plain that a different orientation would have led to greater understanding. Had he had in mind from the very beginning whether these were love or hate relationships, or to what degree the two emotions were intermingled, he need not have concluded that he could not really explain the customs. But he does what many psychologists and psychiatrists do in our own culture, and that is to focus on the relatively observable, even if irrelevant, aspects and leave out the more important questions because they are much harder to answer.

The meaning of love in human existence thus comes out in two different ways. First of all, as a way of life it makes people happy, while hatred on the contrary makes them unhappy. And second, the love–hate dichotomy is the core of all the social sciences. Whether in history, sociology, economics, political science, or even literary criticism, whether the external event makes the person happy or unhappy must always be considered, and this happiness or unhappiness depends very strongly on whether it leads to a happy love life or an unhappy hate life.

LOVE AND NARCISSISM

Love is love for another person, while narcissism is self-love. Obviously the two must be related, but the question is: how? Freud's early paper in 1914 on the topic of narcissism is largely dated; other positions today are equally controversial. There is a widespread belief that this is the "me" generation, a world of narcissists, whereas in the past everybody loved everybody else; this popularization is likewise without any foundation.

When Pulver (1970) came to summarize the disparate views in the field he began by saying: "In the voluminous literature on narcissism, there are probably only two facts on which everyone agrees: first, that the concept of narcissism is one of the most important contributions of psychoanalysis; second, that it is one of the most confusing" (p. 319).

Nor did the work of Kohut do much to eliminate the confusion. In 1978 Judith Teicholz wrote:

> *Freud's ideas on narcissism contained contradictions, inconsistencies and gaps which are still being struggled with in the current decade. . . . But his basic definition and formulations have been maintained by many followers with only minor changes, in spite of major theoretical advances in the rest of psychoanalytic theory. In spite of . . . theoretical complexity and sophistication . . . many leading psychoanalysts still hold to a definition of narcissism that departs very little from Freud's original formulations. [p. 833]*

Part of the difficulty inherent in the psychoanalytic discussions of narcissism is that they leave out of account the social factor, which is more important than anything else. Actually, the version of the Narcissus legend related by Ovid was the most popular story in European literature for several millennia. In Renaissance times it was especially favored.

Paul Zweig (1980) has contributed an excellent summary of the discussions of self-love in the literature from Roman days on. For narcissism is nothing more than self-love. The themes of the Narcissus myth were recounted over and over to warn people of the dangers of self-love. Narcissus was the representative of individualism, and all who cherished individualism or inward autonomy were drawn to his story. Zweig says:

> *Over and over again, he became the figure of a powerful longing for inward autonomy, a sort of spiritual Robinson Crusoe, as in the fantastic poems of the Gnostic sects which competed with early Christianity; or else, a grim figure of warning, a starved lover staring into cold water, a woman gazing into a mirror, representing the medieval sin of luxuria. In Milton's re-working of Genesis, Adam himself became a kind of Narcissus, doomed because he could not live without the "other self" God had made out of Adam's very flesh.* [1980, p. vi]

Zweig then traces the varieties of narcissism that have appeared in history, from the Gnostics to Baudelaire. The alienation of these groups from worldly experience, their antisocial doctrines, and their extreme self-reliance have always involved a conflict with established order. India fostered the doctrine of the inner life more than any other culture, culminating in Buddhism and the philosophy of yoga, while for modern times the Soviet Union (and later China) has been the embodiment of antinarcissism. Arthur Koestler, in his famous book *The Yogi vs. the Commissar* (1981), offers a brilliant description of the eternal problem, the ever-present duality of the individual versus the culture.

The proper approach lies through clarifying the distinction between healthy and unhealthy narcissism. Ideally, the development of love and narcissism can be traced as follows. The earliest relationship, of mother and child, embodies both love and healthy narcissism. Since they are joined by mutual reciprocity, the love relationship fosters the satisfaction of narcissism in both; the mother loves herself because she is gratifying the infant, the infant loves himself or herself because he or she is being gratified and gratifying mother.

Subsequently, love and narcissism can then go on *pari passu*. Healthy narcissism in the child derives from parental approval. When the child does something well (any aspect of the growth process) and mother (or father) offers approval, this reinforces the child's positive self-image, leading to further growth. At times the child may be out of line, or do something poorly; then a correction by the parents will be taken in the proper positive spirit and will not lead to the wild temper tantrums that characterize the dependently narcissistic child.

In all the major developmental lines, this reciprocal relationship between love and healthy narcissism can be traced. Thus in the toilet training period, if training is delayed until between the ages of 2 and 3, the child can be motivated to use the toilet like father and mother, that is, on the basis of a warm, positive identification rather than on the basis of a harsh threat (as in the traditional training system). The child then learns to take pride in his "duty" and in his capacity to "make duty"; very often children brought up with love will at this stage call their parents over to see how well they have done and receive recognition for their efforts.

The narcissism of the mother in turn is bolstered by the feeling that she is bringing up her child (who is after all experienced as part of her body that is now in the outside world) well. In an age when motherhood is under such strong attack, the real joys attached to motherhood (and fatherhood) tend to be forgotten.

In the case of the creative individual, who has long been seen as the epitome of narcissism, the development from the early love relationship with the mother can also be traced. All creative persons ever studied were noted for their achievements early in life. If the parents are positive, this early achievement leads to narcissistic gratification. This narcissistic gratification enables the individual to work at the field in which he or she has shown talent, which leads to further achievement. Again, the new achievement leads to more narcissistic gratification, of the healthy kind, and a creative cycle is set up: Achievement leads to narcissism of the healthy kind and narcissism leads to new achievement. In this process work plays an essential role because no achievement is ever attained without a considerable amount of work. But the feeling about work is positive rather than negative; it is viewed as a pleasure rather than a burden (Fine, 1980).

Again, while this development is an ideal process, it is an ideal that is reached in many areas with a certain amount of frequency. Of course, it is difficult. And if there is some break in the reciprocal cycle of love and narcissism, then the narcissism becomes defensive and pathological. But the literature tends to forget all too often that healthy narcissism does exist as well.

LOVE AND WORK

Again here we shall confine ourselves to depicting an ideal scheme for the development of work gratification, which arises out of the matrix of the early mother–child love relationship.

The early pre-oedipal experiences provide the schema from which later work patterns emerge. Play remains the dominant pre-oedipal experience because the child does not yet have the ego strength to deal with severe external demands. Such a capacity in general matures only at the time of the formation of the superego (school age) and carries with it not only the formation of a superego but also the crystallization of a prized self-image. From now on this superego and self-image take over the regulating functions that were previously handled by the parents. Internalization has gone a good way, though it will continue for a long time to come. Ideally this internalization, in terms of the mother, moves from doing something for love of the mother to loving the activity in which one is engaged. And it is germane to point out here that learning capacity is the best single indicator of ego strength, while vocabulary correlates highest with total intelligence (again viewing language ideally as satisfying communication with the mother).

If work is viewed as the reaction to external demands, in contradistinction to play, which is a reaction to internal wishes, then it can be said that in the pre-oedipal period the ego is limited to the immediate family because of its lack of maturity. It attains the capacity to handle demands of others only at school age, when superego and self-image also become more crystallized.

Ideally, the ability to work develops on the same basis as before, with the distinction that now there is an internal agency regulating reward and punishment as well as external agencies. Thus work is affected by healthy aggression, healthy narcissism, capacity for libidinal control, and approval by the internal regulating agencies (superego, self-image). It now becomes possible to speak of job satisfaction as a result that gratifies the prized self-image. Transferences from the original objects to school and other authorities also play a significant role. However, it is obvious that the child is still protected from the most severe external demands—making a living—and from adult sexual pressures. Nevertheless the basic principle holds: The child must attain a balance between ego and libido. Since no really major libidinal changes occur between the oedipal period and puberty, the latency period may be viewed as a time when ego and superego are consolidated, and a continually growing awareness of the self-image occurs.

Once puberty is reached, the situation changes again, but the components remain essentially the same. The task is to comply with external demands. Reality may decree that many of these demands are onerous and burdensome; the individual or his or her family may have no control or inadequate control over these demands. It is at this point that psychoanalytic theory must combine with sociological and economic realities; however, the psychodynamic factor must always be taken into consideration.

The search for an answer to the work problem has in general moved from emphasis on work to a wider emphasis on the quality of life. It is widely recognized that there is a pressing need to improve the entire quality of life of the worker, not merely his or her productivity or performance on the job.

In a sense, such an emphasis is also in conformance with the Protestant ethic, which dictated a whole way of life, not merely an attitude to work. The way of life that it dictated, however, is not acceptable to modern humanity. Here the analytic ideal moves in again, to replace the Protestant ethic in the search for a good life (Fine, 1984).

In this ideal scheme, work satisfaction derives originally from pleasing the mother. Later, as the ego grows, it becomes enlarged to having a satisfactory role in the family, so that phase-appropriate libidinal gratification, healthy aggression, healthy narcissism, and reinforcement of adequate self-esteem can occur within the framework of the separation–individuation process. At all levels, external demands are placed on the child, who will respond to these with pleasure if they are not beyond the ego's capacity.

As the child grows, and internalization increases, the self-image assumes growing importance. From then on, work satisfaction is found in performing activities that conform to the prized self-image.

Again here we go back to the love relationship with the mother. Satisfaction will occur if the work is an outgrowth of the interpersonal role and intrapsychic gratifications that the child experienced in the family. If there is a clash between the early family role and the later societal demands, then work dissatisfaction will occur.

To be part of the good life, work must also be coordinated with all the other aspects of the analytic ideal. It is no accident that all of these go together.

It will take a long time to reach the analytic ideal. Above all, it must be recognized that, like the Protestant ethic that they are replacing, psychoanalysis and the psychoanalytic ideal represent a program of social reform.

In the meantime there are of course work problems that cannot be wished away. Theoreticians have focused on the work environment and largely neglected internal factors. Work problems, as anyone can see, may also arise from inner conflicts. For such problems I have elsewhere suggested the term *psychoeconomic disorders*: disorders that manifest themselves in work disturbance but that are essentially emotional conflicts. Among the major psychoeconomic disorders may be mentioned: (1) total inability to work; (2) work incapacity; (3) work instability; (4) work dissatisfaction; (5) underachievement; and (6) paradoxical overachievement.

For work problems psychotherapy may be an extremely useful aid. Here another paradoxical conflict arises. In general, unions have been opposed to psychotherapy for workers' grievances, on the grounds that if a worker has troubles, they must be due to something in the work environment. By contrast, employers have taken favorably to the idea, reasoning that if the worker is more stabilized, his or her work performance will improve. By now most of the large corporations support insurance payment for psychotherapy, sometimes 80% or even 100% of the fees for many years. (It is also reported that a very large number of companies have instituted internal counseling for the innumerable cases of work dissatisfaction that are found on the job.)

LOVE AND COMMUNICATION

"If music be the food of love, play on." This well-known quote from Shakespeare's *Twelfth Night* highlights the connection of three basic aspects of communication: music, food, and love. Conversely, in *The Merchant of Venice* Shakespeare states: "The man that hath no music in himself . . . Is fit for treasons, stratagems and spoils . . . Let no such man be trusted." If people cannot communicate, they are full of hatred. The Swedes have an idiom *tiga ihjäl* ("to kill somebody with silence"). In English likewise we speak of giving someone the "silent treatment," which is always felt as a rejection.

That love and communication are closely allied in the adult hardly requires any proof. But that the mother's and child's love are communicated through the early development of speech before the child is in full command of words is also a conclusion that comes out of the recent infant research (see Chapter 6).

A study group at the Hampstead Clinic has delineated five stages in the acquisition of psychologically intentional communication (Edgcumbe, 1981). These are:

Stage 1. This starts at birth. The baby is born with a number of built-in ways of attracting mother's attention to his or her needs and interests, and the mother responds as if the child were doing it deliberately. Without this response from mother, the infant's noises and gestures do not develop into communicative vocalization and words.

Stage 2. There is differentiation in the baby's vocabulary of a range of sounds linked with increasingly specific experiences, and in the value of the mother's sounds in aiding the baby to tolerate delay and frustration: indications that the first steps are occurring in the remembering and ordering of experience. These steps will permit development of the capacity to anticipate, the creation of a primitive representational world, and beginnings of structural development.

Stage 3. The child becomes aware that vocalizing can have specific meanings and can be used to influence the behavior of others. The child now has a primitive image of "mother" whose attention it wants and enough language organization to select appropriate sounds to attract her.

Stage 4. Words are used to express wishes as well as to release impulses and affect; all this implies increasing linkages of words and inner experience, with words helping the process of differentiation among feelings and experiences as well as among objects.

Stage 5. The child's own vocabulary increases. The essential change in this stage is that the child becomes able to communicate to the object, verbally as well as gesturally, a wide range of experiences, questions, and ideas, beginning sometimes to use words as substitutes for action. Internalized concepts now help to sustain the relationship during separation, and words may help the child to recall the image of the absent object.

The shift from the anal–sadistic to the phallic–oedipal level may well be the point at which language normally becomes autonomous from the mother–child relationship.

All of these early stages are guided and moved by mutual feelings of love. In a sense all pathology involves communication disorders; thus Freud's deciphering of the communications of hysterical women showed the sexual origin of the symptoms, so that when these sexual wishes were brought to consciousness via verbalization, the patients improved. The same principle applies today in all psychotherapy. It could be said that neurosis is always, or always involves, a nonverbal communication. Likewise schizophrenia, traditionally described as a thought disorder, is more primarily a love–communication disorder.

The close connection between communication and love has permitted researchers and clinicians to explore more deeply the structure of many forms of psychopathology. In the fascinating book, *The Colors of Rage and Love*, the Norwegian psychiatrist Marie Navestad (1979) described the therapy of a young 23-year-old woman who was suffering from a postpartum depression that had blocked her use of language. Navestad instead treated her with the help of a series of drawings, in which the colors of rage and love were clearly displayed. The therapy was most successful. Others of course have also used nonverbal communication forms in therapy; in addition to drawings, puppets, play materials, even games like chess and checkers and cards have helped patients to bring out feelings that they could not express in words.

From a theoretical point of view the psychopathology inherent in many disorders has been linked with the patients' incapacity to communicate (Freedman & Grand, 1977). Lloyd Silverman has been experimenting for many years with the effect of simple phrases such as "Mommy and I are one" presented tachistoscopically, so that the stimulation is subliminal (Silverman, Lachmann, & Milich, 1982). Thus there is ample clinical and experimental evidence to indicate that adequate verbal communication is a sign of love, while the inability to communicate is the result of a neurotic or psychotic process.

LOVE AND CREATIVITY

The creative artist has always been regarded with awe and wonderment by the average person. Arieti (1976) calls it a "magic synthesis." Some have seen the creative person as a genius, others as insane. Only now is it possible to offer some reasonable psychological explanations of the creative process.

Again we have to begin with the mother–child relationship. If this is a reciprocal love experience, then the child will naturally grow in his or her creative endeavors. When the child experiments with everything around him or her in the second year of life, some have rightly called the child's behavior a "love affair with the world." Ideally such a love affair with the world can be continued all through life.

An essential distinction however must be drawn between inner and outer creativity. Inner creativity represents the inner growth of any individual, whether child or adult, in his or her own terms. The veriest tyro in painting can go through a creative growth process that is far more significant to him or her than the creation of a brilliant masterpiece would be to Picasso. Dewey took this point of view in his position that art should be a form of experience, thus open to everybody.

Ideally, the analytic process is one of inner creativity. The analysand learns new aspects of his or her personality all the time, moves on to all kinds of new experiences, and comes out feeling completely liberated (Fine, 1982). Neurosis has often been defined as a combination of repetition and stereotypy; once these are overcome the natural creative gifts of the patient come to the fore.

Inner creativity is within everybody's reach. Since it is not connected with external approval as such, it is growth related to the person's own potential. It is often more gratifying than outside achievement, which may be spoiled by a bitter element of competitiveness.

Another fact that tends to corroborate the thesis that creativity is inherent in the human being, and that it is intimately connected with his or her love life, is the growing appreciation of works of primitive art, including music, poetry, sculpture, and other forms. Long regarded with disdain by the civilized world, these works have gradually, since the end of the nineteenth century, acquired increasing importance. Many leading modern artists have been deeply inspired by them. To the untutored or less tutored eye they are frequently much more impressive than the rather odd innovations that have characterized so many forms of contemporary art (Biebuyk, 1973). Exhibitions of primitive folk and popular arts can now be found in almost all the museums of the countries of the world. A noteworthy feature of primitive and popular art is that the artist is almost always unknown, which means that it was done for the pleasure of creating, and not for the purpose of impressing an audience or profiting materially.

For creativity to flourish there has to be a creativogenic environment. There is every reason to believe that our culture as a whole, with its emphasis on hatred and destructiveness, often stifles genius and creative abilities (McCurdy, 1958). Ammons and Ammons (1962a) showed that conditions truly favorable to the development of genius arise very seldom. These authors (Ammons & Ammons, 1962b) also present evidence that among persons who are planning to devote their lives to the training or teaching of children there is precious little understanding of the conditions favorable to creativity or genius.

The development of the projective techniques has also shown how much talent goes unused in our society. Thus another effect of the hate culture is a loss of creativity.

Again it is observable here how all the components of the analytic ideal are interrelated. Creativity involves the capacity to work, while the loss of creativity betrays an underlying depression. And in all of them love is the motor that makes the wheels turn.

LOVE AND MENTAL ILLNESS

The basic psychoanalytic explanation of mental illness is as simple as ABC: Love makes for mental health, hatred makes for mental illness. This position is supported by a wide body of evidence, from epidemiology to genetics, from history to anthropology. Yet a widespread denial of the obvious is apparent at all levels of the mental health professions.

We will not reexamine all the arguments pro and con the organic factors in psychiatry (cf. Fine, 1981). Suffice it to say that there is every reason to believe that hate cultures produce mental disorders in large numbers, while love cultures do not.

That Anna O., the first psychoanalytic patient, had never been able to love, and did not develop the ability in the course of her treatment, was Breuer's first observation; it is still the most fundamental of all. The juggling of diagnostic categories is of no particular consequence. The same or similar symptoms have been described in all patients and given different names. There are only differences of degree, a continuum of mental health from the most disturbed to the least. The more serious disorders are generally grouped under schizophrenia, the less serious under neurosis. Schizophrenia has replaced the older terms, such as dementia praecox. Neurosis has been dubbed hysteria, obsessional neurosis, castration anxiety, simply neurosis, masochism, schizoid personality, narcissistic personality, borderline conditions, and many other designations. When the patients are examined more carefully it appears that they differ primarily in deficiencies in various aspects of the analytic ideal (Abend, Porder, & Willick, 1983).

For this reason, the analytic ideal can be taken as the guideline with which to evaluate the condition of any human being. Then mental or emotional disturbance is connected with the lack of love, the conflict about sex, the lack of pleasure, feelings badly managed, an absence or weakness of rational thinking, lack of a healthy family, lack of a role in the social order, lack of a sense of identity, inability to communicate, inability to be creative, and inability to work. Neurosis and psychosis can best be defined as the distance from the analytic ideal.

Critics of organic psychiatry are numerous on the contemporary scene; most of them come from within the profession—they are themselves psychiatrists or psychologists who deplore much that they see in the psychiatric world (Breggin, 1983). With regard to treatment, it is clear that the less severe disturbances are immensely helped by psychotherapy, while the psychoses, particularly schizophrenia, remain hard to approach. Rodgers (1982) states bluntly with regard to schizophrenia: "Our overall outcome in terms of getting patients functioning again hasn't really changed in 100 years" (p. 11).

Tissot, in one of the best reviews of the effects of drug treatment in schizophrenia, concludes: "The outlook remains gloomy" (cited in C. Chiland, 1977, p. 108). Bleuler, who conducted the best conceived and most carefully executed study of schizophrenia in the past generation (Bleuler, 1978), concludes, in radical opposition to what is customarily stated, that: (1) some two-thirds to three-fourths of schizophrenias are benign, and only about one-third or less are malignant; (2) about one-fourth to one-third of the "end states" are long-term recoveries, and about one-tenth to one-fifth are the severe chronic psychoses; and (3) easily half to three-quarters of all schizophrenics, about 10 years or more after onset, attain reasonably stable states that last for many years. Such states then undergo no more dramatic changes. At another point he states that "the overwhelming majority of schizophrenics are physically, and particularly endocrinologically, healthy" (Bellak, 1979, p. viii). Bellak (1979) states that what used to be considered pathognomonic schizophrenic regression is probably largely iatrogenic (p. 4).

With regard to neurosis, it is highly probable that the great majority get better with any kind of reasonable therapy, although the best results emerge with psychoanalytically oriented therapy.

It is becoming increasingly clear that the problem is just as much political as medical, although there are medical questions involved all along the line. But politics, as Aristotle said, remains the fundamental science. The issue is power, not science.

Robitscher (1980) stated: "We cannot expect the medically oriented psychiatrist to become interested in defining and limiting his authority. Until a new, less authoritarian breed of psychiatrists emerges, psychiatry will continue to exert too much power over too many people" (pp. 482–483).

Likewise Murphy (1982), in the most careful and detailed study of epidemiology extant, writes:

> *It continues to be difficult to persuade psychiatrists to examine the mental health of their own society as compared with that of others at the same developmental stage, although it is now much easier to interest them in examining the mental health of societies with which they are less personally identified.* [p. v]

Lest this be taken as concentrating too exclusively on psychiatrists, I hasten to add that these strictures apply to all the mental health professions. Psychiatry is singled out in so many ways only because it happens to be the most powerful; also because most people identify all the mental health professions with psychiatry.

There is no science in which the fundamental tenets can be demonstrated beyond the shadow of a doubt. Physicists are still delving into the atom, astronomers are still puzzled by the universe, biologists still cannot explain creation adequately, in spite of evolution (Mayr, 1982).

The main thesis of this book is that we are living and have been living in a hate culture for thousands of years, that this hatred has caused and is still causing untold havoc among millions of people, and that mental and physical catastrophe can be avoided by moving toward a love culture. It will readily be agreed that this thesis cannot be demonstrated beyond the shadow of a doubt. In spite of that, evidence in its favor, only a small portion of which could be presented in this book, is overwhelming. The pity is only that all the jargon poured out in all the social sciences often obscures the obvious illness and the obvious remedies.

11

*Implications
for Psychotherapy*

There is no doubt that we are the most therapized nation in history. Srole and Fischer (1978), the authors of *Mental Health in the Metropolis*, reported that in the years just before the so-called Midtown Study was launched in the 1950s, an estimated annual total of one million Americans had one or more contacts as a patient with a mental health professional in a hospital, clinic, or office. A decade later the number had doubled, by 1970 it had doubled again, and by 1975 it had probably reached a total of five million. This represents a jump in a quarter of a century from 0.7% to 2.4% of the national population (Srole & Fischer, 1978, p. 469).

The move to psychotherapy is also documented by Veroff, Douvan, and Kulka (1981) in their survey of help-seeking practices among Americans. They found that in gross rates, the use of mental health professionals had more than tripled in the 20 years from 1957 to 1976.

However, the situation is not as simple as it appears. Why people are going to therapists in increasing numbers, what a therapist is, and what therapy is are all complex questions.

In 1971 William Henry and his study group at the University of

Chicago published their survey of 4000 psychotherapists across the country. They included persons from the fields of psychiatry, psychoanalysis, social work, and psychology. Their two major findings were: (1) that the entrants into any of these four systems who finally do become psychotherapists are highly similar in social and cultural background; and (2) that members of each group triumph over the manifest goals of their particular training system and become with time increasingly like their colleague psychotherapists in other training systems. Hence, they all form a new profession, which he called the fifth profession.

In this process, the sharpest conflicts have centered on medical versus nonmedical orientations. In spit of the most intense opposition, two nonmedical professions, clinical psychology and psychiatric social work, have grown since World War II. Even in mental hospitals and community mental health centers, there has been a marked shift from medical to nonmedical administration (Feldman, 1981). In 1971, 55% of the administrators of community mental health centers were psychiatrists; in 1981 it was 19%. An unpublished NIMH study of 43 states in 1979 showed that only 17 required the state mental health commissioner to have a medical degree. Only 9 of 32 states responding to the survey required a medical degree of the state mental hospital director. Feldman also points out that the first administrator of a mental hospital in this country was a layman, James Gall, who opened his hospital in 1773. The American Psychiatric Association was formed in 1844, with the avowed purpose of replacing lay administrators in mental hospitals with physicians; the trend is obviously moving the other way now.

These facts and figures tend to show that the analytic ideal is assuming ever increasing importance in the minds of both professionals and the lay public as the guide to understanding of the mental and emotional disorders. Any number of studies show that socioeconomic status is the most important single component of psychiatric disturbance because of the havoc it plays with the person's emotional life, not because of any medical illness or organic impairment, though that may be present too.

This has been known for a long time; in a sense it has only recently been rediscovered. One is reminded of Freud's remark that if humanity had been able to learn from its observations, his book on sexuality would never have had to be written.

More than a century ago, the leading psychiatrist of that day, Edward Jarvis, was commissioned to do a study of lunacy in Massachusetts. One of his major findings was that there is a close connection between insanity and poverty, then still known as pauperism. He calculated that the pauper class furnished 64 times as many cases of insanity as the independent class. His theoretical summary was as follows:

> *Poverty is an inward principle, enrooted deeply within the man, and running through all his elements; it reaches his body, his health, his intellect, his moral powers, as well as his estate. . . . Hence, we find that, among those whom the world calls poor, there is less vital force, a lower tone of life, more ill health, more weakness, more early death, a diminished longevity. There is also less self-respect, more idiocy and insanity, and more crime, than among the independent.* [1855/1971, p. 52]

Both pauperism and insanity, he held, were traceable to the same source, "an imperfectly oragnized brain and a feeble mental constitution" (1855/1971, p. 56). Jarvis urged that new hospitals be built, to house at most 250 patients, and that those who were likely to get better (i.e., the middle class) be segregated from those who were not (i.e., the paupers). The paupers of that day were the immigrant Irish and the blacks.

Much ink has been spilled in the effort to establish the outcome effectiveness of psychotherapy by fairly simple quantitative studies (Bergin & Garfield, 1978; Lambert, Christensen, & DeJulío, 1983). Psychotherapy researchers have been driven into what Parloff calls an anaclitic depression because their results have generally been ignored by the practicing professional. But this is because psychotherapy is as much a philosophical as a medical process. As Strupp, one of the leading researchers, points out:

> *The issues to be resolved are research tasks only in part. They also involve to a significant degree issues of researchers' beliefs, societal standards, and public policy—which in turn call for a thorough analysis of social values and the manner in which they enter into judgments of "mental health" and therapy change.* [cited in Bergin & Garfield, 1978, p. 16]

Thus, in spite of the vast increase in numbers of patients, the horde of practitioners from various disciplines, and the voluminous literature, the field remains in a state of uncertainty and confusion. Freud (1928) once expressed the hope that a new profession would be established, "of lay curers of souls, who need not be doctors and should not be priests" (p. 126). This profession now exists; it is what Henry calls the fifth profession. But it is fragmented, argumentative, confused, and, let us say it squarely, sometimes simply dishonest. What is needed is not so much statistical refinement, though that can help, as conceptual clarification. It is to this conceptual clarification that the rest of the chapter will be devoted.

THE NATURE OF NEUROSIS AND THE NATURE OF THERAPY

The preceding chapters serve to highlight the fact that there is abundant evidence available for the major thesis of this book, that we live in a hate culture that has produced and produces innumerable mental and physical disorders that could be prevented if we move toward a love culture. Neurosis, in the broad sense of the term (i.e., including conventional normality that masks deep problems and psychosis as well), should be viewed as the distance from the analytic ideal. The whole potpourri of diagnoses, esoteric treatments, and speculative theorizing serves to confuse the issues rather than to clarify them.

In the light of the analytic ideal, with its emphasis on love, pleasure, sexuality, communication, and so on, we can distinguish two major kinds of disorders: the adjustment disorder and the maladjustment disorder. Psychiatry began with the maladjustment disorder (psychosis) but could not shed much light on it until Freud came along to show that most psychiatric disturbances represented failures in development resulting from childhood frustration. Through psychoanalysis, it gradually became apparent that there is also an adjustment disorder, in which the person adjusts himself or herself to the society but suffers from deep inner resentments and frustrations that can be seriously crippling or even fatal. This fact, put in various forms, has made a deep impression on modern people, to the extent that they accept its basic tenets and seek out help when they cannot reach the analytic ideal.

If neurosis is viewed as the distance from the analytic ideal, then its core is the inability to love. But this inability is a relative matter. Those who have never loved anybody in their lives after childhood feel in too much despair about themselves to benefit from anything but very long-term therapy; many times these people stay in therapy all their lives because they have nowhere else to turn. Those who have known some love in their lives can use this positive experience as a basis for further growth. Why one symptom, say, alcoholism, appears in one person, while another symptom, say, hysteria, appears in another is a question that is hard to answer at the present time (the problem of the choice of neurosis). Technically, instead of symptoms we have learned to look at the total character structure (ego strength), and in this character structure the capacity to love is the most important ingredient. Much of the world, however, including the professional world, focuses too exclusively on symptoms and ignores the larger picture, both the individual's character and the social milieu.

What then is a therapist? Here a new dilemma has arisen because of the kind of training system set up. Few people are aware of the fact that the only training system that has a long history, an adequate theoretical rationale, and a large body of practitioners is that of psychoanalysis. Few realize that even today most mental health practitioners merely stumble along in their work, without adequate training, without real supervision, and without any clear idea of what they are doing. On the other hand, the psychoanalytic system, in spite of its theoretical excellence, has also been torn apart by innumerable schisms, battles, feuds, and plain hatred. Psychoanalysts too have to be brought back to recognize the fundamental importance of love, both in their personal lives and in their therapeutic work.

Ideally, then, a therapist is a person who teaches others how to love. To do that, like the child who can learn to love only by being loved, he or she must go through a personal analysis or therapy in which his or her own problems are straightened out so that they do not interfere with his or her therapeutic work. The notion of a "perfectly cured" or "perfectly normal" person was abandoned more than 60 years ago, yet the hope still hangs on.

Most analytic institutes adopt the position exemplified in the *Bulletin* of the New York Psychoanalytic Institute. This states:

> *The preparatory analysis is a requirement for the training in psycho-analysis. Its therapeutic goals are not different from those of a therapeutic analysis. Its educational goal includes freedom from personality factors which would interfere with the ability to conduct psychoanalytic treatment independently. Therefore, no fast rule can be applied to the duration of this preparatory analysis which is determined by the analyzing instructor. It will be seen that any statement of a definite number of hours of analytic treatment is incompatible with this concept.* [1982–1983, p. 11]

The phrase *preparatory analysis* is the last sop that the institute allows itself. What it is really saying is that all candidates have problems in varying degrees, like all persons in our society, and that these problems can be overcome only by a long and difficult analysis. In Janet Malcolm's book *Psychoanalysis: The Impossible Profession* (1981), the protagonist, whom she calls Dr. Arnold Green, has been through 15 years of intensive analysis before being fully equipped, as a mature analyst. This is by no means as unusual as it sounds. It should be interpreted to mean that the analyst is willing to cast all pretensions aside and look at himself or herself with complete honesty, and it should *not* be interpreted to mean that the analyst is desperately sick (as most jokes try to show).

Although only a relatively small percentage of therapists today are fully trained analysts (perhaps 10% at most), psychoanalysis remains the guiding star for the bulk of the profession. In a recent survey of 410 psychologist–therapists, Prochaska and Norcross found the following (1983, p. 161):

1. Over 80% of therapists have had personal therapy and highly value these experiences as preparation for providing therapy.
2. Individual therapy is the most popular therapeutic modality, but over one-half of the sample engage in marital and family therapy.
3. While therapists spend a relatively small percentage of their time doing research, they do as a group publish and present papers.
4. Private practice is the modal affiliation of the sample and may be the most equitable employment setting.
5. Psychodynamic orientations have experienced renewed preference, with eclecticism declining.

In what follows then we shall try to draw all the implications of the major theses of this book for psychoanalytic therapy. For unfortunately, as has been seen, while the first half of Freud's career was devoted to elucidating the principles of his love philosophy, the second half became confused by his poorly developed theories of the death instinct and aggression. Subsequent writers have confused the situation further, so that, surprisingly, even psychoanalysts today have to have their attention called back to the fundamental importance of love.

TRANSFERENCE LOVE, REAL LOVE, AND RESISTANCE

The difference between transference love and real love, as Freud pointed out, is only one of degree. Yet there are obvious differences: The analyst, toward whom the transference love is directed, is consulted as a professional person, the patient has to pay a fee, the visits are regular but come at certain set times and so on. These factors are both gratfying and frustrating, gratifying because the patient has a safe place that he or she can go to for consolation and understanding, and frustrating because this safe haven is rather strictly regulated. Furthermore, even within this haven excessive intimacy is not permitted, as it is in real love.

On the other hand, real love in the outside world has its gratifications and frustrations as well. Since there is no time limit, it tends to foster a clinging, dependent kind of reaction, which is hard to handle; I have called this regression in the service of the spouse. Each partner demands the gratification of all the frustrated childhood demands, which as a rule leads to endless acrimony and bitterness. As we have seen, love in a hate culture is not easy to consummate.

Transference love highlights more than anything else the fact that love in our world is more often a refuge love than anything else. Even the analytic situation becomes a refuge for many people. This obvious fact has been criticized by many people who then call analysis a crutch. What they fail to note is that the refuge is created by the patient, not by the situation; if the analysis did not serve as a refuge, something else would. The difference is primarily that in the analysis the patient's need for a refuge is systematically analyzed, while in other life situations the need for a refuge is systematically exploited.

THE ANALYTIC TRIAD

Freud's discovery of the transference and its concomitant resistance represents a major turning point in the history of psychotherapy, in fact its real beginning as a scientific discipline. Yet it is incomplete in a theoretical sense because it leaves the rest of the world out of account.

In one of his early papers on technique, Freud wrote:

> *Let me express a hope that the increasing experience of psychoanalysis will soon lead to agreement on questions of technique and on the most effective method of treating neurotic patients. As regards the treatment of the "relatives" [the word* Angehoerigen *is put in quotation marks; it is not clear why] I must confess myself utterly at a loss, and I have in general little faith in any individual treatment of them.* [1953–1974, vol. 12, p. 120]

The subsequent course of analytic history has not yielded the agreement on questions of tecnique that Freud had hoped for. In his compilation of articles from the journals, Langs (1976) devotes more than 300 pages to the elucidation of the many different points of view on tranference that have since emerged. In his own summary, Langs writes: "Freud created an ingenious foundation for the study not only of the psycho-analytic but of all therapeutic relationships, and his writings on this subject have spawned a massive and convoluted literature, striking still for its many unresolved issues" (vol. 2, p. 19).

I believe that there are two main reasons for the persistence of the many unresolved issues: First, since Freud, we have learned to treat the relatives, to the extent that they are approachable; and second, analysts have emphasized aggression too much and drifted too far away from the central importance of love.

In the passage from Freud quoted above, Freud uses the word *Ange-hoerigen* instead of the more conventional *Verwandten*. Literally, *Ange-hoerigen* means both "dependents" and "relatives." At any rate, it carries as Freud writes it a wider connotation than "family"; it obviously refers to all those who are close to the patient.

Since, as Freud had already emphasized, transference is present in all human relationships, the transferences to these outside persons must be considered as well as the transference to the analyst. Usually there is a hierarchy of individuals, and one of these is the most important person in the patient's life, apart from the analyst. This creates what I have called the analytic triad (Fine, 1984). I believe that the difficulties and disagreements about the transference among analytic theoreticians to some extent stem from the failure to consider this triad.

In reality, every patient has two major transferences, one to the analyst, and one to an outside person. It is usually almost impossible for the unanalyzed individual to realize that his or her love for spouse or girlfriend or boyfriend is a transference as much as his or her love for the analyst; yet scientifically we know that that is the case. Usually, for technical reasons, the transference to the outside person is not analyzed early unless it seriously interferes with the course of therapy.

Nevertheless, for both theoretical and practical reasons, it is most fruitful to examine *both* transferences; that is, to bear in mind that we are always dealing with a triad, not a dyad. Recent research on child development tends to confirm this point of view (cf. Chapter 6), since it is known that the infant has differential reactions to mother and father as early as the first week of life (Lichtenberg, 1983).

In practice, also, if the other member of the triad is the love partner, which is so often the case, then the recommendation is made that he or she should enter analysis as well. It is safe to say that this recommendation is justified in all cases, even if it cannot always be carried out, because experience, such as the training analysis of the potential analyst, shows over and over again that few persons, if any, in our society have reached the analytic ideal.

Once the love partner enters analysis, special problems arise. With distressing frequency, when there are two analysts, one for each partner, as is usually the case, the battle between the partners spills over into a battle between the two analysts. At other times, the fact that the partner is in analysis leads to a certain amount of passivity on the part of the patient, who then leans back and waits for the partner to change. Other complications may arise. The main point made here is that if the transference problem is approached in terms of the triad, then greater clarity will result.

The other topic is of equal importance: to help the patient clarify his or her image of love. Transference love is a partial love, a compromise between the demands of the outside world and the yearning to return to childhood. Yet it is a real love, in spite of its deficiencies. All authors have agreed that when there is no positive transference, the analysis is virtually a hopeless battle. My own experience is that those patients who display an early positive transference do best in the long run, even though it may be anticipated that later on this will become negative as well; on the other hand, those who are negative from the very beginning are more apt to end abruptly, or to derive less benefit from the whole procedure.

Theoretically, "working through" the transferences and resistances has become (since 1914) the hallmark of a full analysis as contrasted with supportive therapy or analytic psychotherapy. Nevertheless, here too conflicting opinions are found. The recent books on Freud's famous patients, Sergei Pankejeff, who was called the *Wolf Man* (Obholzer, 1982), and the poetess Hilda Doolittle (Robinson, 1982), show that they remained in positive transference to Freud for the rest of their lives. One of the aspects of the battle between the culturalists and the Freudians in the 1950s was the claim of many culturalists (e.g., Alexander, 1961) that some patients developed a dependent transference that could never be broken, while the Freudians held that it was always advisable to analyze the dependent transference until it was satisfactorily resolved (Rangell, 1954).

The dispute ended with a split, which has continued ever since. In the light of the theory outlined in this book, the implications for therapy are that a more consistent discussion of the patient's feelings about love would help to resolve the transference in a more constructive direction.

If transference is a form of love, which it is, then it should be used as a springboard for achieving a more lasting love gratification with some person other than the analyst (the analytic triad). Then the question of whether the transference is ever fully resolved becomes a secondary one; the primary one is what kind of love life the patient achieves.

Resistance should be looked upon as a fight against transference involvement. Freud never wrote a full-length account of resistance, so here too opinions have varied all over the lot.

In terms of the analytic triad, resistance can be viewed as tipping the transference balance to the other person. Indeed, in many cases, in abrupt early termination (often late as well) what happens is that the patient gives way to a transference to the other person in the triad, even when such submission may in the long run be harmful.

Here too the focus should be on love. The patient comes to therapy with a long backlog of disappointments in love; naturally, he or she is afraid that the same disappointment will occur in the analytic situation.

> A woman called the clinic for an appointment. Shortly before the hour set she called again to cancel. When the intake worker inquired why she was canceling she replied that her situation was hopeless. Further inquiry revealed that in a fit of anger she had kicked her son (then about 20) out of the house; he had left. Now she wanted him back but felt that the case was hopeless. No amount of argument could persuade her to come in.

In this case, as in so many, the patient gives up before she has even started. As a matter of fact, there is an enormous amount of resistance to therapy, which is evidenced by the fact that many people never even try to find professional help. It is a well-known truism that the more disturbed the individual, the more resistant he or she is to therapy. Very often, the profession plays into this resistance by declaring these difficult patients inaccessible to therapy. Other forces within the culture feed into the resistance in many different ways. Actually, the same forces that try to maintain the hate culture also fight against therapy, or try to reduce therapy to a symptomatic effort (Fine, 1983). They ignore the larger cultural role of psychiatry and psychology.

Resistance within the culture is approached via general education measures. It has taken a long time, for example, to convince the courts that a person in psychotherapy is not insane and should not be stigmatized. Children's comic books now talk about "shrinks." Perhaps in another generation psychotherapists will be fully acceptable.

LOVE AND TRANSFERENCE

The centrality of the transference shows once more that analysis deals mainly with the peculiarities of the love life. People who have reached a mature stage of love do not seek out a therapist, but, as has been emphasized, in our hate culture few people ever reach such a stage. What happens rather is that some compromise is reached, thereby setting up a neurotic kind of love. In analysis this neurotic love is first destroyed, and then a new and more mature love takes its place.

The learning process involves seeing first of all that previous loves were neurotic in character, and second that a healthier kind of love is possible. This involves as well a consistent search for the factors in the patient that interfere with establishing a gratifying love life.

At all these levels enormous difficulties arise, so that intensive psychotherapy that aims at character change rather than superficial symptom removal is always a long and complex process. It is folly to believe that neurotic problems will disappear by some slick formula (as in EST) or by joining a new or special family (the cult solution—see Chapter 8). There is good reason why the heart of any psychotherapy is referred to as the working-through process.

At bottom, the workings of internal change, which Freud first discovered, are largely a mystery to anyone brought up in our society, with its extreme emphasis on externals, outside forces, denial of internal reality, and the like. Hence, part of the learning process in psychotherapy is to discover that internal change is possible. In a positive transference, quite often after a few months, the patient comes in and says, "I don't know what you've done, but somehow I feel much better than when I started." When that happens, the patient's capacity for exploring internal reality is expanded, and the outlook for a favorable resolution is good.

Much of the time, however, there are three main blocks to learning about oneself: (1) the patient tends to blame the other person; (2) underneath, he or she feels unloved and is terrified to face that feeling; and (3) as a result the patient clings to past love or illusions, hoping against hope that some magical figure will come along and save him or her. A good deal of analysis centers around the elucidation of these three resistances. In all cases, wherever possible, the discussion should be brought to bear on how the individual is handling or has handled his or her love life. Love not only becomes the final goal of the analytic therapy but also should be the central topic of discussion all the way through.

To clarify how these conceptualizations guide the whole therapeutic process, I shall give some actual case material in extenso.

Sally had been married for some 5 years. Her early life was extremely traumatic. Mother died when she was 5; father did not remarry until she was 16. In this interim period he brought her up with a mixture of brutality and seductiveness. For example, when she was a little girl he would punish her by having her undress, beating her with a belt, then embracing her, crying: "My darling child, how could I do such a thing?" Father had also tried to prevent her from going out with boys when she reached adolescence, saying that she should study hard and become a lawyer (his profession).

Shortly before leaving for college, Sally fell in love with one of her classmates. As might have been anticipated, when her father found out about it, he put a stop to the relationship, telling her that all the fellow wanted to do was to use her sexually. (This was father's pattern with women.) The relationship (she had never had sex with the boy friend) ended, and she went off to college.

However, college was too much for her. A breakdown forced her to return home. She was sent to a psychiatrist who evidently had little hope of helping her, since almost nothing was said in the 5 months that she saw him. At home during this period Sally would eat and watch TV, with feelings of hopelessness about her life.

After some 6 months the depression lifted sufficiently to allow her to get a job, though she was not well enough to return to college; it took many years for her to get back to school.

It was in this situation that she met her first husband. He was an agreeable, personable man who did not threaten her and was not aggressive sexually. Sally enjoyed the relationship and agreed to marry him, again against her father's wishes; he wanted her to go back to her studies.

Her husband turned out to be an extremely distant kind of person, who shunned any emotional intimacy. He was most interested in the furniture in the house and would spend much of his time decorating and redecorating. She participated without much enthusiasm.

Sally shared her unhappiness in marriage with a girlfriend, who urged her to get some psychotherapeutic help. Perhaps because of the poor experience with the first psychiatrist, perhaps because of a fear of revealing too much about her father, she put off any visit to a new therapist. It was only after some years that she went to visit one, and then only to see whether her husband could be induced to change. The therapist was willing to see the husband, but he refused any help, saying only that Sally was "oversexed" (the couple at that time was having sex about once every 3 or 4 months).

When the therapist suggested that she could use help, at first she balked, saying that she would think about it. A month later she returned, having decided to start therapy. Once she started, her husband took all the money out of a joint savings account the couple had; there was no apparent reason for this move. Nor did he offer any explanation. This was the final step which led her to separate.

Once she was separated she began an affair with a fellow worker who had been pursuing her for some time. As long as she was married she had not wanted to go out with him. Now she did, and she found that the sexual experience was like nothing she had ever had before. In the therapy she was in positive transference, and life seemed to have taken on a new meaning for her.

However, the new boyfriend did not want to marry her. Instead, another man appeared on the horizon, an engineer. In many ways he was like the first husband: emotionally distant, cool, efficient, well controlled. He proposed to her and she accepted. By this time she was most eager to have sex with him, but he had strong religious scruples about premarital sex (as she later discovered, he was a virgin when they married) and preferred to wait until the wedding night, in the traditional manner. Since he wanted to marry her she put up with the frustration.

In the new marriage Sally quickly had two children. Her feelings for the children, especially the older one, were not particularly friendly; it was understandable that since she had been brought up without a mother, her maternal feelings were not too strong. In fact, she resented the mother role intensely. But since her husband was quite supportive of her, after a while she went back to college and began to become more active in the outside world in amateur theatricals.

During all this time Sally remained in therapy because of her overpowering anxieties. She was always terrified that something awful would happen, that nothing would ever work out, that people would look down on her, and the like.

In spite of her attachment to the therapist, her overt feelings were very negative. She could not really see the point to all this talk, it was such a bother to come in two or three times a week, it cost so much money, and so on. Analytically, the fear of the father was so great that it took her a long time to trust another man unless, like her husband, he offered immediate real-life gratification.

Gradually the sex problem with the second husband began to take on the same proportions as that with her first one. He would ignore her for long periods of time, especially when the children were small. When they did have sex, he ejaculated almost as soon as he entered her, making it difficult or impossible for her to derive much enjoyment from the act.

In this dilemma she began to seek out other men, especially those she had met in school or in her theatricals. A number of affairs followed. With one man, she fell in love, but it was more of a matter of clinging to one another than anything else. He was an unemployed actor, with plenty of time on his hands. The two would get together, drink a lot, and have sex.

To overcome the sex problem, her husband entered therapy. But the net outcome was unexpected: He began an affair with another woman, still ignoring his wife. Shortly thereafter he stopped his therapy.

Gradually, the husband became suspicious of what Sally was doing. He followed her and one day walked in on her when she was in bed with her lover. That put an end to the marriage. The lover also evaporated when he was confronted with the need to make a choice about being serious with Sally. Her husband, who was comfortably fixed, provided her with adequate support.

Sally's love was of the clinging, anxious type, idealizing the strong, powerful man and depreciating herself. It was quite obviously the love of a little girl for a powerful father, which she had lived out all through her childhood. However, it took a long time for her to see this.

In the therapy, the long period of negative transference was coming to an end. She began to appreciate the devotion and understanding of her therapist, and she became known as the analyst of her hometown. Because of her poor experience with the first psychiatrist, she could value the analytic approach of the second one so much more.

Sally was a woman who related to men. So it was not surprising that she soon found a man who was to be her third husband. This time he was active, sexual, and very gratified with her. He too had had a bad time in marriage and had a long and unsatisfactory sex history (he too was a virgin at marriage). But the two managed to achieve a closeness that was better than anything either of them had ever known before. He also accepted the idea of therapy and benefited from it considerably.

When therapy was finished, Sally's love life was in the best shape it had ever been in. While there were still many problems to be ironed out, she could look back on the long years of therapy and be proud of the many ways in which she had changed.

This lengthy history is cited to highlight the way in which the analytic ideal can guide the therapeutic process. The focus is on the love experience, and the patient is brought back to that over and over again. At first she had a deep disappointment in her high school sweetheart. Then with her first husband there was little love feeling, merely a desire to escape from father. But love without sexuality, which was what she was going through, proved to be an impossible solution. She rebelled against it, as so many women are doing today.

The lovers that came in after the first marriage broke up provided libidinal gratification. But they did not relieve her of the ever-present anxiety that had been there from her earliest years. And conflicts arose with each one. For example, one who was rich and handsome had a need to seduce every woman in the office; she was one of the many he had "made." In spite of his reputation, she was eager to go out with him, but he began to do something peculiar. Instead of making dates with her, he would have long telephone conversations with her in which he would tell her of his sexual prowess, of how many women he had conquered, of how beautiful she was, yet he would rarely ask her out. After a while, she began to realize that he was teasing her in order to hurt her: He would excite her and then let her down. The lover who came on after the second marriage (the one with whom she was discovered in bed) was pure sexuality; with him she could let go completely, drink, and have sex. This was like sex without love. Sooner or later this proved to be a disappointment.

In the meantime, the anger and resentment toward the therapist gradually diminished. In the various analytic triads that were formed throughout the therapy, she began to become more aware of the true nature of her transference feelings. This awareness helped her to grow emotionally.

The consistent analysis of the love relationships eventually led to a more wholesome kind of life, in which she felt considerable closeness to her husband, much more affection for her children, and a greatly heightened sense of self-love. For self-love, as has been emphasized, is also an essential part of the love life. Although the result was not ideal, on the whole the analysis, which lasted many years, was a successful one.

In this case, the analysis lends itself to a direct comparison with conventional psychiatric therapy, which she had received from the first psychiatrist. He had evidently "diagnosed" her as a schizophrenic, or psychotic depressive, would not talk to her, used drugs, and provided some slight relief. No insight came, and no real change occurred. The contrast with the second therapy is striking.

The second case to be cited at length is that of a man, a love addict. Here the growth of his love life through analysis will also be traced.

John was the only son of a woman whose husband had left her shortly after the boy was born. She was understandably bitter, but she reacted, to the boy's detriment, by giving up on men altogether and devoting herself to her son. This is the kind of situation that produces men whose lives center around rescue fantasies of the kind that Freud so eloquently described.

As a child John idealized his mother, who brought him up with the conscious idea that as soon as he was old enough he would take care of her. Since he was quite successful in his chosen career of science, he did support her till she died. Underneath, this support engendered a great deal of resentment in him.

Love had been on John's mind as far back as he could remember. When he was 6 years old he fell madly in love with a girl in the neighborhood, and he cried when she took sick. He worshiped his first-grade teacher, acutely aware of her full breasts.

When he reached puberty he felt too shy to go with girls. Of course, his mother's "smotherlove" had a great deal to do with that. On the one hand, he felt that no girl could be as good as mother (a notion she had consciously inculcated); on the other hand, living alone with mother, the incestuous fantasies were so powerful that he felt guilty about wanting any other woman sexually.

His solution, in adolescence, was to split the woman image: There was one girl he worshiped at a distance but could never get himself to speak to; then there were the prostitutes who were readily available in his home town. It was the classic split between the good woman and the bad woman; it took him a long time to realize that "good" women, unlike his mother, could also enjoy sex and love.

In his early twenties he fell in love with one of his classmates and married her very quickly, though neither was really ready, either financially or emotionally. When war service intervened, and he was called up to Vietnam, he spent his free time there with prostitutes, like many of the servicemen, meanwhile daydreaming of his sweetheart back home.

When he got home, he discovered that his wife had been experimenting with a number of drugs and had become seriously depressed; in fact, she had even made a suicide attempt. On top of that, she had acquired a whole host of physical illnesses that interfered with their sex life and made her almost a chronic invalid. The marriage soon ended in divorce.

At this point, John entered therapy. The analyst was a warm, open, kind man for whom he formed an immediate positive transference. The therapy proceeded splendidly. After several years it was terminated, both satisfied with the result.

As might have been anticipated, John then fell in love again, married, and had several children. No sooner had the children come than John fell out of love. His wife no longer had any time for him, the children came first, she had no interest in sex, participated in it mechanically, she let herself go, paying little attention to her appearance, she no longer seemed the joyous, happy-go-lucky creature whom he had married.

Unwilling to break up the marriage, he started an extramarital affair. Again he fell in love with a vivacious young woman who promised him diversion, understanding, and relief from the terrible pressures of marriage. Forewarned by his previous experiences, he decided to resume therapy rather than ask for a divorce.

In therapy he came to realize for the first time that he was repeating in many ways what his father had done: After marriage, leave wife and children for a new love. His second wife was a rather homely woman with few talents; he realized that this was also a rescue fantasy, which could be traced back to the tremendous hold his mother had on him.

The second therapist was also quite different from the first: aloof (his ancestry went back to the Mayflower), correct, punctilious, and lacking the enthusiasm that was so characteristic of his first therapist. This time the transference, though positive, was mixed up with many negative features. His anger at the father who had deserted him was coming out.

In spite of his insights, the pressure to leave the second marriage and marry the new woman friend was enormous. Eventually he did. Then, to his surprise and horror, his wife hired an unscrupulous matrimonial lawyer and instituted a long, drawn-out lawsuit that undermined his financial position seriously. At the end, he found himself with an enormous amount of alimony and child support to pay, coming close to half his salary because the children were so young.

With these handicaps he entered on his third marriage, again confident that love would resolve everything. For a while things went well; then the conflicts with the children began to bother him, especially since his exwife, as so often happens was making it difficult or impossible for him to see the children.

Therapy helped him get over the worst of the conflicts. But the love for the third wife also diminished in time. Eventually he came out more satisfied than he had ever been, but with many unresolved conflicts.

In this case the man's search for mother is quite obvious; his love was for her, and he sought one reincarnation after another of the mother he had idealized so much in childhood. It was only after he had managed to diminish the desire for mother considerably that he was able to settle down in a more comfortable relationship with a woman.

The third case, that of a mother who was too devoted to her son, can be described more briefly.

> Susan was the second of three children of a small rural family. In her conventional childhood, after some early sex play with one of her brothers (he played with her clitoris), she became a tomboy. When she reached adolescence she had a long-standing romance with a fellow student, who dropped her when she refused to have sex with him.
>
> Then one of her brothers was drafted and killed in combat. This drove her mother into a psychotic state in which she spent most of her time trying to commune with the dead. The father became a complete alcoholic.
>
> To escape the home environment, Susan went to New York. There she had her first sexual experience, with a Yugoslav musician whom she did not love. The sex was not gratifying. She had no real success in New York.
>
> Coming home, she found herself courted by two men, one whom she loved, the other whom she did not. When the man she loved changed his mind, she married the other and had a child. There was never any real gratification from her husband, but he was comforting and protective.
>
> When her first child came, a boy, Susan really found the love of her life. She devoted herself slavishly to his life and welfare. In spite of several anxiety episodes and separations, she made a life for herself on the basis of her romance with her son. She never had any real therapy, but the family situation sufficed to carry her through. Eventually, when the boy grew up, Susan resolved her problems by taking her pleasure where she could. The boy grew up satisfactorily, though he was unconsciously held back somewhat by the excessive love of his mother.

These three cases, presented all too briefly [for more extensive case histories illustrating the role of love in psychotherapy, see my books *The Intimate Hour* (1979) and *The Psychoanalytic Vision* (1981)], highlight some of the kinds of neurotic love that have been discussed. In the first, Sally, a young woman with a brutal, domineering, yet protective father and without a mother, submitted to one man after another in adult life in the hope of getting away from father and finding some security in life. Underneath, she remained frightfully anxious as a result of her childhood, and through long-term, intensive psychotherapy she was able to effect major changes in her love life.

The second, a man who was excessively dominated by mother, exemplifies the "falling in love" that is so beloved of the songwriters and balladeers. As far back as he could go, he fell in love with one woman after another, only to be disappointed and hurt by the outcome. Again it took many years of therapy for him to see how his numerous loves were new editions of his desire for his mother, and again eventually he reached a stage of more mature love where his life flowed along more smoothly.

The third is that of a woman whose major love affair in adult life was with her son. After a traumatic childhood in which a beloved brother was killed in an accident, she experienced several severe disappointments with men whom she loved. Her earliest sex experiences were with a man she simply picked for the purpose of losing her virginity. Married to a man she did not love, like Emma Bovary, she fantasized great romances but focused her life on her son. Therapy was superficial and did not get at the real roots of her problems. She resolved her problems with what could be called the Chinese philosophy of *wu wei*—let things come as they do, take life without any real planning.

PERIPHERAL VERSUS CENTRAL THERAPY

Another way of drawing out the implications of the philosophy of love for psychotherapy is to divide the field into peripheral and central therapies. The peripheral are those that deal with an isolated symptom or manifestation; the central therapies are the analytic, which try to restructure the individual's life toward the analytic ideal. The more usual way in which this dichotomy has been expressed is in symptom versus character structure.

Prior to Freud, everything was looked upon as a symptom neurosis, since the idea of a character structure that manifests itself in a variety of symptoms comes from him. The theoretical problem was viewed as one of tracing the symptom to its origin, or using some manipulative device (e.g., hypnosis, or suggestion) to help the patient get better. This was still Freud's approach in the 1890s; it changed only with his development of psychoanalytic theory from the 1900s on.

Today the battle still goes on, with the analytic therapists solidly arrayed against the nonanalytic. For every aspect of the analytic ideal there are available numerous symptomatic therapies that seek to manipulate the patient in much the same way that Freud was doing it when he began in the 1890s; other at that time were working in a similar manner.

Analysts have argued that if one symptom is removed, another will take its place. This will usually happen, though sometimes not. However, a more important point is involved. The symptom therapies are essentially based on a lack of awareness of the whole personality. Every patient, and every person, should be evaluated in accordance with the analytic ideal; neurosis, as will be recalled, can best be defined as the distance from the analytic ideal. When that is done, it immediately becomes obvious that the person is distant in a number of respects; for example, he or she may be unable to communicate properly, or have a disturbed sex life, or a negative self-image. Symptom therapies will not affect these underlying difficulties, in spite of the claims of their proponents.

Deep philosophical–psychological questions come to the fore here. The analytic position, since Freud, has been that the average person is a normal–neurotic (Freud himself once put it as a normal–psychotic). I have tried to rephrase this in terms of the hate culture. Bleuler's (1978) work on schizophrenics suggests that the average person throughout history has been what we would call today a borderline psychotic, with the usual life-style that of a phasic-benign psychotic, that is, a person with episodes of psychotic behavior and episodes of lucid behavior. Certainly, the hate culture throughout the ages has spawned such monstrosities (such as those described in chapters 2 and 3) that any other explanation of history seems highly improbable. As indicated earlier, conventional historians are only now beginning to see how so many historical events have been set in motion as a result of neurotic or psychotic processes.

In the hate culture, love of course always has a hard time. But the need for psychotherapy is strongly felt. Hence, symptom therapy arises, in one form or another. Every culture ever studied has developed some form of therapy; how effective these are no one knows, but they are practiced. Typically in more primitive societies, no distinction is drawn between the somatic and the psychic; and it is worth noting that in our own culture and dominance of medicine in the mental health field has led to the same kind of confusion of the two realms. This is one reason why psychoanalysis has been so bitterly fought by the medical establishment.

In general, the innumerable symptomatic peripheral therapies on the current scene are highly superficial and achieve superficial results, if they achieve results at all. But people still use them and swear by them. Consequently, what we see, outside the analytic sphere, is symptomatic relief, not a radical restructuring of the personality. Since the sights of many professionals have not been raised to a level where they can grasp the significance of a change in character, they are satisfied with the small changes that they can effect. This is one of the factors that produces so much confusion in the current therapeutic environment.

Some examples may make the issues clearer and also show how profound the implications of the love philosophy are for therapy.

In the area of sexual disorders, much attention has been directed to the work of William Masters and Virginia Johnson (1966), the techniques that they evolved, and the clinics that have been set up to follow their lead. The claim is generally made that they succeed in curing a large number of patients of their sexual symptoms in short order.

Yet psychoanalysis after all began with the treatment of sexual disorders. It will be recalled that in the 1890s Freud attributed all neurotic disturbances to sexual conflicts, using sexuality in the genital sense at that time. It was also widely believed in that period that masturbation was the cause of numerous neurotic disturbances, even of insanity in many cases. Later, in the 1900s, Freud attributed the conflicts to the problems connected with infantile sexuality, rather than adult, which led him to try to retrace the patient's entire life history.

In general, Freud achieved a fair amount of success with these techniques and this theory. Here is a typical instance from current practice of how analysis can resolve a sexual problem, in this case impotence.

Myron came to therapy because he had been impotent with a woman whom he loved. She was the one who suggested treatment.

Myron was the only son of refugees from Europe. His father was a college professor, lost in his specialty, but still with warm feelings about Myron. Mother, however, was a seriously depressed woman who had been going from one depression to another all her life. She had had many courses of electroshock treatment, each time with a little relief, then another relapse. She herself blamed her depressions on the birth of her son, which, she said, "tore me apart." Mother had made a number of suicide attempts and eventually killed herself, after Myron had completed his therapy.

With such a background Myron had drifted through life rather aimlessly. He was bright but could not concentrate on his studies. In high school he was sent to a boys' school, where the boys were rigidly observed and controlled. Any sexual material of course was completely forbidden. He kept himself aloof from any kind of social life.

After graduating from college, he tried graduate school for a while, without any clear-cut goal. Soon he dropped out to lead an aimless kind of life, drinking, gambling, and playing chess and cards.

There were few relationships with women. Before his involvement with the woman who sent him to therapy, Myron had had only a few casual dates and sex a few times with prostitutes.

Myron's response to therapy was immediate and dramatic. He formed a strong positive transference that allowed him to make sense of his life and grasp the analytic formulations. In about 2 months his potency returned and he was able to meet various women. The relationship that brought him to therapy broke up because the woman did not want him any more.

After experimenting with a number of women, Myron fell in love with one with whom he was very congenial and married her. The two were very happy together until she unfortunately developed an inoperable cancer and died in short order at a very early age.

In spite of this blow, Myron was able to go on to other women. Not long after his wife's death, he met another woman whom he found very gratifying, and he began to talk love and marriage very quickly. However, the guilt about the speed with which this happened was great, and it made itself felt in the sexual sphere; again he found himself impotent. This time, however, it was only occasional.

Myron then returned to therapy. The guilt about another love was analyzed, and in very short order this bout of impotence also cleared up. He married the second woman and entered another very happy period in his life.

A peripheral therapist (á la Masters and Johnson) might conceivably have cleared up the impotence, but he would never have been able to provide insight into his life history, the dynamics of the depressed—suicidal mother who had made him feel so guilty about sexuality, and the aimless drifting that had been his life-style for 10 years.

Whitman (1980) describes using sex therapy techniques combined with dream analysis to shed light on the underlying conflicts. When he suggested to Masters and Johnson that they should use dreams as well, they refused to consider it. To them it was just a matter of education and manipulation.

Thus, sex therapy becomes another technique of loveless sex, of which there are so many on the market. Actually, the techniques that Masters devised are not radically new; as pointed out earlier, his entire schema is a repetition of what Wilhelm Reich had described 40 years earlier.

What Masters and Johnson added was some anatomical detail, but there was no really substantial change in the whole process.

In the case of Sally, a promiscuous woman (cf. Chapter 1 in Fine, *The Intimate Hour*, 1979b), she had engaged in loveless sex for some 10 years before coming to analysis. She was so skillful at it that Masters and Johnson would have had nothing to teach her. But then she came to grief because she fell in love. Promiscuous sex suddenly became psychologically impossible.

In analysis, a review of her life history revealed what the motivation was for the promiscuous sex. Father and mother had broken up when she was a little girl; after that, father once came along and kidnapped her brother, but ignored her. Then mother remarried twice, each time telling her that men were there to be exploited.

Sally was married, and her husband also had innumerable sexual adventures; that was why the two let each other go their own separate ways. But there was one child, a little boy. In the afternoons, Sally would lie down to take a nap, then wake up screaming that her boy was being murdered; obviously, this was part of her ambivalence about her child.

There were two recurrent dreams. In one, she was on an elevator that went up and down without stopping. In the other, she was trying to get to a party and could not manage to get there. These two dreams were an excellent symbolic description of her plight: The elevator dream showed how she was compulsively rushing around, unable to stop, the party dream that she could not get what she really wanted out of life.

Eventually, the analysis led to a happy resolution: She gave up her lover, who was totally unsuitable, settled down to a more quiet home life with her husband, and had another child.

There are many women who go through promiscuous periods and give them up. But when they change without insight, other problems come to the fore. In the case of Sally, the promiscuity was a defense against her strong feelings of abandonment and worthlessness. It was only when these were worked out that she was able to change in a sensible way.

Many artists come to treatment because of a creative block. A number of such cases are reported in the research study edited by Edrita Fried, entitled *Artistic Productivity and Mental Health* (1964). Here is one case, adapted from her book, which is an excellent example of movement toward the analytic ideal.

Jonathan Norton, a painter, sought treatment because of the multiple work blocks from which he suffered that had virtually choked off all ability to start and complete paintings. In his other areas of activity, teaching and administering the daily life of his family and himself, he seemingly functioned well, even when he entered treatment. However, a peek behind the facade of "normality" revealed that he had daily quarrels with his wife and had woven his intensely competitive and hostile feelings into a somewhat paranoid system that he projected upon colleagues to the point where they cut him off.

In appearance, manner, social relations, and self-image he regarded himself as the "father type" to whom people bring their problems. He had been an excellent art teacher for years. His classes were well attended; it was his major source of income. He would qualify as a good example of an adjustment neurosis.

Several factors in the life history were quite significant. At the time he started treatment he was in his early forties. He had been introduced to painting by his cousin, 12 years older, who had then been living in the parental home. This cousin had then given up painting to become a successful advertising man.

At 14, Jonathan had stolen his cousin's painting and, presenting it as his own, had won a citywide contest. He remembered with embarrassment and humiliation the ridicule of his cousin and others when he said he would be a famous artist some day. In spite of his later successes, he held on to the notion that his cousin, not he, should have been the artist. He lived in vague dread that his cousin would return to painting and outdistance him. This fear was constantly reenacted with fellow artists, with guilt projected as betrayal and injustice.

His father, who died when Jonathan was 22, had been a shadowy figure dominated and humiliated by his wife, and living for the most part in the quiet circle of his music, unrelated to the family. In the last few days of his life he had encouraged his son to become an artist. His mother reprimanded him for not being at his father's bedside when he died, and the "injustice" of her remark contrasted with his father's encouragement.

Jonathan felt that he, like his father, was just a shadow in the house. His cousin was openly preferred and favored. His mother told him that she had tried to abort him. She had felt no need for a child to interfere with her active community life. He recounted this in his usual self-pitying way. Despite this constant detailing of injustices, he was aware of no hostility in himself but saw himself as patriarchal, humorous, and philosophical. Injustice was his fate in life. There was nothing he could do about it. These feelings were cover-all descriptions of his childhood, and he could report few actual memories. He did recall, however, that his cousin said of him that he walked around as though the world were an onion, always crying. Jonathan could not remember this about himself, but he did think he had been lonely, and he poignantly recalled that at art school, where he became aware that he had talent, he felt that he was like a boat entering a harbor of refuge. Art was his refuge.

Upon graduation he looked forward to a year abroad, to be financed by his cousin. When the cousin refused, he had a somatic breakdown, where previously he had always been in excellent health. He had an emergency appendectomy, a hernia operation, a minor complication of the testicles, and following this his first hay fever attack. Later he developed asthma and diabetes, both of which cleared up in the course of psychotherapy.

One of the first concrete activities in treatment was completion of a successful business venture, purchase of a multiple dwelling in a small town near the city, to be used for living quarters, with a studio nearby, and as a source of income from rentals. He discovered that he could handle business matters with skill and ability. At the same time he felt, masochistically, that his fellow artists now regarded him as a businessman rather than a painter.

Dreams were analyzed throughout treatment. At first Jonathan confirmed, in dreams, his feelings of injustice and betrayal. Gradually he saw how he used this defense, as well as others, to guard against real feelings of fear, hostility, and envy. He then began to use dreams in two ways: to clarify his conflicts, and to withdraw from them by denying and detaching himself from his own dreams. He recognized that this detachment occurred whenever new awareness became threatening. Periods of nondreaming were usually periods of even greater resistance, during which the therapist became a new transference figure preliminary to working through the next stage of conflict.

There were many dreams of inadequacy about his body and his genitals. In one, his penis was awkward and he splattered the wall with urine. In another dream, a friend criticized the small size of his penis, as he in reality did with Jonathan's paintings.

In the course of working through his inner conflicts, Jonathan gradually regained his health. Asthma waned. His sugar level, for the first time in years, was normal. He went off insulin, went on a strict diet, and lost 30 pounds.

He now felt equal to his cousin, who began to relate to him as a peer. He said he felt as if at last he had attained his mainhood.

The hostile, oral dependency on the devouring mother had increased, and, freed of much need for and guilt about her, Jonathan formed a strong attachment to a young woman. He related his sexual affair in a detached way—the more involving fantasy lay within his deep longing for this youthful counterpart of his newly found youthful self. He acted out being adolescent, made close friends in a group of adolescents, had parties for them. He lived out in his relationship with his young girl-friend his daughter's first sexual affair. He preferred to be among the young.

Creatively, he was able to make new beginnings, with new forms, new styles. Emphasis had shifted from the compulsion always to begin again, with no feeling of continuity, to the joy and hope of new beginnings and their continuity.

In his second year of treatment he looked forward to an exhibition of his work because he was convinced that the flow of energy would last. When periodically his productivity would lessen, the old tendency to do all kinds of other things was less in evidence. Rather, he studied his finished works and those of other painters, his mind preoccupied with painting and not taking flight into other areas.

At first totally unaware of his intense hostilities, the patient had no idea of the causes behind his compulsion to paint over finished canvases, even those he liked. In the second year of treatment he had a fierce quarrel with his wife. He went to the studio and took out two canvases. One represented two men, one locked in a cave, the other embracing a basket of fruit. The second painting showed a woman bathing. The patient recognized that the two men were himself, and that the woman represented his wife. He then painted over both canvases although they were paintings he admired. Eventually, he was able to see that it was rage that made him paint over finished works many times, thus depriving himself of results. With therapy, the habit totally disappeared.

The most striking changes in his professional work emerged from treatment. When he started he had sold very few paintings. He was ashamed to sell them, on a social basis, and the galleries were less and less eager to represent him because his work had shown no development. In addition, his suspicious manner alienated many gallery owners. He said that he sold himself whenever he sold a painting, and he did nothing worth selling.

Subsequently, he held two one-man shows, and though he told everyone he was doing badly, the facts indicated quite the opposite. At the end of treatment he was looking forward to his third one-man show, predicting that it would be a great success, which it was.

While the main focus in this case history was on the change in his work patterns, there was also a great change in his love life. Relieved of inner conflict, Jonathan began to feel healthy and energetic. Fatigue and all other somatic complaints were infrequent. He found new strength in the reality of gratifying, positive situations that now seemed to be everywhere. There was peace at home with his wife, and excellent relations with daughter, mother, and cousin.

It is not easy to compress the course of analysis lasting many years into a few short pages. Necessarily, much is omitted. Necessarily, certain idiosyncratic features have to be emphasized because they are important to the individual even though they do not occur in others. For instance, in Jonathan's case, there was an unusual occurrence: the theft of the cousin's painting, with which he scored his first success. The theft continued to haunt him all his life until it was finally resolved in treatment.

Another case, this time of a child, may be cited to highlight the nature of communication disorders. (The material is taken from Case 6 of Fine, *The Intimate Hour*, 1979b.)

Sheldon, a 7½-year-old boy, was referred for therapy because he had many fears and an especially acute phobic reaction to movies showing accidents. One time he vomited, and another time he ran out of the room shouting, "No, no!"

In addition, Sheldon had a severe speech problem; he was virtually unintelligible. For this he had been referred to a speech center, which diagnosed him as having "oral inaccuracies" and treated him with speech therapy over a period of several years, with little change. It never seemed to occur to anyone that this speech problem was part of his general personality conflict.

He was the older of two siblings, the younger being a girl 2 years his junior, Heidi. The parents had been married for 7 years before Sheldon was born. In addition, they had had a long courtship at a distance; evidently both had been reluctant to take the plunge into marriage.

The father had no special interests or hobbies; the family did not even have much of a social life. Both parents devoted themselves to their children. The father was impatient with Sheldon and frequently angry at him, but he never hurt him physically.

Shortly after the parents married, the mother became ill. While she was pregnant with Sheldon, it was discovered that she had a uterine tumor. Surgery was postponed until he was about 6 months old, but because of the illness she went back to live with her parents shortly after

he was born. The removal of the tumor was followed by the discovery
of a thyroid disturbance, which also called for surgery. While Sheldon
was still an infant, she had a thyroidectomy, which kept her in the hospital for 2 weeks. Then because of the tumor she was advised to have
another baby as soon as possible. The new baby was colicky and ill and
required a lot of attention. In the meantime, Sheldon was taken care of
by his maternal grandmother. His father was still working in New York
and had little time for his son, even under the best of circumstances.
Not until Sheldon was almost 3 was the family reunited in New York
and the mother able to give her son more attention. Under these circumstances it was not surprising that he could not speak properly; he
literally had no one to talk to. As compensation for his speech problem
he developed an extraordinary capacity to read; at the age of 7 he had a
reading comprehension of 14.

When he was 3, his mother thought he had an orderliness that was
unusual for a child of his age. The unexpected seemed to upset him. If
he played with a toy, he would check it to see if all the pieces were there
when he finished.

When Sheldon was a little under 3, his mother had a second thyroidectomy; this meant another long stay with her parents in Boston. He
sucked his thumb at night until then but abruptly discontinued it while
his mother was in the hospital. On her return he clung to her excessively, asking 20 to 25 times a day, "Are my hands clean?" She assured
him in her usual "reasonable way" that he could be dirty if he wished,
but he continued to cling. Obviously, there was very little mutual reciprocity between mother and child; it is not surprising that he turned in
upon himself, as a defense against the loneliness experienced with her.

When the mother was asked about his sexual interests, she denied
seeing any. Then she said that he did like to watch his sister in her bath.
And lately he had been taking more of an interest in his mother's body,
leaning up against her breasts and playing with her hair. When he did
that, she liked it, but it was not really sex, nor was it when he came into
her bed in the morning to "roughhouse."

In such an environment, it is understandable that he did not develop
the ability to communicate. In the course of the long therapy (5 years)
the unfolding of his capacity to communicate could be observed. It is
on this that the summary of his therapy will focus.

In the first period he hardly talked at all to the therapist. Instead, he
released various grandiose fantasies, such as a story of how an 8-year-old
boy, with scientific and mechanical genius, managed to save the world.

With children, the main technique used is play therapy. The child
is free to use the play materials provided in any way that he or she

wishes, or to talk to the therapist. Sheldon doggedly stuck to the play materials, hardly even noticing the therapist for the first 8 months of treatment, and of course saying almost nothing to him.

Then after 8 months came a dramatic shift. When he came in, he said, "I want to talk to you; I can't sleep lately." He related a number of things about school and his family, but mostly he was concerned with his "bad dreams." From then on the sleep disturbance and the bad dreams came up in almost every session. Intermingled with these were old themes of war, ruling, and rebellion, as well as new themes: He would hint at what was happening in his life or occasionally offer some bit of information about the way his life was going. Then he had good dreams and was concerned with whether the dreams would be good or bad. Each night he would ask his mother to promise him that he would not have any bad dreams, but she, as usual oblivious to his feelings, would ask how she could promise any such thing; after all, she had no control over his dreams.

In his play, war ruled the roost. "If I don't have war I don't get ideas," he explained. He built himself a barricade; inside he was safe, outside he was not.

The next stage was followed by a sudden switch to the normal competitive games that were all over the playroom and that he had hitherto ignored. In these his grandiosity came out in his fanatical desire to win and the variety of tricks that he resorted to if he was in any danger of losing.

But the games that involved the therapist signaled another move away from his narcissism and inability to communicate. He was for the first time relating, even though in an uneven way, to the therapist.

Then came a period when he backed away from the games, falling back on his aggressive fantasies again. This time he used the toy soldiers. For quite a while he exhibited a repetitive pattern of behavior whereby he looked for a traitor, who would be tortured and then put to death, sometimes by being blown up alive.

After this retreat came another switch, a search for physical contact with the therapist. The most common form was to read a comic book while leaning up against the therapist. He persisted in this pattern for almost a year.

Then came another change: He incorporated the analyst into his fantasy world. He had long had a distant country which he ruled, calling it Smithland. Here he appointed courts, ministers, judges, and juries; he called people to account; in short, he was the undisputed master. Now he began to appoint the therapist to various posts in his kingdom.

After this came the building up of lines of communication between him and the therapist. For example, he would build a bridge with pillows to the therapist's chair and then appoint him to high office. The social progress also made him more aware of his speech problems because he was afraid that his fast speech would make the other boys walk away from him. By now his speech was quite intelligible. Once he had verbalized the problem, he was able to bring it under control fairly quickly.

After about 5 years of analysis, when he was almost 13, his fantasy world virtually disappeared and he was able to talk to the therapist quite directly about all the major concerns of his life, including masturbation. At first, though, he spoke mainly of school and the Boy Scouts.

But one day his mother called in great alarm. She had noticed some "strange" sex play of his. When he hinted at this in the sessions and was asked about it, he promptly explained that it was his way of masturbating.

After a 5½-year period, therapy was satisfactorily terminated. Occasional contact was maintained after termination. He ran into some trouble at college but overcame it with a little superficial reassurance. Eventually, he grew up to become a college professor, married, and seemingly led a fairly happy, normal kind of life.

By contrast, his mother, after the children left for college, developed more serious problems. She pulled out all her hair, leaving herself bald; then, ashamed of her appearance, she would not go out. She became quite depressed. Unexpectedly, a sudden attack of ulcers had a fatal outcome. In the beginning of his therapy, treatment had also been attempted with her, but it had been abandoned because she was almost totally unresponsive. Had she been the primary focus, it would have been continued with her, or perhaps family therapy would have been tried, and she might have done better. However, all this is conjecture; the fact is that he did well, while she regressed, especially after the children were out of the house.

The experience with Sheldon again brings up the question of peripheral versus central therapy. It has been noted with him that the formal speech therapy produced little change, while the intensive psychotherapy eventually led him to seek out more social contacts, which in turn brought out the motivation to have people understand him better. It was only then that his speech really began to "grow up." Thus, what he really suffered from was a communication disorder occasioned by a background of a noncommunicating family.

On the current scene, peripheral therapy is far more popular than central. Most people would really much rather work on some isolated symptom, or some one aspect of their lives, such as speech, reading, or the like, than look at their entire life pattern. Again this is one consequence of the hate culture. When people begin to see the hatred in their lives and in that of so many others, a deeply depressing reaction may result. Furthermore, they do not see any easy way out, since therapy, in spite of all the progress that has been made, still carries some stigma attached to it. And also there are many more professionals who are trained in the limited skills required for peripheral therapy and do not grasp the significance of the love life for the growth of the individual, even in terms of the isolated symptoms that come to them. This is but one more way in which the adjustment neurosis is perpetuated throughout a hate culture.

THERAPY AND SOCIAL REFORM

The naive notion is that therapy is only for "deviants," while the "normal" person can get along very well on his or her own. This would be true if we were living in a love culture, in which most people were brought up with love and understanding, while a few, perhaps for organic reasons, perhaps for accidental reasons, missed out on the goodies of life.

But is it clear that nothing could be further from the truth. Take almost any component of the analytic ideal and you will find millions unable to come to grips with it. The world is full of much more hatred than love. Sexual conflicts, again in spite of all the sophistication on display, are rampant. The loveless sex that adolescents practice has produced such phenomena as a routine venereal disease check upon entrance to college. Families are being disrupted at an ever-increasing rate. A sense of alienation hangs over a large percentage of the population. And the incidence of outright psychiatric disorders remains high. Nor has it been possible for good therapy to make much headway. The lack of growth of the American Psychoanalytic Association in the last 5 years may be noted, as well as the comments of some knowledgeable observers that the results in the treatment of schizophrenia have not changed in the last 80 or 100 years, even though a considerable number of these unfortunates could have been saved, or could be saved, with a proper therapeutic approach.

Under such circumstances, in a hate culture, therapy is sought out by an ever-increasing number of people. Where once only the middle class went, now the lower classes are also demanding this avenue to a better life. Slowly the public attitude is changing, toward a greater awareness of the damage that stress and stress-related disorders can do.

Inasmuch as so many people are in need of and seek out treatment, psychotherapy becomes a mean of social reform. Its ideology is that by changing enough individuals, the society will move toward a sense of greater trust and love, and toward truly greater fulfillment in life. Some awareness of this has always been present, in the group therapy sessions of the Oneida community, for example, or the religious meetings of the Quakers. But on a systematic basis the appreciation of therapy as a means of social reform was not understood until the advent of psychoanalysis.

CONCLUSION

To come back to the title of this book: What is the meaning of love in human experience? In all its ramifications, love remains the most profound and important of all human emotions. Above all, its presence makes people happy, its absence makes people unhappy. Love is constructive, hatred destructive. This may seem like a truism, but it has often been the fate of psychoanalysis that it has had to rediscover the obvious.

Love can be defined as an affectionate feeling toward other people, based on mutual reciprocity and functioning within a love culture. Love cannot be divorced from sexuality; sex without love is possible, though not the most gratifying of all human experiences, but love without any sexual desire (contact is not essential) is not. This is why the numerous "saintly" efforts to create a sexless love have all failed and are bound to fail in the future.

The basic distinction in approaching society is that between a love culture and a hate culture. We have tried to show how western civilization has for several millennia been a hate culture. The underlying hatred has always been glossed over; as for instance in the preposterous arguments about whether slavery was "good" for the slaves. Likewise this underlying hatred has nullified almost all attempts at reform, so that only very slow changes are perceptible in the attitudes of human beings toward their fellows. Hopefully, if the hatred ceases to be denied but is instead brought out into the open and analyzed, some real change in humanity's fate can be brought about.

Much of the love seen in the world either covers up hatred or serves as a refuge for the person from the horrors of the outside world. Real love can flourish adequately only in a love culture; hence the efforts of reformers should be directed primarily at transforming the hate culture into a love culture.

Animals, if looked at carefully, live largely in love cultures, but their lives are limited. The old image of the "beast" in the human turns out to be a gruesome joke, since the most destructive of all animals is the human being. Children, as has been seen, learn to love by being loved; if they are not loved, which is usually the case, they grow up with a variety of malformations that are then used to perpetuate the hate culture. Study of other societies reveals that there are many cultures that are far less aggressive and destructive than ours. To produce a love culture, however, changes all along the line are necessary, not mere empty verbal exhortations or platitudes.

Theoretically, if people could live according to the analytic ideal, their lives could move from one love relationship to another; mother to father to peers to the outside world. Obviously, such a state is still very far from realization. Because it is so far away, and because we do live in a hate culture, psychotherapy can serve as a major vehicle of social reform: By analyzing enough people, the culture could move in the direction of more love and kindness.

Finally, since the proper study of humankind *is* humankind, within the study of humankind central significance should also be placed on the role of love in the individual's life. By doing so, all the sciences of humankind, from psychology to history, economics to anthropology, would be revitalized and given a postive direction that they now lack.

Bibliography

Abend, I. M., Porder, M. S., & Willick, M. S. (1983). *Borderline patients: Psycho-analytic perspectives*. New York: International Universities Press.

Adams, R. M. (1983). *Decadent societies*. San Francisco: North Point Press.

Ahlstrom, S. E. (1972). *A religious history of the American people*. New Haven: Yale University Press.

Ainsworth, M. D. S., Blehar, M. C., Waters, E., & Wall, S. (1978). *Patterns of attachment*. New York: Morley.

Alexander, F. (1961). *The scope of psychoanalysis*. New York: Basic Books.

Alitto, G. S. (1979). *The last Confucian*. Berkeley: University of California Press.

Allport, G. W. (1950). *The individual and his religion*. New York: Macmillan.

Almy, M., Chittenden, E., & Miller, P. (1966). *Young children's thinking*. New York: Teachers College Press.

Altman, L. L. (1977). Some vicissitudes of love. *Journal of American Psycho-analytic Association*, 25, 35–52.

American Psychiatric Association. (1982). *Psychotherapy Research: Methodological and Efficacy Issues*.

American Psychoanalytic Association. (1979, 1982, 1983). *Rosters, 1978–1979, 1980–1982, 1982–1984*. New York: American Psychoanalytic Association.

Ammons, C. H., & Ammons, R. B. (1962a). How to prevent genius: McCurdy revisited. *Proceedings of the Montana Academy of Sciences, 21,* 145–152.

Ammons, R. B., & Ammons, C. H. (1962b). How to foster genius: McCurdy extended. *Proceedings of the Montana Academy of Sciences, 21,* 139–144.

Anderson, A. (Ed.). (1975). *Lin Yutang: The best of an old friend.* New York: Mason/Charter.

Andrews, S. R., et al. (1982). The skills of mothering. *Monographs of the Society for Research in Child Development, 47* (6).

Angel, L. L. (1973, August–September). *Paleoecology, paleodemography, and health.* Paper delivered at Ninth International Congress of Anthropological and Ethnological Sciences, Chicago and Detroit.

Annual Review of Sociology, Vol. 8 (1982). Palo Alto, CA: Annual Reviews.

Anthony, E. J., & Benedek, T. (Eds.). (1970). *Parenthood: Its psychology and psychopathology.* Boston: Little, Brown and Co.

Antonov-Ovseyenko, A. (1980). *The time of Stalin.* New York: Harper and Row.

Anzieu, D. (1975). *L'auto-analyse de Freud.* [Freud's self-analysis]. Paris: Presses Universitaires de France.

Arieti, S. (1976). *Creativity: The magic synthesis.* New York: Basic Books.

Aristophanes. (1961). *Lysistrata* (Donald Sutherland, Trans.). New York: Harper and Row.

Aristophanes. (1981). *The complete plays.* New York: Bantam.

Aristophanes. (1925). *The Acharnians.* Oxford: Clarendon Press.

Aristotle. (1908–1952). *Works* (W. D. Ross, Trans., Ed.). Oxford: Clarendon Press.

Arnold, F., et al. (Eds.). (1975). *The value of children: A cross-national study* (5 vols.). Honolulu: East-West Population Institute.

Aron, R. (1975). *History and the dialectic of violence.* New York: Harper and Row.

Asch, S. E. (1952). *Social psychology.* Englewood Cliffs, NJ: Prentice-Hall.

Ashby, P. H. (1963). *History and future of religious thought.* Englewood Cliffs, Prentice-Hall.

Ashmore, H. S. (1982). *Hearts and minds.* New York: McGraw-Hill.

Ashtor, E. (1976). *A social and economic history of the Near East in the Middle Ages.* Berkeley: University of California Press.

Atkinson, J., & Braddick, O. (1982). Sensory and perceptual capacities of the neonate. In P. Stratton (Ed.), *Psychology of the human newborn.* New York: John Wiley & Sons.

Augustine. (1958). *The City of God.* Garden City, NY: Image Books. (Original work dates from 426)

Avalon, A. (1972). *Tantra of the great liberation.* New York: Dover. (Original work published 1913)

Averill, J. R. (1982). *Anger and aggression.* New York: Springer Verlag.

Bachofen, J. J. (1861). *Das Mutterrecht.* [Mother right]. Basel: Benno Schwabe.

Bachrach, H. M. (1983). On the concept of analyzability. *Psychoanalytic Quarterly, 52*, 180–204.

Badinter, E. (1980). *Mother love: Myth and reality.* New York: Macmillan.

Bailey, Msgr. J. G. (1982, October 6). [Letter to the editor.] *New York Times.*

Balint, M. (1953). *Primary love and psychoanalytic technique.* New York: Liveright.

Baroja, J. C. (1965). *The world of the witches.* Chicago: University of Chicago Press.

Bartel, G. D. (1971). *Group sex.* New York: New American Library.

Baumer, F. A. (1977). *Modern European thought.* New York: Macmillan.

Beach, F. A. (1947). Evolutionary changes in the physiological control of mating behavior of mammals. *Psychological Review, 54*, 297–315.

Beach, F. A. (Ed.). (1977). *Human sexuality in four perspectives.* Baltimore: Johns Hopkins.

Beach, F. A. (1976). Sexual attraction, proceptivity, and receptivity in female mammals. *Hormones and Behavior, 7*, 105–138.

Beadle, M. (1974). *A child's mind.* New York: Aronson.

Bean, P. (Ed.). (1983). *Mental illness: Changes and trends.* New York: Morley.

Beavers, W. R. (1977). *Psychotherapy and growth: A family systems perspective.* New York: Brunner/Mazel.

Beck, S. J., & Molish, H. B. (Eds.). (1959). *Reflexes to intelligence.* New York: Free Press.

Becker, C. L. (1932). *The heavenly city of the eighteenth century philosophers.* New Haven: Yale University Press.

Beebe, B., & Sloate, P. (1982). Assessment and treatment of difficulties in mother–infant attachment in the first three years of life. *Psychoanalytic Inquiry, 1*, 601–624.

Bellak, L. (Ed.). (1979). *Disorders of the schizophrenic syndrome.* New York: Basic Books.

Beller, E. A. (1970). The Thirty Years War. In E. P. Cooper (Ed.), *New Cambridge modern history*, Vol. 4 (pp. 308–358). Cambridge, MA: Harvard University Press.

Belmonte, T. (1979). *The broken fountain.* New York: Columbia University Press.

Benedict, R. (1934). *Patterns of culture.* Boston: Houghton Mifflin.

Berg, A. (1973). *The nutrition factor.* Washington, DC: Brookings Institution.

Bergin, A. E., & Garfield, S. L. (Eds.). (1978). *Handbook of psychotherapy and behavior change* (2nd ed.). New York: John Wiley & Sons.

Bergmann, M. (1971). Psychoanalytic observations on the capacity to love. In J. B. McDevitt & C. Settlage (Eds.), *Separation–individuation: essays in honor of Margaret S. Mahler.* New York: International Universities Press.

Bergmann, M. (1980). On the intrapsychic function of falling in love. *Psychoanalytic Quarterly, 49*, 56–77.

Bergmann, M. (1982). Platonic love, transference love and love in real life. *Journal of American Psychoanalytic Association, 30,* 87–111.

Berndt, R. M. (1961). *Love songs of Arnhem Land.* Chicago: University of Chicago Press.

Bertaux, D. (Ed.). (1981). *Biography and society: The life history approach in the social sciences.* Beverly Hills, CA: Sage Publications.

Bertin, C. (1982). *Marie Bonaparte.* New York: Harcourt, Brace and Jovanovich.

Besancon, A. (1981). *The Rise of the Gulag.* New York: Continuum.

The Jerusalem Bible. New York: Doubleday, 1968.

Bibring, G., Dwyer, T. F., Huntington, D. S., & Valenstein, A. F. (1961). A study of the psychological processes in pregnancy and of the earliest mother–child relationship. *Psychoanalytic Study of the Child, 16,* 9–72. New York: International Universities Press.

Biebuyk, D. (1973). *Tradition and creativity in tribal art.* Berkeley: University of California Press.

Biller, H. B. (1981). Father absence, divorce and personality development. In M. Lamb (Ed.), *The role of the father in child development* (pp. 489–582). New York: John Wiley & Sons.

Billington, J. H. (1980). *Fire in the minds of men.* New York: Basic Books.

Birch, H. G., & Gussow, J. D. (1970). *Disadvantaged children.* New York: Harcourt, Brace and World.

Bleuler, M. (1978). *The schizophrenic disorders.* New Haven: Yale University Press.

Bloch, M. (1961). *Feudal society.* Chicago: University of Chicago Press.

Block, N. J., & Dworking, G. (Eds.). (1976). *The IQ controversy.* New York: Random House.

Blum, H. P. (ed.). (1977). *Female psychology.* New York: International Universities Press.

Boakes, R. A., & Halliday, M. S. (Eds.). (1972). *Inhibition and learning.* New York: Academic Press.

Bokenkotter, T. (1979). *A concise history of the Catholic church.* New York: Doubleday.

Bone, C. (1977). *The disinherited children.* New York: Schenkman.

Boswell, J. (1980). *Christianity, social tolerance and homosexuality.* Chicago: University of Chicago Press.

Bott, E. (1971). *Family and social network.* London: Tavistock Publications.

Bowlby, J., et al. (1966). *Maternal care and mental health and deprivation of maternal care.* New York: Schocken.

Bowlby, J. (1969). *Attachment and loss:* Vol. 1. New York: Basic Books.

Brady, I. (Ed.). (1983). Special section: Speaking in the name of the real: Freeman and Mead on Samoa. *American Anthropologist, 85,* 908–947.

Brantl, G. (Ed.). (1964). *The religious experience.* New York: George Braziller.

Brazelton, T. B. (1980). Neonatal assessment. In S. Greenspan & G. Pollock

(Eds.), *The course of life*. Washington, DC: National Institute of Mental Health.

Brazelton, T. B., Koslowski, B., & Main, M. (1974). The origins of reciprocity: The early mother–infant interaction. In J. Lewis & L. A. Rosenblum: *The effect of the infant on its caregiver*. New York: John Wiley & Sons.

Brazelton, T. B., & Als, H. (1979). Four early stages in the development of mother–infant interaction. *Psychoanalytic Study of the Child, 34*, 349–370.

Breggin, P. R. (1983). *Psychiatric drugs: Their hazards to the brain*. New York: Springer.

Breland, K., & Breland, M. (1966). *Animal behavior*. New York: Macmillan.

Brenner, C. (1982). *The mind in conflict*. New York: International Universities Press.

Brett, G. S. (1953). *History of Psychology* (1 vol.). Cambridge, MA: MIT Press.

Briggs, J. (1970). *Never in anger*. Cambridge, MA: Harvard University Press.

Brinton, C. (1965). *The anatomy of revolution*. New York: Random House.

Brody, S. (1956). *Patterns of mothering*. New York: International Universities Press.

Brody, S., & Axelrad, J. (1970). *Anxiety and ego formation in infancy*. New York: International Universities Press.

Brody, S., & Axelrad, J. (1978). *Mothers, fathers and children*. New York: International Universities Press.

Broel-Plateris, A. (1961). *Marriage disruption of divorce laws*. Unpublished doctoral dissertation, Division of Social Sciences, University of Chicago.

Bromley, D. G., & Shupe, A. D. (1981). *Strange gods*. Boston: Beacon Press.

Broom, L. et al. (1980). *The inheritance of inequality*. London: Routledge and Kegan Paul.

Brown, C. (1965). *Manchild in the promised land*. New York: Signet.

Brown, P., & Tuzin, D. (Eds.). (1983). *The ethnography of cannibalism*. Washington, DC: Society for Psychological Anthropology.

Brown, R. (1973). *A first language*. Cambridge, Mass.: Harvard University Press.

Brugger, B. (1977). *Contemporary China*. New York: Harper and Row.

Brumberg, J. J. (1982). Chlorotic girls, 1870–1920: A historical perspective on female adolescence. *Child Development, 53*, 1468–1477.

Bruner, J. S. (1973). *Beyond the information given*. New York: Norton.

Buber, M. (1970). *I and thou*. New York: Scribners.

Burckhardt, J. (1949). *The age of Constantine the Great*. New York: Pantheon Books. (Original work published 1852)

Burnham, D. L., Gladstone, A. L., & Gibson, R. W. (1969). *Schizophrenia and the need–fear dilemma*. New York: International Universities Press.

Burr, W. R., Hill, R., Nye, F. I., & Reiss, I. L. (1979). *Contemporary theories about the family*. New York: Free Press.

Burrows, E. G. (1963). *Flower in my ear*. Seattle: University of Washington Press.

Burton, F. D. (1972). The integration of biology and behavior in the socialization of the *Macaca Sylvana* of Gibraltar. In F. E. Poirier (Ed.), *Primate socialization*. New York: Random House.

Butler, S. (1912). *The notebooks of Samuel Butler* (H. Festing Jones, Ed.). London: Somerset.

Cadoux, C. J. (1982). *The early Christian attitude to war*. New York: Seabury Press.

Cairncross, J. (1974). *After polygamy was made a sin*. London: Routledge and Kegan Paul.

Caldwell, B. M., & Ricciuti, H. N. (Eds.). (1973). *Child development and social policy*. Chicago: University of Chicago Press.

Calef, V., & Weinshel, E. M. (1979). The new psychoanalysis and psychoanalytic revisionism: Book review essay on borderline conditions and pathological narcissism. *Psychoanalytic Quarterly, 48*, 470–491.

Call, J. D., Galenson, E., & Tyson, R. L. (1983). *Frontiers of infant psychiatry*. New York: Basic Books.

Calvin, John. (1954). *Theological treatises* (J. K. S. Reid, Ed.). Philadelphia: Westminster Press.

Capellannus, A. (1941). *The art of courtly love*. New York: Columbia University Press. (Original work published 1180)

Caplow, T., et al. (1982). *Middletown families: Fifty years of change and continuity*. Minneapolis: University of Minnesota Press.

Carlton, D., & Shaerf, Z. (Eds.). (1981). *Contemporary terror*. New York: St. Martin's Press.

Carpenter, G. (1975). Mother's face and the newborn. In R. Lewin (Ed.), *Child alive*. London: Temple Smither.

Cath, S. H., Gurwitt, A. R., & Ross, J. M. (Eds.). (1982). *Father and child*. Boston: Little, Brown and Co.

Cato, Marcus Porcius. (1934). *On Agriculture* (William Davis Hooper, Trans.). Cambridge, MA: Harvard University Press.

Cheetham, N. (1982). *Keepers of the keys*. New York: Scribners.

Chevalier-Skolnikoff, S., & Poirier, F. E. (1977). *Primate biosocial development*. New York: Garland Publishing Co.

Chiland, C. (Ed.). (1977). *Long-term treatments of psychotic states*. New York: Human Sciences Press.

Chiland, C. (1982). A new look at fathers. *Psychoanalytic Study of the Child, 37*, 367–380.

Chilman, C. S. (Ed.). (1983). *Adolescent sexuality in a changing American society*. New York: John Wiley & Sons.

Clark, A. (1982). *Working life of women in the seventeenth century*. London: Routledge and Kegan Paul.

Clark, G. (1961). *The seventeenth century*. New York: Oxford University Press.

Cohen, M. R. (1964). The dark side of religion. In G. Brantl (Ed.), *The religious experience*. New York: George Braziller.

Cohen, Y. (1966). *The transition from childhood to adolescence.* Chicago: Aldine.

Cohn, N. (1975). *Europe's inner demons.* New York: New American Library.

Coles, R. (1970). *Erik Erikson.* Boston: Little, Brown & Co.

Colligan, M. J., Pennebaker, D. W., & Murphy, L. R. (1982). *Mass psychogenic illness.* Hillsdale, NJ: Erlbaum.

Comfort, A. (Ed.). (1972). *The Joy of Sex.* New York: Simon & Schuster.

Committee on Animal Models for Research on Aging. (1981). Washington, DC: National Academy Press.

Condon, W. S., & Sander, L. (1974). Neonate movement is synchronized with adult speech. *Science, 183,* 99–101.

Confucius. (1955). *The Sayings of Confucius* (James R. Ware, Trans.). New York: New American Library.

Conway, F., & Siegelman, J. (1982). *Holy terror.* New York: Doubleday.

Cooper, E. P. (Ed.). (1970). *The new Cambridge modern history: Vol. 4.* London: Cambridge University Press.

Corsini, R. J. (Ed.). (1973, 1979). *Current psychotherapies.* Itasca, IL: F. E. Peacock Publishers.

Coser, R. L. (Ed.). (1964). *The family: Its structure and functions.* New York: St. Martin's Press.

Crawley, A. (1973). *The spoils of war: The rise of Western Germany since 1945.* New York: Bobbs Merrill.

Csikszentmihalyi, M., & Rochberg-Halton, E. (1981). *The meaning of things: Domestic symbols and the self.* New York: Cambridge University Press.

Cuber, J., & Harroff, P. (1965). *The significant Americans.* New York: Appleton-Century.

Cummings, E. E. (1965). *A selection of poems.* New York: Harcourt, Brace, Jovanovich.

Cumont, F. (1956). *Oriental religions in Roman paganism.* New York: Dover.

Curtin, M. E. (Ed.). (1973). *Symposium on love.* New York: Behavioral Publications.

Dally, A. (1983). *Inventing motherhood.* New York: Schocken Books.

Dante. (1977). *The portable Dante.* New York: Penguin.

Darnton, R. (1970). *Mesmerism and the end of the enlightenment in France.* New York: Schocken Books.

Davey, G. (1981). *Animal learning and conditioning.* Baltimore: University Park Press.

Davies, N. (1981). *Human sacrifice in history and today.* New York: William Morrow & Co.

Davis, G. (1976). *Childhood and history in America.* New York: Psychohistory Press.

Dawidowidz, L. (Ed.). (1967). *The golden tradition.* Boston: Beacon Press.

de Mause, L. (Ed.). (1974). *The history of childhood.* New York: Psychohistory Press.

Demos, J., & Babcock, S. J. [Eds.]. (1978). *Turning points: Historical and socio-logical essays on the family.* Chicago: University of Chicago Press.

Descartes, R. (1948a). *The essential works* (Lowell Blair, Trans.). New York: Bantam Books.

Descartes, R. (1948b). *Lettres á Chanut: Oeuvres philosophiques et morales* [Philosophical and moral works]. Bibliotheques des Lettres. Vienna: Imprimerie Aubin.

Descartes, R. (1981). *Philosophical letters* (Anthony Kenny, Trans. & Ed.). New York: Oxford University Press.

Deutsch, H. (1944). *The psychology of women* (2 vols.). New York: Grune and Stratton.

Devereux, G. (1955). A *Study of abortion in primitive societies.* New York: Julian Press.

DeWaal, F. (1982). *Chimpanzee Politics.* New York: Harper & Row.

Dietz, P. E. (1983). Psychiatrists who use and don't use ECT: A comparative study. *Hillside Journal of Clinical Psychiatry, 3,* 149–162.

Ditzion, S. (1969). *Marriage, morals and sex in America.* New York: Norton.

Dobyns, H. F. (1966). Estimating aboriginal American population. *Current Anthropology, 7,* 395–449.

Dobzhansky, T. (1973). *Genetic diversity and human equality.* New York: Basic Books.

Dockes, P. (1979). *Medieval slavery and liberation.* Chicago: University of Chicago Press.

Dohrenwend, B. P., & Dohrenwend, B. S. (1969). *Social status and psychological disorder.* New York: John Wiley & Sons.

Dohrenwend, B. P., et al. (1980). *Mental illness in the United States: Epidemiological estimates.* New York: Praeger.

Donne, John. (1966). *Selected poetry.* New York: New American Library.

Douglas, A. (1977). *The feminization of American culture.* New York: Avon Books.

Douglas, M. (1978). *Purity and danger.* London: Routledge and Kegan Paul.

Douglas, N., & Slinger, P. (1981). *The pillow book.* New York: Destiny Books.

Dover, K. J. (1978). *Greek homosexuality.* New York: Vintage Books.

Drekmeier, C. (1972). *Kinship and community in early India.* Stanford: University Press.

Driver, H. E. (1969). *Indians of North America.* Chicago: University of Chicago Press.

Eaton, J. W., & Weil, R. J. (1955). *Culture and mental disorders.* Glencoe, IL: The Free Press.

Edgcumbe, R. M. (1981). Toward a developmental line for the acquisition of language. *Psychoanalytic Study of the Child, 36,* 71–104. New Haven: Yale University Press.

Edwards, M. U. (1975). *Luther and the false brethren.* Stanford: Stanford University Press.

Ehrenfels, Joseph Karl Von. (1907). *Sexualethik* [Sexual ethics]. Wiesbaden: J. F. Bergman.

Ehrenreich, B. (1983). *The hearts of men.* New York: Doubleday.

Ehrenreich, B., & English, D. (1978). *For her own good.* New York: Anchor Press.

Ehrlich, H. J. (1973). *The social psychology of prejudice.* New York: John Wiley & Sons.

Eibl-Eibesfeldt, I. (1979). *The biology of peace and war.* New York: Viking.

Ekstein, R. (1966). *Children of time and space, of action and impulse.* New York: Meredith Publishing Co.

Ekstein, R., & Motto, R. (1969). *From learning for love to love of learning.* New York: Brunner/Mazel.

Eliade, M. (1978). *A history of religious ideas.* Chicago: University of Chicago Press.

Elias, N. (1978). *The history of manners.* New York: Pantheon Books.

Emde, R. N., & Harmon, R. J. (Eds.). (1982). *The development of attachment and affiliative systems.* New York: Plenum Press.

Engels, F. (1980). *The condition of the working class in England.* New York: Granada. (Original work published 1845)

Entwisle, D. R., & Deering, S. G. (1981). *The first birth: A family turning point.* Baltimore: Johns Hopkins.

Epstein, B. L. (1981). *The politics of domesticity.* Middletown, CT: Wesleyan University Press.

Erhardt, C. O., & Berlin, J. E. (Eds.). (1974). *Mortality and morbidity in the U.S.* Cambridge, MA: Harvard University Press.

Erikson, E. H. (1950). *Childhood and society.* New York: Norton.

Erikson, E. H. (1958). *Young man Luther.* New York: Norton.

Erikson, E. H. 1968). *Youth identity and crisis.* New York: Norton.

Eysenck, H. J. (1965). The effects of psychotherapy. *International Journal of Psychiatry, 1,* 99–142.

Feldman, S. (1981). Leadership in mental health: Changing the guard for the 1980's. *American Journal of Psychiatry, 130,* 1147–1153.

Fenichel, O. (1945). *The psychoanalytic theory of neurosis.* New York: Norton.

Ferenczi, S. (1950). *Sex in psychoanalysis: Contributions to psychoanalysis.* New York: Basic Books.

Ferin, M., Halberg, F., Richart, R. W., & Vandewiele, L. (Eds.). (1974). *Biorhythms and human reproduction.* New York: John Wiley & Sons.

Ferrante, J. (1975). *Woman as image in Medieval literature.* New York: Columbia University Press.

Fine, R. (1972). The age of awareness. *Psychoanalytic Review, 59,* 55–71.

Fine, R. (1973a). *The development of Freud's thought.* New York: Jason Aronson.

Fine, R. (1973b). Review of Evelyn Hooker's studies on homosexuality. *International Journal of Psychiatry, 11,* 471–475.

Fine, R. (1979a). *A history of psychoanalysis.* New York: Columbia University Press.

Fine, R. (1979b). *The intimate hour.* New York: Avery Publishing Company.

Fine, R. (1980). Work, depression and creativity. *Psychological Reports, 46,* 1195–1221.

Fine, R. (1981). *The psychoanalytic vision.* New York: Free Press.

Fine, R. (1982). *The healing of the mind.* New York: Free Press.

Fine, R. (1983a). *The logic of psychology: A dynamic approach.* Washington, DC: University Press of America.

Fine, R. (1983b). The Protestant ethic and the analytic ideal. *Political Psychology, 4,* 245–264.

Fine, R. (1983c). Reply to Wallerstein's review of *The Psychoanalytic Vision. International Review of Psychoanalysis, 10,* 237–240.

Fine, R. (1983d). The cultural role of psychiatry. *Professional Psychology,* pp. 855–868.

Fine, R. (1983e). The Protestant ethic and the analytic ideal. *Journal of Political Psychology, 4,* 245–264.

Fine, R. (1984). The analytic triad. *Current Issues in Psychoanalytic Practice, 1,* (3).

Fine, R. (1986). *The forgotten man.* New York: Haworth Press.

Finley, M. I. (1963). *The ancient Greeks.* New York: Penguin Books.

Finley, M. I. (1977). *Aspects of antiquity.* New York: Pelican Books.

Finley, M. I. (1979). *The world of Odysseus.* New York: Penguin Books.

Finley, M. I. (1981). *Economy and society in ancient Greece.* New York: Penguin Books.

Fishman, R. (1977). *Urban utopias in the twentieth century.* New York: Basic Books.

Flugel, J. C. (1921). *The psychoanalytic study of the family.* London: Hogarth Press.

Fortes, M. (1969). *Kinship and the social order.* Chicago: Aldine.

Fortes, M. (1977). Custom and conscience in anthropological perspective. *International Review of Psychoanalysis, 4,* 127–154.

Fortune, R. (1932). *The sorcerers of Dobu.* New York: Dutton.

Foster, J. L. (1974). *Love songs of the new kingdom.* New York: Scribner's.

Foster, M. L., & Brandes, S. H. (Eds.). (1980). *Symbol as sense.* New York: Academic Press.

Foucault, M. (1979). *Discipline and punish.* New York: Vintage Books.

Fowlie, W. (1967). *Climate of violence.* New York: Macmillan.

Fraiberg, S., & Fraiberg, L. (1979). *Insights from the blind.* New York: New American Library.

Freedman, E. B. (1982). Sexuality in nineteenth century America: Behavior, ideology and politics. In S. I. Kutler & S. N. Katz (Eds.), *The promise of American history.* Baltimore: Johns Hopkins.

Freedman, J. L., Sears, D. O., & Carlsmith, J. M. (1981). *Social psychology*. Englewood Cliffs, NJ: Prentice-Hall.

Freedman, N., & Grand S. (Eds.). (1977). *Communicative structures and psychic structures*. New York: Plenum Press.

Freud, A. (1963). The concept of developmental lines. *Psychoanalytic Study of the Child. 18*, 245–265.

Freud, S. (1953–1974). 1892–1939. *The Standard Edition of the Complete Psychological Works of Sigmund Freud*. (24 vols.). London: Hogarth Press and the Institute of Psychoanalysis.

Freud, S. (1928). *Psychoanalysis and faith*. New York: Norton.

Freud, S., & Andreas-Salome, L. (1972). *Letters*. New York: Harcourt Brace Jovanovich.

Fried, E. (Ed.). (1964). *Artistic productivity and mental health*. Springfield, IL: C. C. Thomas.

Friedan, B. (1963). *The Feminine mystique*. New York: Dell.

Friedan, B. (1981). *The second stage*. New York: Summit Book.

Friedl, E. (1967). The position of women: Appearance and reality. *Anthropological Quarterly, 40*, 97–108.

Friedrich, O. (1982). *The end of the world: A history*. New York: Coward, McCann and Geoghegan.

Frings, H., & Frings, M. (1977). *Animal communication*. Norman, OK: University of Oklahoma Press.

Frisch, K. Von. (1965). *Tanzsprache und orientierung der bienen* [Dance language and orientation of bees]. New York: Springer Verlag.

Fromm, E. (1956). *The art of loving*. New York: Harper.

Fuller, M. (1974). *Woman in the nineteenth century*. Columbia, SC: University of South Carolina Press.

Fullwinder, S. P. (1982). *Technicians of the finite*. Westport, CT: Greenwood Press.

Furman, E. (1974). *A child's parent dies*. New Haven: Yale University Press.

Furman, E. (1982). Mothers have to be there to be left. *Psychoanalytic Study of the Child, 37*, 15–28.

Galenson, E. (1980). Characteristics of psychological development during the second and third years of life. In S. Greenspan & G. Pollock (Eds.), *The Course of Life: Vol. 1*. Washington, DC: National Institute of Mental Health.

Gallagher, J. M., & Easley, J. A. (Eds.). (1978). *Knowledge and development: Vol. 2. Piaget and Education*. New York: Plenum Press.

Gandhi, M. (1957). *Autobiography*. Boston: Beacon.

Gardell, B., & Johansson, G. (Eds.). (1981). *Working life: A social science contribution to work reform*. New York: John Wiley & Sons.

Gardner, R. A., & Gardner, B. T. (1969). Teaching sign language to a chimpanzee. *Science, 165*, 664–672.

Garibay, K. (Ed.). (1970). *La literatura de los Aztecas* [The literature of the Aztecs]. Mexico City: Editorial Joaquin Martez.

Gay, P., & Webb, R. N. (1973). *Modern Europe*. New York: Harper.

Gedo, J. E. (1979). *Beyond interpretation*. New York: International Universities Press.

Gedo, M. M. (1980). *Picasso: Art as autobiography*. Chicago: University of Chicago Press.

Gelles, R. J. (1974). *The violent home*. Beverly Hills: Sage.

Gelles, R. J. (1978). Violence in the American family. In J. P. Martin [Ed.], *Violence and the family*. New York: John Wiley & Sons.

Gelles, R. J., Steinmetz, S. K., & Straus, M. A. (1981). *Behind closed doors*. New York: Anchor Books.

Gener, P. (1880). *La Mort et le Diable*. Quoted in Jones, p. 225.

Genovese, E. D. (1979). *From rebellion to revolution*. New York: Vintage Books.

Georges, R. A., & Jones, M. O. (1980). *People studying people*. Berkeley: University of California Press.

Gernet, J. A. (1982). *A history of Chinese civilization*. New York: Cambridge University Press.

Gibb, C. A. (Ed.). (1969). *Leadership*. Baltimore: Penguin Books.

Gibbon, E. (1963). *The decline and fall of the Roman Empire* (abridged ed.). New York: Dell. (Original work published 1788)

Giglioli, P. P. (1972). *Language and social context*. New York: Penguin Books.

Gil, D. G. (1970). *Violence against children*. Cambridge, MA: Harvard University Press.

Gilligan, C. (1982). *In a different voice*. Cambridge, MA: Harvard University Press.

Gillman, R. D. (1982). The termination phase in psychoanalytic practice: A survey of 48 completed cases. *Psychoanalytic Inquiry, 2*, 463–472.

Gilman, C. P. (1975). *The living of Charlotte Perkins Gilman: An autobiography*. New York: Harper Colophon Books.

Girard, R. (1977). *Violence and the sacred*. Baltimore: Johns Hopkins University Press.

Glaser, R. (Ed.). (1971). *The nature of reinforcement*. New York: Academic Press.

Glass, G. V., McGaw, B., & Smith, M. L. (1981). *Meta-analysis in social research*. Beverly Hills: Sage Publications.

Gluckman, M. (1955). *Custom and conflict in Africa*. Oxford: Basil Blackwell.

Goddard, D. (1966). *A Buddhist bible*. Boston: Beacon Press.

Goldberg, B. Z. (1958). *The sacred fire: The story of sex in religion*. New York: University Books.

Goldfarb, W. (1961). *Childhood schizophrenia*. Cambridge, MA: Harvard University Press.

Goldman, M. (1983). *U.S.S.R. in crisis: The failure of an economic system*. New York: Norton.

Gonsiorek, J. C., Paul, W., Weinrich, J. P., & Hotvedt, M. E. (1982). *Homosexuality: Social, psychological and biological issues*. Beverly Hills: Sage Publications.

Goode, W. J. (1978). *The celebration of heroes: Prestige as a control system*. Berkeley: University of California Press.

Goode, W. J. The theoretical importance of love. *American Sociological Review*, 24, 38–47.

Goode, W. J. (1982). *The family*. Englewood Cliffs, NJ: Prentice-Hall.

Goodman, M. E. (1952). *Race awareness in young children*. Cambridge, MA: Addison-Wesley.

Gould, R. (1972). *Child studies through fantasy*. New York: Quadrangle.

Grant, M. (1975). *The twelve Caesars*. New York: Scribner's.

Grant, M. (1977). *Jesus: An historian's review of the Gospels*. New York: Scribner's.

Grant, M. (1978). *A History of Rome*. New York: Scribner's.

Grant, M. (1982). *From Alexander to Cleopatra*. New York: Scribner's.

Grant, R. M. (1970). *Augustus to Constantine*. New York: Harper and Row.

Grant, R. M. (1977). *Early Christianity and society*. New York: Harper and Row.

Green, R. J., & Framo, J. L. (Eds.). (1981). *Family therapy: Major contributions*. New York: International Universities Press.

Greenspan, S. I., & Pollock, G. H. (Eds.). (1980). *The course of life*. Washington, DC: National Institute of Mental Health.

Greenwald, H. (1970). *The elegant prostitute*. New York: Walker and Co.

Griffin, D. R. (1976). *The question of animal awareness*. New York: Rockefeller University Press.

Grigson, G. (1976). *The goddess of love*. New York: Stein and Day.

Gronbech, V. (1964). *Religious currents in the nineteenth century*. Carbondale, IL: Southern Illinois University Press.

Grosser, P. E., & Halperin, E. G. (1978). *The causes and effects of anti-Semitism*. New York: Philosophical Library.

Grossman, F. K., Eichler, L. S., & Winickoff, S. A. (1980). *Pregnancy, birth and parenthood*. San Francisco: Jossey-Bass.

Gruchmann, L. (1977). *Der Zweite Weltkrieg* [The Second World War]. Munich: Deutsche Taschenbuch Verlag.

Grunebaum, H., Weiss, J. L., Cohler, B. J., Hartman, C. R., & Gallant, D. H. (1975). *Mentally ill mothers and their children*. Chicago: University of Chicago Press.

Hallie, P. P. (1982). *Cruelty*. Middletown, CT: Wesleyan University Press.

Hallpike, C. R. (1977). *Bloodshed and violence in the Papuan Mountains*. Oxford: Oxford University Press.

Hammer, S. (1982). *Passionate attachments*. New York: Rawson Associates.

Hanby, J. (1976). Sociosexual development in primates. In P. P. G. Bateson, and P. H. Klopfer (Eds.), *Perspectives in ethology: Vol. 2*. New York: Plenum Press.

Hansen, J. (1900). *Zauberwahn, inquisition und hexenprozess im Mittelalter* [Magical delusions, inquisition and trials against witches in the Middle Ages]. Quoted in Jones, p. 192.

Hansen, M. L. (1961). *The Atlantic migration, 1607–1860.* New York: Harper Torchbooks.

Hansson, C., & Liden, K. (1983). *Moscow women.* New York: Pantheon.

Harlow, H. F. (1974). *Learning to love.* New York: Aronson.

Harnack, A. (1957). *What is Christianity?* New York: Harper Torchbooks. (Original work published 1900)

Harner, M. (1973). *The Jivaro.* New York: Anchor Books.

Harris, M. (1968). *The rise of anthropological theory.* New York: T. Y. Crowell.

Hartmann, H., Kris, E., & Loewenstein, R. (1946). Comments on the formation of psychic structure. *Psychoanalytic Study of the Child, 2,* 11–38. New York: International Universities Press.

Hartup, W. W. (Ed.). (1982). *Review of child development research: Vol. 6.* Chicago, University of Chicago Press.

Hay, M. (1975). *Thy brother's blood.* New York: Hart Publishing Co.

Haywood, Bill. (1929). *The autobiography of Big Bill Haywood.* New York: International Publishers.

Hazo, R. G. (1967). *The idea of love.* New York: Praeger.

Heer, F. (1962). *The Medieval world.* New York: New American Library.

Heer, F. (1972). *Europe: Mother of revolutions.* New York: Praeger.

Hegel, G. (1942). *Philosophy of right* (T. M. Knox, Trans.). Oxford: Clarendon Press.

Helfaer, P. M. (1972). *The psychology of religious doubt.* Boston: Beacon Press.

Hendin, H. (1964). *Suicide and Scandinavia.* New York: Grune and Stratton.

Henry, W. E. (1971). *The fifth profession.* San Francisco: Jossey-Bass.

Herdt, G. H. (Ed.). (1982). *Rituals of manhood.* Berkeley: University of California Press.

Herman, S. N. (1977). *Jewish identity: A social psychological perspective.* New York: Henzl Press.

Hermann, Imre. (1936). Sich-anklammern-auf-suche-gehen [To cling to and to go in search]. *Internationale Zeitschrifte fuer Psychoanalyse, 22,* 349–370.

Herzog, A. R., et al. (1982). *Subjective well-being among different age groups.* Institute for Social Research, University of Michigan.

Herzog, J. M. (1982). On father hunger: The father's role in the modulation of aggressive drive and fantasy. In Cath, Gurwitt, & Ross (Eds.), *Father and child.* Boston: Little, Brown & Co.

Hibbert, C. (1981). *The days of the French Revolution.* New York: Morrow Quill Paperbacks.

Hillel, M., & Henry, C. (1977). *Of pure blood.* New York: McGraw-Hill.

Hillerbrand, H. J. (Ed.). (1968). *The Protestant Reformation.* New York: Harper.

Hiltebeitel, A. (1976). *The ritual of battle.* Ithaca, NY: Cornell University Press.

Himmelfarb, G. (1984). *The idea of poverty*. New York: Knopf.

Hinde, R. A. (Ed.). (1972). *Non-verbal communication*. New York: Cambridge University Press.

Hinde, R. A., & Stevenson-Hinde, J. (1973). *Constraints on learning*. New York: Academic Press.

Hitschmann, E. (1952). Freud's conception of love. *International Journal of Psychoanalysis, 33,* 421–428.

Hoch-Smith, J., & Spring, A. (Eds.). (1978). *Women in ritual and symbolic roles*. New York: Plenum.

Hoffer, P. C., & Hull, N. E. H. (1981). *Murdering mothers*. New York: New York University Press.

Holbrook, D. (1965). *The quest for love*. University, AL: University of Alabama Press.

Homans, G. C. (1965). Group factors in worker productivity. In H. Proshansky & L. Seidenberg (Eds.), *Basic studies in social psychology*. New York: Holt.

Homer. (1950). *The Iliad*. New York: Penguin Books.

Honig, W. K., & James, P. H. R. (1971). *Animal memory*. New York: Plenum Press.

Hooker, E. (1957). The adjustment of male homosexuals. *Journal of Projective Techniques, 21,* 17–31.

Hooker, E. (1958). Male homosexuality in the Rorschach. *Journal of Projective Techniques, 22,* 33–54.

Hopkins, K. (1978). *Conquerors and slaves*. New York: Cambridge University Press.

Horney, K. (1928). The problem of the monogamous ideal. *International Journal of Psychoanalysis, 9,* 318–331.

Hostetler, J. (1974). *Hutterite society*. Baltimore: Johns Hopkins.

Houpt, K. A., & Wolski, T. R. (1982). *Domestic animal behavior for veterinarians and animal scientists*. Ames, IA: Iowa State University Press.

Howard, M. (1976). *War in European history*. New York: Oxford University Press.

Howarth, J. (1982). *The Knights Templar*. New York: Atheneum.

Howell, E., & Bayes, M. (1981). *Women and mental health*. New York: Basic Books.

Huizinga, J. (1956). *The waning of the Middle Ages*. New York: Doubleday. (Original work published 1950)

Hume, D. (1896). *A Treatise of Human Nature*. Oxford: Oxford University Press.

Hunt, M. (1959). *The natural history of love*. New York: Knopf.

Hurley, N., Rev. (1983, September 24). [Letter to the editor]. *New York Times*. Anchor Books.

Hutchison, K. (1966). *The decline and fall of British capitalism*. Hamden, CT:

Jackson, M., & Jackson, J. (1981). *"Your father's not coming home anymore."* New York: Ace Books.

Jackson, W. T. H. (1971). *The anatomy of love.* New York: Columbia University Press.

Jahoda, G. (1982). *Psychology and anthropology: A psychological perspective.* New York: Academic Press.

James, R. R. (1979). *The British Revolution, 1880–1939.* New York: Knopf.

James, W. (1950). *The principles of psychology.* New York: Dover.

James, W. (1902). *The varieties of religious experience.* New York: Random House Modern Library.

Jarvis, E. (1971). *Report of the Commission on Lunacy.* Cambridge, MA: Harvard University Press. (Original work published 1855)

Jencks, C., et al. (1979). *Who gets ahead?* New York: Basic Books.

Johansen, B., & Maestas, R. (1979). *Wasi'Chu: The continuing Indian wars.* London: Monthly Review Press.

Johnson, C. (1982). *Revolutionary change.* Stanford, CA: Stanford University Press.

Johnson, J. T. (1981). *Just war tradition and the restraint of war: A moral and historical inquiry.* Princeton, NJ: Princeton University Press.

Johnson, W. S. (1975). *Sex and marriage in Victorian poetry.* Ithaca, NY: Cornell University Press.

Johnson, W. S. (1979). *Living in sin.* Chicago: Nelson-Hall.

Joint Commission on Mental Health of Children. (1970). *Crisis in Child Mental Health.* New York: Harper and Row.

Jones, E. (1929). Psychoanalysis and psychiatry. In E. Jones, *Collected Papers on Psychoanalysis* (5th ed.). London: Bailliere, Tindall and Cox, 1948.

Jones, E. (1931a). The concept of a normal mind. In *Collected Papers on Psychoanalysis* (5th ed.).

Jones, E. (1931b). *On the nightmare.* London: Hogarth Press.

Jones, E. (1937). Love and morality. *International Journal of Psychoanalysis, 18,* 1–5.

Jones, E. (1948). *Collected Papers on Psychoanalysis* (5th ed.). London: Bailliere, Tindall and Cox.

Jones, E. (1953–1957). *The life and work of Sigmund Freud.* New York: Basic Books.

Josephus, F. (1959). *The Jewish war.* New York: Penguin Books.

Journal of the American Psychoanalytic Association Index: Vols. 1–22. New York: International Universities Press, 1976.

Kamerman, S., & Hayes, C. D. (Eds.). (1982). *Families that work.* Washington, DC: National Academy Press.

Kaplan, L. (Ed.). (1973). *Revolutions: A comparative study.* New York: Vintage Books.

Kardiner, A., Karush, A., & Ovesey, C. (1959). A methodological study of Freudian theory. *Journal of Nervous and Mental Disease, 79,* 1–4.

Kaye, K. (1982). *The mental and social life of babies.* Chicago: University of Chicago Press.

Kazdin, A. E., & Tuma, A. H. (Eds.). (1982). *Single-case research designs.* San Francisco: Jossey-Bass.

Kelly, A. (1978). *Eleanor of Aquitaine and the four kings.* Cambridge, MA: Harvard University Press.

Kelly, H. A. (1975). *Love and marriage in the age of Chaucer.* New York: Cornell University Press.

Kempe, C. H., & Kempe, R. S. (1984). *The common secret: Sexual abuse of children and adolescents.* New York: W. H. Freeman.

Kempe, C. H., Silverman, F. N., Steele, B. S., Droegemuller, W., & Silver, H. (1962). The battered child syndrome. *Journal of the American Medical Association, 181,* 21–24.

Kendler, H. H., & Spence, J. T. (Eds.). (1971). *Essays in neobehaviorism.* New York: Meredith Corp.

Keneally, T. (1982). *Schindler's list.* New York: Simon and Schuster.

Kernberg, O. (1974a). Barriers to falling and remaining in love. *Journal of the American Psychoanalytic Association, 22,* 486–511.

Kernberg, O. (1947b). Mature love: Prerequisites and characteristics. *Journal of the American Psychoanalytic Association, 22,* 743–768.

Kernberg, O. (1976). *Object relations theory and clinical psychoanalysis.* New York: Jason Aronson.

Kernberg, O. (1980). Love, the couple and the group: A psychoanalytic frame. *Psychoanalytic Quarterly, 49,* 78–108.

Kestenberg, J. S. (1975). *Children and parents.* New York: Aronson.

Khayam, Obar. (1971). *Rubaiyat.* New York: Grosset & Dunlap. (Original work dates from twelfth century)

Khruschchev, N. (1970). *Kruschchev remembers.* Boston: Little, Brown and Co.

Kiell, N. (1964). *The universal experience of adolescence.* New York: International Universities Press.

Kinkade, K. (1973). *A Walden Two experiment.* New York: Morrow Paperbacks.

Kinsey, A. C., Pomeroy, W. B., & Martin, C. E. (1948). *Sexual behavior in the human male.* Philadelphia: W. B. Saunders & Co.

Kinsey, A. C., et al. (1953). *Sexual behavior in the human female.* Philadelphia: W. B. Saunders & Co.

Klein, M., et al. (1952). *Developments in psychoanalysis.* London: Hogarth Press.

Klemer, J. D. (Ed.) (1959). *Chinese love poems.* Garden City, N.Y: Hanover House.

Koestler, A. (1981). *Bricks and babel: Selected writings.* New York: Basic Books.

Kohut, H. (1971). *The analysis of the self.* New York: International Universities Press.

Kohut, H. (1977). *The restoration of the self.* New York: International Universities Press.

Kollontai, P. (1960). *The autobiography of a sexually emancipated Communist woman.* New York: Norton. (Original work published 1926)

Komarovsky, M. (1967). *Blue-collar marriage*. New York: Vintage Books.

Konvitz, M. R. (1980). *Judaism and the American idea*. New York: Schocken.

Kotaskova, J. (1982). Social development: A survey of European Longitudinal studies. In W. W. Hartup [Ed.], *Review of Child Development Research: Vol. 6*, pp. 325–348.

Kracke, W. H. (1978). *Force and persuasion*. Chicago: University of Chicago Press.

Kriesberg, C. (1970). *Mothers in poverty: A study of fatherless families*. Chicago: Aldine.

Kung, H. (1968). *On being a Christian*. New York: Simon & Schuster.

Ladner, J. A. (Ed.). (1973). *The death of white sociology*. New York: Random House.

Ladurie, L. R. (1978). *Montaillou: The promised land of error*. New York: Braziller.

Ladurie, L. R. (1981). *The mind and method of the historian*. Chicago: University of Chicago Press.

Lamb, M. E. (Ed.). (1981). *The role of the father in child development*. New York: John Wiley & Sons.

Lamb, M. E. (1982). *Nontraditional families: Parenting and child development*. Hillsdale, N.J.: Erlbaum.

Lambert, M. J., Christensen, E. R., & De Julio, S. S. (Eds.). (1983). *The assessment of psychotherapy outcome*. New York: John Wiley & Sons.

Langs, R. (1976). *The therapeutic interaction* (2 vols.) New York: Jason Aronson.

Lannoy, R. (1971). *The speaking tree*. New York: Oxford University Press.

Lapidus, F. W. (1978). *Women in Soviet society*. Los Angeles: University of California Press.

Laslett, P. (1972). *Household and family in past time*. London: Cambridge University Press.

Latourette, K. S. (1962). *The Chinese: Their history and culture*. New York: Macmillan.

Lazarus, A. A. (1971). Where do behavior therapists take their troubles? *Psychological Reports, 28*, 349–350.

Lea, H. C. (1966). *Sacerdotal celibacy*. New York: University Books. (Original work published 1907)

Leach, W. (1980). *True love and perfect union*. New York: Basic Books.

Lederer, N. (1968). *The fear of women*. New York: Harcourt, Brace, Jovanovich.

Lefebvre, G. (1962). *The French Revolution*. New York: Columbia University Press.

Levi-Strauss, C. (1962). *Totemism*. Boston: Beacon Press.

Levy, B. H. (1979). *Barbarism with a human face*. New York: Harper Colophon.

Levy, L. W. (1981). *Treason against God: A history of the offense of blasphemy*. New York: Schocken Books.

Levy, R. I. (1973). *Tahitians*. Chicago: University of Chicago Press.

Lewis, C. S. (1958). *The allegory of love*. New York: Oxford University Press.

Lewis, J. M., Beavers, W. R., Gossett, J. T., & Phillips, V. A. (1976). *No single thread: Psychological health in family systems*. New York: Brunner/Mazel.

Lewis, M., & Rosenblum, L. A. (Eds.). (1974). *The effect of the infant on its caregiver*. New York: John Wiley & Sons.

Lewis, N., & Reinhold, M. (1966). *Roman civilization: A source book* (2 vols.). New York: Harper Torchbooks.

Lewis, O. (1970). The culture of poverty. In *Anthropological Essays*, Chap. 4. New York: Random House.

Licht, H. (1932). *Sexual life in ancient Greece*. London: Abbey Library.

Lichtenberg, J. D. (1973). *Psychoanalysis and infant research*. Hillsdale, NJ: Erlbaum.

Lichtenstein, H. (1970). Changing implications of the concept of psychosexual development. *Journal of the American Psychoanalytic Association, 18*, 300–318.

Lidz, T. (1963). *The family and human adaptation*. New York: International Universities Press.

Lidz, T., et al. (1965). *Schizophrenia and the family*. New York: International Universities Press.

Liebowitz, M. R. (1983). *The chemistry of love*. Boston: Little, Brown & Co.

Lifton, R. J. (1969). *Thought reform and the psychology of totalism*. New York: Norton.

Lind, J. D. (1983). The organization of coercion in history. *Sociology 1983*, pp. 1–29. San Francisco: Jossey-Bass.

Linden, E. (1974). *Apes, men and language*. New York: Dutton.

Ling, T. (1968). *A history of religion east and west*. New York: Harper Colophon Books.

Ling, T. (1952). *The Buddha*. New York: Scribner's.

Lorenz, K. (1952). *King Solomon's ring*. New York: New American Library.

Lorenz, K. (1963). *On aggression*. New York: Harcourt.

Lorenz, K. (1981). *The foundations of ethology*. New York: Simon and Schuster.

Lovejoy, P. E. (Ed.). (1981). *The ideology of slavery in Africa*. Beverly Hills: Sage.

Luther, Martin. (1883). *Werke*. Weimar Ausgabe.

Luther, Martin. (1955–1976). *Works* (Joroslay Pelikan, Ed.). Saint Louis: Concordia Publications House.

Luther, Martin. (1971). *Works*. Philadelphia: Fortress Press.

Lutz, C. (1983). Parental Goals, ethnopsychology, and the development of emotional meaning. *Ethos, 11*, 246–282.

Lynch, J. J. (1977). *The broken heart*. New York: Basic Books.

Macaulay, J., & Berkowitz, L. (Eds.). (1970). *Altruism and helping behavior*. New York: Academic Press.

MacDonald, M. (1982). *Mystical bedlam: Madness, anxiety and healing in 17th century England*. New York: Cambridge University Press.

MacFarlane, A. (1975). Olfaction in the development of social preferences in the human neonate. In CIBA *Foundation Symposium 33*, 103–117. Amsterdam: Elsevier.

Mackay, C. (1932). *Extraordinary popular delusions and the madness of crowds.* New York: L. C. Page and Co. (Original work published 1841)

Madaule, J. (1967). *The Albigensian Crusade.* New York: Fordham University Press.

Mahler, M. (1968). *On human symbiosis and the vicissitudes of individuation.* New York: International Universities Press.

Mahler, M., et al. (1975). *The psychological birth of the human infant.* New York: Basic Books.

Malcolm, J. (1981). *Psychoanalysis: The impossible profession.* New York: Knopf.

Mannix, P. P. (1958). *Those about to die.* New York: Ballantine Books.

Manuel, F. E. (Ed.). (1966). *Utopias and utopian thought.* Boston: Beacon Press.

Manuel, F. E., & Manuel, F. P. (1979). *Utopian thought in the western world.* Cambridge, MA: Harvard University Press.

Marlow, H. C., & Davis, H. M. (1976). *The American search for woman.* Santa Barbara, CA: Clio Books.

Marmor, J. (1980). *Homosexual behavior: A modern reappraisal.* New York: Basic Books.

Marshall, D. S. (1971). Sexual behavior on Mangaia. In D. J. Marshall & R. C. Suggs (Eds.), *Human Sexual Behavior.* New York: Basic Books.

Marshall, D. J., & Suggs, R. C. (Eds.). (1971). *Human Sexual Behavior.* New York: Basic Books.

Martin, E. W. (1971). *The History of the great riots and of the Molly Maguires.* New York: Augustus Kelly.

Martin, J. P. (Ed.). (1978). *Violence and the family.* New York: John Wiley & Sons.

Martin, M. R., & Beckett, S. (Eds.). (1968). *The world's love poetry.* New York: Bantam Books.

Masters, W. H., & Johnson, V. E. (1966). *Human sexual response.* Boston: Little, Brown and Co.

May, R. (1969). *Love and will.* New York: Dell.

Mayman, M. (Ed.). (1982). Infant research: The dawn of awareness. *Psychoanalytic Inquiry, 1,* 104.

Mayr, E. (1982). *The growth of biological thought.* Cambridge, MA: Harvard University Press.

McCord, J. H. (Ed.). (1969). *With all deliberate speed.* Urbana, IL: University of Illinois Press.

McCurdy, H. C. (1958). *The childhood pattern of genius.* Washington, DC: Smithsonian (Smithsonian Publication 4373).

McIntyre, T. J., & Obert, J. C. (1979). *The fear brokers.* Boston: Beacon Press.

McNeill, W. H. (1974). *The shape of European history.* New York: Oxford University Press.

McNeill, W. H. (1976). *Plagues and peoples.* New York: Doubleday.

McNeill, W. H. (1982). *The pursuit of power.* Chicago: University of Chicago Press.

McPherson, J. M. (1982). *Ordeal by fire: The Civil War and Reconstruction.* New York: Knopf.

Mead, M. (Ed.). (1961). *Cooperation and competition among primitive peoples.* Boston: Beacon Press.

Mead, M. (1935). *Sex and temperament in three primitive societies.* New York: New American Library.

Mead, M., & Wolfenstein, M. (Eds.). (1955). *Childhood in contemporary cultures.* Chicago: University of Chicago Press.

Mead, M. (1930). *Growing up in New Guinea.* New York: Morrow.

Meeks, W. A. (1983). *The first urban Christians.* New Haven: Yale University Press.

Meisner, M. (1977). *Mao's China.* New York: Free Press.

Menzel, E. W. (1974). Communication and aggression in a group of chimpanzees. In R. Pliner, L. Krames, & T. Alloway, *Nonverbal Communication of Aggression: Vol. 2.* New York: Plenum Press.

Mercer, C. (1983). *Honorable intentions: The manners of courtship in the 80's.* New York: Atheneum.

Merleau-Ponty, M. (1969). *Humanism and terror.* Boston: Beacon Press.

Merser, C. (1983). First night sexual niceties. *Self*, pp. 106–109.

Messmer, S. F. (1983). Regional and racial effects on the urban homicide rate: The subculture of violence revisited. *American Journal of Sociology, 88,* 997–1007.

Metcalfe, J. J. (1953) *Love portraits.* Garden City, NY: Doubleday & Co.

Milgram, S. (1963). Behavioral study of obedience. *Journal of Abnormal and Social Psychology, 67,* 371–378.

Miller, P., & Johnson, T. H. (Eds.). (1963). *The Puritans.* New York: Harper Torchbooks.

Minar, D. W., & Greer, S. (Eds.). (1969). *The concept of community.* Chicago: Aldine.

Mitchell, G. (1981). *Human sex differences: A primatologist's perspective.* New York: Van Nostrand Reinhold.

Mitchell, J. (1974). *Psychoanalysis and feminism.* New York: Vintage.

Mommsen, T. (1958). *The history of Rome.* New York: World. (Original work published 1854)

Montagu, A. (1979). *Touching.* New York: Columbia University Press.

Montagu, A. (Ed.). (1973). *Man and aggression.* New York: Oxford University Press.

Montagu, A. (1974). Aggression and the evolution of man. In R. E. Whalen (Ed.), *The neuropsychology of aggression.* New York: Plenum.

Montagu, A. (1976). *The nature of human aggression*. New York: Oxford University Press.

Montagu, A. (Ed.). (1978). *Learning non-aggression*. New York: Oxford University Press.

Moore, J. F., & Myerhoff, B. G. (Eds.). (1975). *Symbol and politics in Communist ideology*. Ithaca, NY: Cornell University Press.

Morgan, R. (Ed.). (1970). *Sisterhood is powerful*. New York: Vintage Books.

Morley, J. (1980). *Vatican diplomacy and the Jews during the Holocaust*. New York: KTAV.

Morrison, S. E. (1972). *History of the American people*. New York: Oxford University Press.

Mortimer, E. (1982). *Faith and power: The politics of Islam*. New York: Random House.

Moss, C. (1982). *Portraits in the wild*. Chicago: University of Chicago Press.

Mosse, G. L. (1981). *Nazi culture: A documentary history*. New York: Schocken Books.

Murdock, G. P. (1949). *Social structure*. New York: Free Press.

Murphy, G. (1953). *In the minds of men*. New York: Basic Books.

Murphy, H. B. M. (1982). *Comparative psychiatry*. New York: Springer-Verlag.

Murphy, T. P. (Ed.). (1976). *The holy war*. Columbus: Ohio State University Press.

Nagel, E. (1961). *The structure of science*. New York: Harcourt & Brace.

Nance, J. (1975). *The gentle Tasaday*. New York: Harcourt Brace Jovanovich.

Nasr, J. H. (1975). *Ideals and realities of Islam*. Boston: Beacon Press.

Nathan, L. (Ed.). (1976). *The transport of love*. Berkeley: University of California Press.

Natterson, J. M. (Ed.). (1980). *The dream in clinical practice*. New York: Jason Aronson.

Navestad, M. (1979). *The colors of rage and love*. Oslo: Universities Forlaget.

Nelson, J. C. (1958). *Renaissance theory of love*. New York: Columbia University Press.

New York Psychoanalytic Institute. Bulletin, 1983.

Nietzsche, F. (1968). *The Portable Nietzsche* (W. Kaufmann, Ed.). New York: Penguin Books.

Nisbet, R. (1980). *History of the idea of progress*. New York: Basic Books.

Nordhoff, C. (1965). *The Communistic societies of the U.S.* New York: Schocken Books. (Original work published 1875)

Norman, C. (1966). *Come live with me: Five centuries of romantic poetry*. New York: David McKay.

Noyes, J. H. (1966). *History of American socialisms*. New York: Dover. (Original work published 1870)

Nunberg, H., & Federn, E. (Eds.). (1962–1975). *Minutes of the Vienna Psychoanalytic Society* (4 vols.). New York: International Universities Press.

Nygren, A. (1982). *Agape and eros*. Chicago: University of Chicago Press. (Original work published 1932–1939)

Obholzer, K. (1982). *The Wolf-man sixty years later*. New York: Continuum.

Offer, D., & Sabshin, M. (1974). *Normality*. New York: Basic Books.

Offer, D., Ostrov, E., & Howard, K. I. (1981). *The adolescent: A psychological self-portrait*. New York: Basic Books.

Ogilvie, R. M. (1980). *Roman literature and society*. New York: Penguin Books.

O'Keefe, P. L. (1983). *Stolen lightning*. New York: Vintage Books.

Ortega y Gasset, J. (1957). *On love*. Cleveland: World Publishing Co.

Osofsky, J. D. (Ed.). (1979). *Handbook of infant development*. New York: John Wiley & Sons.

Otto, H. A. (Ed.). (1972). *Love today*. New York: Association Press.

Ovid. (1968). *Amores* (Guy Lee, Trans.). New York: Viking Press.

Oxford Dictionary of Quotations (2nd ed.). (1906). New York: Oxford University Press.

Pagels, E. (1981). *The Gnostic Gospels*. New York: Vintage Books.

Paige, K. E., & Paige, J. M. (1981). *The politics of reproductive ritual*. Berkeley: University of California Press.

Palmer, R. R. (1971). *The world of the French Revolution*. New York: Harper and Row.

Papousek, H., & Papousek, M. (1982). Integration into the social world: Survey of research. In P. Stratton (Ed.), *Psychobiology of the human newborn*. New York: John Wiley & Sons.

Parker, G. (1982). Some recent work on the Inquisition in Spain and Italy. *Journal of Modern History*, *54*, 519–532.

Parkes, C. M. (1972). *Bereavement*. New York: International Universities Press.

Parsons, T. (1952). The superego and the theory of social systems. *Psychiatry*, *15*, 15–24.

Patai, R. (1973). *The Arab mind*. New York: Scribner's.

Patterson, O. (1982). *Slavery and social death*. Cambridge, MA: Harvard University Press.

Pavlos, A. J. (1982). *The cult experience*. Westport, CT: Greenwood Press.

Peters, E. (Ed.). (1980). *Heresy and authority in Medieval Europe*. Philadelphia: University of Pennsylvania Press.

Peto, E. (1949). Infant and mother: Observations on object relations in early infancy. *International Journal of Psychoanalysis*, *30*, 260–264. (Originally published in Hungarian in 1937)

Petroni, F. (Ed.). (1968). *Poesia d'amore*. Bologna: Gherardo Casini Editore.

Petronius. (1965). *The Satyricon*. New York: Penguin Books.

Pfister, O. (1924). *Love in children and its aberrations*. New York: Dodd, Mead and Co.

Pfister, O. (1948). *Christianity and fear*. London: Allen and Unwin. (German ed., 1944.)

Piaget, J. (1973). The affective unconscious and the cognitive unconscious. *Journal of American Psychoanalytic Association, 21,* 249–261.

Plaidy, J. (1969). *The Spanish Inquisition.* New York: Citadel Press.

Plato. (1927). *The works of Plato* (selected and edited by Irwin Edman). New York: Simon and Schuster Modern Library.

Pliner, P., Kramer, L., & Alloway, T. (Eds.). (1975). *Nonverbal communication of aggression.* New York: Plenum Press.

Plutchik, R., & Kellerman, H. (Eds.). (1983). *Emotion: Vol. 2. Emotions in early development.* New York: Academic Press.

Polansky, N. A., Burgman, R. D., & De Saix, C. (1972). *Roots of futility.* San Francisco: Jossey-Bass.

Polisensky, J. W. (1971). *The Thirty Years War.* Berkeley: University of California Press.

Pollack, H. (1971). *Jewish folkways in Germanic lands (1648–1806).* Boston: M.I.T. Press.

Pomeroy, S. B. (1975). *Goddesses, whores, wives and slaves.* New York: Schocken.

Portmann, A. (1961). *Animals as social beings.* New York: Viking.

Pound, E., & Stock, M. (Trans.). (1962). *Love poems of ancient Egypt.* New York: New Directions Publishing Co.

Praz, M. (1933). *The Romantic agony.* New York: World Publishing Co.

Premack, D. (1970). The education of Sarah. *Psychology Today, 4,* 55–58.

Premack, D. (1976). *Intelligence in ape and man.* Hillsboro, NJ: Erlbaum.

Premack, D., & Premack, A. (1983). *The mind of an ape.* New York: Norton.

Prochaska, S. O., & Norcross, J. C. (1983). Contemporary psychotherapists: A national survey of characteristics, practices, orientations and attitudes. *Psychotherapy, 20,* 161–173.

Psychosocial Treatments Research Branch, NIMH 1980—Psychotherapy of Depression Collaborative Research Program. Unpublished research project.

Pulver, S. F. (1970). Narcissism: The term and the concept. *Journal of American Psychoanalytic Association, 18,* 319–341.

Pulver, S. E., & Jaffe, D. S. (Reporters). (1976). Survey of psychoanalytic practice 1976: Some trends and implications. *Journal of American Psychoanalytic Association, 26,* 615–631.

Putnam, J. J. (1971). *James Jackson Putnam and psychoanalysis: letters.* Cambridge, MA: Harvard University Press.

Radin, P. (1957). *Primitive man as philosopher.* New York: Dover.

Rado, S., et al. (Eds.). *Zehn Jahre Berliner Psychoanatytisches Institut* [Ten years of the Berlin Psychoanalytical Institute]. Vienna: Internationaler Psychoanalytischer Verlag, 1930. Reprinted 1970 by Verlag Anton Hain KG, Meisenheim; edited by G. Maetze.

Rajecki, D. J. (Ed.). (1983). *Comparing behavior: Studying man through animals.* Hillsdale, NJ: Erlbaum.

Raju, P. T. (1962). *Introduction to comparative philosophy.* London: Feffer and Simons, Inc.

Ramsey, P. (1961). *War and the Christian conscience.* Durham, NC: Duke University Press.

Randall, J. H. (1976). *The making of the modern mind.* New York: Columbia University Press.

Rangell, L. (Reporter). (1954). Psychoanalysis and dynamic psychotherapy—similarities and differences. *Journal of American Psychoanalytic Association,* 2, 152–166.

Rank, O. (1952). *The myth of the birth of the hero.* New York: Brunner. (Original 1909)

Rawson, P., & Legeza, L. (1973). *Tao.* New York: Avon Books.

Redican, W. M., & Taub, D. M. (1981). Male parental care in monkeys and apes. In M. Lamb (Ed.), *The role of the father in child development.* New York: John Wiley & Sons.

Reich, A. (1940). A contribution to the psychoanalysis of extreme submissiveness in women. *Psychoanalytic Quarterly,* 9, 470–480.

Reich, W. (1927). *The function of the orgasm.* New York: Orgone Institute Press.

Reik, T. (1941). *Masochism in modern man.* New York: Farrar, Strauss.

Reps, P. (1961). *Zen flesh, zen bones.* New York: Doubleday Anchor.

Rexford, E. N., Sander, L. W., & Shapiro, T. (Eds.). (1976). *Infant psychiatry.* New Haven: Yale University Press.

Rheingold, H. L. (Ed.). (1983). *Maternal behavior in mammals.* New York: John Wiley & Sons.

Rheingold, J. C. (1967). *The mother, anxiety and death.* Boston: Little, Brown and Co.

Rheingold, J. C. (1964). *The fear of being a woman.* New York: Grune and Stratton.

Rheinstein, M. (1972). *Marriage stability, divorce and the law.* Chicago: University of Chicago Press.

Ribble, M. (1943). *The rights of infants.* New York: Columbia University Press.

Richard, A. F., & Schulman, S. R. (1982). Sociobiology: Primate field studies. *Annual Review of Anthropology,* 11, 231–255.

Ridley, M. (1978). Paternal care. *Animal Behavior,* 26, 904–932.

Riesman, D., Glazer, N., & Denney, R. (1969). *The lonely crowd.* New Haven: Yale University Press.

Roberts, P. E. (1971). *The new communes.* Englewood Cliffs, NJ: Prentice-Hall.

Robinson, J. S. (1982). *H. D.: The life and work of an American poet.* Boston: Houghton Mifflin Co.

Robitscher, J. D. (1980). *The powers of psychiatry.* Boston: Houghton Mifflin.

Rodgers, J. E. (1982). "Roots of madness." *Science* 82 (3), 85.

Rogers, Daniel. (1982). *Matrimonial honor.* London:

Roheim, G. (1932). Psychoanalysis of primitive cultural types. *International Journal of Psychoanalysis,* 13, 2–224.

Roheim, G. (1950). *Psychoanalysis and anthropology*. New York: International Universities Press.

Rorabaugh, W. J. (1979). *The alcoholic republic*. New York: Oxford University Press.

Rosen, B. (1972). *Witchcraft*. New York: Taplinger.

Rosen, R. (1982). *The lost sisterhood: Prostitution in America 1900–1918*. Baltimore: Johns Hopkins University Press.

Rosenberg, C. E. (Ed.). (1975). *The family in history*. Philadelphia: University of Pennsylvania Press.

Rosenberg, S. D. (1983). Review of Neale and Oltmanns: "Schizophrenia: the science and politics of psychiatry." *Contemporary Psychiatry*, 2, 10–13.

Rosenblatt, J. S. (1975). Prepartum and postpartum regulation of maternal behavior in the rat. In M. O'Connor (Ed.), *Parent-infant interaction*, 17, 39. Amsterdam: Elsevier.

Ross, J. B., & McLaughlin, M. M. (Eds.) (1949). *The Portable Medieval Reader*. New York: Penguin Books.

Ross, J. M., Cath, S. H., & Gurwitt, A. R. (Eds.). (1982). *Father and child*. Boston: Little, Brown and Co.

Ross, N. (1970). The primacy of genitality in the light of ego psychology. *Journal of American Psychoanalytic Association*, 18, 267–284.

Roustan, M. (1969). *The pioneers of the French Revolution*. New York: Howard Fertig.

Ruiz, R. E. (1980). *The great rebellion*. New York: Norton.

Rumbaugh, Duane (Ed.). (1977). *Language learning by a chimpanzee*. New York: Academic Press.

Rushton, J. P., & Sorrentino, R. M. (Eds.). (1981). *Altruism and helping behavior*. Hillsdale, NJ: L. Erlbaum Associates.

Ruskin, J. P. (1983). Romantic malnutrition—solving America's number 1 emotional craving. *Self*, 5 (4), 65–67.

Russell, B. (1961). *The basic writings of Bertrand Russell*. New York: Simon & Schuster.

Russell, D. E. H. (1974). *Rebellion, revolution and armed force*. New York: Academic Press.

Russell, J. F. (1972). *Witchcraft in the Middle Ages*. Ithaca, NY: Cornell University Press.

Saadawi, Nawal el. (1980). *The hidden face of Eve*. Boston: Beacon Press.

Sagan, E. (1979). *The lust to annihilate*. New York: Psychohistory Press.

Salisbury, H. E. (1972). *The eloquence of protest: Voices of the 70's*. Boston: Houghton Mifflin.

Sanders, G. S., & Suls, J. (1982). *Social psychology of health and illness*. Hillsdale, NJ: Erlbaum.

Sandler, J., Kawenoka, M., Neurath, L., Rosenblatt, B., Schurmann, A., & Sigal, J. (1962). The classification of superego material in the Hampstead Index. *Psychoanalytic Study of the Child*, 17, 107–27.

Sapir, S. G., & Nitzburg, A. C. (Eds.). (1973). *Children with learning problems*. New York: Brunner/Mazel.

Sarlin, C. N. (1970). The current status of the concept of genital primacy. *Journal of American Psychoanalytic Association, 18,* 285–299.

Schafer, R. (1968). *Aspects of internalization*. New York: International Universities Press.

Schaller, G. B. (1967). *The deer and the tiger*. Chicago: University of Chicago Press.

Schlegel, A. (1977). *Sexual stratification*. New York: Columbia University Press.

Schneidau, H. N. (1976). *Sacred discontent: The Bible and western tradition*. Baton Rouge, LA: Louisiana State University Press.

Schopenhauer, A. (1969). *The world as will and idea*. New York: Dover.

Schopler, E., & Reichler, R. J. (Eds.). (1976). *Psychopathology and child development*. New York: Plenum.

Scott, D. M., & Wishy, B. (Eds.). (1982). *America's families*. New York: Harper and Row.

Scott, J. P. (1983). *Animal behavior*. New York: Doubleday Anchor.

Scott, J. P., & Senay, E. C. (1973). *Separation and depression*. Washington, DC: American Association for the Advancement of Science.

Sebald, H. (1978). *Witchcraft*. New York: Elsevier.

Seguin, C. A. (1965). *Love and psychotherapy*. New York: Libra Press.

Seligman, B. B. (1968). *Permanent poverty: An American syndrome*. New York: Quadrangle.

Seligman, N. (1948). *Magic supernaturalism and religion*. New York: Pantheon Books.

Sellin, J. T. (1976). *Slavery and the penal system*. New York: Elsevier.

Seneca, L. A. *De Beneficius*. (On Benefits). In Lewis and Reinhold, eds.: *The Roman Empire*, Vol. II, p. 94.

Serafica, F. C. (Ed.). (1982). *Social-cognitive development in context*. New York: Guilford Press.

Shakespeare, W. (1957). *The love poems and sonnets*. Garden City, NY: Doubleday & Co.

Shakespeare, W. (1963). *Hamlet*. New York: Norton.

Shaw, G. B. (1971). *Saint Joan*. New York: Bobbs Merrill Co. (Original work published 1924)

Sheehy, G. (1977). *Passages*. New York: Dutton.

Shepher, J. (1983). *Incest: A biosocial view*. New York: Academic Press.

Shirer, W. L. (1960). *The rise and fall of the Third Reich*. New York: Simon & Schuster.

Shorter, E. (1975). *The Making of the modern family*. New York: Basic Books.

Shorter, E. (1982). *A history of women's bodies*. New York: Basic Books.

Shostakovich, D. (1979). *Testimony* (S. Volkov, Ed.). New York: Harper Colophon Books.

Siegel, L. (1978). *Sacred and profane dimensions of love in Indian traditions*. New York: Oxford University Press.

Silver, D. (Ed.). (1983). Commentaries on Parens "The development of aggression in early childhood." *Psychoanalytic Inquiry, 2* (2).

Silverman, I. (Ed.). (1981). *Generalizing from laboratory to life.* San Francisco: Jossey-Bass.

Silverman, L. H., Lachmann, F. M., & Milich, R. H. (1982). *The search for oneness.* New York: International Universities Press.

Simis, K. (1982). *USSR: The corrupt society.* New York: Simon & Schuster.

Singer, I. (1977). *Mozart and Beethoven: The concept of love in their opera.* Baltimore: Johns Hopkins University Press.

Skinner, B. F. (1971). *Walden Two.* New York: Macmillan.

Skinner, B. F. (1971). *Beyond freedom and dignity.* New York: Knopf.

Skinner, B. F. (1972). *Cumulative record.* New York: Appleton-Century-Crofts.

Skocpol, T. (1979). *States and social revolutions.* New York: Cambridge University Press.

Skultans, V. (1975). *Madness and morals.* London: Routledge and Kegan Paul.

Slotkin, R. *Regeneration through violence.* (1973). Middletown, CT: Wesleyan University Press.

Smith, H. S. (1972). *In His image, but . . .* Durham, NC: Duke University Press.

Smith, M. L., Glass, G. V., & Miller, T. I. (1980). *The benefits of psychotherapy.* Baltimore: Johns Hopkins University Press.

Socarides, C. (1974). The sexual unreason. In *Book Forum, 1,* 172–185. Rhinecliff, NY: Hudson River Press.

Solomon, R. Z. (1982). Report of committee on social issues. *Journal of American Psychoanalytic Association,* pp. 982–983.

Southwick, C. H. (1963). *Primate social behavior.* New York: Van Nostrand.

Spacks, P. M. (1981). *The adolescent idea.* New York: Harper Colophon Books.

Spence, K. W. (1956). *Behavior theory and conditioning.* New Haven: Yale University Press.

Spengemann, W. (1980). *The forms of autobiography.* New Haven: Yale University Press.

Spiro, M. E. (1959). Cultural heritage, personal tensions, and mental illness in a South Sea culture. In M. N. Opler (Ed.), *Culture and mental health.* New York: Macmillan.

Spiro, M. (1970). *Buddhism and society.* New York: Harper and Row.

Spitz, R. A. (1952). Authority and masturbation. *Psychoanalytic Quarterly, 21,* 490–527.

Spitzer, R. L., & Klein, D. F. (Eds.). (1976). *Evaluation of psychological therapies.* Baltimore: Johns Hopkins University Press.

Sprenger, J., & Kramer, H. (1928). *Malleus malleficarum.* London: John Rodker. (Original 1486)

Srole, L., & Fischer, A. K. (1978). *Mental health in the metropolis.* New York: New York University Press.

Starr, C. G. (1982). *The Roman Empire.* New York: Oxford University Press.

Starr, C. G. Review in *New York Times Book Review*, September 19, 1982.

Starr, P. (1982). *The social transformation of American medicine*. New York: Basic Books.

Stendhal. (1957). *De l'amour*. Paris: Le Divan. (Original work published 1853)

Stern, D. N. (1974). The goal and structure of mother–infant play. *Journal American Academy Child Psychiatry*, 13, 402–421.

Stern, D. V. (1977). *The first relationship*. Cambridge, MA: Harvard University Press.

Stern, M., & Stern, A. (1980). *Sex in the USSR*. New York: Times Books.

Stevenson, J., & Quinault, R. (Eds.). (1975). *Popular protest and public order*. New York: St. Marten's Press.

Stevenson, J., Hutchison, R. E., Hutchison, J., Bertram, B. C. R., and Thorpe, W. H. (1970). Individual recognition by auditory cues in the common tern (*Sterna hirundo*). London: *Nature*, pp. 226, 562–563.

Stierlin, H. (1978). The transmission of irrationality reconsidered. In L. C. Wynne, R. C. Cromwell, & S. Matthysse, *The nature of schizophrenia*. New York: John Wiley & Sons.

Stone, L. J., Smith, H. T., & Murphy, L. B. (1973). *The competent infant*. New York: Basic Books.

Stone, L. (1975). *Family and fortune*. London: Oxford University Press.

Stone, L. (1979). *The family, sex and marriage in England 1500–1800*. New York: Harper Colophon Books.

Stone, L. (1982). Madness. *New York Review of Books*, 29 (20), 28–36.

Strassburg, Gottfried von. (1960). *Tristan* (A. T. Hatto, Trans.). Hammondsworth.

Strasser, S. (1982). *Never done: A history of American housework*. New York: Pantheon.

Stratton, P. (1982) (Ed.). *Psychobiology of the newborn*. New York: John Wiley & Sons.

Suetonius, G. (1957). *The twelve Caesars* (Robert Graves, Trans.). New York: Penguin Classics.

Sugiyama, Y. (1967). Social organization of Hanuan Langurs. In S. Altmann (Ed.), *Social communication among primates*. Chicago: University of Chicago Press.

Sullivan, H. S. (1939). *Conceptions of modern psychiatry*. New York: Norton.

Sussman, M. B. (Ed.). (1972). *Non-traditional family forms in the 1970's*. Minneapolis: National Council on Family Relations.

Svejda, M. J., Pannabeccker, B. J., & Emde, R. N. (1982). Parent-to-infant attachment: A critique of the early "bonding" model. In R. N. Emde & R. J. Hannon (Eds.), *The development of attachment and affiliative systems*. New York: Plenum Press.

Tacitus. (1977). *The annals of imperial Rome*. New York: Penguin Books.

Tannahill, R. (1980). *Sex in history*. New York: Stein & Day.

Tapp, J. T. (Ed.). (1969). *Reinforcement and behavior*. New York: Academic Press.

Tawney, R. H. (1952). *Religion and the rise of capitalism.* New York: Harcourt Brace. (Original work published 1926)

Teichholz, J. (1928). A selective review of the psychoanalytic literature on theoretical conceptualizations of narcissism. *Journal of American Psychoanalytic Association, 26,* 831–861.

Temerlin, M. K. (1975). *Lucy: Growing up human.* Palo Alto, CA: Science and Behavior Books.

Terhune, C. B. (1979). The role of hearing in early ego organization. *Psychoanalytic Study of the Child, 34,* 371–383.

Terrace, H. S. (1979). *Nim: A chimpanzee who learned sign language.* New York: Washington Square Press.

Terrill, R. (Ed.). (1979). *The China difference.* New York: Harper and Row.

Thomae, H., Coerper, K. W., & Hagen, E. (1954). *Die Deutsche Nachkriegskinder* [The German post-war children]. Stuttgart: Thieme.

Thomas Aquinas. (1977). The end of man. In Ross and McLaughlin (Eds.), *The medieval reader.* New York: Penguin Books.

Thomas, A., & Chess, S. (1984). Genesis and evolution of behavioral disorders: From infancy to adult life. *American Journal of Psychiatry, 141,* 1–9.

Thomas, K. (1983). *Man and the natural world.* New York: Pantheon.

Thomis, M. I. (1972). *The Luddites.* New York: Schocken Books.

Thompson, E. P. (1963). *The making of the English working class.* New York: Vintage Books.

Thorpe, W. H. (1972). A comparison of vocal communication in animals and man. In R. A. Hinde (Ed.), *Non-verbal communication.* New York: Cambridge University Press.

Thucydides. (1982). *The Peloponnesian Wars.* New York: Penguin Books.

Tiger, L. (1970). *Men in groups.* New York: Vintage Books.

Tillich, H. (1974). *From time to time.* New York: Stein and Day.

Tillich, P. (1968). *A history of Christian thought.* New York: Simon and Schuster.

Tinbergen, N. (1951). *The study of instinct.* Oxford: Clarendon Press.

Tjossem, T. D. (Ed.). (1976). *Intervention strategies for high risk infants and young children.* Baltimore: University Park Press.

Tracy, P. J. (1980). *Jonathan Edwards, pastor.* New York: Hill and Wang.

Treece, P. (1982). *A man for others: Maximilian Kolbe, saint of Auschwitz.* New York: Harper and Row.

Treurniet, N. (1983). Psychoanalysis and self psychology: A metapsychological essay with a clinical illustration. *Journal of American Psychoanalytic Association, 31,* 59–100.

Troeltsch, E. (1966). *Protestantism and progress.* Boston: Beacon Press. (Original work published 1912)

Truax, C. B., Carkhuff, R. R., & Kodman, F. J. R. (1965). Relationships between therapist-offered conditions and patient change in group psychotherapy. *Journal of Clinical Psychology, 21,* 327–329.

Tschanz, B. Trottellumen [Young guillemots]. Z. *Tierpsychologie, 4*

Tuchman, B. W. (1978). *The calamitous 14th century.* New York: Knopf.

Tucker, R. C., (Ed.). (1977). *Stalinism.* New York: W. W. Norton & Co.

Turnbull, C. (1966). *Tradition and change in African tribal life.* New York: World.

Turnbull, C. (1972). *The mountain people.* New York: Simon and Schuster.

Turnbull, C. (1978). The politics of non-aggression. In A. Montagu (Ed.), *Learning non-aggression.* New York: Oxford University Press.

Turnbull, C. (1983). *The human cycle.* New York: Simon and Schuster.

Turner, V. (1969). *The ritual process.* Ithaca, NY: Cornell University Press.

Tuzin, D. F. (1982). Ritual violence among the Ilahita Arapesh. Berkeley: In G. H. Herdt (Ed.), *Rituals of manhood.* University of California Press.

Tweedie, J. (1979). *In the name of love.* New York: Pantheon Books.

Ulam, A. B. (1981). *Russia's failed Revolutions.* New York: Basic Books.

Vaillant, F. C. (1950). *Aztecs of Mexico.* Garden City, NY: Doubleday & Co.

Valency, M. (1961). *In praise of love.* New York: Macmillan.

Van Lawick-Goodall, J. (1971). *In the shadow of man.* Boston: Houghton Mifflin Co.

Vann, R. T. (1969). *The social development of English Quakerism, 1655–1755.* Cambridge, MA: Harvard University Press.

Vantage Press. *New Voices in American Poetry, 1977.* New York: Vantage Press, 1977.

Veroff, J., Kulka, R. A., & Douvan, E. (1981). *Mental health in America.* New York: Basic Books.

Veroff, J., Douvan, E., & Kulka, R. A. (1981). *The inner American.* New York: Basic Books.

Veysey, L. (1978). *The communal experience.* Chicago: University of Chicago Press.

Wallerstein, R. S. (1978). Perspectives on psychoanalytic training around the world. *International Journal of Psychoanalysis, 59,* 477–509.

Wallerstein, R. S. (1983). [Letter to the Editor]. *International Review of Psychoanalysis, 10,* 240.

Ware, J. R. (Ed.). (1955). *The sayings of Confucius.* New York: New American Library.

Washington, J. R., Jr. (1969). *The politics of God.* Boston: Beacon Press.

Wasser, S. K. (Ed.). (1983). *Social behavior of female vertebrates.* New York: Academic Press.

Wax, M. (1983). How Oedipus falsifies Popper: Psychoanalysis as a normative science. *Psychiatry, 46,* 95–105.

Weber, M. (1947). *The theory of social and economic organization.* New York: Free Press.

Webster's Third New International Dictionary. (1969). Springfield, MA: G. C. Merriam Co.

Wedgwood, C. V. (1938). *The Thirty Years War.* New York: Methuen.

Weintraub, K. J. (1966). *Visions of culture.* Chicago: University of Chicago Press.

Weisbrod, C. (1980). *The boundaries of utopia*. New York: Pantheon.

Welch, H. (1966). *Taoism: The parting of the way*. Boston: Beacon Press.

Werner, E. E., & Smith, R. S. (1982). *Vulnerable but invincible*. New York: Mc-Graw-Hill.

Wesson, R. G. (1963). *Soviet communes*. New Brunswick, NJ: Rutgers University Press.

Westley, W. A., & Epstein, N. B. (1969). *The silent majority*. San Francisco: Jossey-Bass.

Whitehead, A. N. (1955). *Adventures of ideas*. New York: New American Library.

Whitman, R. M. (1980). The dream in sexual dysfunction therapy. In J. M. Natterson (Ed.), *The dream in clinical practice*. New York: Jason Aronson.

Whyte, W. H. (1956). *The organization man*. New York: Simon and Schuster.

Wickler, W. (1972). *The sexual code*. New York: Doubleday.

Wilson, B. R. (1973). *Magic and the millennium*. New York: Harper and Row.

Wilson, E. O. (1978). *On human nature*. Cambridge, MA: Harvard University Press.

Withey, L. (1982). *Dearest friend: A life of Abigail Adams*. New York: Free Press.

Wolf, L. (Ed.). (1968). *Voices from the love generation*. Boston: Little, Brown.

Wolff, R. L., & Hazard, H. W. (Eds.). (1969). *A history of the later Crusades*. Milwaukee: University of Wisconsin Press.

Wolfgang, M. E., & Ferracutti, F. (1982). *The subculture of violence*. Beverly Hills: Sage.

Wood, A. D. (1983). The fashionable diseases. *Journal of Interdisciplinary History, 4*, 25–52.

Woods, R. L. (Ed.). (1953). *A treasury of Catholic thinking*. New York: Thomas & Crowell.

Wynne, L. C., Cromwell, R. L., & Matthysse, S. (1978). *The nature of schizophrenia*. New York: John Wiley & Sons.

Yee, M. S., & Layton, T. N. (1981). *In my father's house*. New York: Berkley Publishing Corp.

Yerkes, J. (1983). *The Christology of Hegel*. Albany, NY: State University of New York Press.

Yutang, Lin. (1937). *The importance of living*. New York: John Day.

Zablocki, B. (1980). *Alienation and charisma: A study of contemporary American communes*. New York: Free Press.

Zigler, E., & Valentine, J. (Eds.). (1979). *Project Head Start*. New York: Free Press.

Zinberg, N. E. (Ed.). (1977). *Alternate states of consciousness*. New York: Free Press.

Zinn, H. (1980). *A people's history of the United States*. New York: Harper-Colophon Books.

Zuckerman, M. (Ed.). (1983). *Biological bases of sensation seeking, impulsivity and anxiety*. Hillsdale, NJ: Erlbaum.

Zweig, P. (1980). *The heresy of self-love*. Princeton, NJ: Princeton University Press.

Author Index

Subject Index

Academy of love, Freud on, 286, 315
Acquisitive love, 276
Adjustment neurosis, in children, 181
Adolescence, 188–192
    rebellion in, 231
    romantic love in, 319
Adult roles, in adolescence, 189–190
Affectional ties, love as, 129. *See also* Animals, love and
Agape, 126, 274
Aggression, 1
    in adolescence, 190
    in animals, 155–157
    in children without fathers, 176–177
    Freud on, 287
    Mbuti and, 255
    Tahitians and, 257–258
    universality of, 15
    see also Hate cultures
Albigensian Crusade, 67

American Psychiatric Association, 340
American Sign Language, chimpanzees learning, 154
Anabaptist movement, 88
Analytic ideal, 308–309
    communication and, 332–334
    creativity and, 334–336
    family and, 319–322
    hate culture and, 309–312
    hatred and, 317–318
    mental illness and, 336–338
    narcissism and, 327–329
    neurosis and psychosis as distance from, 337, 342
    pleasure and reason and, 318–319
    sexuality and, 312–317
    society and, 322–327
    work and, 330–332
    see also Psychotherapy
Analytic triad, 345–349

413